Youthscapes

21⁹⁵

Youthscapes

The Popular, the National, the Global

*Edited by Sunaina Maira
and Elisabeth Soep*

PENN

University of Pennsylvania Press

Philadelphia

10   9   8   7   6   5   4   3   2   1

Published by
University of Pennsylvania Press
Philadelphia, Pennsylvania 19104-4011

Library of Congress Cataloging-in-Publication Data

Youthscapes : the popular, the national, the global / edited by Sunaina Maira and
Elisabeth Soep.
    p.   cm.
  Includes bibliographical references and index.
  ISBN 0-8122-3834-6 (cloth : alk. paper) — ISBN 0-8122-1896-5 (pbk. : alk. paper)
  1. Youth—Social conditions.   2. Youth—Cross-cultural studies.   3. Popular culture.   I.
Maira, Sunaina, 1969–   II. Soep, Elisabeth.

HQ796.Y88   2005
305.235—dc22   2004052635

Contents

Foreword
Midnight's Children: Youth Culture in the Age of Globalization

George Lipsitz

Joy de la Cruz died in a car crash on a Nevada highway on October 6, 2003. She was only twenty-five years old. A much-admired spoken-word performer and feminist activist, her brilliant potential will now never be realized fully. She grew up as part of the first truly transnational generation of youth, an immigrant daughter whose first language was Tagalog. For those of us who knew her in San Diego where she went to college or in the San Francisco Bay Area where she was raised, Joy was our "morning star"—a planet that burns so brightly in the eastern sky that everyone who sees it knows a new dawn is coming. She was quiet in class, but loud on the mic. An outspoken spoken-word warrior, she fought ferociously for a future that she will now never see.

The pain of losing Joy de la Cruz is directly proportional to ways she delighted us in life. Her parents named her Elaine, but she adopted her middle name, turning herself into Joy. "Don't postpone Joy," she counseled on her website, and whether performing her art on stage or working behind the scenes as the key organizer of the annual University of California Women of Color conference, she made us happy and gave us heart.

In her short life, de la Cruz witnessed the worst and the best this world has to offer. Like so many of the young people whose consumption patterns, creative endeavors, and critical thinking are chronicled in the pages of *Youthscapes*, she hungered for a more just and joyful existence. It hurt her to think about the women in the Philippines working as prostitutes to U.S. service men, to see the campus custodial staff working midnight shifts trying to feed their families on the $6.25 an hour that an extremely rich university paid them, to learn about the power of what she called "the isms"—racism, sexism, classism, heterosexism, capitalism. Yet her art and activism were powered by more than politics: they emerged from her struggle to build a self worth respecting, from the very doubts she had about herself. She would laugh about her insistence on writing outside the lines on sheets of lined paper, ruefully admit she watched too much television, and enjoy her powerful response to a particular music video (by the handsome hip-hop artist and actor D'angelo, apparently naked but filmed only from the waist up), which she described as "the one that makes all the women I know sit up taller as if looking at the television screen from a higher angle might allow us a peek at what's just below the bottom edge . . . that makes us nod our heads or flutter our hand like that might make the camera pan down."

After reading Maya Angelou's challenge to think about what we would say if we knew we were going to die, de la Cruz wrote a poignant and prophetic immigrant daughter's lament,

> I haven't always been the best daughter
> I've prided myself on fierce independence but all that gets me is alone
> My rationale: I tired of not meeting expectations of success
> Though I guess all parents push their children to do well in school
> To get good grades
> To be a good student to get into college to get a good job to make
>   decent money to earn a living to feed themselves and their family
>   and have a good life to not have to work as hard to not have to work
>   as much and to not have it as hard
> As they did

On June 15, 2001 de la Cruz went to jail. She had been part of a contingent of University of California, San Diego students who staged a non-violent obstructive demonstration blocking traffic at a busy intersection near campus to support efforts by the largely immigrant janitorial work force on campus to win medical benefits, a raise in pay, and union representation. Upon her release from incarceration that evening, she sent out an e-mail explaining how she overcame her fears and chose to allow herself to be arrested. Her e-mail told about how difficult it was for her to pay her rent and buy her economical rations of Top Ramen on the seven to eight dollars an hour she made from her job on campus, more than the wage paid to workers with families to support. In her e-mail, de la Cruz talked about the student activists who preceded her, those who had been arrested in a similar demonstration in 1996 while protesting against the end of affirmative action in California, and about her strong desire that Asian Americans in general, and Pilipinas in particular, stand in solidarity with the largely Latino/a workforce. "But it was hearing the Tagalog chant that really gave me strength," she wrote, "and that almost brought tears to my eyes. That might sound corny but it's true. *Ma ki ba ka . . . wag ma ta kut!* Hearing *aking mga kaibigan at kababayan* (my friends and country men/*la raza*) remind us that 'the struggle continues . . . don't be afraid'—hearing not only Spanish, but MY first language—helped me not be so nervous."

In the patrol wagon on the way to jail, Joy broke out with one of her spoken word pieces. Brian Babbs, another one of the young people arrested that day, had not known before that moment that de la Cruz wrote poetry. "She made me forget I had handcuffs on," he said, meaning literally what many of us who knew her felt figuratively as well.

Youthscapes surveys the problems, possibilities, injustices, and imaginings that made Joy de la Cruz into the person she became, that shape the contours of life for young people around the globe in our age of transnationalism. From the graffiti writing on the walls in a Midwestern U.S. Chicano barrio to the transnationalism of political mobilization and cultural expression by gang members deported from Los Angeles to El Salvador, from young women selling Amway cosmetics as a strategy to escape the bonds of tradition in northern Thailand to students in San Francisco making videos about their intercultural connections and conflicts, *Youthscapes* presents ideas and analyses about how young people are living the contradictions of their time.

More than a century ago, in another time of tumult and fear, African American social justice activist Sojourner Truth informed an 1881 women's rights convention, "I am sittin' among you to watch; and every once and awhile I will come out and tell you what time of night it is" (Truth 1962).[1] *Youthscapes* is a book that performs that task for our own time, a book that lets us know exactly what time it is. The authors in this volume report about youth cultures from around the world. They show us how creative young people are making meaning for themselves under circumstances they do not control.

For many youths around the world today, the hour is midnight. Structural adjustment policies imposed on Africa, Asia, Latin America, as well as on poor communities in North America and Europe by the World Bank and the International Monetary Fund secure unearned advantages for the wealthy and powerful while wreaking havoc in the lives of vulnerable children. Every day, some thirty thousand youths under the age of five die from malnutrition or completely curable diseases. Thirty thousand deaths a day means ten million per year, one every three seconds (Millen, Irwin, and Kim 2000, 5). More than one billion people in poor countries lack access to safe drinking water (Millen, Irwin, and Kim 2000, 4).

The number of children living on the street in Africa now exceeds one million (Maxted 2003, 56). On a continent where more than two million people have been killed in wars over the past twenty years, where deaths from AIDS occur most often among the generations most likely to be parents, and where destruction of state-sponsored education, health care, and housing programs forces children to wander in search of work, children wielding automatic weapons have become a growing percentage of the troops in mercenary armies (Maxted 2003, 51–69). Undernourished Latin American, Caribbean, and Asian children work in sweatshops for starvation wages making sweat-suits and running shoes favored by affluent suburban children and their parents who are trying to stay physically fit on diets laced with sugar and fat (Kernaghen 1999, 18). Promoters of "sex tours" profit from global income inequality by inviting European and North American predators to the Caribbean and Asia for the purpose of having sex with desperately poor adults, teens, and children (Kempadoo 1999).

Even for children in wealthy countries, the clock is striking midnight. Despite an avalanche of talk about family values, educational reform, the sanctity of human life, abuse by pedophiles, and the need "to put children first," young people in affluent societies can see that they do not count. No one seems to care what they think, or if they think. Public policy and mass media discourses on youth position young people largely as a problem, as a population to be controlled and contained. A seemingly endless stream of negative messages urges them to say no to drugs and no to sex, to give up graffiti writing and gang violence, to clean up their tattoos and take the rings out of their noses and navels. But by and large they are not given important work to do, not invited to say yes to anything except consumption.

Of course, not all children in wealthy countries are wealthy themselves. The same forces that create inequality across countries generate it within countries, and almost always it is young people who suffer the most because of it. Young people from poor and working-class communities can see that they are society's lowest priority just by looking at the neighborhoods in which they live, the buses they ride, and the schools they attend. Some of the greatest injuries they experience come from environmental pollution and inadequate health care, from forces that are felt, but rarely seen. African American children in the United States are twice as likely as white children to be born with low birth weights and twice as likely to die in infancy (Edelman 2001, 11). Navajo teenagers develop reproductive organ cancer at seventeen times the national average (Wenz 1996, 66). Farm workers and their children grow the food that nourishes others, but suffer disproportionately from malnutrition (Shields 1996, 8).

The problems faced by young people around the world are severe, daunting, and deadly. But the contributors to *Youthscapes* show that the darkest hour of midnight can also be seen as the start of a new dawn. Young people who are burdened—but not beaten—by the present emerge in these pages as people preparing themselves for the future. They seem to think that the things that kill can also cure, as they appropriate the raw materials of globalization—its commodities, mass mediated messages, and displacements—and turn them into tools for building community and critique. Like the Native Americans who made jingle dresses (originally designed to heal the sick) out of discarded Copenhagen tobacco tins, or the Trinidadians who made a perfectly blended rhythmic and harmonic instrument out of discarded oil drums, young people in these pages take the very items that most symbolize their subordination and use them for their own purposes (Buff 2001). As the first generation raised in and around hip-hop, they appreciate the art of talking back. Surrounded all their lives by the scrawls of graffiti, they have learned to read the writing on the wall. Often confined to ghettos, barrios, or the more affluent but equally contained world of the suburbs, they dance their way out of their constrictions, accessing entry in local sites to processes, practices, circuits, and networks that are global in scope.

Four decades ago, Martin Luther King Jr. told the nation and the world what time of the night it was. It was midnight within the social order, within the psychological order, and within the moral order, he declared (King 1981, 60–61). Pushing the metaphor, King declared that midnight was a confusing hour, a time when it was difficult to keep the faith. Yet "the dawn will come," he declared, noting "disappointment, sorrow and despair are born at midnight, but morning follows" (King 1981, 68). Today we are not so sure. Too many hopes have been dashed, too many expectations unmet, too many hearts broken, too many lives destroyed to sustain a simple faith in the future. Those who say that "it is always darkest just before dawn" may know too little about real, real dark. But if a wishbone won't work, maybe some backbone will. Youth cultures today evidence very little utopian optimism, but they seem to draw sustenance and power from a radical negativity, from a will to fight that does not depend on the expectation to win.

Young people who have been handed the worst of everything continue to make something beautiful out of the hand they've been dealt. The San Diego writers group known as the Taco Shop Poets, the St. Louis hip-hop artist Nelly, and the members of the Laotian Youth Project in Richmond, California demonstrate in different ways exactly what young people are up against and what they are doing in response.

In San Diego, a recent study by the Environmental Health Coalition found thirty of thirty-nine homes tested in the Chicano/a neighborhoods of Sherman Heights and National City exceeded the national standards for levels of toxic lead. Tests given to children under the age of six in these areas revealed that 19 percent of the youths had elevated levels of lead in their bloodstreams. Throughout the county, public health officials announce approximately one hundred cases of lead poisoning per year—84 percent of them in Latino children. The actual numbers are much higher because the county and the state do so little testing—even though they are required to do so by law. In Barrio Logan, Sherman Heights, and Logan Heights, neighborhood industries release three million pounds of toxic pollution into the air every year. This area is small, containing only 2 percent of the residents of San Diego County, but more than a third of the county's hazardous wastes are generated or stored there, some 32 million pounds per year. Twenty-eight percent of the children living in these neighborhoods and the ones adjacent to them in southeast San Diego have been diagnosed with probable or possible asthma, a level of infection more than four times greater than the national average (Air salta 2000, 5; Environmental racism 2000).

Homi Bhabha says that out of every emergency, there's an emergence. The San Diego Taco Shop poets come from their city's polluted neighborhoods. They teach in the local schools, write for local newspapers, ride the area's inadequate and underfunded public transportation, and hang out in its commercial establishments. Their goal is to turn the aspirations and experiences of their neighbors into art, to take poetry out of the coffee shops and bring it into the taco shops. Their brilliant interlingual and international spoken-word art offers a privileged optic on globalization from their perspective on an international border, from the end of the continent and the end of the streetcar line (Taco Shop Poets and de la Torre 2000).

Impoverished African American children in cities across the United States live in dwellings with lead-based paint on interior and exterior walls and windowsills, exposing them to toxic levels of lead. In 1998, medical authorities in St. Louis discovered 1,833 new cases of childhood lead poisoning, estimating that somewhere between 20 and 25 percent of local youths have toxic amounts of lead in their bloodstreams—nearly six times the national average. In some black neighborhoods the number of infected children was closer to 40 percent. Yet the city of St. Louis only spends enough money to test less than half of the children requiring screening for lead poisoning every year (Higgins 2000, 17). For every hundred students who begin the ninth grade in St. Louis schools, only thirty graduate. Eight-five percent of the students in the St. Louis school system are so poor they qualify for federally funded school lunches. Eighty percent of them are African American (Portz, Stein, and Rones 1999, 18).

St. Louis is also the home of the rapper Nelly and his crew, the St.

Lunatics. To the hip-hop cognoscenti, Nelly is just another bland but best-selling corporate rapper, singing lascivious lyrics about "pimp juice" and craving commodities. But in St. Louis, his global prominence validates local cultures of place, enables young people who have been invisible in the media to see and hear their surroundings broadcast to a wider world. Nelly's song "Country Grammar" holds out the hope that ordinary people from out-of-the-way places, even those (in Nelly's words) "whose grammar be's ebonics," can get paid, make it big, and stay true to the neighborhood at the same time. The song serves as an emblem of inner-city identification, solidarity, and pride. In his song, Nelly celebrates "making my living from my brain instead of [co]caine now, running credit checks with no shame now." Moreover, he imagines that he can carry his community with him. Although screaming "let me in" to Bill Gates and Donald Trump, Nelly boasts, "we spin now, I got money to lend my friends now, we in now."

In the city of Richmond, California (in Contra Costa County near San Francisco) oil refineries, waste incinerators, and factories producing pesticides, fertilizer, and other chemical products pollute the air, land, and water. The area has experienced thirty-five major industrial accidents and thousands of minor incidents since 1989 as well as a deadly series of explosions, oil spills, chemical leaks, fires, and releases of toxic gases. The Chevron Oil refinery in Richmond stores more than eleven million pounds of corrosive, toxic, and explosive chemicals in sites near residential neighborhoods. The plant had more than three hundred accidents between 1989 and 1995.[2]

Nearly ten thousand Lao, Khmu, and Mien immigrants live in the western part of Contra Costa County (Nguyen 2001, 31). Immigrant children find themselves forced to live near toxic hazards because of racial segregation and their own poverty. The traditional modes of subsistence they bring with them from Laos often expose them to unexpected dangers in North America. They cultivate vegetables in contaminated soil and catch fish from polluted waters. Laotian immigrant women have the highest rate of death from breast cancer of any group in Contra Costa County.[3] Children and the elderly suffer particularly pronounced effects from their repeated exposure to sulfur dioxide and other toxins, experiencing chronic nausea, rashes, and respiratory problems (Nguyen 2001, 32).

The Laotian Youth Project targets immigrant daughters and encourages them to take leadership roles in the community. Fam Linh Saechao joined the project when she was thirteen because she craved "a place where we can come together and identify as Asian women. It gives us a place to be both Laotian and American, some kind of middle ground to talk about the struggles we have with our families, no matter if we are

Lao, Mine, Hmong, or Khmu" (Parr 1999, 1). The Laotian Organizing Project persuaded county officials to replace the monolingual English telephone alerts with a multilingual system capable of serving the needs of the region's Southeast Asian immigrant population.[4] They succeeded in securing five million dollars for the Martin Luther King Jr. Medical Center to treat their mothers' breast cancer and address other community needs. While inspired by many sources—by the Asian American feminists who recruited them into the group, by indigenous traditions of struggle they brought from Laos and those they learned from and with their African American and Latino neighbors in Richmond, by the environmental movement at large—they also drew upon popular culture references and played with their audiences' unfamiliarity with their identities when Fam Linh Saecho started calling herself Fam Mulan (Saechao 2003, 65–66).

By focusing on popular culture, national ideologies, and global markets, Sunaina Maira and Elisabeth Soep present us with a collection that delineates the category of youth as a social achievement, not so much a given category based on biological age but a social position structured by the simultaneous powers of consumption, creativity, schooling, citizenship, surveillance, and social membership. This book blends ethnographic observation and cultural critique. It offers perspectives on youth and youth culture from close up and from far away.

Youthscapes is a book for our time that is right on time. It comes to us in the midnight hour to tell us what time of the night it is. But it also reminds us that while we stand in this life at midnight, we're always on the verge of a new dawn (King 1981, 58–68).

Introduction

Sunaina Maira and Elisabeth Soep

Youth, it seems, are everywhere and nowhere. They are the focus of moral panics and appear regularly in the media in the guise of "folk devils" (S. Cohen 1972): the gun-toting high-schooler, the Palestinian rock-thrower, the devious computer hacker, the fast-talking rapper, the ultra-fashionable Japanese teenager teetering on platform heels. Youth in these incarnations personify a given society's deepest anxieties and hopes about its own transformation. Such characterizations of youth are continually invoked within contemporary popular, political, and theoretical debates. Ironically, though, in many fields of academic research, the actual experiences of youth are not always considered important sites for developing theory and methodology and are seen as secondary in importance to the actions and imaginations of adults.

"Youthscapes"

The essays collected in this volume trace young people's movements across literal and imagined spaces, specifically analyzing the intersections between popular culture practices, national ideologies, and global markets. This is an under-theorized intersection in the existing literature in these three areas, but one that is vital for developing a new model for youth culture studies. The approach suggested by these chapters conceptualizes local youth practices as embedded, in both obvious and unexpected ways, within the shifts in national and global forces marking the late twentieth and early twenty-first centuries. This is what we mean in our title by a "youthscape." We use youthscape to suggest a site that is not just geographic or temporal, but social and political as well, a "place" that is bound up with questions of power and materiality (Dirlik 2001/2002; Soja 1989). In this sense, we hope to push the agenda of youth culture studies in a direction that can account for some of the most pressing theoretical concerns in an era of globalization and born-again nationalisms, while also keeping our focus on the social and political implications of young people's responses as well as the methodological questions raised by our own regimes of observation. The metaphorical concept of youthscapes draws most directly from models of globalization, but in doing so it also lends itself to analysis of the related processes of nationalism and popular culture. The work on youth collected here links the three themes of the book's subtitle in various ways, in some cases, speaking directly to two of the issues while alluding to the third more implicitly. It is in the assemblage of these various perspectives across the different essays that a complex and rich youthscape emerges.

In his theory highlighting the cultural dimensions of globalization, Arjun Appadurai (1996) used the idea of a "scape" to account for the deeply perspectival and uneven character of the forces behind globalization. Ethnoscapes, technoscapes, financescapes, mediascapes, and ideoscapes were the terms he introduced to describe dimensions of global cultural flows that are fluid and irregular, rather than fixed and finite. Ethnoscapes comprise the shifting circuits of people who animate a given social world; technoscapes draw attention to high-speed channels connecting previously distant territories; financescapes encompass new systems for accumulating and moving money; mediascapes refer to the dispersal of images and texts to small and vast audiences; and ideoscapes embody the "imagined worlds" produced through intersections between and among all of the above. Clearly we are taking some conceptual liberties in appropriating Appadurai's terminology, to the extent that youth is a social category that belongs to all five of his units of analysis. Young people participate in social relations; use and invent technology; earn, spend, need, desire, and despise money; comprise target markets while producing their own original media; and formulate modes of citizenship out of the various ideologies they create, sustain, and disrupt. Therefore we use the notion of a *youthscape* in the epistemological spirit of Appadurai's framework, while conceiving of youth as a shifting group of people that is simultaneously a deeply ideological category.

Appadurai's framework is, of course, just one way to theorize cultural globalization, which is itself a particular slice of the free-wheeling debates about globalization in political, economic, and social realms and the one with which this book is particularly concerned, connecting as it does to the everyday cultural practices of youth. Globalization, for that matter, is also only one term, and a particularly broad and sometimes amorphous one, used by those concerned with thinking beyond nation-states—an interest that has produced concepts such as "diaspora" (Clifford 1997), "transnationalism" (Basch, Glick Schiller, and Szanton Blanc 1994), and "cosmopolitanism" (Cheah and Robbins 1998). The rubric of diaspora has emerged most strongly as a pivot for theoretical work in the humanities, literary studies, and area studies, but has sometimes implicitly included in its definition an attachment, however imaginary, to an originary nation-state, a point of departure, rather than a place of residence. Theories of cosmopolitanism are generally more engaged with philosophical debates centered on humanist and universalist ideals, which remain bound up with questions of loyalty and allegiance, even when they include local and materialist perspectives (Clifford 1998; Robbins 1998). The notion of transnationalism emerged most clearly out of ethnographic work and by social scientists and immigration scholars (Basch, Glick Schiller, and Szanton Blanc 1994) attempting to delineate concretely the social, economic, and political ties spanning two or more nation-states.

Overall, a wide range of conceptual and methodological tools have developed out of these perspectives to study the transnational social networks, cultural forms, economic strategies, and citizenship models emerging in official and everyday realms in response to the changing relationship between the nation-state and global capital (Basch, Glick Schiller, and Szanton Blanc 1994; García Canclini 2001; Gupta and Ferguson 1997a; Hall 1997; Hannerz 1996; Jameson and Miyoshi 1998; Massey 1994). Taking just a few examples from this vast and growing body of literature, theorists have offered notions of "flexible citizenship" (Ong 1999b) and "discrepant cosmopolitanisms" (Cheah and Robbins 1998; Clifford 1998) and suggested research methods such as multisited ethnography to study the links between "local" everyday practices and "global" macro-forces (Buroway 2000; Marcus 1998). While distinct in terms of methodology as well as theoretical orientation, analyses tend to converge on a set of factors characterizing this particular era of globalization: for example, speed of real and virtual movement, a compressed sense of space, and newly permeable borders, which are, in some cases, also more heavily policed as a result of their greater porousness to flows of people, media, and commodities (Beynon and Dunkerley 2000; Harvey 1990).

This growing body of work on globalization, while highly relevant to studies of youth including those collected here, leaves key questions about an entire generation largely unanswered or in some cases, unconnected. How can youth studies offer new models or methods for studying border politics and commodity cultures in an era of global capitalism and changing patterns of coerced and voluntary migration? What might studying youth reveal about social identities being remade through transnational popular culture and new communication technologies in the context of debates about cultural authenticity, renewed nationalisms, and free-market relations? How is the category of youth reshaped in settings where young people are on the front lines of wars within and between nations, or when particular groups of youth bear the brunt of violence, profiling, and incarceration by the state, and find themselves caught between various models of childhood and human rights that are often manipulated by state and nongovernmental agencies for political and material ends? These are the kinds of questions that emerge when youth are recognized for their varied roles in this moment of globalization, as they move within and between territorialized nation-states while still tied to centralized sites of power and engaged within everyday life worlds.

Youthscape, therefore, refers not just to a generational term, but to a conceptual lens and methodological approach to youth culture, which brings together questions about popular culture and relations of power in local, national, and globalized contexts. In this sense, a youthscape is not a unit of analysis, as in Appadurai's framework of "scapes," but an approach that potentially revitalizes discussions about youth cultures and social movements while simultaneously theorizing the political and social uses of youth to maintain repressive systems of social control. We imagine the category of youth as a *social achievement* rather than a given psychological stage that children naturally pass through en route to adulthood. It might seem counterintuitive to evoke achievement with respect to a category so often associated with delinquency by mainstream scholars, resistance by progressive and radical thinkers, and failure by researchers alarmed by apparent patterns of academic and moral decline (McDermott 1987; Varenne and McDermott 1999). Achievement does not necessarily mean a positive outcome, but it does connote a condition that is produced, over and over again, by various parties and institutions participating—whether they know it or not—in the concerted activity of producing youth. The actual practice of recognizing and treating a given subset of individuals as youth, a category associated with specific vulnerabilities, rights, desires, and dangers, entails considerable work and coordination. Relevant forces include, but are not limited to, parents, peers, schools, juvenile justice systems, social welfare and labor policies, military apparatuses, marketing schemes, and media and entertainment industries (Wyn and White 1997). When the process of achieving youth as a designation applied to certain bodies or groups is obscured or overlooked, it is all too easy to undertheorize the local and global practices—including apparently trivial micro-interactions as well as heavily regulated institutionalized procedures—that render youth a viable cultural construction.

Our purpose, in collecting the essays that follow, is to take a step toward redressing the undertheorizing of youth as key players in dynamics surrounding the nation and globalization, who are both more and less than the familiar images of mass audience members, savvy consumers, junior citizens, and folk devils. Too often, the field of youth culture studies itself is taken as the epistemological folk devil of academic knowledge production, the sensationalist sideshow that is simply an echo of the main act, or the site where extreme manifestations of widespread phenomena are vividly described. Youth culture practices are not simply handy examples, suggestive cases to note in passing, or celebratory testaments to popular culture's possibilities. Youth is, after all, often the ideological battleground in contests of immigration and citizenship as well as the prime consumer target for the leisure industry. Even when young people are not themselves traveling across national borders, or leaving their own bedrooms, they can find themselves implicated within transnational networks. When mothers migrate across continents to look after other people's children, youth on both sides of that care-giving relationship are brought up within globalized networks for care and domestic work, whether by virtue of absence or presence, as well as the influx and expenditure of money (Parreñas 2001, see also Haney and Pollard 2003). While branches of the beauty and entertainment industries uphold youth as a repository of desire, young people themselves fuel those industries not simply by embodying and buying the message, but often by doing the service work to sell it, for salaries at or well below a living wage, while at the same time influencing, subverting, and otherwise transforming the products in circulation (Tannock 2001).

Youth, then, are at the center of globalization. However, rather than pushing for a rightful centering of youth studies in relation to an implicit margin, we argue that youth culture studies itself has much to teach us about the production of cultural centers or margins, about which bodies and which discourses are privileged, condemned, or overlooked. "We need to learn from people and cultures that have been forced to make themselves as mobile, flexible, and fluid as transnational capital, yet still capable of drawing upon separate histories, principles and values," writes George Lipsitz (2001, 20) in his analysis of the present "dangerous moment" confronting American studies and cultural studies more broadly. Analyses of youthscapes reveal how youth are drawn into local practices, national ideologies, and global markets while always occupying an ambiguous space within and between them. For instance, Murray Forman, in this volume, writes of the lives of refugee youth who have fled war-torn nations to resettle in the United States or Canada, where state and school authorities attempt to "suture" them into civic and national communities, a process that highlights the contradictions at the heart of racial and national ideologies in North America and one that these youth actively renegotiate on a daily basis. All the essays in this volume, in fact, address in one way or another the shape and meaning of this "suturing" process—and the tensions or renegotiations it entails—between local, national, and transnational communities in the lives of youth. As such, this book contributes to work on transnationalism, immigration, and cosmopolitanism that has not adequately addressed questions about youth. In the sections that follow, we identify new directions for theory, research, and analysis that emerge when youth culture studies is juxtaposed with the three strands of the book—globalization, national ideologies, and popular culture—and conclude with a reflection on the collection's methodological interventions and thematic organization.

Youth Culture and Globalization

Clearly, there is a large and growing body of work that deals with culture and globalization, and many of the shifts in cultural processes that are discussed in this literature shape the lives of, if they are not partly produced by, youth in various local and national contexts. Here, we are not attempting to provide a comprehensive overview of the debates about cultural globalization, a task that would be beyond the scope of a short essay, and one that is already the subject of many book-length works. Instead, we do want to allude to the ways in which questions about youth culture shed light on some of the key tensions in studies of cultural globalization, such as issues of cultural diffusion versus localization (Hannerz 1996), unidirectional versus multidirectional flows of culture, and the framing of cosmopolitanism as privileged physical and imaginary mobility versus coerced displacement (Cheah and Robbins 1998, Ong 1999b). Issues of youth culture seep into these studies by way of their attention to popular culture, media, and cultural change. We have found, however, that there is much less focus directly on youth per se, and particularly on the ways young people *themselves* understand or grapple with globalization. For example, the edited volume *The Anthropology of Globalization* (Inda and Rosaldo 2002a), an important contribution to the literature, includes a few chapters that touch on young people's lives and practices, but there is less attention to conceptualizing youth as itself both a force and a product of globalization. Some might suggest that searching for the presence or absence of young people may harden an arbitrary boundary around youth, who are after all constantly implicated in discussions of modernity, migration, and cultural flows. However, we would argue that assuming youth are present, even in their absence, in these discussions actually allows youth to be yoked constantly to the ideology of progress and change, reinscribing rather than deconstructing the very social and state processes that produce youth as a marginal category of actors.

Youth culture studies, for its part, certainly has a strong tradition in materialist analysis, crystallized most clearly—if not unproblematically—in the analyses of the Birmingham school theorists of youth subcultures. More recent work in youth culture studies that is transnational in scope adds to this strong foundation on which youth researchers interested in globalization can build. *Cool Places* (Skelton and Valentine 1998) is a collection of essays using conceptual tools from the field of cultural geography to study young people's local practices in sites around the world. In *Youth Cultures: A Cross-Cultural Perspective* (1995), Vered Amit-Talai and Helena Wulff take an anthropological approach, arguing that an ethnographic focus on the lived experiences of youth is necessary to advance theoretical debates. Jonathon Epstein's introduction to *Youth Culture: Identity in a Postmodern World* (1998) reconsiders the sociological concept of alienation attached to "Generation X" in a collection including several essays focused on youth subcultures in their encounters with global media and music. Even a U.S.-based historical anthology such as *Generations of Youth* (Austin and Willard 1998) offers a global perspective to the extent that a few of the essays do account for the ways in which diasporic communities have helped contribute to what are recognized as U.S. youth cultures. Because of popular culture's imbrication with global processes of production and consumption, it is apparent that a transnational context is often at least implicit within youth culture studies, and in fact some may argue that youth culture scholars have been studying globalization for years. At the same time, though, much of this work has remained wedded to a local or national frame of reference, or has undertheorized the specific processes whereby global currents help shape regional and national contexts as well as ethnic and racialized identities.

Given that there seem to be strong substantive and theoretical linkages between youth culture and globalization studies, why have these two fields seemingly evaded each other for so long? Why have scholars of globalization not taken questions of youth culture more seriously, and flipping the question over, why have not more youth culture scholars theorized globalization? We speculate that a partial answer lies in the social meanings attached to youth, an association that seems doggedly to follow youth across various national contexts, even historical periods, and that is both part of the cultural construction of youth *and* a reason why they are not taken seriously by scholars of globalization. The most salient, and troublesome, of these social meanings is the portrayal of youth as inadequately formed adults, as subjects lacking in the presumably desired qualities of adulthood, rather than as subjects in their own right with specific (even if they are not always unique) needs and concerns. Much work on globalization and transnationalism has tended to focus largely or explicitly on adults, and youth are assumed to be incomplete social actors, or subjects less able to exert agency in the face of globalization that some scholars are, understandably, eager to document. To be sure, youth are engaged in an ongoing process of social and cognitive development and do, in fact, acquire more rights and responsibilities as they move into adulthood. However, there is often an assumption in traditional work on youth and citizenship, for example, that young citizens—to the extent that they have rights, which are often limited—must be socialized into adult norms of political involvement rather than being thinking agents who may express important critiques of citizenship and nationhood (Buckingham 2000, 13).

Yet developmental assumptions about youth are embedded in a broader theoretical framework that actually hinges youth culture analyses in interesting ways to the study of globalization, and, in fact, throws into relief the ways in which the two fields share some key paradigms—in particular, a problematic logic of development. Research on adolescence, particularly in the field of psychology but also in anthropology, has generally assumed a stage-based model of youth and of identity; in fact, this approach assumes that identity is the exemplary question associated with youth, as in the classic identity development theory of Erik Erikson (1968) that posits adolescence as a moment of identity crisis. In the theories of identity development inspired by this approach—many of which have not questioned their own cultural specificity—development is, if not a linear, at least a teleological process. Erikson granted that adults may return to earlier crises not fully resolved at the appropriate "stage," since his theory proposed an epigenetic model of development, but there is still at least an implicit tenet that youth are proceeding toward a desirable end-goal, which is to be realized only and always in adulthood.

Globalization, too, is often framed in the context of arguments about "progress," resting on assumptions of development of a different sort; even if these arguments are discussing economic and political, and not psychological, development, they still are embroiled in debates about the desired end-goals. By now, of course, most scholars concede that globalization is not a linear process, but is inherently and deeply uneven. However, while some critics say that the notion of globalization as development is acknowledged as an undeniable failure on the levels of both metanarrative and concrete social policy, an ideology of development is clearly alive and well in many places around the world, in particular as applied to those experiencing economic expansion (Ferguson

2002, 145). Our point here is not to overstate the homology between youth as maturation and globalization as development, but to argue for the ways in which the processes of *both* youth and globalization need to be considered together, always with an effort to avoid the tendency to frame the two as stages or moments along a forward-moving continuum. The flows of people, goods, capital, and media images across national borders are embedded in, and produce, social and material inequalities that in turn drive further immigration and displacement. Youth are necessarily caught in this loop, in this movement of people and the mobilization for justice and equity, and in this cycle of production and consumption.

Clearly, youth display a wide range of responses to globalization, and the book itself offers examples of youth who want to benefit from globalization and who do so in some spheres of their lives even as they are also positioned as marginal workers in places where globalization's inequities are deeply apparent. Perhaps the most publicized response by youth to globalization in the U.S. mass media was the spectacle of the 1999 blockage of the World Trade Organization meetings in Seattle, Washington. Coverage of those events revealed a striking ambivalence that goes to the heart of the duality projected onto youth: the suspicion that young people are not mature citizens who can act effectively, and simultaneously, the fear that they are actually citizens with the power to effect change that some may not desire (Shepard and Hayduk 2002). This kind of deep social ambivalence has, of course, long existed as moral panics about youth (S. Cohen 1972). Without veering into a functionalist analysis, it might be safe to say that these panics are projected onto young people because of the association of youth with liminality, in anthropological terms, so that societies both reject those who critique their norms as "deviant" but also tolerate, and even incorporate, them as citizens existing somewhere between one space or status and another (Dannin 2002, 16).

Citizenship and Consumption

The construction of youth as a "transitional" category of citizenship reveals the role of the state in defining youth and points to what Philip Mizen calls "the importance of age to the political management of social relations" by the state (2002, 6). "Liminality," in this view, is not to be taken for granted nor is the very notion of "age" or the process of "growing up" under various economic systems. The notion of "youth-as-transition" is not only culturally constructed, but also necessary to the division of labor and the hierarchy of material relations specific to various forms of the capitalist state. In the shift from the welfare state to the privatization of state services in Britain, Mizen argues that youth remains important as a category that is part of the broader age-graded relations that underpin systems of labor, education, criminal justice, taxation, property, marriage, and family, and this is certainly true in other state models around the globe as well. Such a perspective on youth implicitly draws on a Foucauldian analysis of how "age provides a precise method of calibration for state administrative practices as the means to define subordinate populations in order to effect their control" (Mizen 2002, 12). At the same time, the state is constituted not of an abstract or static disciplinary power but of social relations and of people's imaginings of the state as being powerful, necessary, limited, irrelevant, or disruptive. Young people, too, imagine the state in all of these ways, in the contexts of schooling, immigration, policing, social services, or the prison system. As Thomas Hansen and Finn Steputat observe, ethnographies of the state show "how the state tries to make itself real and tangible through symbols, texts, and iconography" and examine its "everyday and local-ized forms" that may move "beyond the state's own prose, categories, and perspective" (2001, 5). Maira's study, in this volume, of South Asian Muslim youth in Cambridge, for example, focuses on how young work-ing-class immigrants grapple with the limitations and opportunities of two or more nation-states in their transition to the United States, partic-ularly in a post-9/11 moment where they are the target of the state's domestic, as well as foreign, "war on terror" and its accompanying pro-gram of detention, deportation, and surveillance. At the same time, they desire the economic and political benefits they believe citizenship offers as legal and material protection from the state's own disciplining and terrorizing policies.

Theorists of citizenship point to the emergence of the model of the citizen as consumer with the increasing privatization of services pre-viously offered by the welfare state; liberal conceptions of individualized citizenship mesh well with the notion of individualized consumption in capitalist democracy (Miller 1993, 129–30; see also Giroux 2000). This is apparent in the ways in which popular culture functions as an arena in which individual consumer-citizen identities are constructed, a process clearly applicable to youth as they grapple with the meanings of the state and citizenship in their everyday lives, for if they are supposedly alien-ated from traditional, public forms of political participation, so is the vast majority of the populace in a country such as the United States. Nés-tór García Canclini argues that "for many men and women, especially youth, the questions specific to citizenship, such as how we inform our-selves and who represents our interests, are answered more often than not through private consumption of commodities and media offerings than through the abstract rules of democracy or through participation in discredited legal organizations" (2001, 5).

The essays in this volume, therefore, all explore in different and often nuanced ways the tensions that young people experience between their identities as citizens and as consumers, and the politics associated with both locations. In northern Thailand, for example, Ida Fadzillah finds that young women are recruited by multinational corporations, such as Amway, to sell beauty products that are perceived as opening up a world of mobility and autonomy, in contrast to Thai-produced commodities and village marketplaces that affirm a certain cultural nationalism in the face of shifts in labor and consumption. In a different vein, Nicole Fleetwood examines how youth media producers both recreate and contest ideologies of "realness" projected onto urban, racialized, U.S. youth by activist video projects as well as a film and music industry that is increasingly globalized. Youth often enter the discussion of globalization only as consumers in a global marketplace, but it is clear to those observing carefully on the ground that, as cultural producers and members of a global labor force, youth are also always helping to manufacture and distribute consumer products while actively negotiating their circulation within complex media worlds (Ginsburg, Abu-Lughod, and Larkin 2002). Approaching these processes from a variety of angles, the essays in this volume all raise the question, in one form or the other, of what is at stake for youth in this tension between consumption and citizenship.

García Canclini suggests that we need to be more attuned to the new forms that citizenship takes in an era where relations of social belonging are "steeped in consumption," acknowledging the ways in which young people, among other social actors, may express political motivations or aspirations through their use of the media rather than assuming, a priori, that the space of consumption is opposed to that of citizenship (2001, 20; see also McRobbie 1994). Yet García Canclini remains critical of the limits of a liberal model of citizenship and of the need for the privatized state to produce consumers through technologies of governmentality, civic virtue, and individual self-interest, rather than of communitarian self-making (see also Miller 1993). He suggests, in fact, that the sociality associated with consumption needs to be harnessed to activate a progressive model of citizenship that aims "to reform the state," "to reconceptualize the public sphere," and to realize "the right to participate in the remaking of the system, that is, to redefine the very arrangement in which we desire to be included" (García Canclini 2001, 21, 154–55).

This challenge—of how to work in and through popular culture toward a transformative politics on local, national, and global scales that would connect the cultural to the material—is taken up by several of the essays in this volume. Alexandra Schneider uses a case study of a Tamil refugee boy adopted by a Swiss family to show how his fan relationship with Jackie Chan, the Hong Kong film icon, and his own film production help him mediate between ideologies of race, nationalism, and masculinity. Gustavo Guerra Vásquez's research on Salvadoran gang-involved youth in both Los Angeles and El Salvador shows how the youth-led organization Homies Unidos not only recognizes the transnational migration flows that link youth in both nations but also draws on the production of cultural commodities to respond to the criminalization of Latino youth in California and the scapegoating of Salvadoran American youth in El Salvador. There is, arguably, a new form of youth citizenship emerging here, one that crosses national borders to link processes of cultural consumption and migration to a critique of state-sponsored violence and detention. Susan Shepler uses her ethnographic research to argue that child soldiers in Sierra Leone are caught between models of "innocent" childhood imported by nongovernmental organizations and UN programs, which are working to rehabilitate youth in a post-civil war society, and local notions of youth. Her essay highlights the responses of youth themselves to violence, images of masculinity, and global commodity culture and their strategic uses of popular culture and public discourse about children's rights. All three of these essays, and others in the book, suggest the potential limits of cosmopolitanism for youth who know only too well that the specificity of national and local ideologies and practices of governmentality require equally specific—if also disruptive—models of citizenship, affiliation, and community. It is also apparent that there is a range of arguments about the meanings of globalization or cosmopolitanism for youth in the work featured here, and that a "youthscapes" approach does not imply a formulaic analysis.

Youth Cultures and National Ideologies

The cosmopolitan or transnational imaginaries of youth culture are always in dialectical tension with both national ideologies and local affiliations. In fact, the new research featured here demonstrates the ways in which youth produce localized understandings of national ideologies as well as state policies. Mica Pollock, for example, offers a critique of federal and state policies that call for "colorblindness" based on her study of everyday racial practice in an urban U.S. high school, where students use race labels to expose inequality even as they call into question the very existence of racial categories. Authors throughout the volume confront the question of when youth respond to a shared social condition as a form of politics, and what politics would or does mean for them in specific contexts. In many cases, it is apparent that youth respond to national ideologies in ways that may not be considered traditionally "political" but that are critical, even when these youth are considered to be nationalism's "other" and are targeted as such by the state, as in Maira's research on South Asian Muslim immigrant youth in post-9/11 Cambridge, Massachusetts. The anti-immigrant sentiment in the United States has centered on new targets of suspicion, namely, young Muslim or Arab American men or those presumed to belong to these groups. However, the surveillance and detention policies consolidated in the name of the "war on terror" at the present moment are part of a continuum of state measures that had previously been developed in response to what has been described as an "invasion" of immigrant "hordes" from the Caribbean, Latin America, and Asia, and a growing bilingual, multiracial population—not to mention similar anxieties about immigration in western Europe since the 1990s. It is important to situate the "new racism" directed at Muslim or Arab American youth in the context of the history of ongoing racial profiling, surveillance, and detention of other youth of color in the United States, and the ways in which those practices have historically secured a national consensus around a particular definition of citizenship. To do so means examining how domains are constructed as "public" or "private" realms of expression and exploring how state and foreign policies work in conjunction with cultural discourses and practices in different national contexts.

Clearly, many young people are ambivalent about the nation-state—and in many cases, more specifically, the state, although renewed nationalisms after 9/11 may have changed this for some—but they still draw on nationalism as a resource or model. The chapter by Ralph Cintron describes how gang-involved Latino youth in Angelstown strategically recreate the structure of the nation-state in what he calls a "shadow system" within the syntax and visual production of street gangs, which Cintron considers a potentially subaltern counterpublic sphere. This mimicry of nationalism, organizationally or discursively, is an important point to juxtapose with the progressive impulses of youth movements that many of the essays in this volume seem to point to, for the face of the nation is often reflected or reworked in the forms of collective identity that young people produce. Cintron's essay suggests that the discourse or topos of nationhood remains potent for youth because of its narrative power, much as Bhabha (1990) has argued, to provide stories of cohesion, stability, and hierarchy.

In some of the essays here, it becomes apparent that discourses about masculinity or femininity often seep into the stories about nationhood or collective culture; gender and nationalism are of course deeply interconnected, and youth cultures are no exception to this larger phenomenon. Studying a multiracial group of teenage boys who make camcorder movies in overnight production sessions in the San Francisco Bay Area, Elisabeth Soep contrasts the producers' fictional characters and plots, which draw heavily on transnational blockbuster movie tropes that valorize "hard-core" masculinity, with the boys' moment-to-moment interactions. Their actual discourse is in fact intensely collaborative and intimate, evoking linguistic features coded as "feminine" in both popular language ideologies and sociolinguistic scholarship. Masculinity and queer sexualities are a focus also in Todd Ramlow's essay, which links questions of disability to race and sexuality, through analysis of popular media texts as well as events such as the Columbine High School shootings. He argues, for example, that responses to the rapper Eminem's performances reveal a racialized anxiety about male sexuality and its place in the social order, which is deeply embedded in U.S. national ideology.

Rereading the United States

In considering the relationship of youth culture to national ideologies, it must be acknowledged that more than half of the essays here focus on the U.S. national context, even while the book includes new work based in Canada, El Salvador, Sierra Leone, Switzerland, and Thailand. Not surprisingly, in every instance, the research from Central and North America, Africa, Europe, and Asia examines in some way the impact of U.S. media, immigration policy, and human rights frameworks, suggesting the ways in which youth culture makes sense of these cultural and structural forms. Globalization, in fact, can be analyzed within local and national sites, as more and more American Studies scholars in particular are acknowledging, by viewing U.S. culture as itself globalized, rather than only looking outward to places that presumably absorb or are transformed by U.S. cultural exports. For example, the new journal, *Comparative American Studies*, aims to read America by "repositioning discussions about American culture within an international, comparative framework . . . whilst also fully attending to multi-ethnic comparisons within the U.S.A." (www.sagepub.com/journal.aspx?pid = 355). Perhaps, then, the essays focused on the United States in this collection contribute as much to advancing a literature on globalization as do the chapters based elsewhere; globalization happens in, and not only by, the United States.

As other theorists have pointed out (Gupta and Ferguson 1997a; Massey 1994), "the local," after all, is not simply the binary opposite of "the global"—traditional, fixed, authentic, grassroots, progressive, and, often, feminized—even if it can take on these representations for young people who may, often strategically, draw on the meanings of multiple "locals" in their lives. Youth culture helps shift, sometimes even distort, an easy mapping of local/national/global. In some cases, it seems that localism is dismissed even as it remains the site of important moral frameworks that guide young people's decisions, if only to try to escape them, as in Fadzillah's essay on young women working for Amway in a Thai village. Such analyses of the local, emerging from an analysis of the institutions that youth inhabit or (re)create, could help radically rethink debates about place, power, and culture, for they link systems of meaning and structures of production that have not always been yoked together.

In fact, a youthscapes approach articulates discussions of localism and regionalism with the national and the global. Some of the essays in this book (Fleetwood, Guerra Vásquez, Pollock, Soep) foreground the ways in which California, for example, has emerged as a fascinating and politically charged regional site in which young people are grappling with the meanings of globalization in response to immigration from Latin America and Asia, border cultures and linguistic creolization, demographic shifts, and punitive state legislation targeting immigrants and youth. In fact, we were struck while editing this book by the number of submissions we received from scholars doing research in California, in particular, that dealt with questions of youth culture and transnationalism. It seems to us, aside from the factor of our own places of residence and local connections, that one reason why California seems to have emerged in our book as a prominent site for studies of youth culture and globalization is because it is a region in which a confluence of social, political, and economic factors have conspired to produce a setting ripe for research on new youth movements. The rich and growing body of work on youth culture by researchers, often young scholars, in California may partly be due to the strong presence of ethnic studies and cultural studies programs within the state that encourage interdisciplinary and critical studies of youth. Institutional factors and regional and national contexts for the production of knowledge shape the intellectual genealogies of youth culture theories, as is apparent in the various strands of work represented in the book.

Youth Subcultures and Popular Culture

The most prominent tradition of youth studies that lends itself to an analysis of local, national, and global issues, as well as to social movements and questions of politics, is that of the Birmingham school. This is clearly not the only model of youth culture studies, or even the only one that has influenced the work represented in this book, in which authors draw on frameworks ranging from gender studies to linguistic anthropology to critical pedagogy. However, the work of the Centre for Contemporary Cultural Studies (CCCS) at Birmingham in the 1970s (by Stuart Hall, Dick Hebdige, Phil Cohen, John Clarke, Tony Roberts, Angela McRobbie, Jenny Garber, Simon Frith, and others) was seminal in bringing serious attention to the meanings of youth subcultures at a time of social transition in post-war Britain. Their work was based, for the most part, on ethnographic studies that focused on the rituals that youth create within the context of popular culture consumption and performative practices (Clarke et al. 1976). Bringing together structuralist and semiotic analyses, this early intervention demonstrated how collectivities of youth used the rituals they had created around cultural commodities such as music or clothing to respond, if only imaginatively or symbolically, to the material contradictions shaping their lives.

This work from CCCS has its antecedents in the United States in the qualitative research produced by the sociology department at the University of Chicago from the 1920s through the 1950s (Thornton 1997, 11). Ethnographers such as Robert Park, Paul Cressey, Howard Becker, and Albert Cohen focused on social interactions in an urban environment, and while they did not focus exclusively on youth, their analysis highlighted issues of social status, collective problem solving, and "deviancy" as a symbolic solution underlying the emergent formulation of "subcultures." While these scholars analyzed "deviant" behavior as a response to problems of social (class or racial) status, they did not undertake the kind of Marxist analysis of capitalism that critiqued the very production of "class" and of "youth," and that was able to explore how the two categories were articulated, not to mention link them to analyses of race, nation, and gender. Furthermore, youth remained associated with deviant or delinquent subcultures rather than shifting focus to other forms of social interaction or subcultural identification in the home, family, or leisure arena. Sarah Thornton (1997, 15) argues that it was studies such as Jock Young's *The Drugtakers* (1971), which drew on Herbert Marcuse's analysis of work, leisure, and productivity, that provided the transition to the Birmingham school's concerns with youth as mediating both class culture and mass culture. But others also point to the continuities between both schools, which focused on urban, working-class young men and on spectacular forms of subcultural or street-corner activity (S. Cohen 1997, 150).

Resistance and Disappointment

The Birmingham school theorists, of course, have been critiqued for overinterpreting the working of "resistance" and for focusing largely on the experiences of white, working-class young men (S. Cohen 1997, Gelder 1997, Turner 1996). Youth culture scholars since then have looked more carefully at the contradictory political meanings of subcultures and "oppositionality," and have also critically examined constructions of gender, sexuality, and race (Duncombe 2002; D. Gaines 1990; Kelley 1997b; Leblanc 1999; Lipsitz 1994; McRobbie 1994, 1999, 2000; Rose 1994; Thornton 1996). We would also argue that while our understandings of resistance clearly need to be complicated—and have been, given the work of Michel Foucault, Ernest Laclau, Chantal Mouffe, and James Scott, among others—the issue of resistance is still on the table. Theorists may have grown weary of the dichotomous framing of resistance, which can pit oppositionality against appropriation, or the micro-politics of popular culture against formal, organized activism. These binaries may be familiar and perhaps frustrating, to the extent that they can lead to a semantics game of sorting particular actions into very subtle abstract categories, making distinctions, for example, among acts that are "oppositional" or "transgressive," "authentic" or "imposed," in the process losing touch with the actual, complex meanings and consequences of these actions in the lives of youth.

It seems that a common cultural studies argument, applied to a variety of sites, is that even apparently progressive cultural forms can in fact be complicit with the very forces participants aim to overthrow. And while this argument may lead academics to throw up their hands in theoretical fatigue, there is still value in drawing attention to the fact that this is how power, in relations of race, gender, and nation, continues to operate, and that resistance may indeed take recognizable forms. We cannot give up on this analysis of resistance simply because the tradition may feel well established and therefore not "new." Furthermore, young people themselves are very much seeking vernaculars for dissent, and we may be missing the depth and subtlety of their critiques, sometimes out of our own fears of pinning our politics and hopes for a new theory of resistance onto young people. Yet perhaps what is most powerful or instructive are the nuanced ways in which young people express disappointment in the gaps they perceive between the potential for expressive forms and political movements to achieve change, and the complex realities of how that potential can be redirected or diffused. Maybe this idea of disappointment, which young people express in myriad ways, unsettles the binaries of resistance and cooptation, and in a sense resonates with the disappointment of academics longing for theories to reinvigorate our own sense of political efficacy.

We clearly see the ways in which popular culture is a space for contesting ideas about national identity, belonging, or patriotism, as well as the ways in which the space for expression is sometimes constricted to project a national consensus. The notion of "the popular" is fraught at this moment, as it inevitably is in times of national and international crises, so it is worth drawing on the essays in this book to think about the ways in which the political meanings of popular culture are produced and critiqued by youth, in the face of images of Gen-X (or Gen-Y) political apathy. Many young people may indeed feel alienated from the forms of politics they see around them, but it is still worth investigating the frameworks that popular culture offers youth, or the frameworks they themselves create through cultural production to understand the political world, if not to question it. In this, we have been inspired by the work of theorists such as Lipsitz, Robin Kelley (1994, 1997b), and also Juan Flores (2000), who have argued for a definition of popular culture that is temporal, not just spatial, and that complicates old distinctions of high/elite and low/popular. Drawing on Johannes Fabian's work on anthropology and popular culture, Flores (2000, 20) urges us to "think of popular culture not so much as an entity comprised of products and processes, or as a bounded social space such as low or marginal, but as a relation or system of relations. Rather than marking off boundaries and defining separate spheres of cultural practice, perhaps popular culture is about the traversing and transgressing of them, and characterized by a dialogic among classes and social sectors, such as the popular and non-popular, high and low, restricted and mass."

Fabian, grappling with questions of democracy and popular culture, offers the notion of "moments of freedom," observing that "the problem of freedom poses itself within, not only between, high and popular, dominant and dominated culture" and concluding that "there can never be a freedom as a state of grace, permanent, and continuous. . . . Freedom, in dialectical parlance, comes in moments" (1998, 20–21). This idea, of moments of freedom—decidedly plural—in popular culture is one that is still provocative to us, especially when juxtaposed with the insights of the various essays in the book that each theorize the relation between popular culture and the political in some way. We think the works here speak best for themselves, given the range of arguments and theoretical possibilities they suggest, and that they attest to the continuing importance not just of the question of politics in youth culture studies, but also of youth culture studies as a political project.

Organization of the Book

The sections that organize the book knit together the different structural and analytic dimensions of the chapters they contain. The first section, "Documents and Tags," offers a range of examples of how young people negotiate policies of the state, and of nongovernmental organizations, that regulate youth through notions of citizenship, racial classification, and "rehabilitation." "Documents" suggests the regimes of governmentality that young people are forced to negotiate, whether as refugee youth, high school students, or targets of state profiling. This term highlights the paradoxes faced by youth as they attempt to respond creatively to the spaces these institutions carve out for them, infusing these sites with their own imaginings of citizenship or struggles with democratic ideals. "Tags" evokes the work of graffiti artists who move through urban space leaving marks of their presence in neighborhoods that are often considered by outsiders to be devoid of art or cultural vitality, or on public transportation that carries graffiti through other neighborhoods, even when artists themselves "stay home." "Tags" also evokes the labels or systems of classification imposed on youth, from census categorizations of race to government initiatives defining youth itself to other markers of social difference. It suggests the possibilities, but also limits, of playing with alternate identities in the public sphere.

"Movements and Outbreaks," the second section, operates on at least two levels. First, several authors in this section describe new trajectories of youth that are forming in relationship to consumption, the state, and violence, where identity categories are used strategically as potentially fluid or transnational bases for organizing and reshaping the very notion of youth and family. Throughout this section, youth use diverse resources, ranging from rap lyrics to statistical instruments to fashion statements, to advance their particular and unpredictable movements into and across boundaries. Second, there is the more indirect reference in this section to movement in the sense of new modes of mobility—ideological, physical, and economic—that young people experience through their encounters with, and in some cases critiques of, globalizing or state forces. The essays in this section that address criminalization, deportation, and social stratification point to the structural and imaginary limits of these movements that motivate some "outbreaks" and prevent others.

The final section, "Icons and Retakes," contains a set of essays that relate, in one way or another, to identities that young people manufacture and assume through their relationships with and against "established" or iconic personas, such as Jackie Chan, Eminem, and Spike Lee. Each of these chapters comments on a form of doubling, from the "retakes" of video production to the rereading of lyrics by hip hop audiences to the rewriting of Chan's aesthetic in a young fan's media archives. Retakes could also imply the re-creation of family and the back and forth of migration, as in Schneider's essay, which focuses on a young refugee boy growing up in a Swiss foster family after his father returns to Sri Lanka.

Methodologies, Texts, Disciplines

As authors in this volume experiment with diverse techniques of inquiry, youth emerge sometimes as the "figure," the central focus of discussion, and sometimes as the "ground," a cultural category that lends itself to the interrogation of key themes in social theory, such as citizenship, cosmopolitanism, gender, race, or visuality. In this sense, methodological and disciplinary orientation constitute a kind of subtext against which one might read the chapters' substantive theoretical contributions. This shifting methodological and disciplinary subtext seems especially fitting given youth culture studies' own contested position within the academy.

The study of popular cultures within local, national, and globalized contexts is itself, then, never outside institutional tensions pertaining to place, power, and culture. In this sense these essays carry on the long-standing search within cultural studies for ways to avoid vulgar empiricism, on the one hand, and sterile textual criticism, on the other, by developing and employing methods that seem consistent with Stuart Hall's assumption that "culture will always work through its textualities—and at the same time . . . textuality is never enough" (1996, 271; see also Grossberg 1996, Kelly 2000). Textuality is a major point of provocation for cultural studies scholars, given the continued use of methods derived from the humanities alongside what appears to be something of a move toward reflexive or critical ethnography (Cohen and Ainley 2000). These methodological interventions clearly make their mark in the chapters of this book. Authors use diverse approaches to studying cultural production, such as combining textual and psychoanalytic methods with discourse analysis and ethnographic techniques. Parallel frames of analysis run through these essays, as authors examine media content, explore social context, and reflect critically on their own involvement within their sites of study. In this sense, they point to both the limitations and possibilities of methodological eclecticism, bringing together modes of inquiry born of different, and in some cases not so easily integrated, disciplines.

In many ways the interdisciplinarity of a youthscapes approach, in terms of theory and methodology, aligns with broader trends across the academy to draw on diverse conceptual frameworks and modes of analysis when carrying out research. What stands out here, in particular, is the extent to which authors bring young people's own innovative epistemologies and theoretical resources into conversation with ideas drawn from published literature. Concepts gleaned from daily life and vernaculars within these authors' research sites, and in some cases literally quoted from individual youth, are used not simply as "raw" materials to be interpreted but as already developed grounded theories that fuel further analysis.

The collection does not consolidate in a single, clear picture of what interdisciplinarity looks like within youth culture studies, and it is also evident that there are works that point to the strengths of training in a particular disciplinary approach or theoretical tradition. The institutional context of the academy, the ways in which departments and programs are formed in relation to disciplines and tenure is awarded and evaluated, inevitably shape the possibilities of interdisciplinary work in a field such as youth culture research. The essays here suggest a call for scholars to be ever vigilant and generous in what they take as data, how they conduct analysis, and what really counts as a worthwhile theoretical contribution. For interdisciplinarity here means not only venturing into areas that fall within a different academic department, but also listening for theories that may rarely if ever appear as such in any literature, but which play an important role in shaping the lives of young people and their real, imaginary, and institutionalized "others" (Lipsitz 2001). To conduct youth culture studies in ways that connect with questions of national ideologies and global processes means, in many cases, pulling theory through analyses, embedding conceptual insights within sources ranging from ethnographic descriptions to visual images to the discourses of youth engaged in moment-to-moment interaction. In this sense the book is uniquely suited to integrate fine-tuned studies of everyday life and popular culture with broader critiques of the local, national, and global. Youth are not merely products of the interconnections among these spheres of social life—sectors easily, and misguidedly, cordoned off from each other as "micro" and "macro" levels of analysis. Rather, young people forge those connections in their daily lives as they move through the institutions that shape how we and they live together in the deep and uneven relations that surface in this volume.

Part I
Documents and Tags

Chapter 1
Straight Outta Mogadishu: Prescribed Identities and Performative Practices Among Somali Youth in North American High Schools

Murray Forman

I open with a research anecdote: while explaining his school's daily operations and the "work" of engaging youth in their education and school life, a public high school principal quietly lamented the fact that his school was acquiring a local reputation as "a dumping ground" for the immigrant and refugee children spilling into the city.[1] He rattled off a list of global hot spots, places rife with civil war, civic unrest, and from which vast swaths of the populations desperately sought escape, noting with a shrug of resignation that teenagers from these countries would eventually end up at the door to his school; time proved him right. His perception was based on the school's diverse student body, often characterized as a "mini United Nations," which was increasingly comprised of youths displaced by violence in eastern Europe and Africa. As this principal explained, the teaching mission at his school had undergone a substantial shift with the arrival of a massive influx of Somali immigrant and refugee youth, veering from a traditional educational process of teaching and vocational training toward meeting new exigencies that circumscribe and define the boundaries of nation, race, and citizenship.

As I will argue, the public education systems in Canada and the United States serve a particular function in the transformative ideological project that attempts to revise or realign Somali youth identities. I will further explain that schools also provide a primary setting where these global teens—teens whose forced peregrination is on a global scale—actively engage in the self-aware processes of renegotiating their individual and collective identities among their peers. They do so by many means: watching television and music videos, carefully observing the sartorial codes of their classmates and neighbors, developing "westernized" musical tastes and consumer patterns or acquiring a facility with the slang of the day. It is frequently in the hallways and grounds of public schools where immigrant and refugee teens enact their identity "performances," exploring new and radically altered versions of themselves on the stage of teen expressivity. Official institutional authorities and teen peers are each crucial to the processes of transformation among foreign students and must be approached as dual (and often dueling) forces influencing the experiences of Somali youths.

Somali Youth: A Brief Profile

In Canada and the United States, Somali youth are situated within an institutional nexus comprised of the family, religion, and the school. In many cases, fathers and uncles—the foundation of the Somali patriarchal family structure—have either been killed in battle or were unable to exit the country with their families due to years of civil war and internal clan violence, at times resulting in the premature ascendancy of male children in the family hierarchy.[2] This has produced extreme pressures on single mothers who have managed the transit and welfare of their children (Affi 1997). Many fragmented Somali families have landed in North America after arduous and extremely dangerous exits from their homeland, navigating the militias, land mines, and roving bandits as well as the legitimate and the corrupt factions that monitor and control the stream of refugees crossing their national borders. By 1995, the inflow of Somali immigrants and refugees in designated settlement communities in both Canada and the United States had resulted in high neighborhood concentrations of Somalis, altering the character of these specific locales.

The Somali family structure has consequently suffered immeasurably, causing considerable stress on maturing teenagers. Islamic tenets provide a cohesive force in the Somali community and it is often the adherence to practices of the Muslim faith that links Somali teens in their new cultural environments. As some youth have expressed, in a world where so much has been taken from them, where all that was once certain has been rent apart, Islam provides the single most stable force in their daily lives. After a period of initial bewilderment, school staff members have learned to accommodate the prayer needs of observant Muslim students by, among other things, permitting access to restrooms to wash before prayer sessions and providing classroom space for mid-day prayers.

The inevitable culture clashes that erupt take multiple forms as immigrant teenagers become acclimatized to their new surroundings. Due to the strife in Somalia, many teenagers have been unschooled for several years and, among the more extreme cases, younger teens have been almost entirely lacking any formal education. Acquiring English language skills and learning to negotiate the Westernized institutional environments of their schools and communities, teens gradually begin to drift away from the core values of the family and of Islam, producing a generational dissonance that is not easily resolved. As the anchoring "grand narratives" of Somali nationalism and Islamic values wane among Somali teens, there is a corresponding sense of cultural erosion and loss among Somali elders. As one Somali parent who was an active member of the parent-based school council explained, "You know, a lot of values are getting less binding because of the influence of the main culture. There are a lot of things from Somali culture we'd like to keep and sometimes these come at a cross with the main culture."

Iain Chambers describes the dialogical character of immigrant nomadicism encompassing interactions between oneself and the cultural Other and between one's present self and the resonating cultural forces of the past that are diminished or abandoned: "Faced with the loss of roots, and the subsequent weakening in the grammar of 'authenticity,' we move into a vaster landscape. Our sense of belonging, our language and the myths we carry in us remain, but no longer as 'origins' or signs of 'authenticity' capable of guaranteeing the sense of our lives. They now linger as traces, voices, memories and murmurs that are mixed in with other histories, episodes, encounters" (1994, 18–19). The point here is that Somali teenagers are frequently adrift between cultures, as are all immigrants, refugees, and postnational wanderers. Yet, because of their specific political, geocultural, and ethnic character, Somali youths are also positioned in a turbulent nexus of institutional influences. While many Somali youth claim that they are either unable or unwilling to maintain heritage traditions, they continue to feel the resonating effects of a cultural past in their "new" lives in North America. According to one Somali student, "People stick with people because they speak the same language, because they have the same backgrounds. The only time I talk to other people is in the classroom. Other people don't trust those who are different." As a result of cultural incertitude, many youths encounter considerable difficulties in establishing stability within a transitional mode that is shaped by an array of competing agendas.

First Encounter: The Public School

Schools constitute a primary port of entry for young global migrants and teen refugees who arrive in North America, providing a sociocultural threshold through which displaced youths must pass as they enter into the North American social mainstream. Reinforcing this point, a school vice-principal articulated the school's role as a culturally disciplining force, stating "this is Canada, so we have to use our standards." It is also in schools that immigrant and refugee youth most directly encounter the formal and informal integrating forces of their new society, where the structured discourses of nationalism, conveyed through the educational curriculum and other facets of public schooling, converge with the unwieldy discourses of contemporary popular culture. Within these sites of convergence observers can note "the connection between student alienation and classroom resistance to new narrative forms currently being constructed in the domain of the popular" (McLaren and Giroux 1997, 36). High schools subsequently emerge as a point of contact and as a site of a particularly intense nature where the collision of cultures and competing discourses occurs, giving rise to a variety of interpretations and expressions of postmodern, if not necessarily postnational, citizenship for displaced global youth.

Public high schools attempt to manage strategically the education and cultural transformation of their immigrant and refugee students through a series of suturing practices. The idea of suture refers, in one sense, to a school's attempts to help the mending process, especially among refugee youth, closing their psychological wounds and rejuvenating young people whose spirits have been shattered by turmoil and terror. It also describes the process of accumulating young people from around the world and suturing them into the school as a learning community and, by extension, into the local civic community and the wider nation. This includes drawing them in more closely to public agglomerations of different scales through specialized curricula as well as through extracurricular activities that inculcate school and national spirit and otherwise bind young people together at the level of experience and affect.

It is true, as Michael Olneck suggests, that immigrant or refugee encounters with schools are "conditioned by local school cultures. . . . Immigrants do not enter into undifferentiated 'American' [or Canadian] schools. They enter into specific schools whose immediate contexts, histories, memories, and commitments shape their organization and practices" (1995, 315). The school sites of this study exemplify the transitions occurring within their school catchment areas, encompassing a demographic shift from predominantly white, middle-class constituencies to mixed-race, multiethnic, and mixed-income populations. These (and many other) schools are consequently affected in new ways by shifting world conditions, and are, thus, repositioned within what Kevin Robins terms "the global-local nexus," involving diverse tensions

that are exerted at the level of scale: "Globalization is, in fact, also associated with new dynamics of re-localization. It is about the achievement of
a new global-local nexus. . . . It is important to see the local as a rela-
tional, and relative, concept. If once it was significant in relation to the
national sphere, now its meaning is being recast in the context of globalization" (1991, 34–35). In response to the localized impact and varie-
gated manifestations of such pronounced demographic shifts, what one
principal describes as "a revolution, not an evolution," these urban
schools, like many others throughout North America, must continually
restructure and reimagine themselves to accommodate the diversity of
incoming students.

Underfunded and undersupported, these "international" schools frequently battle with school board trustees over the numbers of foreign
students assigned to them. Trying to do "more with less" emerges as a
common expression among administrators, yet for all their efforts they
generally end up doing less with less (Butler-Kisber and Forman 1998).
Compounding matters, such schools are often debilitated by unscrupu-
lous interschool maneuvers and the back room dealings of principals,
parent committees, and school board trustees who work in tandem to
ensure that the influx of immigrants and refugees is channeled and contained in one or two schools rather than affecting/infecting the entire
system.[3] This includes providing easy exit options among mainly white
students seeking transfers, resulting in what one principal described as
a "ghettoizing" effect.

Immigrant and refugee students, as well as those who are native born,
chafe under the negative labels and reputation that their schools bear
due to unethical containment practices. They are subject to verbal ridicule by students from other schools and are painfully aware of enhanced
public scrutiny and negative judgment (Butler-Kisber and Forman
1998). As one Somali male student claimed, "People say there are so
many fights, but I don't see it. People blame our students for disruptions
everywhere," to which other attendant Somali students concurred,
explaining, "Other schools make fun of us" and "They all laugh at me
for going here." A tenth-grade Somali male student narrowed his interpretation of external derision, claiming that the dominant public perception was that the school was "violent and dirty," further suggesting
that these epithets were also readily traced onto the predominant
Somali student body. The Canadian school where Somali enrollment
hovered near fifty percent was widely disparaged by city youths who
referred to it as "Mogadishu High." Students also communicated the
belief that their overall quality of education suffered as a result of dis-
criminatory practices and policies, undermining their opportunities in
the competitive job market and post-secondary school admissions. One

eleventh-grade female student who had attended the high school for only one year remarked, "We can't choose, but if I could, I wouldn't come here." While students within the school may feel that "it's friendly and open," they are also frustrated and angered by the prevailing racial and cultural stereotypes that diminish their status and ignore their collective achievements. The student respondents frequently reacted to the atmosphere of discrimination they felt, explaining in focus group interviews, "it's not right" and "it's not fair."

"First world" and "third world" comparisons are not uncommon in either school context, with North America's sheltering capacity or its vaunted reputation as a land of wealth and opportunity emerging as facets of a standard classroom discourse. Securing the host nation's authority is a strategic achievement and from the moment they enter their new schools, immigrant and refugee students encounter the disciplining forces of the nation that are articulated through the regulating powers of the school. One means of maintaining such distinctions was conveyed through the discourse of "standards" as teachers and administrators continually judged "third world" educational systems as being substandard to the North American system.

Teachers validate the international status of their students, yet they are just as capable of inflecting the dynamics between the host nation and students' heritage nations within hierarchical relations of domination and subordination. An expression of authority is evident in the way that immigrant and refugee students are required to stand silently for the playing of the American or Canadian national anthems even though they lack a sense of identification with the nation. Such tendencies are implicated in the mapping of subject positions available to immigrants, refugees, and minority youth as well as defining the terms of citizenship to which these constituencies are coerced to adhere. Addressing the delineation of authority and dissent in relation to a nation's master codes of citizenship, Renato Rosaldo writes, "Cultural citizenship attends, not only to dominant exclusions and marginalizations, but also to subordinate aspirations for and definitions of enfranchisement" (1999, 260). In this sense, many Somali students verbally imply that they frequently "go along" with the school rules as a means to "get along" in their new nation. The aforementioned Somali parent who was a member of the school council acknowledged the difficulties young Somali students encounter, uttering with a sense of resignation, "I think it's not easy for these kids when they're living in two worlds."

Nation, Discourse, and Otherness

Many cultural analysts have noted that, where immigrant populations are involved, dominant national discourses are aggressively mobilized and overlaid with convergent discourses of racial difference that produce negative structuring effects (Omi and Winant 1994; Giroux 1996; Walcott 1997; G. Clarke 1998). Henry Giroux points to this tendency within nationalist discourses when he writes, "National identity is structured through a notion of citizenship and patriotism that subordinates ethnic, racial, and cultural differences to the assimilating logic of a common culture, or, more brutally, the 'melting pot'" (1996, 190). In a viable articulation of the conditions of contemporary education in multicultural situations, Michael Omi and Howard Winant explain that "the state is inherently racial. Far from intervening in racial conflicts, the state is increasingly the preeminent site of racial conflict" (1994, 82). In this context, existing school systems can be regarded as extensions of state authority; each school operates in pact with the state to circulate the dominant national discourses and to fulfill the national agenda while responding to localized conditions whereby incoming Somali students confront their racial identities anew.

During this study, it was evident that, among secondary school educators (who are generally well intentioned) in both Canada and the United States, "nation" is discursively structured within a relatively monolithic vision of unity. Among most high school educators, nation is evidently still generally conceived as a singular and coherent entity, despite the ruptures and counterexamples that abound. During the project's data-gathering stage, there was certainly no sign of teachers trumpeting the decentering of the nation as a binding construct and celebrating the arrival of "postnationalism" with its attendant libratory potentials (Chambers 1994). Still, despite the adherence to a generally homogeneous conceptualization of what the nation is and a commitment to its maintenance, there was no single unified *expression* of nation or national identity that was streamlined for propagation among the students; schools and curricula plainly are not that well organized. The image of the idealized nation is, in practice, portrayed unevenly and inconsistently within each school, creating fissures in the national narrative. The dilemmas of defining and disseminating idealized constructs of national identity are exacerbated when, in the United States, competing ideological forces (embodied, for example, in the Democratic and Republican parties) are in tension or, in Canada, when historically rooted debates about national identity (across regional and linguistic divides) remain unresolved. Though each country presents its own timeworn rituals of nationhood, these rituals are also often carefully orchestrated in institutional settings as part of the strategic attempt to mitigate the impact of fractious ideological conflicts.

Within a dominant discursive frame, the multiple, contingent meanings of "nation" are accentuated by the various idiosyncratic interpretations upon which teachers base their lessons and through which they convey national ideals. This is not to say, however, that Somali youth are not perceptive observers. The fact that most child refugees in North America have escaped from the violence of national conflict and civil war should not be overlooked. In Canada, where the confusion over nation and national identities is more explicit than in the United States, inconsistent appeals to an ostensibly stable, unified image of the nation rapidly become obvious to even the most disengaged immigrant and refugee student. Somali students admit to not always understanding the details of Canada's apparent national identity crisis, but they do recognize it as a crisis. Their incomprehension is not related to the realities of a nation divided by cultural and ethnic differences. As they made clear time and again, what they struggle to understand within their own frame of Somali experience is how it does not result in full-scale war.

George Clarke (1998) takes this one step further, noting that the discourse of Canadian national identity structures a narrative positing French and English heritages as the core of national belonging. He suggests that this not only facilitates the erasure of Canada's First Nations aboriginal population but also its global immigrant constituencies. As he notes, in Canada and the United States the nation is a racialized construct that privileges whiteness.[4] The conservative interpretation of the national crisis can be—and too often is—defensively articulated toward the immigrant and refugee populations, ascribing a causal relationship between the arrival of global immigrants and refugees and perceived national erosion. This sentiment was given voice in one unfortunate discussion with a white teacher who, in defining the perceived problems in her school, expressed the attitude that "there are too many of one color here."

Immigrant and refugee youths are regularly denied adequate opportunities in society or their schools to implement the values of their experiences and to collaborate meaningfully in the redefinition and reinvention of "the nation." Though this is true for most students, it is intensely so for foreign students who are already often marginalized by their lack of English language skills or, insidiously, by their race or ethnicity. The vice-principal at one school elaborated on the importance of introducing preestablished rules and regulations that did not invite student collaboration or input: "Kids buy into rules quickly. . . . Teenagers are interesting. If you make a rule and explain it, if they understand it, they buy into it. If the rule is there, especially if it's already in place, they'll buy it."

An alternate example can be seen in the manner in which Somali youths were invited, again and again, to recount publicly their harrowing tales of escape, journey, and arrival in North America. On the surface this would seem like a positive empowering exercise allowing students to articulate their experiences and identities publicly in a performative mode. That it was requested of the students by their teachers, however, is reminiscent of the colonial condition in which the voice of the subjugated Other is reproduced within the authoritative structures of the dominant class, directed toward conversations of nation and identity that are already established within unequal and imbalanced power relations. The teachers unfailingly provided the conclusion to these tales by amplifying the message that North America is a safe haven and, implicitly, a superior national culture for its comparative stability and democratic underpinning.

The stories further serve as a means of positioning students, locking them into their "refugee" or "immigrant" roles and relegating them to an objectified identity that is oddly dependent on their own histories. Escaping a repressive system or dangerous context and living to tell the tale may, thus, produce a prison of another, discursive form. The students' own experiential narratives become a binding force, an ideological shackle that constrains their capacity to redefine and transform their subjective identities within their new national loci on their own terms as they actively—even desperately—seek to realign themselves according to what Arjun Appadurai (1996) describes as "postnational loyalties" and "transnational identities."

Belonging and Fitting In

As the Somali school council member, community elder, and parent of two teenagers explained, "This is the first generation that has come to Canada. We need to be a plus to Canada; we don't want to be a minus. We have to work strong and hard to prove that we are a plus, that we belong here." This adult attitude, however, differs from that expressed by many Somali students for whom "fitting in" is of more immediate concern, suggesting a generational division that is exacerbated by exposure to new cultural contexts and their accompanying exigencies. Belonging and fitting in are each aspects of suturing practices applied to young foreign students, though in this articulation suture is not necessarily aligned with the formal practices of institutional authorities but is more accurately an intentional effort initiated by Somali youths operating according to their own interests, needs, and longer term agendas.

Belonging is aligned with the agendas of the state that dictate processes of establishing citizenship or legitimate national subject status. To belong, individuals embrace the dominant values and meanings of the nation while proving their worthiness (and personal worth) so that they will, in turn, be accepted into the nation. Belonging involves pride and it also entails fulfilling the prescribed obligations to the nation that, for students, also means being respectful of one's teachers, submitting to the rules of the school and the laws of the land, or excelling scholastically.

Belonging is also related to the hegemonic relations between the immigrant and the state and the battle for consent that precedes one's induction as a "naturalized" citizen. It is significant to note that in the school research sites, the Somali students whose sense of belonging was most pronounced were also among the highest academic achievers and were the most directly engaged in academic life and student leadership. They observed the rules and their inclusion was predicated on their ability to meet prescribed standards and simultaneously conform to the ideals of the school and the nation. An unfortunate outcome emerged during field observations and interviews, however, when Somali students attained a positive status in the eyes of teachers and administrators and were subsequently subjected to new pressures by virtue of their capacity to succeed according to predefined terms. Weighted with "the burden of representation," they were repeatedly selected out of the student body or the Somali student population, isolated by staff members as examples of immigrant student capability. They were cast as the "good" Somali students and elevated as role models among their peers, even though their unrequested status at times resulted in ostracization or more obscure forms of marginalization among both their Somali peers and their native-born classmates. These students struggled with the additional expectations placed upon them, gaining a critical understanding of the manipulative potentials of institutional authority as well as learning the price of success in their new cultural environment.

Fitting in is entirely different than belonging; it is more contingent. One may fit in but never really belong. Conversely, one may never quite fit in among peers yet, with duration and exposure to the nation's symbolic systems, one may develop a sense of national belonging. Fitting in is prone to shifting affinities, marked by gestures, expressions, and mannerisms that bespeak a certain urgency. Fitting in involves a lived process that unfolds across the images and ideals of the nation but is not easily reducible to them. It does not require an established commitment to the nation per se, but operates through the formation of subnational allegiances and subcultural alliances, the "microcultures" that encompass various milieus and localized sites of significance. As Helena Wulff writes, "Microcultures are flows of meaning which are managed by people in small groups that meet on an everyday basis. . . . The particular combination of personalities, the localities where they meet, and certain momentous events that they experience together, are three kernel elements in every microculture (1995a, 65)." Becoming Canadian or American is not, for most Somali teens, as important as establishing a peer identity and participating in the elaborated practices of teen-oriented production and consumption. In both the U.S. and Canadian contexts, numerous students from various ethnic backgrounds pointed to their school as offering a preferable environment for peer interaction and ease of fitting in; as one tenth-grade female student recounted, her school had "an advantage compared to other schools because of the different cultures. The social life is better here," citing a perception of snobbishness and racial intolerance at several of the city's other high schools.

School curricula and the institutional discourses of nation and otherness often reinforce structures of difference that define relations of authority and subordination between institutions and individuals, between native citizens and foreign immigrants, between adults and youths, between whites and nonwhites. Daily, Somali teens listen to teachers reproduce the mainstream curricula; they are taught by adults who operate under the assumption, whether true or not, that Somali students "desperately want to be North American," as one school administrator suggested. Between classes and in the breaks, however, these students experience the dynamics of teen culture and learn to read across the symbolic and codified distinctions of subcultural difference. Thus, they are rapidly exposed to a complex range of ideas and experiences that require radically different cultural maps than those presented by their teachers. Somali teens subsequently observe with great care the myriad performative modes of other teenagers. Taking cues from those surrounding them, Somali teens develop complex strategies of identity (trans)formation, working within the semiotic systems of youth style and meaning as a method of fitting in. This involves what Paul Willis describes as "symbolic creativity," the individual or collective activity that "transforms what is provided and helps to produce specific forms of human identity and capacity. Being human—human be-ingness—means to be creative in the sense of remaking the world for ourselves as we make and find our own place and identity" (1990a, 11).

Performing Contemporary Black Youth Identities

Somali students suggest in interviews and conversations that in their homeland they are not interpolated as "black" according to the various competing meanings of the term in North America. It is upon their arrival in Canada and the United States that they encounter informal social practices and formal institutional structures that inscribe them as black youth. For some, this is a disorienting revelation that demands considerable introspection and self-evaluation. They do not always fully comprehend the racial basis of their new social status nor do they easily process the North American discourses of racial and generational difference that marginalize and socially construct them as Other. The phenomenon leads many Somali teens to interrogate what North American blackness is, how it is manifested in its many forms, and how they might fit into a system that has historically discriminated against minority youth.

Jody Cohen writes, "Although identity development is not in the curriculum, teenagers continually formulate, act out, and revise identities. . . . Interwoven with individual identity formation is the development of cultural identity, in our society closely linked with racial identity" (1993, 293). The effects of the cultural encounter with North American racial hierarchies are further exacerbated outside the school when, as a young Somali male explained, a bigoted white landlord yells at Somali teens, employing racial epithets as he does so, or when a white police officer interrogates them for no apparent reason; in a focus group discussion, references to these and similar incidents elicited knowing nods of agreement among the small group of assembled Somali respondents. These frequent expressions of racial intolerance or cultural miscomprehension resonate with Walcott's important observation that Somalis in Canada are located "outside the Canadian imaginary" while they are simultaneously "being forced into the North American black criminal paradigm" (1997, 87). Such forces of surveillance and policing are also highly evident in the schools themselves. One Somali girl in eleventh grade criticized a vice-principal's vigilance as being "like a dog waiting to get you" and a Somali male freshman claimed that the senior administrators "know how to play the game . . . they have the screws in ya while they're smiling." Another boy summarized the critical scrutiny of Somali male students as being unjustified, stating, "They're evil, like the devil . . . they encourage you to drop out." In many instances (usually during informal field interviews), accusations of institutional racism targeted against Somali youths were explicitly articulated by the student respondents.

Somali youths receive a rapid education in North American racial politics with their accompanying Canadian and U.S. nuances, and concurrently experience firsthand the realities of a contemporary social system that regards minority youth and immigrant populations as a problem, as part of a "crisis" (Hall et al. 1978; Gilroy 1987; Acland 1995; Forman 2002). As a result, with the gradual enhancement of their English language skills and growing comfort with their public identities, Somali teens also begin to conjoin their critical resistance with that of their black peers, voicing their opposition to real or perceived inequities in terms that strongly conform to those of North American black youth.

Among Somali youths this involves gradually adopting the mantle of blackness, consciously and unconsciously adapting the codes of North American black youth culture in the formation of their own evolving teen identities. Fitting in, in this context, is structured across a shared ideological and discursive system of racial values and political convictions.

Further defining this range of alignments, the transformative character among many Somali youth can be connected to the expressions of hip-hop culture that encompass "a whole way of life."[5] While hip-hop has evolved into a prominent facet of teen culture in general, spanning a broad racial and class spectrum, the most intense concentrations of involvement, whether as producers or audience consumers, are among urban black and Latino youth constituencies. As members of this "Hip Hop generation" (MEE Foundation 1993; Kitwana 2002), a term describing youths who were born after approximately 1978, young Somalis are increasingly steeped in an awareness of the multiple activities of hip-hop while connecting to a larger nation-based system of hip-hop attitudes, values, and meanings. This might be framed within a notion of fracture, though not simply the bifurcated "two-ness" bridging race and nation as W. E. B. DuBois suggested in his classic text *The Souls of Black Folk* (1903), but today bridging multiple loci of identity, which in the Somali case includes allegiances to more than one nation and a plurality of racial constructs that are summoned contingently, within specific contexts and conditions.

Although it is not commonly framed in such a manner, Somali teens entering North American neighborhoods and schools also encounter the hegemonic authority of hip-hop culture. Hip-hop is a dominant cultural form among contemporary black youth and it is primarily within its fields of discourse that the problematic articulations of racial and cultural authenticity are most frequently expressed (Boyd 1997; Kelley 1997b; Forman 2002). Michael Eric Dyson notes, "Many of the divisions in black life—especially those based on gender, class, sexuality, authenticity, and generation—come together in debates about the virtues and vices of hip-hop culture. Hip-hop artists furiously debate the politics of authenticity; many artists have as a motto to 'keep it real'" (1996, xii). Indeed, the question of "real" black identities is given voice in complex and often vitriolic terms in hip-hop, especially in the lyrics of rap songs and in hip-hop's ancillary press.

While the authenticity debates are rampant, it is a fact that there is a prevailing and pronounced American bias in the articulations of black identity. Somali teenagers eagerly consume images of a particular kind or character of blackness that has as its heritage the cultural past of blacks in the United States, although this heritage may or may not be understood and articulated among hip-hop's young practitioners in explicitly historical terms. In this context, Somali teens in Canada also respond more fully to icons and symbols of U.S. black popular culture that are defined and disseminated within hip-hop, although they frequently imply that they are aware of the cultural distinctions across the border (especially in the instance of gun or gangster-related themes that are stereotypically associated with U.S. urban youth). The contemporary ghetto also functions, problematically, as a geocultural signifier of black authenticity. The spaces and places of the ghetto or "the 'hood" have, since at least 1988 and the rise of the powerfully compelling gangster rap subgenre, become identified in the minds of youths across the racial spectrum with exoticized ideals of danger, threat, and survival amid adversity (Forman 2002). This phenomenon is of significance among Somali immigrant and refugee youth who, due to their often precarious economic status, inhabit low-income housing projects in their settlement communities that are also home to many low-income black Canadian and U.S. families. By tuning into specific media texts that valorize the constrained environments of "the 'hood," Somali youth encounter cultural meanings and values that inform attitudes and practices among their peers and their immediate neighbors, many of whom are also their classmates.

Somali youths quickly recognize that hip-hop establishes many of the norms and values currently defining "authentic" black identity among youths, and, moreover, they rapidly determine that these informal (that is, noninstitutionally grounded) articulations of blackness are organized alternatively and often in radical opposition to the formally structured discourses of race and nation as they are communicated in the schools. They enter into these issues, however, with virtually no historical sense of North American cultural politics and a general lack of familiarity with race, identity, and difference in North American contexts. Somali teens learn from their North American peers that, as some recorded lyrics proclaim, "real niggaz make the world go 'round." In the Canadian school, however, Somali students are also exposed to a Caribbean student population and in the U.S. school there is a sizable Latino contingent (consisting primarily of youth of Puerto Rican and Dominican lineage).

The Somali teens observe various distinctions in style, argot, and cultural tastes in their encounters with these students, discerning the nuances of blackness that are influenced by national heritage, yet among the Caribbean and Latino cohort—especially those of Jamaican extraction—and among a smaller group of white students, the primacy of African American hip-hop remains identifiable. Other in-group factors, such as the cultural tendency among Somali girls to be more physically expressive with one another, also set them apart from their student peers, including the hip-hop-identified black or Latino classmates who may remain suspicious of their differences. In one instance, during a school assembly, a group of American black female students was seen shunning a lone Somali girl clad in a hijab and traditional robes, joking among themselves that they didn't want her touching them when the lights went down. She subsequently sat alienated and alone, lending credence to Dyson's comment that "hip-hop's homophobia is vicious and downright depressing" (1996, xii).

The question, then, is how do Somali youths enact their interpreted versions of black youth identities? How do they reconcile their Somali heritage and their black youth status in their schools, in this new land? How do they attain citizenship in the "imagined" hip-hop nation even as they vie for citizenship documents in the official nation-state? Manthia Diawara provides one analytic option when he describes the shift away from what he terms "black oppression studies" toward "black performance studies." This approach emphasizes "the ways in which black people, through communicative action, created and continue to create themselves within the American experience. Such an approach would contain several interrelated notions, among them that 'performance' involves an individual or group of people interpreting an existing tradition—reinventing themselves—in front of an audience or public; and that black agency in the U.S. involves the redefinitions of the tools of Americanness" (Diawara 1993, 265). More specifically addressing Canadian cultural contexts, Walcott isolates black performativity "as something that is continually provisional and an act of doing—verbing," explaining that performance strategies are inexorably tied to a politics of racial identity that is prone to constant revision (1997, 100).

Somali youths generally arrive on this continent with limited "cultural capital" in relation to international cultural repertoires. They consume the images and styles of their teen counterparts in acts of symbolic creativity, inflecting them with their own relevant meanings in a performative mode with the school conforming to Diawara's notion of a performative space. Clearly, there is a process of reinterpretation and reinvention underway. For example, the male teenagers in the Canadian school who are most explicitly aligned with the hip-hop culture regularly wore camouflage sports gear and rugged wear that were then current, displayed in hip-hop magazines and music videos. For them, it had dual significance: it allowed them to fit in with other teenage hip-hop fans wearing similar gear but it also maintained a continuity with the military garb that is common among fighting men in the militias and clan forces of the Somali capital, Mogadishu. The Somali boys inhabited the style as a masculine statement of identity, reinforcing their "thug" image with the swagger and intonations of hip-hop. Their clothing was not a benign fashion statement, however, as it drew from, and was influenced by, several overlapping elements of teen identity and youth rebellion that meet in the cultural conjunctions of the Somali immigrant and refugee experience. This sartorial gesture is, therefore, part of a symbolically loaded performance that cannot easily be dismissed.

These youths were incensed by the administration's sudden rule against wearing camouflage to school, a decision that was (I learned, upon consultation with the school administrators) based on the belief that it could cause discomfort among other Somali students as well as students from various war-torn nations. In voicing their disapproval and dissent, several of the male students—one of whom summoned the spirit of the late rap star Tupac Shakur in his self-definition as a "thug nigga"—cited a wider and more complex range of problems, from the fact that the rule was inadequately explained and harshly imposed upon them, to the claim that the administration and staff are racist and discriminate against Somali students, especially the males, and even more precisely, the group whose hip-hop affiliations were most evident. For them, their stylistic choices are part of a fundamental identity issue; the freedom and ability to dress in the subcultural style that is most meaningful has important implications for their sense of self in relation to their cultural roots and their location within the hierarchies of the school and the wider teen community.

Difference looms large in the performative practices of teen identity politics and, in making their case, these Somali youths confirmed that they were gradually internalizing the systems of racial distinction and the accompanying cartographies delineating the terrains of subcultural affiliation. This was also evident as they articulated their resistance and questioned the legitimacy of the administrative rules by pointing to white students whose own sartorial tendencies included the prominent display of corpses, skeletons, and skulls as an expression of their involvement with other subcultural scenes (such as the goths). As one older Somali student stated, "Why can't we wear camouflage? . . . sometimes I just wonder if [the administrators] know what they're doing. Wearing camouflage don't hurt nobody. There are more serious things . . . Why can't we wear no camouflage but the other students can wear the punk-Nazi stuff. They wear tattoos, boots, black clothes." This, the Somali youths argued, was a horrifying and much less acceptable fashion statement, having acquired new social relevance as a potential signifier of teen nihilism in the aftermath of the April, 1999, Columbine High School massacre in Littleton, Colorado.

Cultural Consumption, Mass Media, and Identity Transformation

The initial experiences among Somali youths in North America involved a widespread "sampling" of cultural forms, including musical genres, learning the codes, signs, and symbols through which North American teenagers communicate, and developing media literacies that inform their sartorial style, argot, and general comportment. During focus group discussions, Somali students frequently cited the importance of school events, including music performances and dances, as contributing inestimably to their knowledge and awareness of North American youth tastes. John Shepherd addresses the particular power of music in this context: "Music is ideally suited to coding homologously, and therefore to evoking powerfully yet symbolically . . . because music can enter, grip, and position us symbolically, it can act powerfully to structure and mediate individual awareness as the ultimate seat of social and cultural reproduction (1993, 52)." In practice, the media function as central elements in the postmodern and postcolonial processes that shape Somali teen identities in North America. In Somalia, teen contact with North American popular culture is constrained by cultural barriers (that is, Islam) and the prevailing turmoil that restricts access to international popular media. Referring to rap music, Somali youths in the U.S. high school explained that, while they were familiar with the genre before exiting Somalia, they did not have sufficient access to tapes or CDs to develop a broad aesthetic appreciation of the music, nor were they able to form fan-based affiliations around individual artists. Within the Canadian school, I was told by one boy that some Somali teens have attempted to rap in their native tongue but the results were not particularly successful in his evaluation; unlike Spanish or French in which rap is commonly performed, the Somali accent and cadence seem ill-suited to its appropriation.

Many Somali teens, and the young women certainly, are discouraged or forbidden from participating in extracurricular school dances or events that traditionally occur in the evenings. Upon realizing that Somali cultural norms forbade girls from attending school dances or evening events, the staff and student council at the Canadian school rescheduled some of these events for the hours immediately following the day's last class in order to accommodate their Somali student population. This was deemed acceptable—and commendable—among Somali parents and students alike. Describing their parties at teen youth centers or community functions, Somali youths stated that they listen to a mix of musical styles, with American rap and Jamaican dance hall reggae figuring prominently, as well as playing tapes and CDs by popular Somali artists as they are available.

As one Somali teenager in Canada suggested, after immigration there is an initial process of socialization that involves the perusal of North America's pop cultural menu. He described his encounters with a range of musical styles, including country, classic and college rock, reggae, and rap, and the various teen subcultures, audience formations, or "affective alliances" (Grossberg 1992) that are shaped in and through these genres. For him, rap fit his personal taste patterns and those of most of his friends yet he expressed uncertainty when asked if there were extenuating social influences guiding his taste and gravitation toward rap and the stylistic elements of hip-hop. He acknowledged his awareness that rap is, at its base, black music and there was a sense of comfort—even a sense of security—in this student's identification with hip-hop. It seemed that hip-hop was the stronger preference in part due to its symbolic messages, its inherent blackness. Most Somalis interviewed in this study admitted that the images of black youth emanating from hip-hop music videos and the dynamic "hard-core" narrative themes of street life portrayed in rap have more to do with their drift toward the music than anything about the music itself, although they clearly love its "beats and rhythms."

Herman Gray has observed, "Within the mediascape of contemporary consumer culture, black youth constantly use the body, self-adornment, movement, language, and music to construct and locate themselves socially and culturally" (1995, 149). Visual style produces an interesting cultural hybrid among Somali teenage girls who display a sartorial blend of traditional Somali garb (such as the hijab or wrapped headdress) and hip-hop street wear (including oversized name-brand sports gear). In the Canadian school, divisions among Somali girls could be charted along the lines of adherence to either hip-hop or Muslim style codes. Some girls were unabashedly "Westernized" in their consumption and style decisions, whereas others navigated the cultural boundaries more cautiously, in some cases arriving at school wearing their hijabs, removing them and storing them in their lockers until it was time to return home. In the U.S. school, where the general level of cultural incorporation evolved more slowly, it was common to see girls wearing long, brightly colored clan robes, although this was also evident among the more recent arrivals at both the Canadian and U.S. schools.

Both male and female Somali students, of whom many are enrolled in special language courses, regularly infuse their speech with the highly debated "ebonics" or "black English" forms of American black youth vernacular that they openly acknowledge is derived from recorded rap, film, and television as well as from their American or Canadian-born classmates. This is not a simple case of reaction against formal language systems (that is, not a case of celebratory resistance against the tongue of authority), nor is it an unconscious adoption of black linguistic styles. Rather, it can be interpreted in practice as an experiment in language performance that engages with central issues of signification at the juncture between Somali, black, American, and Canadian points of identity, in the sense implied by Homi Bhabha, who writes, "Culture as a strategy of survival is both transnational and translational" (1995, 48).

While at ease in the hallways and school yards, the Somali teens flex their new language loudly and confidently, although at times imperfectly; in the Canadian school, one vice-principal explained, "I hate to point to one group, but when Somalis talk in the hallways, they're loud . . . you'd think there was a riot." In the U.S. site, I witnessed a small group of African American boys laughing quietly (though not maliciously) among themselves as they observed several Somali teens struggling to phrase properly their hip-hop-inflected expressions. It is worth noting, however, that disparate approaches to language education in the Canadian and U.S. contexts have produced quite different results in terms of the ways that Somali teens enter into both their schools' youth cultures and the hip-hop vernaculars that inform language practices among North American black youth.[6] With time, male and female students converse easily among themselves and with classmates and staff in both English and Somali, switching between languages effortlessly. As their English language skills improve, Somali "homeboys" and "homegirls" become more clearly aligned with hip-hop's particular expressivity and are much more fluent in the vernaculars of their black peers. Moreover, they were seen to be more confident and aggressive in articulating their dissatisfaction with school governance and were more capable of expressing their hybrid identities across a range of contexts.

Conclusion

The high school context offers an important public space where identities are forged, often under great duress, and where powerful formal and informal discourses compete. The situation is changing rapidly, however, as the first generation of Somali immigrant students has graduated and a new generation of high school students—their younger siblings—enters the system. The current wave of Somali high school students, many of whom arrived from Somalia as young children or preteens, has in most cases already become accustomed to North American schooling and education. They know what is expected of them in class and they enter high schools with better English language skills and a more thorough comprehension of North American cultural norms and values. They are also more prone to recognize themselves within the dominant contours of "the nation," positioned within the institutional discourses of national belonging and located along the prevailing spectrum of racial identity and youth practices. Indeed, the manner in which younger Somalis today understand racial and subcultural differences and express their subjective agency or define their identities adhere to different strategies than those of their elder brothers and sisters. These distinctions produce separate tiers within the Somali community.

The local institutions and authorities are also now more familiar with their young Somali wards and there is a more fluid interaction between disparate communities who have attained a basic level of familiarity, if not necessarily greater tolerance and respect toward one another. Finally, hip-hop, as an underlying influence in the social processes through which Somali youths express their agency, reinvent their individual and collective identities, and "become" black, is itself undergoing continual reinvention. The discourses and accumulation of signs and imagery emanating from black popular culture industries offer fluctuating ideals to which teens might aspire, repositioning the meanings among eager Somali teen audiences.

With each successive wave of Somali youth moving through North American high schools, the social development and individual and collective sense of national allegiance or belonging will undergo transformation, as will the methods employed as Somali youths attempt to fit in alongside their classmates and peers. By apprehending the tensions between the formal and informal discourses and expressions of nation and identity that converge with undeniable force in the social spaces of contemporary North American high schools, it becomes possible to illuminate the mechanisms through which Somali immigrant and refugee youths align themselves within larger social formations. Although the high school exists as but one social setting among many, its central role in the lives of this youth group makes it an important site in which to undertake the research on African communities in North America. Beyond a narrow comprehension of "the African condition" in this continent, the encounters, struggles, and dynamics of transnationalism and cultural resistance with which Somali teens regularly engage can better expose the constructed characters of Canada and the United States as multiethnic and multiracial nations.

Chapter 2
Gangs and Their Walls

Ralph Cintron

More than twenty years ago while walking through a Mexican American neighborhood somewhere in San Antonio, Texas, a good friend and I passed by a house whose front yard had become a cluttered gallery of homemade concrete folk art. Scattered within this fantastic scene were real mesquite trees, shrubs, vines, a dwarf tree or two, and potted plants and flowers. Narrow paths tried to make their way through the clutter but were soon defeated. The lot was small, but oh so intense. The clutter wrapped around both sides of the house to create an even bigger heap of the back yard. This scene was from long ago, and now I cannot remember if the figurines and other odd, concrete sculptures contained a set of themes that may have unified this enormous, wild collection. What I distinctly remember to this day was a sign over the doorway of the house. It announced the artist's name, followed by the word "MAKER." Makers; the process of making; made things as cultural displays or performances; the economic, social, and political contexts of made things; the circulation of such things through the imaginations of a community and a culture—these issues constitute major themes in this chapter.

One of this essay's controlling questions is *how does one create respect under conditions of little or no respect?* Where I did fieldwork, it seemed sometimes that the difficulty of conditions—or their perceived difficulty—encouraged a kind of hyperbolic need for respect. The result was that some versions of creating respect were incompatible with other versions. People created different kinds of respect that were constantly backfiring in the eyes of others.

At this level, as I explore how people made and unmade themselves and how these makings were received by different audiences, the essay, as well as the larger study on which it draws (Cintron 1997), is traditionally ethnographic. I consider the project an ethnography of a Latino/a community approaching thirty thousand people who live in a city I call Angelstown, a city of approximately one hundred thousand located close to Chicago. However, I would also like my readers to consider the essay a project in the rhetorics of public culture or the rhetorics of everyday life. The first term in particular is my own, but both terms try to name an approach that, consistent with the discipline of rhetoric, is interested in the structured contentiousness that organizes, albeit fleetingly, a community or a culture.

Street-Gang Graffiti: Lexicon and Syntax

There are no other gang experts except participants.
—*Sanyika Shakur, AKA Monster Kody Scott,* Monster: The Autobiography of an L.A. Gang Member, *p. xiii*

The above quotation by Shakur is an important critique of anyone presuming to comment, as I will shortly, on street gangs and their graffiti.[1] I will discuss street gangs even though, at most, my research assistants, Edmundo Cavazos and Dan Anderson, and I scuttled along the periphery of a few gangs. We interviewed those individuals who accepted us and became friends with a few, and occasionally we stumbled onto caches of information that we had no right to see. I never aspired to being a gang expert. I turned to street-gang members, however, because, in my interpretive scheme, they embodied the question of *how does one create respect under conditions of little or no respect?* with an intensity that acted like a search light revealing the rest of the community. Street-gang members explicitly wrote out their needs for respect, and the more I realized this particular fact the clearer it became to me that this most glaring manifestation of desire, frustration, and the appeal of the hyperbolic highlighted the common structure, the single story under the many.

What is necessary to understand first are the syntactic elements and lexicon of Angelstown's graffiti and how that syntax and vocabulary operated in a variety of other media to create a thick semiotic full of redundant messages. I will concentrate on the lexicon of the Almighty Latin King Nation because I know more about this organization. The emblem of the Latin Kings was either the five-pointed or the three-pointed crown with the five-pointed being more common. Members of the nation referred to the crown as *la corona*. Each point of the *corona* was jeweled and represented a particular ideal. Oftentimes the figure of a man with longish hair, trimmed mustache, pointed beard, and a tear drop was drawn wearing the crown. This figure was called *el rey*, "king," and associations with "Christ the king" or the "king of kings" were not uncommon. (The term "king of kings," however, was also used for the highest leader of the King Nation, a leader who was rumored to have visited the area at least once.) Not appearing in graffiti but still an important emblem of the Latin Kings was the lion, the *king* of the jungle.

The colors of the Latin Kings were black and gold. All street gangs in Angelstown used black as one of their colors, but for the Kings, black signified the "dominant color of the universe," the "darkness of the immense night," and the "alpha and the omega." Gold represented the sun and the "brilliance of the mind." Black and gold were described as the two colors of creation, "existing since the beginning of time and enduring forever."[2]

The number that ruled over the Latin Kings was five (five-pointed crown, for instance), and their abbreviations were ALKN (Almighty Latin King Nation), LKN, and LK. Again, not appearing in graffiti but still an important part of "representing" oneself as a Latin King was the left side of the body, as in wearing an earring in the left ear, cocking one's baseball cap to the left, or folding one's left arm over one's right. The number five, the phrase "All is well," and "representing" to the left were also used by a larger alliance of gangs called the "People," which in Angelstown consisted primarily of the Kings, Vicelords, and, for a while, the Insane Deuces. The other gangs in this alliance, however, had different colors and symbols. For instance, the colors of the Vicelords were red and black, and their symbols were typically a pyramid, a crescent moon, a cane, a tophat, and a martini glass. The Insane Deuces, in contrast, used green and black as their colors, and their symbols were dice, the spade playing-card, and the number two.

Battling against the Latin Kings were rival gangs belonging to another confederation called the "Folks." In Angelstown, the Folks' gangs were primarily different branches of Disciples, and these included Black Gangster Disciples, Satan's Disciples (sometimes called Spanish Disciples), and Maniac Latin Disciples. These gangs all "represented" to the right and used a variety of symbols such as pitchforks, six-pointed stars, a devil's tail and horns, and a heart with wings. As I said earlier, graffiti was only one medium to make use of the basic lexicon. Hand signs, tattoos, jewelry, clothes, oral language, and miscellaneous objects used the same vocabulary to signal one's gang affiliations and to insult other gangs.

The most conspicuous way to mark one's affiliation, however, was to wear one's colors. A goal of a young Latin King, for instance, might be the assembling of as many clothes as possible referencing the colors and emblems of the Kings. Basketball shoes worn with five holes left open (five being the ruling number), Pittsburgh Pirates baseball hats (black and gold with a P signalling "People"), a sports jacket from the Iowa

Hawkeyes (black and gold) or the L.A. Kings hockey club, or any item from Miller Genuine Draft Beer (black and gold) might be used. Other gangs, of course, appropriated their own mainstream symbols according to their special lexicons. For instance, the red and black of the Chicago Bulls were suited to the Vicelords, and the green in Notre Dame and Oakland Athletics paraphernalia was suited to the Insane Deuces.

In short, the possibilities for appropriating mainstream symbols and recontextualizing them into new meanings were almost endless.[3] These appropriations pointed to one of the most important characteristics of Angelstown's street gangs and, I believe, American street gangs in general. In the public sphere, street gangs and particularly "hard-core" gang members may be viewed as a kind of antisociety (Halliday 1978), as barbarous and vermin-like, so completely outside the fold of the human community that they deserve to be removed. Indeed, as I will show, street gangs for very understandable reasons sometimes played with this very rhetoric, creating from it hyperbolized images in which the mainstream could witness its deepest fears. In gobbling up the images, the mainstream felt that it had the evidence that proved the legitimacy of its views. But, I would argue, constructing such legitimacy was based on the mainstream positioning itself atop a moral high ground from which to judge and punish. What quickly disappeared in this moral scenario was a more accurate and complex picture, namely, that, even as a street gang adopted its transgressive pose, the gang was structured with numerous appropriations from the mainstream. In other words, the appropriations of mainstream material, so visible during a gang member's display of his or her colors, might be understood as a kind of synecdoche of an entire system of appropriations through which street gangs constructed themselves. Therefore, to understand the display of colors was to understand that the mainstream's cultural material was the very fund that a street gang tapped in order to make its meanings. The mainstream may have circulated its fund of cash and iconography,[4] but the street gang performed a symbolic conquering of the mainstream when mainstream meanings gave way to gang meanings. For the most part, the mainstream could not interpret gang meanings, and thus a secret, esoteric, subterranean world was made. Here, then, in this most common of gang gestures, the display of colors, was the ambiguous structure of the street gang, borrowing from the mainstream even as it formulated a radical departure.

Continuing the linguistic metaphors, I will turn to the "syntax" of graffiti. The most prominent syntactic elements were a group of markers that might be called "negative morphemes." To a certain extent, these morphemes also operated across media. Two of these morphemes were reversals and upside downs. For instance, to reverse a letter in a rival gang's abbreviation or to draw a rival gang's symbol upside down was to disrespect that gang. A reversed "K," therefore, beside an upside down *corona* meant that someone was disrespecting the Latin Kings. Similarly, to "throw down" the hand sign for the Latin Kings was to disrespect the Kings. Or, taking another example, to disrespect the Insane Deuces one might draw an upside-down spade alongside an upside down 2 (the spade and 2 being two of the primary symbols for the Deuces) alongside a reversed "D." Because the Deuces and Kings were battling each other, one would expect to see alongside the disrespected symbols the other gang's symbols drawn in conventional fashion.[5] Disrespect, therefore, was syntactically marked through reversals and upside downs—negative morphemes, if you will, "non," "un," or "not"—whereas respect was unmarked. Indeed, the notion of respect relied on the conventions of standard writing in so far as street-gang graffiti was typically written linearly from left to right and followed standard spelling. This last point is important, for it suggests that convention in signaling respect was the baseline on which a transgressive order was manufactured.

Two other negative-like morphemes characterized graffiti. These consisted of "K," meaning "killer," and a squiggly line that cancelled a rival gang's graffiti. To draw such a line was to "crack" the graffiti. For instance, imagine that the Latin Kings had drawn their *corona* and written beside it their initials, ALKN. A rival gang member could disrespect the Kings by "cracking" the *corona* with a squiggly line drawn through its middle and by adding a "K" after ALKN. In short, such a gang member would be announcing himself or herself as an Almighty Latin King Nation Killer. "Killer" and "love" were structured opposites equivalent to the "throwing down" of a rival gang's hand sign and, in contrast, the "throwing up" of the hand sign of one's own gang.

So far, I have been examining the "lexicon" and "syntax" of gang graffiti. But also very observable in graffiti were certain stylistic elements. Those who put up graffiti, as I was told often, had special talents. The major purpose of graffiti was to enact explicitly a degree of violence against another gang or to do so implicitly by celebrating the power of one's own gang. Much graffiti went unsigned, but, signed or not, at times there were stylistic characteristics performed with flair that garnered for the graffiti writer considerable respect. One such characteristic was called "Old English script" by gang members and entailed a considerable amount of fancy lettering reminiscent, perhaps, of that found in illuminated manuscripts. Stylistic elaboration, then, of the core symbols and abbreviations of one's gang was at the heart of the very decorative Old English script.

However, I know of at least one example of another kind of elaboration that did not follow the "look" of Old English script. This particular example of elaboration used conventional lettering to create visual puns to amplify a set of redundant meanings. This piece of graffiti was particularly frightening on first viewing. It was drawn by a Latin King (King Sinister, I presume), whom I did not know, at a time when the Kings were being gunned down by the Disciples, the Spanish Disciples, the Insane Deuces, and the Maniac Latin Disciples. Done in blood red with a thick application that sometimes dripped, this stretch of graffiti seemed to capture stylistically in ways that I had never seen before the violence and paranoia of the moment. In the left-hand corner, as if introducing the graffiti, was a jingle: 5 King's Gunning/10 Deuces Running. (I presume "Deuces" was meant, but since the lettering only provided a reversed "D," it is possible that "Disciples" was also being punned.) The juxtaposition of this structure, a kind of childlike rhyme, with such a violent semantic amplified the haunting and threatening quality of this stretch of graffiti. Throughout the graffiti the "i" was typically dotted with five pointed stars, the number "5" being one of the numbers identified with the Kings. In fact, "5" occurred in various places: for instance, below the *corona* and in various arrangements of red dots above the *corona* and other places. In other words, the number "5" echoed throughout the stretch of graffiti, thickening one of its central, if implicitly understood, messages: *King love.* Put downs of at least four gangs (Deuces, Spanish Disciples, Maniac Latin Disciples, and Gangster Disciples) were just as thickly and redundantly placed.

Most graffiti lacked the stylized elaborations of either Old English script or the idiosyncratic visual puns just described. Since this stylized, ornate work was especially respected, it deserves further comment. So-called Old English has a long precedent in American street-gang life. Rodriguez (1993: 51–52), for instance, talks about "old English" among Latino street gangs in the 1960s and 1970s in Los Angeles: "I had on a T-shirt, cut off at the shoulders, with "The Animal Tribe" in old English lettering on the back written in shoe polish. . . ." He also describes the use of the word "Thee" in such street-gang names as Thee Impersonations and Thee Mystics: " 'Thee' being an old English usage that other clubs would adopt because it made everything sound classier, nobler, *badder*" (Rodriguez 1993, 41–42). For Rodriguez and other gang members, then, this oral and written style they called "Old English" was classy and noble. As an emblem of a romanticized past, Old English allowed its purveyors to rupture the humiliation of the present. In this sense, Old English was a site for creating the stylized difference of street-gang life. In appropriating this style, gangs made it their signature writ large. Moreover, Old English was part of a larger iconography that included thumpers, Too Low Flows,[6] hair and clothing styles, and so on, each one a special site for creating an exaggeration that might be awarded respect. This iconography, then, represented a kind of confluence in which Old English as evocation of the past blended with other styles that evoked the modern. Each style was a site that could offer the remaking of one's world—or at least a rhetorical remaking behind which lay a version of the real world, biting hard, insisting that it be made over through any means necessary.

Graffiti, as part of the warfare between rival gangs, was the use of language in the place of—although, at times, as a kind of—weaponry. It could be used, for instance, to proclaim a particular gang's territory or the courage and audacity of a rival gang member who had dared to enter enemy territory to disrespect the local gang. Under these conditions, inscription often led to erasure either by a property owner or rival gang member, which, in turn, often followed by another round of inscription and erasure. In short, the ephemeralness of graffiti meant that an evening's work could disappear only to reappear again the next night. When graffiti became layered in this way, one message atop another, a wall became dense with authors. Authors had found a way to scribe themselves over each other in their need to make themselves individually and socially known. This system of inscription and erasure resulting in layered messages, then, was the physical trace that one could read, if one knew how, of the system of respect and disrespect that could rightfully be called the emotional origins behind the warfare of graffiti. Or it was the logic of violence, the need to take the moral high ground at the expense of another, written out on the walls of the city.

Other physical characteristics of graffiti included its size as well as the varied surfaces that it could occupy. These characteristics helped to create a special presence in the midst of public space. Graffiti, of course, could occupy a variety of surfaces: interior or exterior walls, fences, dumpsters, concrete supports of expressways, garage doors, doors, and so on. It could even turn the corners of buildings. In taking over these spaces, it created a kind of "rulership"—a loaded and potent term in the context of gang life. Such rulership declared through the medium of graffiti not only who controlled the 'hood, but simultaneously and implicitly established a new set of rules that violated those of conventional print space. Graffiti implicitly declared metaphorical ownership wherever it desired and in the face of property owners whose own system of rules was being rendered impotent. It is no wonder, then, that graffiti in Angelstown quickly became an issue in the larger battle for control of public spaces. Indeed, while I was doing research, graffiti surfaced during city council meetings. Council members discussed graffiti resistant paints, youth agencies that might be used to remove graffiti, and, finally, passed an ordinance that compelled, among other things, property owners to clean up graffiti on their premises.

Street Gangs, the Public Sphere, and the Topos of Nationhood

When graffiti declared ownership of a particular 'hood by a particular street gang, that ownership functioned as part of a "shadow" system that had no legitimacy inside the system world. Since ownership in the system world was certified during the exchange of cash, the ownership that graffiti declared was, in comparison, metaphorical, or might be called a tactical response, in de Certeau's (1988) sense, to the system world.[7] Street-gang graffiti and its inherent bravado and the willingness to back up that bravado with force were substitutes for cash, its metaphor so to speak—but a metaphor that individuals willingly spilled blood for.

The more Dan Anderson and I looked at street-gang graffiti, the more we were convinced that it was not only a tactics of action (metaphorical ownership) but also a tactics of language. By "tactics of language," I mean that graffiti was an important narrative "tactic" available to gang members for the public expression of their subjectivities, subjectivities that were constantly being suppressed by the public sphere. Indeed, if my earlier descriptions of street-gang graffiti relied heavily on linguistic terms such as "syntax" and "lexicon," it was to prepare the foundation for describing graffiti as a special kind of narrative genre whose deeper meanings were not explicit but which rested on a large substratum of related but private oral and written texts. In short, graffiti was the condensed narrative of more subterranean narratives and the only one of these to enter public spaces.

In order to clarify the point that graffiti might be interpreted as condensed, public narratives whose roots reached into subterranean texts consisting of more elaborated, private narratives that circulated through the shadow system of street gangs, I will turn to the fact that the term "nation" appeared in both kinds of narratives. The term "nation" or its abbreviation "N," as in ALKN (Almighty Latin King Nation), was commonly written out in the graffiti of Angelstown. Moreover, I have already explained how major gangs referred to themselves as nations or organizations as in the Insane Gangster Satan's Disciples Nation (also known as Spanish Disciples) and the Maniac Latin Disciples Nation. It should be no surprise, then, that terms such as "nation," "empire," and "organization" were part of the daily talk and the official written documents that circulated among gang members. To make my point, I take the following example from a letter authored by a gang leader and widely dispersed to gang members in other chapters of the same gang: "All sections of our Nation must come together to form this structure of power, to put all minds, hearts, and dedication to help this organization structure grow stronger." And notice the word "empire" and continuing emphasis upon solidarity in related documents: "My brothers, this is just the beginning of our Empire. This is a new era of the 90's, which we shall improve with time, to become a great organized power. That we will use to build a predominant (having superior strength, influence, or authority,) Empire." (All quotations from street-gang documents, their spelling, syntax, and so on, are exact.)

Why should the trope or *topos* of nationhood hold such a special place in the shadow system of street gangs? In my interpretive scheme, the *topos* of nationhood provided the shadow system one more way to mimic the system world. But why should the same trope be so important for both the overarching nation as well as the many gang nations in its confines? What sort of need does this shared trope satisfy? What sorts of imaginings does it rhetorically conjure? An illuminating set of essays collected in *Nation and Narration* makes a case for the discursive construction of nationhood among nation states of the system world.[8] A shared perspective of these authors is that authority busily composes "its powerful image" by constructing such "national objects of knowledge" as "Tradition, People, the Reason of State, High Culture," and so on and represents these "as holistic concepts located within an evolutionary narrative of historical continuity" (Bhabha 1991, 3). Ernest Renan (1991, 19) in 1882 discussed the strategy that such narratives might take:

The nation, like the individual, is the culmination of a long past of endeavours, sacrifice, and devotion. Of all cults, that of the ancestors is the most legitimate, for the ancestors have made us what we are. A heroic past, great men, glory (by which I understand genuine glory), this is the social capital upon which one bases a national idea. To have common glories in the past and to have a common will in the present; to have performed great deeds together, to wish to perfom still more—these are the essential conditions for being a people. One loves in proportion to the sacrifices to which one has consented, and in proportion to the ills that one has suffered.

It may be that the *topos* of nationhood incorporates something of Renan's strategy wherever it is found. At any rate, one can hear it fully inherited in a street-gang document describing the annual picnic honoring the birthday of the gang's founder, their "Beloved King," as if the distances of time, culture, and socioeconomic context could not separate Renan's heroic, historical Europe from that of an American street gang in the 1990s:

On this day we shall all give thanks to our Beloved King, the day in which the heavens had sent Him down among us, to bring us together as a family.

This very Special Day is when all of our family comes together, to show the Honor, Love, Respect, and Greatfulness, we all have for the Beloved King. Having Him among us is a blessing, because it's Him who loved us enough to show this Nation the way to a key, which opens the door to Life.

He never gave up the struggle or hopes of this Nation to become as great as it is now. Holding on was a must, and holding on He has did, never letting the Family fall.

As we, given Him the power and strength, He in return gave us the knowledge and understanding to believe in who and what we can become. The one powerful Nation of an Organization, and a Great Loving Family of Sisters and Brothers.

The *topos* of nationhood—perhaps, in whatever context it should appear—would seem to be, at best, subtly coercive, for its task is to have disparate, individual wills voluntarily meld themselves into a community (brotherhood/sisterhood). At worst, for instance, in a totalitarian state, the coercion is far more blatant. At any rate, in the enumeration of nostalgic legends, heroes, and a common lineage, of shared sorrows, sacrifices, cultural *topoi*, institutions, language, rituals, honor, and so on, the past is constructed as a kind of animus that continues to—or ought to—inspire the present and make it virtuous long into the future. In short, a dedicated community—a "Loving Family of Sisters and Brothers"—can span the continuum of time and transcend the forces of decay, and it is this dedication that the *topos* of nationhood tries to instill in the very depths of the individual will as an identification that is more than merely persuasive. If the *topos* of nationhood can evoke such dedication, then the human longing for continuity, cohesion, stability, and power becomes satisfied, and in this forming of an enduring community we abate our aloneness and our fear of chaos so that even death, particularly in the case of war, can be reinterpreted as sacrifice. It is in these ways and others that the *topos* of nationhood attempts to create a kind of single photograph of countless people that is passed around as everyone's reality.

At some point, however, if the *topos* of nationhood should cease to inspire dedication, then the many fault lines hidden below its coercive efforts begin to stir. Some of the most disturbing fault lines would be those invented by street gangs: declarations of independent nationhood via rival geographies, laws, traditions, and systems of authority in the very belly of the overarching nation. In making such declarations, the shadow system mimics or turns itself into a metaphor of the system world, and in that mimicry the system world sees the chaos that its veneer of continuity, cohesion, stability, and power were meant to seal. The irony is that in having pursued the *topos* of nationhood, the system world set the stage for its own attempted assassination. For the *topoi* of a culture are available to everyone, and during those times when the rhetoric of the overarching nation fails to inspire some of its citizenry with the mystique of solidarity, the rhetoric of a gang nation is ready to work out its version of the same magic as one response to the increasing organizational status of rival gang nations. It is at these moments that the system world becomes terrified. One of our gang-member friends captured it this way when describing to Dan the picnic/celebration day of his gang. Our friend spoke of two thousand of his brothers and sisters wearing "a sea of baby blue and black" at a state-wide gathering. The police had the area circled but kept their distance, knowing they were outnumbered. Meanwhile, the gang members and their families ate free food and played games provided by the leadership. From the perspective of the lifeworld of the gang members, the scene was "righteous" in so far as it asserted a defiant and just empowerment of their nation over and against the system world's more bankrupt authority.

The view of gang nationhood I have been describing appears to be mostly oppositional, as if a shadow system had specifically emerged to oppose the system world. Such a view, I believe, is misleading for two reasons. First, gang nationhood in the Chicago area, it seems to me, was a formidable response to the threats posed by rival gangs who had been amassing over time their own organizational status. In short, it was largely within a system of gang rivalry—rather than a way to defy the overarching nation—that street gangs imagined their nationhood. This view of nationhood as rivalry was particularly true for young gang members, who, in my view, were politically self-conscious only intermittently. However, the gaining of a kind of political self-consciousness might occur through the experience of jail. For some, the experience of jail could function as a kind of rite of passage in which one could get, as one gang member told me, "wisdom." "Wisdom" and "360 degrees of enlightenment," which was a concept that circulated through at least two gangs, might lead to seeing one's gang nation as specifically opposed to the overarching nation. To experience imprisonment was to experience the oppressions of society in their most concentrated form. In addition, jail provided one the opportunity to read the politically sophisticated lore that had been written over the years by the more mature brothers from one's gang. In short, I am trying to avoid the suggestion that all gang members saw their nationhood as explicitly opposing the overarching nation. Second and more significantly, since opposition is rarely whole and seamless, characterizing street gangs and others as necessarily and defiantly opposed to the overarching nation misses important subtleties. The term of choice in this text has been "appropriation," more so than "opposition." For instance, in contexts of power differences, "opposition" suggests only resistance and its strategies, whereas the term "appropriation" suggests a use of "tactics," in de Certeau's sense, as well as envy on the part of the less powerful for the more powerful. It is from such an understanding that one can make sense of how being a policeman or a marine or, I have no doubt, fighting in a war defending the United States might be seen as desirable occupations and actions despite the fact that one's gang nationhood expressed implicit opposition to the overarching nation.

Or take the fact that at least one gang saw its nationhood largely, although not entirely, in the context of improving its efficiency in organized crime, and, thus, urged its members to get an education. I quote from official documents again:

> The gangbanging, getting locked up, or getting high on hard drugs, isn't the way anymore. Education is the key to our success, in everyway. All organizations have become powerful with this key to knowledge. Now it's time for us to reach out and take hold of this key, that will open all doors to give opportunities to the Organization as well as yourself.
> What we are trying to accomplish, they call it organized crime. There will be those that will try to stop us. . . .

These examples suggest that in the construction of gang nations the *topos* of nationhood seemed to have functioned with different ends in mind. For instance, it functioned rhetorically, mobilizing the rhetoric of menace, strength, and independence for at least two audiences: other gangs and the overarching nation; but it also mobilized the rhetoric of solidarity and status for a third audience: the gang's own membership. Similar rhetorical conjurings are evoked, for all practical purposes, by nations of the system world. In short, it was as if the shadow system, during its mimicry of the system world, had found the *topos* of nationhood and in so doing fashioned for itself a kind of hyperbolic pose that could be aimed at three audiences.[9]

In short, street gangs of Angelstown, even in their marginalization, are part of a continuum, a thought system, if you will, that is more than just the history of gangs in the United States. In their appropriation of a variety of *topoi*, gangs represent a contemporary incarnation of thought systems ingrained in the society at large.

Limits of the Public Sphere

Nancy Fraser (1993, 15) wants to believe that a subaltern counterpublic has emancipatory potential and constitutes "a good thing in stratified society." Insofar as a counterpublic represents an oppositional interpretation to the status quo and its concentration of power, Fraser would hope that here lies the fertile ground for the emergence of a dialectic between the subordinate world and the system world.

I am not sure that Fraser and others would allow street gangs to be called a subaltern counterpublic. Indeed, maybe here is the test case, a most difficult one, for a Fraser-like interpretation of the public sphere.

In short, at what point do well-intentioned theorists defend and honor a subaltern group as a legitimate "counterpublic" and at what point does a group become labeled criminal and lose almost all participatory privileges? Or the problem might be phrased this way: How expansive can any participatory democracy be when, lying at the farthest limits of its embrace, there exists criminality that is, at least, partially determined by the same socioeconomic and power differences that give rise to subaltern counterpublics? For instance, I have described gang graffiti as "condensed narratives" that emerge from a "shadow system" to occupy public spaces. Graffiti is the evidence of an intense need to acquire power and voice. From this perspective, then, gang graffiti might be considered part of the public evidence of a larger subaltern counterpublic formed as one response to socioeconomic disparities. Graffiti becomes criminal, however, because it functions outside the economic and message-making rules of the system world. Its illegality, of course, is not particularly serious, but the shadow system from which it emerges, the subaltern counterpublic, so to speak, is, in the eyes of most people, seriously illegal when it entails killings and drug dealing.

For the most part, the public sphere in Angelstown was fundamentally closed to gang graffiti writers and street gangs. As evidence, I offer a series of events that occurred between the summers of 1990 and early fall 1991 while Edmundo Cavazos and I were conducting fieldwork off and on. On June 4, a black member of one of Angelstown's primarily Latino street gangs was shot and died a day later. Two other members were shot during the episode. A few days after the shooting, a street ceremony was improvised by gang members who had lost their "brother." The ceremony was staged at the location where their comrade had fallen. The ceremony included flowers that were the same colors as the gang's, large memorial candles, flower-covered crosses, and a placard with a religious saying as well as the street names of other gang members. The local newspaper reported the event, interviewed some of the participants, and took a picture showing about four gang members crouched before the shrine and wearing "hoodies" (street term for sweat shirts with hoods) that helped to cover their faces. Many of the gang members were clearly throwing down (disrespecting) the hand sign of the rival gang responsible for the shooting. The picture and article appeared on the newspaper's front page on June 7.

The newspaper received numerous complaints, and letters were published in the "Letters to the Editor" section. One letter was from the departing president of the local chapter of Mothers Against Gangs.[10] (I have changed the name of the town as well as the name of the newspaper and have not included the actual names of the letter writers. I have also slightly edited the letters and other texts in this section in order to convey their central points more efficiently.)

As if the city of Angelstown does not already have enough problems with gangs, the *Gazette* has to go and promote gangs with a large, front-page photo and story concerning the death of a gang member.

We are shocked that the *Gazette* would lend credibility to a pack of vicious hoodlums by printing their hateful nicknames and colors.

Sure, a young man is dead, but he made his choice to belong with the criminal faction of this city. The *Gazette* does not need to glorify his death or his friends . . .

Come on, *Gazette,* we need your support in ridding Angelstown of vermin, not promoting their evil ways.

A variety of letters before, after, and much later conveyed a sense of dismay concerning street gangs and a general lack of awareness about the natures of gangs. For instance, the following letter suggests that what the prior writers feared concerning the newspaper's role in promoting the death threats of one gang actually came to pass. The connection, however, is highly suspect since the writer seems to be unaware that the gang rivalry in Angelstown at that time was not primarily between blacks and Latinos but, in fact, between two primarily Latino gangs (the Latin Kings and the Insane Deuces). Moreover, it is not even certain which gang the accused men belonged to or if they were, indeed, even gang members.

I read an article in the *Gazette* on June 7 about a young black man killed by two Hispanic men, members of a rival street gang, on June 4.

. . . The next day, a group of black men, members of a street gang, came to the Century Lane neighborhood, romping the street at night and terrifying the neighborhood. The new screen door to my house was destroyed.

I am not a member of a gang, I am not Mexican or Puerto Rican, and I do not have any business with them.[11] I would like to know why I have been included in their hate. Why do gang members destroy property of innocent people? . . .

On June 20, the newspaper published as an editorial the following apology to the complaints that had been received.[12]

We strive continually neither to sensationalize nor underplay the news we report.

Occasionally, however, we stumble. That, in essence, is what happened June 7, when we published a front-page article about a makeshift roadside service conducted in memory of youth gunned down in an apparent gang-related attack.

The problem was not so much the written account—a narrative we hoped would bring home the senselessness of the loss of life it connoted—as it was the photo, containing both gang "colors" and symbols, which accompanied it.

. . . Gang activity is a problem for all of us, and it will take all of us working together to minimize, if not eradicate completely, this blight upon our own home turf. . . .

During the next year, numerous articles, editorials, and letters to the editor concerning street gangs were published in the newspaper. One particular editorial published thirteen months (July 1991) after the above editorial stands out because of how it defends the social order.

Park District Sends Gangs Good Message

An ounce of prevention, as Ben Franklin's "Poor Richard's Almanac" reminded more than two centuries ago, truly is often worth a pound of cure.

Thus, . . . Park District Board recently tried to give area park goers their own ounce of prevention, by means of a new set of policies designed to ban gang activity at all of its family recreation areas. . . .

New rules ban gang colors, insignia, signs

Primarily, the new security rules prohibit all who are wearing known gang colors, emblems and insignia, or who attempt to communicate with gang-related hand signs, from entering and loitering at any park district property.

This is nothing particularly new in what park district police have long sought to accomplish.

However, with so much negative feelings seemingly so rampant about the overall status of the social order these days, it is good to see the district's trustees formally codify what long has been standard practice.

The next step, of course, is to ensure that these new official policies translate into the same kind of aggressive enforcement effort that thus far has marked the first weeks of operation of the park district's beautiful . . . Family Aquatic Center at Howell Place and Montgomery Road in Angelstown.

Indeed, a fine control and enforcement effort there has kept the facility free of incident and helped ensure it remains the inviting family recreation center it was designed to be.

It also, of course—as do the newly passed anti-gang policies—sends a loud and clear message to society's less-desirable elements that this is indeed our community, and they are not welcome.

That's a good message to send.

During this same year, the newspaper reported disagreements between the newly hired police chief and the mayor. In time, the police chief lost the confidence of the mayor and the city council and eventually resigned. The mayor was paraphrased as saying that the police chief had come under criticism for not effectively attacking the "city's gang crime problem" and for not addressing the "morale problems within the police ranks." By August 1991, a new police chief had been chosen, and by early September the new chief had installed a "zero-tolerance" crackdown on gang violence. One measure raised the number of officers assigned to "full time gang patrol" from eight to twenty-five. This new unit represented "about one-sixth the department's combined patrol officers and investigators." Other measures included special tactics such as "street-reclaiming neighborhood sweeps" and the promise "to seek aggressive prosecution of gang members accused of crimes—and stiffer sentences for those who are convicted." These measures and others were seen as fulfilling some of the pledges made by the new police chief, pledges that were meant to appease a very nervous city council whose agitated constituencies, concerned about crime and street gangs, had already influenced recent elections.[13]

What, if anything, does this selection of newspaper articles spanning more than a year's time provide? I suggest that it provides one kind of window unto the public sphere, but the view through this window is of dramatic events whose depths remain hidden. Whereas real people lived out these events with anger, fear, sorrow, dismay, and so on, the newspaper—trapped by advertising revenues, deadlines, economic pressures, the need to respect conventional morality, and who knows what else—never entered the emotional turbulences that coursed through a variety of opposing voices, *including those of gang members.* The result is washed-out life and a bleaching-out of the potential of a participatory public sphere. If the public sphere is that "theater in modern societies in which political participation is enacted through the medium of talk" (Fraser 1993, 2), the *Gazette* could not open its pages to the full range of talk—much less the emotional life behind the talk—so as to begin opening the possibility of political participation. The public sphere as institutionalized openness was not the *Gazette*'s goal, even though it could have helped in this role. Instead, its editorials attempted to shape the public sphere according to conventional views and thereby glossed over the potential critiques of the conventional that might have emerged.

The best example of not undoing the conventional was the *Gazette*'s willingness to bend to the pressures of those who protested the publication of the photograph of the street-side funeral. I will offer my summary and interpretation of the public arguments that eventually led to the *Gazette*'s apology. According to the letters to the editor and the apology itself, the two central arguments were 1) that gangs were being glorified, and 2) that the *Gazette* unwittingly had become a conduit for sending a death threat from the Kings to the Deuces and in so doing was intensifying gang violence. These arguments were coded in such terms as gangs being given "free advertising" and "credibility." The "Christian believers" made a third argument, namely, that the depiction of a fallen gang member as a kind of "religious martyr" was blasphemous and indicated the newspaper's insensitivity to Christians in the community. This argument, however, was not mentioned in the Gazette's apology, hence my claim that only two arguments were central.

Did the credibility and death-threat arguments have weight? On the one hand, both arguments seemed viable. The media, for instance, are sometimes accused of promoting the social ugliness that they witness. Hence, American television audiences are never shown the innocuous streaker who crosses the baseball diamond. More seriously, television stations during, say, a riot may have to determine the fine line between reportage and their potential contribution to incitement if it is possible that nearby viewers may participate. Current practices and policies, therefore, seem to acknowledge that the media may encourage certain actions. On the other hand, it is probably impossible to determine the amount of encouragement, glorification, or credibility that the media might induce. Certainly, the power of the media to encourage streaking and rioting is not as potent as the personal and social conditions that motivate streakers and rioters. Moreover, the media do not stop reporting wars, suicide attempts, terrorist bombings, and so on because they are fearful of encouraging these actions. Was the street-side funeral a significantly different event? Not really. Hence, it is doubtful that running the picture of the funeral had any long-lasting effect on the intensity of the gang wars, or that it encouraged a young person to join a gang. Gang-related actions emerged more from particular emotional frameworks and social conditions than from pictures in the *Gazette*. It is also doubtful that the *Gazette* conveyed a significant death threat that the rival gang didn't already know about. The Deuces, for instance, did not need a newspaper to tell them that the Kings were disrespecting them. Any argument that maintains that the media glorifies, gives credibility to, or encourages the social nastiness that they report on—in short, that some individuals imitate the news, and some do—has to coexist with the equally or more powerful argument that consumers of the media also interpret, discard, ignore, or remain significantly unaware of whatever spectacles the media may present. The bridge that runs between the media and individual consciousness is full of obstacles and detours so that public consciousness remains multiple. Indeed, some of its variations perversely resist the shapings that power of any kind would like to fabricate.

But is it not a tedious and unfair project to judge as false or irrelevant the arguments belonging to people one disagrees with, particularly if this means failing to understand the emotional frameworks that are attempting to speak through the arguments? From this perspective, arguments cannot be lightly discarded as illogical or groundless. Indeed, they are more like indirect pathways through emotional life, and they can be traversed so that they no longer hide what needs to be heard. In this sense, the argumentive talk that comprises the public sphere and from which policymaking emerges is less an arena of rationality than an arena of obscured fears. At any rate, in my view, the arguments made in the letters to the editor and the editorial apology can be traversed so as to reveal important aspects of how real public spheres work. For instance, the funeral occurred in a small and already deeply concerned, even perplexed, community, for the city had never experienced frequent street-gang slayings. The letters and apology, then, seemed to reflect a kind of emotional overload neatly captured in the July 1991 editorial: "so much negative feelings seemingly so rampant about the overall status of the social order these days." And, as if to retrieve some semblance of social order, the same editorial evoked numerous stable icons: for instance, a founding father of American tradition, Ben Franklin, and his "an ounce of prevention . . . is often worth a pound of cure"; the hallowedness of family; and the idea of a community as cordoned-off from "nuisances" and "less-desirable elements." These evocations of stable order helped to justify the enforcement policies of the park district. The irony, however, was that in protecting *public* property in the name of the status quo, the property no longer seemed so *public.* In short, the maintenance of social order is also the maintenance of exclusion. In these letters and editorials, the public—and by extension the public sphere—remained exclusive because at the limits of any defined public lies a fence line of fear electrified by a need for self-preservation. The boundaries of the fence line remain murky because public liberalism may espouse a code of tolerance whereas public conservatism may espouse less tolerant measures. Wherever the fence line lies, however, many who are excluded are magnetized to it, for in testing it one derives power, a power that is otherwise ensconced among those who maintain or abide by the social order. Power derived from testing the fence line might be called reversed power. Hence, those who test may be represented in the public sphere as wild-eyed mavericks toppling the social order, and the self-representations devised by the excluded, as I have suggested among street gangs, oftentimes hyperbolize the maverick label through the *topoi* of nationhood and madness/disorder in order to test with even more power the very fears that limit the public sphere.

What is important to remember is that the public sphere of modern stratified societies, whether imagined as impossibly comprehensive and bourgeois or imagined as sets of feisty subaltern counterpublics with their own argumentive styles and ways of being, is constrained by whatever becomes its collective fear. Locate the anxiety of a public sphere, and one will have located the limit for engaging in rational discourse and, hence, for constructing a participatory democracy. In this sense, a public sphere cannot "think" beyond what terrifies it. And certainly it is the very stratification of society itself that fosters the emergence of systemic fears, for fears tend to consolidate around divisions and differences and to make these more "real" than what might otherwise be the case. Fear in these instances, then, becomes a kind of touchstone, deriving substance from vagueness, invisibly infecting the possibilities of policymaking, and shaping, also invisibly, much of the style and substance of resistance. From all this, I am left with two conclusions. First, the articulation of virtues that occurred in the pages of the *Gazette* was a kind of circling of the wagons by which Angelstown's "law-abiding citizenry" began unconsciously to consolidate communal fears in the guise of virtues and thereby passed a flurry of anti-graffiti ordinances and police actions claiming "zero-tolerance" of gangs. Second, in articulating those virtues, the nonvirtues were simultaneously, if sometimes implicitly, articulated. Thus, on the one hand, those in power could now more easily recognize (and sometimes overrecognize) what they hoped to prevent; and, on the other hand, those most deeply alienated from majoritarian power could now more easily mobilize the styles and substance of hyperbolic resistance. Did any of the new city policies work? Given the fact that gang-related homicides increased in the following years, one might say that the policies did not, but such a reply is probably too much of a generalization. What I am left with instead is a metaphorical interpretation that is grounded somewhat in the complexity of city life but not as completely as one might like: The city's policies nourished in their cores cancerous fears that were never eradicated and thus consistently prevented other policies from emerging, and because of this incomplete understanding of what was happening inside its social body, the city could not realize the cure that it desired. What specific policy might have worked? I am approaching quicksand on this one, but if I were to maintain the faintest of hopes in broad public discourse, and I doubt that I do, I would argue for pushing further back the fence line electrified by fear by encouraging gang leaders and membership to participate in public forums with majoritarian society, by insisting on careful documentation of the assumptions and beliefs of all parties so that they could be later deconstructed, and by insisting that these forums move toward concrete truces, programs, and proposals. Such an approach, I realize, tumbles back into the optimisms of Fraser. In the Angelstown of 1990 and 1991, such an approach would have been outrageous. The approach then and continuing through 1996 has been the unremitting enforcement of powerlessness upon those whose actions speak of a need for power. The assumption behind this approach, of course, was not to recognize the maverick or to give him or her voice because in doing so maverickness itself will be encouraged across the entire social body until all icons of stability collapse; better to stamp it out until it is extinguished.

Conclusion

Here at the end of this chapter I encounter, it seems to me, one of the central conundrums of critical ethnography. The approach taken by the city, that of unremitting enforcement, offered itself as the only "real" solution. Other solutions run the danger of appearing anemic, eccentric, or groundless. For instance, my reading of street-gang graffiti through the lenses of linguistic metaphors (lexicon, syntax, condensed narratives of subjectivity) runs violently counter to any "commonsense" understanding grounded in the property rights of law-abiding citizenry. I also realize that my interpretations of street-gang culture butt heads against a "commonsense" understanding of criminality. My analyses derive from and argue for a big-picture version of social justice. In this picture, one can all too easily afford generosity and compassion. But there is also a more immediate picture, a local picture, and when we find ourselves in it, we often quickly discard the big one, for the local is urgent and pressing. It squeezes us painfully, annoyingly, and it disciplines us into a kind of honesty concerning the limitations of ourselves and others. From its perspective, the big picture looks like a waste of imaginary labyrinths, a sense of social justice that has never been and never will be. Anglestown's experience with graffiti and street gangs is a powerful example of a local picture shrinking any possibility of a bigger picture of social justice. Are there ways to dodge the conundrum? Can one argue critically for a big picture of social justice and simultaneously find solutions that make sense from the perspective of the local? I think so. The rhetorical trick might be to find insights and solutions that are not inconsistent with the reigning ideology but whose implementation has the slow-moving power to alter insidiously the existing institutions and ideologies that constitute the local. The solution presented in the prior paragraph lacks the necessary subtlety, perhaps, and yet rhetorical invention must begin somewhere.

Chapter 3
Race Bending: "Mixed" Youth Practicing Strategic Racialization in California

Mica Pollock

At the turn of the twenty-first century, more and more U.S. residents are becoming versed in the twentieth-century anthropological deconstruction of biological race groups as human-made "myth."[1] Popular magazines occasionally tackle the very concept of "race," reminding readers that the nation's "racial groups" are more genetically diverse *within* than *between* themselves (see *Newsweek* 2000). The American Anthropological Association has launched a new public education program contesting biological notions of "so-called racial" difference (AAA 1998) and it has now become almost routine in U.S. academic discourse to call racial difference a "social construction." Indeed, contesting the very existence of "racial" difference is increasingly everyday popular practice in the contemporary United States (see Jackson 2001). In a most explicit demonstration of race's constructed nature, an increasing number of U.S. youth proudly claim "mixed" parentage, in the process hinting that supposedly distinct "race groups" have always had blurred boundaries (see Root 1996; Sollors 2000).

Given these increasingly routine challenges to foundational U.S. notions of simple racial difference, many U.S. residents now express uncertainty about the very validity of using "race" labels to categorize human beings—and as this uncertainty infiltrates U.S. equality ideology, it is having a major impact on the nation's racial politics. Indeed, some public figures—a few even citing directly the anthropological rejection of biological race—have begun to argue publicly that using race labels to describe people is inherently "racist," and that to achieve equality, people should no longer speak in race terms at all. Although such calls for ignoring race (typically called "colorblindness") have long been a part of American popular ideology and legal discourse (see Guinier and Torres 2002), this is the first time that public figures have argued widely that racial categorization has effectively reached its endpoint: Quests to *delete race words altogether* from national inequality discourse are for the first time characterizing U.S. public policy. Anti-affirmative action figurehead Ward Connerly, for example, a University of California regent who teamed up with an anthropologist in the 1990s to promote California's "colorblind" Proposition 209 (also known as the Equal Opportunity Initiative, which began the process of dismantling race-based affirmative action policies in the state), was in 2003 backing another state proposition (Proposition 54), designed to eliminate *all* racial data-gathering by the State of California. I term such moves "colormuteness" rather than colorblindness, as such actions seek to erase race words from public discourse in an *exceedingly* race-conscious way (Pollock 2004).[2] Although Connerly's Proposition 209 outlawed "discriminating against" or granting so-called preferential treatment to "any individual or group" in California "on the basis of race," this new initiative declared that "the state *shall not classify* any individual by race, ethnicity, color or national origin in the operation of public education, public contracting or public employment" (emphasis added).

Adult framings of equality co-opt youth in such official discourse about race. For just as adults placed the imagined desires of youth of color at the center of the state's 1990s affirmative action controversy (Proposition 209 proponents argued that youth felt stigmatized when recruited to colleges through racially conscious outreach programs), they placed "multiracial" youth's imagined needs at the center of this new controversy over racial politics. As one think-tank reported on a public speech from Connerly on the initiative in April 2002:

Mr. Connerly (like so many Californians) is a prime example of the absurdity of racial classification. His heritage includes Irish, African and Choctaw native American ancestors. His wife is Irish. His son married a Vietnamese girl. "But when people find out my grandchildren are Ward Connerly's grandchildren, they often say, 'Oh, you're black,' " he told the audience. "*This initiative is for the growing population of kids who don't know what box to check—and shouldn't have to decide. Please give them freedom from race and let them just be Americans.*" (American Civil Rights Coalition 2002; emphasis added)

As some California adults call for deleting race categories from public policy in the name of "freedom" for the state's "kids," however, some "mixed" California youth offer quite a different version of the nation's equality ideology. They demonstrate that given a national inequality system in which opportunities have long been distributed along simple "racial" lines, strategically using race labels one alternately acknowledges as reductive still often seems necessary to make things "fair." Indeed, acknowledging quite directly on occasion the nation's legacy of simple racializing practice, the "mixed" youth I came to know over several years of teaching and fieldwork in California knowingly treated race labels paradoxically, employing simple racial identifications for inequality analysis even as they contested their accuracy for understanding complex identities. In doing so, they exposed daily a paradoxical reality of U.S. racialization, one that adult analysts such as Connerly all too quickly dismiss: We don't belong to simple race groups, but when it comes to inequality, we do (Pollock 2004).

California, long on the cusp of U.S. demographic diversity, is a key site where public policies hoping to erase race words from inequality analysis are clashing with the complex realities of everyday racialized practice (Pollock 2004). Many such clashes over race have centered on institutional sites serving young people: schools. This is unsurprising, as U.S. schools are particular places where people both distribute opportunities along racial lines and form identities in racial terms. Indeed, schools are key sites where U.S. young people and adults, in a striking "institutional choreography" (Fine 1997), actually "*make* each other racial" (Olsen 1997).[3] Clashes over race in America, too—from laws denying basic literacy to slaves, to battles over desegregating "the races," to contemporary debates on college admissions—have long taken place in and around schools. As many ethnographers have shown, schools are institutions where people encounter, struggle with, and reproduce many such received systems of difference and inequality: schools in the United States and elsewhere also (re)produce young people who are "ethnic" or "indigenous" (Luykx 1999), classed (Willis 1977), gendered (Luttrell 2002), citizens of nations (Levinson 2001), and "abled"/"disabled" (Mehan 1996; Varenne and McDermott 1998). Since all such categorizations are (re)birthed within existing systems of inequality, young people themselves also often wield these categories compensatorily to garner resources in school, responding to local inequalities with a received equality logic. At an urban California high school in the 1990s, youth used and challenged race labels strategically rather than deleting them unthinkingly, and in doing so they modeled a practical and theoretical strategy crucial for dealing with race thoughtfully in twenty-first century America: they kept race words in the daily inequality analysis even while alternately calling the very existence of "race groups" into question.

To better understand such everyday race theorizing, I looked ethnographically at youths' everyday *talk* of race at Columbus High School in California City (both pseudonyms), where I taught Ethnic Literature from 1994 to 1995 before returning there as an anthropologist in 1995–

1997. My ethnographic focus on everyday race talk was not just academic fascination: Columbus youth, going to school in a state and nation full of adults struggling fiercely over the very future of racial language, indicated unmistakably in their daily discourse that race talk itself mattered to how racial orders were shaped and challenged (Pollock 2004).

In using everyday race talk for analyzing everyday practices of racialization, I also build here upon prior theories of the everyday (re)production and challenging of social structures: As Ortner (1996, 2) writes, social scientists have long argued that "human action is made by structure, and at the same time always makes and potentially unmakes it." While race structures are remade daily through various human actions that include complex habits of body movement, social association, taste, speech variation, and economic distribution, my more restricted focus on race-label use as a key racializing practice echoes many scholars of language, who have long viewed talk as an everyday action that shapes the world as well as describes it (see, for example, Duranti and Goodwin 1992; Tedlock and Mannheim 1995). Indeed, self-described "mixed" Columbus youth *became* single-race-group members in school, even as they negotiated so becoming, every time they described themselves or others in simple racial terms. Ethnographic work has long examined the everyday re-creation of "classes of people" (Frake 1980) through such naming practices (see, for example, Moerman 1968). Further, a rich tradition of historical work has shown us people actively building (and contesting) a racial structure through the use of basic racial labels throughout American history (see, for example, Davis 1997; Haney Lopez 1996; Roediger 1991). Youth is an important time for such paradoxical reproductions of race: much literature on youth culture has examined how young people actively redraw received lines of racialized difference even as they erase and blur them (Bailey 2000; Gilroy 1993a; Hebdige 1979b; Maira 2002; Perry 2002; Roediger 1998). I call youths' everyday strategic use of race labels "race-bending": Columbus youth, far from accepting their nation's race categories wholesale, alternately contested and strategically accepted the ability of simple racial categories to describe complex people.

In describing themselves purposefully at times as members of single "races," Columbus students temporarily prioritized simple, equality-minded "racial" *identification* over complex, personal racial *identity*, a distinction Lee Baker (2000) found similarly central to the late 1990s controversy over a proposed mixed-race category of the U.S. Census (see also Cose 1997). Although proponents of the mixed-race category demanded that the Census allow "mixed" individuals finally to accurately record their complex personal identities, opponents argued that distributing resources equally in the United States still necessitated the bureaucratic boxes of lump-sum racial identification, precisely because resources were still denied along simple race lines. By sometimes listing multiple terms to describe themselves (the Census's final solution), sometimes creating new racialized words to describe "mixed" youth accurately, and sometimes applying single, simple race labels to describe their own diversity, Columbus's "mixed" youth, too, employed simple race words strategically to cope with an already racialized, racially hierarchical world. In so doing, they demonstrated that deleting race altogether from U.S. equality talk is a premature proposal—that, in fact, negotiating equality still requires using the discourse of simple race even as at other moments we openly defy the very notion of "race" itself.

Method

Capturing the shifting race talk of Columbus youth required a special self-consciousness about ethnographic method. Scholars studying race too often treat the talk they gather as simply quoted opinion or static "truth," more rarely examining the complex situational politics and shifting scripts of racial talk. I conducted far more interviews with youth and adults during this research than I eventually used, having become convinced that formally prompted race talk was packaged particularly statically for a researcher and that the "informal logic of actual life" (Geertz 1973, 17) was best demonstrated by more naturalistic interaction with both students and adults. Youth race talk at Columbus alternately highlighted complexity and imposed a simple categorical order, and being an *ex*-teacher made me particularly likely to experience both forms of race talk with Columbus youth. Although my newly informal presence at Columbus made me available for unprompted "race bending" games with Columbus youth, as a former teacher I still routinely participated with youth and adults in the simple race talk of Columbus's more institutionalized racial equality discourse.

Notes on my teaching year in 1994–1995 were taken from a personal journal I kept in the hopes of writing a (never finished) first-year teacher memoir; over time, this diary provided an important window into the race talk of teacher-student interactions in Columbus classrooms. During my subsequent years as a researcher at Columbus (1995–1997), I also spent almost every day embroiled in more informal, impromptu research discussions with students and adults in hallways, on outside benches, and in empty rooms; I reconstructed these research conversations on paper immediately after they occurred. I thus participated in much of the race talk I present here, and in both out-of-classroom and in-classroom talk, my own "whiteness" unquestionably influenced the situational emergence of Columbus youths' race-challenging talk *and* their strategically simple race talk. For one, my presence occasionally prompted youth to discuss and debate the very category "white"—and in doing so, they articulated some central realizations about the need to retain simple race labels in monitoring racial equality.

Describing Youth at Columbus

To a newcomer watching Columbus students emerge at the end of a typical day, these youth might have appeared stunningly diverse, an urban population that seemingly embodied the country's breathtaking demographic complexity. Many Columbus students or their parents had immigrated to California City from Central and South America, various Philippine islands, Cantonese- and Mandarin-speaking regions of China, and Samoa; recently or some decades earlier, the relatives of many African American students had headed to California City from the U.S. South. Just a handful of students, most with ancestors from western Europe, were called "white" at Columbus; as in many tracked urban communities, white parents in California City sent their children to so-called "academic," application-only schools rather than to "comprehensive" schools such as Columbus. And at Columbus, complex, "mixed" parentage was so common that "What are you mixed with?" was a matter-of-fact student question. Even students who did not consider themselves "mixed" would acknowledge that it was often quite hard to tell "what" anybody at Columbus "was"; many young people listed strings of multiple words to describe themselves, and if you were to ask any Columbus student "what" he or she "was," you would likely find that he or she offered different answers at different times of the day, week, or year.

Hanging around Columbus for a few days, though, you as an observer would realize that the confusion of such endlessly criss-crossed parent-group and national boundaries coexisted with the discursive simplicity of six described "groups." Despite the "mixed"-up roots and global routes (Gilroy 1993b) central to the Columbus youth experience, these young people, in conjunction with the adults around them, worked daily in school to squash their diversity into six groups they called "racial." Although identities at Columbus were infinitely complex, racial identification was an accepted process of social simplification. In the mid-1990s, there were six words that Columbus youth used to describe the school's main student and adult "races": "black," "Latino" (occasionally conflated with "Mexican," to the consternation of "Latinos" with other Latin American origins), "Filipino," "Chinese," "Samoan," and "white" (this last category included mostly adults, including myself). A student who told me in one conversation that he was both "black" and "mixed with Puerto Rican" thus still wrote for a class this poem describing Columbus's complexity with easy numbers:

> 4 good teachers, with two bad ones a day
> every 5 bad kids copping one great student
> 2 fights, 0 body breaking them up
> 6 different groups, and nobody cares about anything
> over 1500 people different to the bone

In identifying daily these "6 different groups," notably, Columbus students called "racial" even the labels scholars typically term "ethnic" or "national" ("Filipino," "Chinese," "Latino," and "Samoan"). One day, for example, a student-made poster appeared on the walls of Columbus ranking "The Top Five Races of the Week," bluntly listing the five most demographically prominent student "groups" at Columbus:

1. Samoan
2. Filipino
3. African American
4. Latino
5. Asian

Rules: Do things positive with your race to get moved up on the chart like perform in a rally or play football in the quad or just about anything just get along with one another. Congratulation Samoans

While some scholars would criticize this conflation of race, ethnicity, and nationality, eliding and negotiating between the three systems of difference was a process key to Columbus students' daily social analysis; indeed, it is a daily process for young people in many areas of the world, one intertwined intimately with negotiations over social and political power (see, for example, Gilroy 1993a; Sansone 1995; Sharma 1996). At Columbus, although these "race" terms indeed described six groups assumed to look somewhat physically different, rarely did students suggest that they saw these six "racial" groups as inherently biological entities. Rather, calling all these groups "racial" indicated primarily that they were competitive parts in a local, shifting social hierarchy of groups. As Rumbaut (in press) notes, youth negotiating local power struggles often label as "races" their self-categorizations of national origin or ethnicity; at Columbus, calling all these groups "racial" indeed demonstrated that notions of racial difference—as opposed, for example, to the more unranked notion of ethnic difference (Sanjek 1996)—always denoted socially ranked populations vying for resources. As Fine (1997, 64) argues, "race" groups in schools and elsewhere are always interconnected in such unequal structural relationships, never simply "different" or "distinct, separable, and independent," but rather "produced, coupled, and ranked." Many scholars have noted that people of all ages strategically employ simple self-categorizations to wield power within such racialized inequality contexts (Omi and Winant 1994), calling such tactics finding "strategic places from which to speak" (Sharma 1996, 34, citing Stuart Hall), "strategic essentialism" (Spivak 1987), "anti-anti-essentialism" (Gilroy 1993b), and "the politics of recognition" (Taylor et al. 1994).

When talking to one another *about racial classification itself*, then, Columbus students almost always wound up contesting easy accounts of race group membership; it was in talk about racial *equality*, particularly with adults, that contestation over group membership ("*Is* he Samoan?" "Who *is* 'white'?") vanished. In such equality talk, students demanded the equal curricular and social representation of six racialized groups, reifying these groups as things they should "learn about" in equal amounts in Columbus classrooms and events. Indeed, in an analytic convergence that indicated a shared simple diversity system employed for distributing limited resources, this student framing of a handful of Columbus "races" was central to district and legal discourse on educational equality in California City as well. The California City Unified School District (CCUSD) used roughly these same six labels to describe what it called Columbus's "racial/ethnic groups"; the district, laboring under a desegregation court order, scattered a set of nine such "groups" of students districtwide in proportional amounts. Accordingly, in 1994–1997, district demographic records reported that Columbus enrolled students classified as Filipinos (28 percent), Latinos or Hispanics (29 percent), African Americans or blacks (22 percent), Chinese (8 percent), other nonwhites, a catch-all category that included Columbus's Samoans (8 percent), and other whites, a category that for the district primarily meant white (5 percent). Columbus's teaching staff—also monitored for racial/ethnic balance—was listed as 54 percent other white, 15 percent African American, 10 percent Filipino, 13 percent Latino, 5 percent other nonwhite, and 3 percent Chinese.

Policies in place throughout the district in the mid-1990s quietly compared the achievement and disciplinary records of these simple student groups: Although district personnel typically employed these "racial/ethnic" labels in formal written texts or uttered them anxiously in safe locations far away from schools, the equality-minded *logic* of simple race comparison was central to district and legal thinking about the distribution of resources and educational achievement (Pollock 2001). Only rarely did outside adults struggling with inequality orders indicate confusion over these "racial/ethnic" categories' boundaries. Near the beginning of California City's desegregation history, for example, a judge had suggested in one legal opinion that the city's public school population consisted of "at least four, and as many as nine distinct racial/ethnic groups," momentarily indicating that he could not say conclusively how many such "distinct" "groups" actually existed; after this momentary stumble, he proceeded to argue confidently that desegregation would provide the city's students with "meaningful opportunities to know members of different races." Similarly, in the 1990s, the CCUSD publicly acknowledged in one way only that the nine simple categories central to its desegregation policy might not adequately describe the city's infinitely complex student population: The district allowed parents to change their children's recorded "racial/ethnic" classifications up to two times to facilitate their enrollment in particular schools. Of course, students were allowed simply to shift from one simple race category to another—that is, as long as parents could produce some (unspecified) "proof" of category membership.

The project of balancing resources and attention *between* these simple racial "groups," then, was a staple legal and policy concern in California City (as academics reviewing the city's desegregation plan put it classically in the 1980s, "An improved plan . . . will not subtract from some groups to pull others up"). Policymakers would eventually bury such tensions over simple racial equality altogether within generalized talk of schooling for "all students" in California City, a de-racialization of policy talk that would, as I describe elsewhere, make inequality analysis impossible (Pollock 2004). In contrast, Columbus students continued to openly employ their six basic race labels to compare resources given to "blacks," "Filipinos," "Latinos," "Samoans," "Chinese," and "whites"— even while at less inequality-charged moments, as we see first here, they often talked as if their peers did not belong to such simple "groups" at all.

Students Contesting Simple "Racial" Classifications—Even while Employing Them

The first informal conversations presented here, which I documented as a researcher, demonstrate students talking directly about their own shifting self-classifications. (As an ethnographer interested in "race" at Columbus, I focused immediately on capturing such *student* self-descriptions, seeking to discover how important "race" was solely to Columbus students' identities and more rarely noting the racialized roles Columbus and district *adults* were playing in school life. Research questions about race and schooling regularly frame "race" in this way as the implied property of students of color, rather than as a communal practice involving people of all ages and "races"; once I made race words themselves the unit of analysis, I came to see the institutional choreography that had all players inside and outside Columbus racializing school life together.) As I wandered around tables one day in a library study hall at Columbus, I ended up in an impromptu conversation about classification with several students I had never met. A small, wiry, light brown-skinned boy with a pointed nose and freckles, enveloped in baggy clothes and a big black ski cap, looked up at me and without prompting started a guessing game:

"Does that girl over there look Mexican to you?" he asked. "I don't know, do you think she does?" I asked. "Don't you think she looks Mexican?" he repeated. "I guess so, why?" I asked. " 'Cause she's not Mexican, she's Samoan!" he said, smiling. "Samoan and white, with some black," he added. "Hey, don't be pointing!" the girl yelled over at us, smiling slightly. "I ain't no Mexican!" she added. "How do you know so much about her?" I asked him. "She's my cousin. And she's his cousin too, and he's mine!" he said, pointing to a guy sitting next to him who was somewhat bigger, with curlier hair, less freckles, and a wider nose. "So are you Samoan too?" I asked. "Yeah, Samoan . . . and part white, and part Chinese," he said. "So do you call yourself Samoan?" I asked. "Yeah . . . and part white, and part Chinese!" he said, laughing.

The girl next to him said, "I'm Samoan, black, Puerto Rican, Filipino, and Indian." She was tall, freckled, with long braid extensions wrapped up into a loose knot on her head; I had met her earlier that day. "Indian from India, or Native American?" I asked, pointing at the table to mean the United States. "Native American," she said, mimicking my gesture. "How do you know all this about yourself?" I asked her. "My mom! My mom tells me," she replied. "What does she call herself?" I asked. "Others," she said matter-of-factly. "What?" I asked. "Others, like that's what she puts down," she said. "Oh, on forms and stuff. What do you put?" I asked. "Other," she said. "That's what I put, too," said the small guy, adding, "I don't know what to put. Or I put 'Polynesian.' "

"What'd you say you were?" called over a girl with straightened-looking hair and slightly darker skin. "Samoan, black, Puerto Rican, Filipino, and Indian," the freckled girl repeated. "Hey, you tryin' to be like *me*," the other girl called back, smiling slightly. "Nobody's tryin' to be like nobody," said the small boy. "I bet I can tell what everybody is," he said. "Like you, you're black and Filipino, right?" he said to a guy down the table. "What?" the guy replied. "You're black and Filipino, right?" he repeated. "Yeah," this guy said, nodding slowly. "And he's part Samoan and part white," the small boy said, gesturing toward a guy with a long braid sitting two seats away. "What's your dad?" a girl asked this braided kid. "He's French," he replied, very softly. "I can always tell a Samoan," said the small guy, shaking his head and smiling. "How?" I asked. "I just can," he said.

"Are you from Western Samoa or American?" the small guy asked the five-ethnicity girl. "American," she said. "Is there a difference?" I asked. "Yeah," the boys said. "Then there's Tongans, and Fijians," he said. "Are Tongans different?" I asked. "Yeah—we don't eat horses!" said the bigger guy. Several people laughed. "*We* eat the pig, and chicken," he continued. "Everyone eats chicken!" said the smaller guy. "And ———, and ———," continued the guys, naming foods in Samoan and laughing. "Who's 'we'?!" I asked. "Samoans," they answered. "And Tongans have big noses," added the small guy. "Like some

Samoans, too, hella big!'' added the bigger guy. A girl at the table raised her head from her magazine (*Ebony*) and said, "Don't be putting us down like that, I ain't no Tongan, we don't got noses nearly that big."

Group boundaries were fundamentally blurred here—and simultaneously reinscribed. The students kept returning over the course of the conversation to expose race group memberships as infinitely malleable and multiple, yet somehow through all this contestation the single category "Samoan" survived. As the discussion of "forms" indicated, the complexity of multiple origins at Columbus was often literally boxed in by the simplistic options of bureaucratic documents from the outside requiring students to "put down" such single-word identifications; yet even in everyday student conversations challenging the very notion of simple "groups," such single-race categories also were sporadically and voluntarily invoked. Here, the stated nuances of lines of nation (such as the distinction between Western and American Samoa), as well as the gleeful chaos of unexpected familial mixtures and unclassifiable appearances, evaporated finally into a "Samoan" "we." Such simplifications were fueled, to some degree, by my own classifying questions ("Do you call yourself Samoan?" "Are Tongans different?"). While I proceeded throughout my study with the methodological commitment to always let others drop race labels into conversations first, in asking students questions such as "Who's we?" in the midst of conversations in order to get them to articulate their running classifications of self and others, I often found students imposing the idea of racial categorization upon the very people who defied the concept. Indeed, even to answer routine peer or adult questions such as "What are you mixed with?" and "What are you?", students had to describe themselves or others using one or multiple simple race terms, as the sum of numerable matter-of-fact parts. Tautologically, students also especially brought such single categories into race-bending conversations when comparing (and informally ranking) simply bounded groups; and in the end, the basic structure of available "race" categories remained sturdy, even while games of "guessing" indicated that one could always "guess" wrong (see also Root 1996).

Students sporadically imposed race categories on one another in the midst of debates about racial classification without direct adult influence as well. Occasionally, for example, as I found one summer school day visiting a teacher friend at a nearby junior high, students even merged existing race terms into new race terms to racially identify "mixed" people. Of course, my notes' own imposed, physically descriptive language ("Filipino-looking," "black guys") demonstrated a cultural context in which racialized phrases seemed almost required shorthand for describing people:

A Filipino-looking guy is speaking to two black guys and one Filipino looking guy sitting in an informal circle. He says, "I know who's a niggapino—my auntie. And that one guy, he's a niggapino; my cousin's a pino; she's (points across room) a japapino."

In inventing such new race terms (and to me, disturbing ones, in the case of using "nigga" to denote a category I presumed to be "black") to describe the complex "mixture" of specific people, students were indicating that the very practice of racial classification was a human act that could be actively contested. Still, they retained race labels as dominant descriptive tools, hinting that the context of simple race categorization was simply too pervasive to be escaped. Students thus bent race categories in such debates rather than breaking them apart altogether. In a discussion about "assumptions" in one of my own classes in 1994, similarly, one student's assertion that she could "tell who's Filipino 'cause I'm Filipino" prompted a conversation about the actual difficulties of "telling" Columbus people's "race," yet all but one of us still left the conversation racially identified:

Lani:	I can tell who's Filipino 'cause I'm Filipino.
Nando:	Yeah, I can tell who's Latino 'cause I am. Like her (points to Anita), she looks white but I know she's Latino 'cause of how she talks. . . . Like you, I can tell you're, well, white 'cause of the color of your hair (reddish brown). Michael, I can tell he's white, just 'cause.
Michael:	But I'm not.
Me (to Michael):	How would you describe yourself? (He shrugs) Okay, you don't want to? (He shakes his head) Okay, he doesn't have to.
Carrie:	You can't always tell—people never know I'm Hawaiian.
Me:	Do you think you look Hawaiian?
Carrie:	(She shakes her head) I look white.
Nando:	Really? I would've thought you were white or Latino.
Me:	Do people assume anything about you when they find out you're Hawaiian?
Carrie:	No, 'cause they hardly ever find out or guess.

Michael, who proved through his silence that "race" was indeed not always something you could "find out or guess," said to me a year later in an informal interview that although he himself "*appeared* white," "there are hecka races in me." He now called himself a "white black kid," adding that he got along with "black kids" because he grew up with them and with "Filipino kids" because he had "Filipino cousins." He had no interest in hanging out with "Samoans," though, he said—they always "caused trouble." While talk about racial classification itself had Michael observing his own blend of "hecka races," then, his sudden social rankings had him slotting others into simple racial groups: When not focused explicitly on contesting the very idea of classifying people racially, Columbus students often simply went ahead and classified. Similarly, outside in the main quad one day in 1995, I ran into Robert, a former student who had typically labeled himself "Latino" in my classroom. Only once our matter-of-fact conversation about the merits of his Latin American Studies class at the nearby community college turned into a discussion of racial categorization itself did he reveal to me for the first time his own complex roots:

I asked what he was reading and he showed me *Down These Mean Streets* by Piri Thomas, saying he liked it. "What's it about?" I asked. "A Puerto Rican kid growing up," he said. "Do you feel like you relate to it at all?" I asked. "Yeah—the gangs and stuff. Not that I really relate to gangs, but like that stuff, and the fights he gets into," he said. "Do you relate to the Puerto Rican part?" I asked. (*An unusually leading question for me, but with an unexpected race-bending answer.*) "Yeah, 'cause I'm actually part Puerto Rican," he said. "Really?" I asked (he hadn't mentioned this last year in class). "Yeah—my mom's Filipino and Puerto Rican, and my dad's Mexican and Puerto Rican, so I'm mostly Puerto Rican," he said. . . "'Cause I don't even remember you mentioning this in class," I said. "'Cause I didn't *know* I was Puerto Rican!" he said, smiling. He continued, "I thought I was Hawaiian, but I was curious about my grandfather's last name. I asked my mom, 'cause I was like, that doesn't sound Hawaiian. And my mom said no, he was born in Puerto Rico." "You never mentioned the Hawaiian part in class either," I said, smiling. "No—I was all confused last year. What did I say I was?" he asked. "Uh, I think Mexican and part Filipino, you definitely didn't mention Hawaiian," I said. "I didn't? I thought I did," he said.[4]

In most assignments in my Ethnic Literature class the previous year that had prompted written self-identification, Robert, despite his now admitted "confusion," had actually just described himself simply as "Latin." The classroom world typically took little time for debating the subject of racial classification itself, more often proceeding using a logic of single-group identification. As my own year of teaching Ethnic Literature at Columbus proved, classroom life typically prompted a discourse of lump-sum groups, alternately called "races," "ethnicities," and "cultures" in the presence of adults. And as students and adults proceeded using these simple race terms in their shared public life, their simple race discourse intertwined always with a key shared race concern: equality.

Students Using Simple Race Talk in Conversation with Adults

When I arrived to teach at Columbus in 1994, I learned quickly that the social studies curriculum, designed to explore each of Columbus's groups' histories in turn, was to begin with a unit on pre- and post-colonial Africa, and then turn to units on Latin America and the Philippines; as the Ethnic Literature teacher, I was to lead concurrent examination of "African American," "Latino," and "Filipino" literature (as the Samoan population in the tenth grade happened to be particularly small, we had no "Samoan unit"; "Chinese" literature would be covered in a brief unit on immigration; and Europeans would be covered most explicitly in an end-of-the-year unit on the Holocaust). Moving sequentially from group to group, it seemed, was an expected format for a teacher of Ethnic Literature. As one white teacher would say several years later of her own Ethnic Literature class, "We're moving from Hispanic to Asian poetry, and then we'll be doing crazy white guys, the Beat poets."

Wielded by both students and adults, a Columbus discourse of "learning about other cultures" took the placement of people into clear-cut "cultures" for granted—and those students in my classes who considered themselves "mixed," I found out over time, typically left the full complexities of their identities outside the classroom. Seth, a former student who told me in one interview that he considered himself "a melting pot" (his father was "African American," his mother was "Italian," his grandmother was "Irish and Italian," and his dad's parents were "black and Filipino"), revealed that in our class discussions the previous year, he had simply "picked Italian" because he had more ties with his mother, never mentioning his African American, Irish, or Filipino "parts." ("Most people knew," he explained, since outside class students routinely asked him what he was "mixed with.") I myself silently recalled Seth framing himself simply as "white" in the classroom. He now said emphatically that he was, if anything, "*not white.*"

At Columbus, curriculum played a key role in simplifying the local taxonomy of student "races"; as Suárez-Orozco and Suárez-Orozco (2001) have noted generally, the very "entry into American identities today is via the culture of multiculturalism," which often quickly socializes young people into the nation's simplified "racial regime" (Suárez-Orozco 2001, 357). In my own classroom curriculum, simple lines delineating people into the school's small handful of "races" persisted to the end of the school year, despite my intermittent attempts to have discussions challenging the very concept of racial classification. In response to the year's last assignment, in which I asked students to bring in music that they felt "represented themselves" or had something to say about "ethnicity," students squashed the complexity of their everyday media usage into neat racialized categories, announcing that Tupac Shakur songs were about being "black"; "corridos" were "Mexican"; traditional folk songs expressed the experience of "Samoans"; national songs made one "very proud to be Filipina"; and music from the Chinese New Year demonstrated, as one student put it, "what my culture's mostly about." Robert brought a song that, as he put it, "represents how Latins have come up a long way from Christopher Columbus." Although some students of all "groups" brought in the same hip-hop songs on this last day of Ethnic Literature, demonstrating the border-crossing appeal of the genre (Leslie, a self-identified "black" student, summed up paradoxically that "It's my ethnicity—everybody that's my ethnic group and that isn't listens to it"), most students throughout that day still talked as if music were designed for uncontested racial or "ethnic groups." My assignment to "represent" through music, of course, had prompted such simple identifications even while suggesting that students be their complex "selves" (see also Gilroy 1993a; Perry 2002; Roediger 1998).

In Columbus classrooms, then, as in classrooms across the United States, adults and students typically "learned about other cultures" one at a time. And with such sequential discussion of distinct "races" or "cultures" or "peoples" came another crucial question—namely, whether each group was equally represented. Pleas or demands for equal racial representation in Columbus school events, too, were routine—and such demands rarely suggested that race groups had negotiable boundaries. As inequality in racial "representation" seemed to pattern out in simple-group ways, achieving equality accordingly required simple-race groups. As Winant (1998, 90) writes, the very concept of "racial" difference serves both to allocate resources *and* to "provid[e] means for challenging that allocation"; and when students were considering the allocation of curricular resources, their talk of simple racial identification always trumped considerations of complex or multiple identities.

One afternoon in 1996 at a traditional assembly where juniors parodied seniors, an equity-minded call from the audience caught my attention: "Where're the black people at?" I had noticed the same pattern myself: out of around twenty juniors performing on stage, only two regularly identified themselves as "black." One of the two was the event's emcee, and when he greeted the audience, several students, all of whom looked African American, stood up and shouted out, "reeeeee!"—it was Columbus students' colloquial form of the word "represent." Moments later, I heard a girl next to me ask another, "Why don't they do any black people?"

In 1998, I called Tina, a former student who had graduated the previous spring, to ask her opinion about this question of racial "representation" in Columbus life. In my classroom, Tina had described herself as "black and Filipino" in a few conversations that had touched on racial classification itself; in later years, as she finished up at Columbus and went to college, she repeatedly described herself to me as "black." Notably, she did so again during our telephone conversation, while suggesting that people at Columbus had neither adequately represented "black people" in school nor assisted her to "learn about" *other* "cultures" adequately:

"It would have been nice if we would have had some African American history," she said. There was "no black history until February, and then suddenly all the black people came out—and as soon as February was over they put them back in the closet again. And the only people you ever heard about were Martin Luther King and Malcolm X." In her history classes, she said, they "never learned anything about black people, Latin people, Filipino, Chinese— immigrants—nothing about culture really." . . . I mentioned to her that at the senior parody I had heard students say things like, "Where're the black people at?" "Mm-hmm," she replied. "But who organized that event? All Filipinos," she added, who only portrayed their friends.

While students describing themselves in detail sporadically admitted the nuances of their own "mixture," analyses of social and curricular resource distribution had them comparing (and slotting themselves into) a short list of simple race groups. When articulating their needs for material and educational resources, students similarly prioritized simple racial identifications over the nuances of national origin. Carlo, who at many other moments called himself "Nicaraguan," argued fervently one day for more "Latino" history by contrasting "Latino" representation in school with the overrepresentation of "blacks" and "whites":

He mentioned the conquistadors, and I asked where he had learned about them. "Not in school—we don't learn about our race," he said decisively, adding, "Most teachers worry about keeping the blacks and the whites happy. They give blacks a whole month—for us, it's one day." "One day," his friend Miguel (*who had arrived a few years earlier from El Salvador*) echoed, "Cinco de Mayo . . ." "They just teach us black history and white history," Carlo finished.

Comparing the resources given "our race" to those given other "races," Columbus students fit themselves and one another into simple race groups for the very purpose of comparison. Michael (the student of "hecka races") suggested in a private conversation with me and a "Latina" teacher after school one day that this logic of simple racial equality extended far beyond the Columbus walls. He actually had to "pick" a culture, he said, in part to acquire resources within an adult-run structure of distributing financial aid:

"I feel like I don't have a culture. My mom's Mexican and Irish, my dad's Filipino and, uh, Portuguese," he says. "You're American then, it doesn't get more American than that," Ms. Duran says. "My dad says, 'You're white,' and I'm like, 'No I'm not, just 'cause *you* wanna be white,'" he says. . . . "My mom doesn't tell me stories like about rituals and stuff, so I don't have a culture. But I have to pick one." "Why do you have to choose?" asks Ms. Duran. "Well, it says 'other white' on my transcript. And I can't get *any*thing with that," he smirks, adding, "even though I live in the projects or whatever."

Noting the structural constraints of resource distribution inside and outside Columbus, students selected single racial identifications within a finite system of options. And as students strategically appropriated racial identifications for themselves, adults struggled circularly to equalize resources distributed to the school's six "groups." In navigating the school's omnipresent discourse of equal racial representation, as Tina and Carlo demonstrated, adults *and* students could always be accused of "bias." Michael himself had demonstrated this directly one day the previous year, when his class, having finished a unit on Africa and African Americans, began a unit "on Latin America and Latinos in the United States":

Lizzie ("Filipina"):	"How about the Philippines?"
Me:	"They're last."
Lizzie:	"Why they gotta be last?"
Me:	"Someone has to be last."
Michael (smiling):	"You're biased!"

Given the omnipresent possibility of unfairly underrepresenting one of Columbus's "groups," public schoolwide activities (organized by both students and adults) were meticulous about presenting sequential appearances by students representing the six major groups of Columbus's simple race taxonomy. Looking more closely at the details of these "multicultural" assemblies, of course, one could notice that racial categorizations were actually leaking all over the place. Although performances often involved Samoan students in grass skirts performing traditional dances, Latino students dancing merengue in billowy shirts, and black students rapping, Latino students also sometimes rapped in these performances, Filipino students sometimes played hard rock, an occasional black student danced merengue, and Samoan students routinely sang rhythm and blues tunes. Still, talk *about* "multicultural" events and classroom curriculum continually referenced simple racial groups *as if* these groups had clear-cut borders: In a sense, so-called multicultural rites were *about* simplification, *about creating an equalizable set of "groups."* Indeed, talk of equal representation in events and texts itself seemed to organize students into measurable racial groups, even as everyday actions repeatedly demonstrated the blurred complexity of racial practice. For example, when I showed *Menace to Society* (a movie whose cast appeared almost entirely "black") as a class reward one day, Carlo approached my desk to say that he himself owned the video and had seen it countless times. But anyway, he complained, he "thought this was supposed to be Latino week!"

Such conflict, what we might call competitive diversity, sometimes seemed part and parcel of sequential curricular units and "multicultural" events. As one self-described "black" teacher remarked of "multicultural" assemblies, "Now in assemblies, it's the same old thing all the time—see who can outclap who." In meetings the summer after my teaching year, my partner teachers and I similarly discussed how setting up our own curriculum as a series of "ethnic" units had seemed to foster what we called "ethnic cheerleading": if all "cultures" were not given equal time, students had sometimes stated, they didn't want to learn about "other cultures" at all. As Lipsitz (1998, 66, 252) argues, simplifying practices of "encouraging allegiance to [single] group interests" and "investment in individual group identities" can, often unintentionally, inhibit cross-"racial" allegiances and even "run the risk of reifying the very categories they seek to destroy." In truth, equity-minded, sequential presentation of simple race groups did seem paradoxically to prime people to measure such representation as unequal, as I described in my diary as a teacher after one "multicultural fair." Takisha and Frankie, both of whom usually labeled themselves "black" (Frankie sometimes called himself "Jamaican"), had grumpily measured the unequal representation of "blacks":

Takisha: This school's *racist,* I swear.
Frankie: The rapper didn't even get to finish!
Me: But the sound system broke, Frankie.
Takisha: It didn't break down during the *other* performances.
Me: You think they broke it on purpose?!
Frankie: He was gonna do free flow, they didn't let him do it.
Takisha: And the Samoan group got hella time!

Many U.S. observers critique so-called "multicultural" curricula for setting up precisely these sorts of race-group conflicts (Schlesinger 1998), in part *by* oversimplifying the infinite complexity of human diversity (McCarthy 1998). Yet multicultural education scholarship itself increasingly critiques the very concept of distinct "cultures," *even while* still setting out unapologetically at times *to* represent basic "groups" in sequence to remedy a history of ignoring these very "cultures" in schools (see Nieto 2000 on multicultural education's project of actively "affirming diversity"). The typical "multicultural" tactic of sequential presentation, however, sets up a constant dilemma: as Gonzales and Cauce (1995) wonder most generally, "How does one recognize ethnic differences and support ethnicity as an important dimension of self-definition without paradoxically encouraging group divisions and inter-group tensions that often result when ethnic categories are empha-sized?" (140–41).

As a teacher selecting books, films, and projects, I indeed had repeat-edly found myself arguing defensively that in our attempts to "do" one racial group "before the next," we were learning about these groups in equal amounts—and the very act of balancing curricular time between simple racial groups often had us ignoring the identity complexities that Columbus students articulated when discussing racial classification itself. Yet as my students and I struggled to equalize the proportions of simple-race-group representation, of course, these very shared processes of racial simplification also served to clarify when resources *were* distrib-uted equally: in the very act of reproducing together a reliably simple racial taxonomy, that is, we clarified the set of "groups" to which equal resources could be distributed and ensured that all Columbus students would feel in some way represented. In fact, confronting a local world and nation in which resources always appeared inequitably distributed along simple racial lines seemed to *require* the compensatory use of sim-ple race terms, and Columbus students sometimes acknowledged as much explicitly. Notably, they did so with particular insight when they were given the space to debate racial classification itself—and especially when they were adding the category "white" to the analysis. Lipsitz (1998, 1) argues that simple-race "identity politics" often leave "white" people unmarked, never acknowledging the particular role whiteness plays "as an organizing principle in social and cultural relations"; and indeed, interrogating the very category "white" often led us immedi-ately to an analysis of racial identification itself as a process intertwined with struggles over power. When we started discussing the category "white" most directly in my own classroom near the end of my teaching year, for example ("White people? Let's *do* this!" one student exclaimed), within moments Michael, the student of "hecka races," had offered the year's most piercing structural analysis of the racial identifi-cation process:

Michael says: "They say all people from Europe are supposed to be white, right? And all the people from Africa are supposed to be black, right? And all the people—Indians are supposed to be red, right? And all the Asian people are supposed to be yellow, right? These are the colors people are givin' 'em. So it seems just like sports—they put 'em all in teams, like categories," he says. "*Yes!!* And why do they put 'em into teams?" I ask. "To make 'em compete!" he finishes.

Although people didn't necessarily belong to simple race categories, "they" had already lumped together the people who were "supposed to be" racially similar—and now, the categories were bricks in a wall of power relations. Accepting the idea that race categories existed, of course, itself helped maintain this artificially simple racial structure—but as Columbus youth themselves demonstrated, people now also had to remain racial in order to make things "fair."

Conclusion

Some analysts have predicted that contemporary U.S. youth, by professing self-consciously "mixed" ancestry and often by associating seemingly easily with one another (when desegregated demographics allow), sound the death knell for American racial categories writ large (Heath 1995). Yet even our most diverse youth populations employ simple "race" categories daily, in concert with the adults around them—especially for the purposes of negotiating toward "fairness," and perhaps particularly in school. Indeed, as Columbus students reproduced daily a structure of simple, six-group "race" difference despite their stunning diversity, they activated a finding central to national equity policy and law: the persistent paradoxical need to employ, in equity efforts, the very systems of difference Americans have long naturalized to make people unequal (Minow 1990). By alternately challenging the very notion of simple racial difference and strategically utilizing race categories to identify human beings in their discourse, however, Columbus students also indicated the importance of fostering such race-bending discourse in our schools. Adults, too, can spearhead far more conversations in schools *about racial categorization itself,* bringing to light the youth contestation of "race groups" occurring already in the margins of our institutions in order to expose the lines we draw around "races" as human-made. Adults can also highlight the intersections and blurred borders between "races" when structuring school curricula and performances, even while discussing with youth how after several centuries of treating one another unequally along racial lines, Americans must often employ race labels purposefully in our attempts to make things equal.

At largely "mixed" Columbus, then, the shifting nature of youth identity did not erase simple-race identifications as crucial social ordering devices. Both defying and employing the racial logic available for use in America, Columbus students demonstrated that racial classification itself is always a process intertwined with struggles over power—and that creating local versions of equality in a nation with a legacy of simple-race logic will for a time require speaking categorically even while interrogating the very reality of categories themselves. Indeed, as Guinier and Torres (2002, 42) warn, people who *continually* question the existence of race groups cede analysis of race's relevance to those who would like to "purge legal and political discourse of *all* racial references and who may be indifferent to whether this move preserves unjust hierarchies" (emphasis added).

As some California adults hasten to delete race words from equality talk, then, youth proceed strategically with race talk and with "racial" equality demands. Daily, Columbus youth both challenged the very idea of simple-race categorization *and* temporarily sacrificed the detailed complexities of racial "identity" to a national habit of simple racial identification, as a strategic response to an inequitable nation that has for generations bluntly asked us what we "are." While demonstrating that "races" are indeed a mind-boggling oversimplification of human diversity, young Americans still practice this oversimplification daily—in part to learn how to strategically challenge an existing simple race system in which the distribution of social and tangible resources remains perennially unequal.

Chapter 4
The Intimate and the Imperial: South Asian Muslim Immigrant Youth After 9/11

Sunaina Maira

In ethnic studies as well as in American studies (and the two fields increasingly intersect), an interest in globalization has stimulated a more transnational or comparative perspective that forces attention to the ways in which forms of culture, community, and subjectivity spill over national borders. Young people are often held up as compelling examples of how individuals increasingly shape forms of culture, community, and subjectivity in relation to two or more nation-states, or beyond nation or state altogether. Yet there is still a cautious acknowledgment that nationalist identities and territorialized nation-states play a powerful role in the lives of presumably transnational or immigrant youth. The tensions between nationally bounded and transnational experiences in the lives of individuals are mirrored in the debates about balancing the specificity of area studies with the global reach of transnational studies.

The hinge between these two levels of analysis, in my view, is that hidden behind these debates is an institutional, material force that needs to be made explicit: that of U.S. empire. Globalization cannot simply be understood as an amorphous decentered phenomenon unmoored from the interests of any single nation-state; it is fundamentally shaped by the economic, military, and economic power exercised increasingly unilaterally by the United States (Marable 2003, 6; Panitch and Gindin 2003). This is a moment when the word "empire," in relation to the United States, has come out of the closet. But I will argue that the word imperialism needs to be outed as well, for it is attached to a critique whose political import represents more than a subtle semantic difference between the two terms. (As a commentator on the occupation of Iraq noted at a benefit concert in Berkeley for the anti-occupation "Wheels of Justice" bus tour in December 2003, the United States seems to be the only "nonimperialist empire"!) On the level of the academy, the formation of area studies in the United States has been understood in relation to its Cold War interests in particular regions of the world that were mapped in accordance with specific foreign policy agendas. The internal critique of this national defense and intelligence agenda in area studies and anthropology has been complemented by the analyses produced by ethnic and American studies scholars of U.S. racial formation and gendered and classed nationalisms that work in tandem with the state's foreign policy.

Furthermore, in the last couple of years, there has emerged a new kind of area studies of the United States, a post-9/11 area studies, if you will. It was evident in the profusion of books in the aftermath of the events of September 11, 2001, works by academic scholars that focused on Islam and on the impact of 9/11 on various communities and local sites, primarily, and also on analyses of political rhetoric and media discourses, with varying political persuasions and approaches to the role of the U.S. state.[1] In this post-9/11 area studies, there are various ways of positioning Muslim Americans: as adherents of Islam, as immigrants (to be placed within the framework of assimilation or multiculturalism), as transmigrants or transnational subjects (with the complex and potentially charged implications of dual allegiances that that implies), as victims of the state's war on terror and the latest group to be racially profiled and so to be inserted somewhere in the ambiguous matrix of U.S. race politics, or as a target population to be mapped and identified by the state. This last approach, even if only implicit, is a troubling one especially given the various projects of surveillance and documentation of Muslims in the United States, such as the now revised Special Registration program that required nationals of twenty-four predominantly Muslim countries to register annually with federal immigration and submit to interrogation and fingerprinting.

The project of documentation of Muslim Americans after 9/11 is fraught with political and ethical questions, echoing earlier questions during the Cold War era of area studies that I will return to in the conclusion. A current instantiation of the ideological dimensions of this debate is H.R. 3077, the legislation proposed by the U.S. Congress to regulate Title VI funding for area studies through an International Education Advisory Board constituted by no less than members of the Department of Defense, the National Security Agency, and the infamous Department of Homeland Security. The areas of knowledge explicitly targeted by hearings on this bill were postcolonial theory, Middle Eastern studies, and Edward Said's work, in particular, which was accused of being anti-American. It is, of course, the case that theories of postcoloniality and Orientalism are critical of imperialism, but it becomes apparent that post-9/11 area studies, and area studies in general, exist in uneasy relation with studies of U.S. empire and with state policies for disciplining knowledge production and the subjects of empire. I would argue that shifting the focus from "globalization" studies to "empire studies" or "post-9/11 area studies" helps to make the implications of these relations somewhat clearer.

My research demonstrates that the experiences of Muslim immigrant youth in the United States after the events of 9/11 reveal a critique of empire grounded in vernacular modes of citizenship that deviate from the dominant, patriotic nationalism as well as from liberal notions of cosmopolitanism. The essay also suggests that it is the reflexive relationship of the researcher to the "research subject" in such a project that illuminates the ways in which empire acts as the hinge between the institutional matrix of knowledge production and the everyday political understandings of immigrant youth. Social scientists and area studies scholars have always had to struggle with the nature of forms of "intelligence gathering" in relation to state policies of profiling, interrogation, and detention/internment at home and military intervention overseas, and H.R. 3077 makes it clear that in the current moment the stakes are high enough to warrant overt government regulation. What can be revealed, or how one is identified, are questions intimately bound up with a moment of empire in which the secrecy/surveillance of the state's "homeland security" policies and the interrogation/detention of selectively targeted immigrant subjects makes knowledge feel like a slowly burning fuse. Methodologically, it seems to me that such a moment demonstrates the need for researchers to situate themselves in the context of their research, though I also argue that such a moment is not exceptional in U.S. history but simply highlights ongoing tensions for researchers over modes of identification and revelation, collusion and betrayal, intimacy and evasion. My use of "post-9/11" to discuss the emergence of a new kind of area studies, and to situate my own research, is not meant to signify a radical historical or political rupture, but rather a moment of renewed contestation over ongoing issues of citizenship and transnationalism, religion and nationalism, civil rights and immigrant rights. The assault on immigrant rights crystallized in the PATRIOT Act actually extended measures put in place in 1996 with the Anti-Terrorism and Effective Death Penalty Act and the Illegal Immigration Reform and Immigrant Responsibility Act, which heightened distinctions between the civil rights afforded to citizens and noncitizens (Moore 1999, 95).

Cultural Citizenship

This essay is based on an ethnographic study that I began in the fall of 2001 focusing on working-class Indian, Pakistani, and Bangladeshi immigrant students in a public high school in Cambridge, Massachusetts.[2] In my ongoing analyses of this research, I have used the lens of cultural citizenship to examine the "behaviors, discourses, and practices that give meaning to citizenship as lived experience" in the context of "an uneven and complex field of structural inequalities and webs of power relations," the "quotidian practices of inclusion and exclusion" (Siu 2001, 9). Cultural citizenship becomes an important construct to examine because legal citizenship is clearly no longer enough to guarantee protection under the law with the state's War on Terror, as is clear from the profiling, surveillance, and even detention of Muslim Americans who are U.S. citizens.

The concept of cultural citizenship has been developed by those, such as Latino studies scholars Renato Rosaldo (1997) and William Flores and Rina Benmayor (1997), who take a new social movement-based approach to immigrant and civil rights. It has also been developed, from a Foucauldian perspective, by cultural theorists such as Aihwa Ong who are concerned with citizenship as a regulatory process, and who define cultural citizenship as "a dual process of self-making and being-made within webs of power linked to the nation-state and civil society" (1999, 738). Some writing in this vein, such as Toby Miller (1993), has been skeptical about the possibility for using citizenship as the collective basis for political transformation—given its increasingly individualized, privatized definition—but is still open to its potential. My work, in a sense, bridges these two approaches, for I am interested in the critical possibilities of cultural citizenship for galvanizing struggles for civil and immigrant rights, particularly for young immigrants, but within the limitations of state-sponsored and increasingly privatized citizenship as circumscribed by both liberal multiculturalism and the inequities of global capital (Miller 1993; Hutnyk 2000). Research on youth and citizenship is meager and generally tends to come out of the traditions of developmental psychology or functionalist socialization theory, both of which assume a limited definition of what constitutes the "political"; more recent work challenges these assumptions and pays attention to young people's own understandings of politics and the ways they negotiate relationships of power in different realms of their everyday lives (Bhavnani 1991; Buckingham 2000).

In this essay, I deviate somewhat from a coherent, predetermined theoretical frame, for the last few months of my fieldwork have caused me increasingly to wonder about ways to define the "field" for my ethnographic research. The way I have ended up defining the site of my fieldwork is reflexively, in terms of the sites in which I am present but also those that I unsettle or am complicit in producing, as well as those in which I am not present but in which this project is inevitably embedded. This is not just a question of multisited ethnography—it is a question of how even to begin to define the notion of a site, temporally, spatially, and socially, when its very conceptualization (as "Muslim America," for example) is so much of a part of the ideological war that is being waged currently through very specific state and media discourses and regimes of govermentality. My aim then, is to raise some questions related to issues that I am grappling with at present as I work myself out of a single totalizing frame. Questions of citizenship remain threaded throughout my reflections, implicitly and explicitly, for I have not abandoned these theoretical interests, but they exist, uneasily at moments, in tension with questions of dissent and empire. How do young people express moments of dissent in relation to ideas of citizenship and practices of the state at a moment of U.S. empire? How do I, as a researcher, understand and write about these engagements given their politically charged and ethically fraught nature? These are the fundamental questions underlying this chapter, but they are questions, as will become apparent, that are not easily answered.

The Study

Cambridge is an interesting site for this research, for while media attention and community discussions of racial profiling were primarily focused on South Asians in the New York/New Jersey area, there were hundreds of incidents around the country in places where South Asians have not been as visible in the public sphere or as organized, as in the Boston area. It is also interesting to focus on communities, such as Cambridge, that are known to be more politically liberal to understand what kinds of responses such a setting both allows and does not allow, particularly for youth. The Cambridge public high school—there is only one in the city—has an extremely diverse student body reflecting the city's changing population, with students from Latin America, the Caribbean, Africa, and Asia. Students from India, Pakistan, Bangladesh, and Afghanistan constitute the largest Muslim population in the school, followed by youth from Ethiopia, Somalia, and Morocco.[3] There are about sixty students of South Asian origin, including a few Nepali and Tibetan youth, who are almost evenly split between immigrant and second-generation youth.

The South Asian immigrant student population is predominantly working- to lower-middle class, recently arrived (within the last five to seven years), and with minimal to moderate fluency in English. As such, these youth generally seem to socialize predominantly with other South Asian immigrant youth and with other immigrant students in the bilingual education program. The majority of the Indian immigrant youth are from Muslim families, most from small towns or villages in Gujarat in western India. Several of the South Asian students are related to one another as their families have sponsored relatives as part of an ongoing chain migration, recreating their extended family networks in the same apartment building in Cambridge. The parents of these youth generally work in low-income jobs in the service sector, and they themselves work after school, up to thirty hours a week, in fast food restaurants, gas stations, retail stores, and as security guards. At least half of the South Asian immigrant youth in the school live in (public and private) high-rise apartment complexes in North Cambridge. The remainder live in the Central Square area, an ethnically and racially diverse neighborhood that is undergoing gentrification. The families of these South Asian (Sunni) Muslim youth are not very involved in local Muslim organizations or mosques that draw a diverse Arab, North African, Asian, and African American population. They tend to socialize mainly with people from their own ethnic community, but they do not seem to affiliate with the Indian American or Pakistani American community organizations in the Boston area either, which tend to involve mainly middle- to upper-middle-class suburban families.[4] Thus the responses of these immigrant youth are rooted in the specificities of their urban, working-class experience, an experience that is often completely unknown to their more privileged South Asian American counterparts in the area. In fact, my own parents lived in an affluent, predominantly white suburb of Boston for about twelve years; I lived in the Cambridge area for about the same time, having moved to the United States for college, and so witnessed the shifts in the South Asian community's composition in the 1990s and experienced myself the consequences of the class cleavages for community organizing after the events of 9/11.

Not all the immigrant youth in this study have been directly targeted by the War on Terror, but I found that in one way or another all of them have had to grapple with the scapegoating of Muslims, the demonization of Islam, and the fear of suspicion and surveillance after 9/11. I also found that some youth, rather than accepting uncritically the premises of the state's War on Terror, domestically and overseas, were critical of its responses to 9/11 from the perspective of global human rights, thus reframing the basis of citizenship. I have argued elsewhere that young Muslim immigrants' understandings of citizenship shed light on the ways in which nationalism in the United States is defined in relation to transnationalism and globalization ("flexible citizenship"), multiculturalism and polyculturalism ("multicultural citizenship"), and, increasingly overtly, the links between domestic and foreign policy that underlie U.S. imperial power (through their expression of what I call "dissenting citizenship").

Here, I will not discuss these three, vernacular modes of citizenship at length, but will only provide a brief summary as a backdrop for the analysis that follows. These youth all desired U.S. citizenship as part of a long-term, family-based strategy of migration that entailed sponsoring relatives for visas and setting up transnational family businesses. This is what researchers have called *flexible citizenship*, as has been argued for affluent Chinese migrants by Aihwa Ong (1999). Migrants increasingly use transnational links to provide political or material resources not available to them within a single nation-state (Basch, Glick Schiller, and Szanton Blanc 1994). For these young immigrants, the very notion of citizenship was flexible and contingent, shifting with context, and they used this strategically to reconcile questions of national allegiance after 9/11.

One of the most pervasive, and also widely challenged, discourses of cultural belonging in the United States today, especially in education, is that of multiculturalism. So not surprisingly, many of these youth talked about ideas of cultural difference and relationships with others in terms of *multicultural citizenship*, even if only implicitly. For most of them, it was important to emphasize that they "get along" with students from other immigrant or ethnic groups. But it is also true that there are moments of tension among these different groups of youth. Since 9/11, some of the South Asian immigrant youth, particularly the Muslim boys, have felt targeted as Muslims by other high school youth. Accusations such as "you're a terrorist" or "you're a bin Laden" enter into what might otherwise be just an outbreak of youthful aggression among boys, but is now part of a political discourse about Islam sanctioned by the doublespeak of George W. Bush, whose policies and rhetoric have targeted a "foreign" enemy but also an enemy within, despite his verbal attempts to assuage Muslim American and liberal voters.

These working-class South Asian youth sense a connection with other youth of color based on their shared sense of distance from normative (white, middle-class) Americanness, even as they struggle with the challenges that Muslim identity has posed to liberal multiculturalism. The responses of these youth seem to suggest a more critical understanding of multicultural citizenship, a potentially *polycultural citizenship*, based not on the reification of cultural difference that multiculturalism implies, but on a complex set of political affiliations and social boundary crossings, as Robin Kelley's (1999) notion of polyculturalism suggests. This nascent polycultural citizenship is embedded in the messiness and nuances of relationships of different groups with each other and with the state, and one that allows for a political, not just cultural, resonance based on particular historical and material conjunctures.

The post-9/11 moment has seen a stronger conflation of "Arab/Muslim/Middle Eastern" with "terrorist" and "noncitizen" than ever before (Volpp 2002), even though this designation has long existed in the United States in relation to its foreign policy and crystallized at particular historical moments, from the Iran hostage crisis to the first Gulf War and throughout the ongoing, U.S.-backed Israeli occupation (Green 2003; McAlister 2001; Shaheen 1999). Leti Volpp points out that after 9/11, a "national identity has consolidated that is both strongly patriotic and multiracial" (2002, 1584), absorbing African Americans, East Asian Americans, and Latino(a)s. So, despite the potential of polycultural affiliations, there is no easy reading of the fissures and alliances formed after 9/11, and many Arab and South Asian Muslim Americans themselves have been compelled to affirm a patriotic national allegiance to the United States, for reasons of fear, denial, and a desire for belonging and assimilation (see Hing 2002, Prashad 2003). However, some South Asian immigrant youth are willing to voice political views, even publicly, that some middle-class community leaders have not been willing to express. It is this notion of a potentially dissenting citizenship that I want to begin to explore in this essay.

Dissent

An incident with a Pakistani boy, Samir, helped me think about the modes of political dissent expressed by youth in this community and the complexity of identifying political subjectivity for youth. This is an excerpt from my field notes in September 2002:

I'm sitting in the International Student Center when Samir comes in, so I ask him about his website and he sits down [at one of the computers] and pulls it up. It has links to Lollywood [Pakistani] films, Bollywood film music, and also to "funny pictures." I ask him to look up the funny pictures, and when he clicks on the link, pages and pages of pictures of [George] W. [Bush] appear, a row of him wiggling his hips, a row of him looking like a chimp, a row looking like Superman. I start giggling profusely, and Samir is clearly tickled that I'm enjoying it.

"This is great," I say. "So you and I think the same thing about Dubya!" Samir doesn't seem to understand the reference, and he also doesn't respond.

"So you don't like George Bush?"

"No," he says, "I just saw these and I thought they were funny."

Then he scrolls down and there's a picture of a turbaned Bush looking like Osama [bin Laden], and a picture of the Statue of Liberty draped in a hijab. I had seen these after 9/11, both in the context of anti-Islamic humor and recirculating as trivia on the Internet. I ask Samir what he thinks of them and how he chose to put them up, and he just says that someone sent them to him. He has nothing to say about their meaning or his political views. Yet these are the only "funny" images he has up, and also the only images of America. They are clearly, grotesquely about 9/11 and about the president. So what does it mean that he has them on his personal website?

I spent a long time wondering about Samir's choice of these images, his response to me, and the political thinking it could imply: Was this implicitly a mode of dissent? Despite his verbal denial, was Samir situating this image on his website as a way of expressing an implicit critique of Bush, if he on some level recognized that the image, though problematic, played visually with the question of who the "real" terrorist is? Was this Samir's nonverbal way of grappling with a moment that seemed so layered for him with anti-Islamic caricatures that he was responding with his own somewhat opaque visual layers, resituating them on a website that is pro-Islamic, swathed in green with greetings of "asamalekum"? Or is it simply that Samir thought these images were amusing and he "happened" to find them? It seems that the contradictory juxtaposition of his Pakistani pride and these images is not totally accidental, that there is a way in which "the political" seeps into his play with these images via technology, wrapped in his nostalgia for Pakistan through popular culture, his national pride, and his Muslim identity. Samir was not one of the students who had overtly political views; his family was religious and conservative, but he had not talked to me before about politics in an explicit way. This incident was one of the encounters I had with these youth that gave me the most pause, for it made me think about the ways in which young people engage with the political, and the often subtle ways in which they may express a range of responses to questions of power, the state, and resistance. Clearly, these images are subversive, in some way, even if it is not clear exactly how they function for Samir. Yet it is these kinds of moments of ambiguous dissent, expressed from multiple locations and against various forces, that are important to consider when thinking about the political subjectivity of youth, especially of Muslim and immigrant youth who cannot speak out and are increasingly, and justifiably, afraid of doing so.

A more overt moment of political discussion that I witnessed occurred in May 2003, when Samir and other students watched a documentary, *Bridge to Baghdad*, as part of a workshop organized by the South Asian Mentoring and Tutoring Association (SAMTA) in the high school. I had been involved with SAMTA since 9/11 as a volunteer organizer of biweekly workshops on academic, cultural, and political issues for South Asian students in the bilingual program. As such, I very much realized that I was helping to shape the context in which the questions I was interested in exploring in my research were emerging. *Bridge to Baghdad* was shot just before the invasion of Iraq occurred, and focused on an exchange, via satellite TV, of a group of college-age youth in New York and Baghdad. The students were mesmerized by the film and a couple of the boys were particularly excited by the interview with a young Iraqi man who had a heavy metal rock band—and an irreverent persona—and whose father was in the Iraqi army. The girls laughed when an articulate young Iraqi woman in hijab swore in response to a question from an American youth about whether or not she had dated anyone before. When the debate about the imminent war became a heated exchange among some youth, the young woman in hijab asked the American students how they would feel if an army, "say an Iraqi army," came to invade their country and remove their leader. A young anti-war activist of color in New York responded that she would actually be happy if an army came to get rid of Bush. The students laughed. Later, in a discussion between the SAMTA volunteers and the students about the film, an Afghan boy said that he liked the Iraqi woman's comment. An Indian Muslim girl made a similar remark, saying, "It's not right that the war will affect innocent people." But the Afghan boy also wanted to know what happened to the Iraqi youth, or to their fathers in the military, now that war had begun. We, of course, simply said we did not know. It was particularly poignant because this question was voiced by the young Afghan refugee, who personally understood the meanings of war and invasion.

The gendered response to the film was also apparent in the identification of the girls with the issues of dating and the boys with the young metal rocker. On the face of it, this response fits neatly with the dominant way in which issues of gender among Muslim American youth have been discussed in the mainstream U.S. media, pinning the question of hijab and social control onto young Muslim women, and the image of rebelliousness, implicitly tied with a presumably Western mode of modernity, onto young Muslim men. It was not always clear to me how gender inflected understandings of cultural citizenship for these youth, for boys and girls showed very little difference in their expressions of dissenting citizenship. Yet it is certainly apparent that the scrutiny of Muslims in the United States after 9/11 has had a gendered shade, a preoccupation with women in hijab or presumably "oppressed" Muslim women requiring liberation from their tradition in order to be brought into the fold of the nation, and a deep anxiety about young Muslim men as potential terrorists and religious fanatics disloyal to the nation and, unlike women perhaps, ultimately unassimilable. It was in a peculiarly reflexive moment in my research that I realized the extent to which the everyday gendered representations of Muslim identity after 9/11 perform a classically Orientalist role in the present moment. This example is interesting, for although it did not involve "youth" directly, it is clear that young immigrants respond to social forces in relation to adult actors and that the experiences of these South Asian Muslim youth cannot be isolated from the larger political context in which they are embedded, which was also shaping my own understandings of their expressions of dissenting citizenship.

I was at a meeting of the New England Immigrant and Detainee Response Network, a coalition of immigrant and civil rights activists, in Boston in the spring of 2003, to get trained as a monitor of the Special Registration process.[5] A white American woman, who is a civil rights lawyer, wondered aloud what it meant that the largely female group of volunteers from the South Asian community were working on behalf of Muslim males. Some of us laughed at this comment and said that this might challenge the immigrant men's conceptions of gender roles, but I was unsettled by this question for I did not fully know what it meant; also, I did not quite agree with the response, but did not immediately know why. Later, it occurred to me that it was the location of the observer who made the comment that was the key. For me, and for most other South Asian American women I know who have been doing immigrant and civil rights work after 9/11, we are not simply working on behalf of "our men." While we may feel a particular commitment to working with our community, I think many of us feel strongly that we would organize on behalf of men of other communities.

In fact, emphasizing the connection between gender and ethnic or national community—the women on the outside helping "their men" on the inside—implicitly sets up an Orientalist framework of emasculated Muslim males, helpless and impotent in prison, degraded and humiliated (which they are) by representatives of state power. The comment implies that the relationships of Muslim immigrant men with "their women" are imprisoned by tradition but are liberated in a (colonially) perverse way by the crisis created by U.S. state power and the agency of women. This is part of a prevailing mainstream, state-sanctioned discourse of Muslim masculinity but it is not necessarily a discourse that resonates with all the female activists or the men involved, based on my conversations with others who were present at the meeting or involved in immigrant/civil rights organizing. It is complicated, certainly, for there are ongoing issues of gender relations and contestations, but I think further thought needs to be given to the implicit Orientalism that underlies dominant constructions of Muslim masculinity vis à vis the state and that seeps into even progressive sites where state policies are presumably being challenged. In this instance, it was the reflexivity of the research process and my own involvement with this local immigrant rights coalition that forced me to think about the ways in which civil rights issues were being connected to state power and local acts of resistance in gendered ways, and the ways in which I was implicated in these processes. The "liberal Orientalism" that seeps into discussions of civil rights organizing is one layer of the social, political, and legal fields that shape the experiences of Muslim immigrant youth in the United States. After all, the civil rights of South Asian/Arab/Muslim American youth are very much at stake at this moment—and they are the subject of legal initiatives, organizing campaigns, and social scrutiny permeated by ideological representations of Muslim and Arab "others."

But local civil rights organizing initiatives also revealed other kinds of tensions around modes of dissent and conceptions of citizenship after 9/11 that framed the responses of Muslim immigrant youth. Communities of dissent were formed in the Boston area that, as in all moments of organizing, had shifting boundaries and bases for alliances. What is interesting after 9/11 is the ways in which Muslim civil rights have become the focus of organizing initiatives, creating unique coalitions and forcing questions of secularism, the racialization of religious identity, nationalism, and class into discussions of civil rights. Anwar Kazmi is president of the Massachusetts chapter of the American Muslim Alliance, an organization that focuses on encouraging Muslim Americans to get involved in electoral politics. After 9/11, Kazmi said that AMA began getting involved with the peace movement, and its members attended rallies protesting the war in Iraq. His niece, Salma Kazmi, who is the outreach director at the Islamic Society of Boston, commented on the "desire to know what are the true limitations and restrictions in terms of being Muslims and citizens" after 9/11 and the perceived need to have "a newer generation of Muslim civil rights leaders at the forefront, who are without an accent, or women in hijab." She felt that she herself had become a poster child in this project of defining Muslim American citizenship, which seems to rest on a need to prove allegiance and assimilation into the nation. For example, Imam Talal Eid of the Islamic Center of New England proclaimed at an anti-war rally in Boston in November 2001 that Muslims want to be a part of the United States and contribute to its "civilization," an interesting turn on Samuel Huntington's (1996) anti-Islamic argument about the "clash of civilizations"—"Islam" versus "the West"—but one that nonetheless defends Muslim Americans on the premise of assimilation into U.S. citizenship.

Working-class South Asian Muslims in the Boston area are generally not involved in Muslim activist organizations or community initiatives, which draw on the suburban, middle- and upper-middle-class South Asian community, but the youth I spoke to connected with political debates in other sites. Farid, a Gujarati Muslim boy who had grown up in Cambridge, identified the most with hip hop culture among the students in SAMTA and was also a practicing Muslim. He spoke forcefully and eloquently at a workshop one day against the U.S. occupation of Palestine, saying that his tax dollars were being used to kill "his people" and arguing with a Pakistani boy who was defending the U.S. attacks on Afghanistan. When I asked Farid later how he knew so much about Palestine, he said that he had heard discussions at the mosque but that most other students in the school did not seem to care about politics, or at least global politics, although he acknowledged that teachers in the school tried to talk about current events. This was indeed the case, I found on my visits to classes, especially for teachers in the bilingual program but also for other progressive teachers.

There were other moments of overt political discussion in my conversations with students when they offered an analysis of 9/11 and the U.S. government's bombing of Afghanistan, speaking of it in terms of culpability and justice and resisting the nationalization of 9/11 and the U.S. response. Jamila, a Bangladeshi girl, said, "I felt bad for those people [in Afghanistan] . . . because they don't have no proof that they actually did it, but they were all killing all these innocent people who had nothing to do with it." Aliyah, a Gujarati American girl who could very easily pass for Latina, chose to write the words "INDIA + MUSLIM" on her bag after 9/11. For her, this was a gesture of defiance responding to the casting of Muslims as potentially disloyal citizens: "Just because one Muslim did it in New York, you can't involve everybody in there, you know what I'm sayin'." This critique of the anti-Muslim backlash was pervasive among the South Asian Muslim youth after 9/11.

After an anti-Muslim incident in the high school in the fall of 2001, the International Student Center organized a student assembly featuring two Pakistani boys and a Gujarati Muslim girl who delivered eloquent speeches condemning racism to an auditorium filled with their peers. Amir said that when he was threatened by some young white men in Boston after 9/11, "I could have done the same thing, but I don't think it's the right thing to do." Amir is a muscular young man and his call for nonviolent response was a powerful one at that assembly, and could be taken to be a larger political statement about the U.S. response as well. Samiyah stood up in her *salwar kameez* and said, "We have to respect each other if we want to change society. You have to stand up for your rights." South Asian youth are being visibly drawn into antiracist politics and civil rights debates in the local community, although it is not clear yet what the impact of this politicization will be over time. But a year later on the anniversary of 9/11, when the International Student Center organized another student assembly, two Gujarati Muslim girls voluntarily made similar speeches that were reported in the local press.

Even though these working-class youth do not have the support of, or time to participate in, community or political organizations, they have become spokespersons willing to voice dissent in the public sphere. Other Muslim American youth have been forced to play the role of educators as well, giving speeches at their schools and in community forums about Islam. A coordinator of a Muslim youth group at the Cambridge mosque pointed out that it is a role that is not without pressure or fatigue for young Muslim Americans. I do not want to suggest here that these youth are somehow a hidden political vanguard; understandably some of them are hesitant to speak publicly about political issues given the climate of surveillance and fear and this anxiety has only increased with time. Yet I have found these Muslim immigrant youth to be engaged in a practice of dissenting citizenship, based on a critique and affirmation of human rights that means one has to stand apart at some moments, even as one stands together with others outside the borders of the nation.

Dissenting citizenship is a variant of what Paul Clarke has called "deep citizenship," an ethics of care that is fundamentally about a moral and political engagement with the world and extends beyond the state (1996, 4). In my conceptualization, however, dissenting citizenship can be, and is, fundamentally bound up with practices of the state. These Muslim American youth have been forced, by historical events and specific state policies, to engage politically with the world, which they understand locally, nationally, and globally. This is perhaps a moment of making what Clarke calls "citizen selves." Youth are a category of citizens whose rights and representations, in the media but also in policy and in public discourse, are always primarily negotiated for them by others such as institutional authorities or family adults. Yet vis à vis their families, these immigrant youth model a version of deep citizenship that is not always available to their parents and have become spokespersons about race, religion, and civil rights.

Furthermore, the perspective of Muslim immigrant youth is very much rooted in their identities as Muslims, who are targeted as such by the state, and sheds light on the links between U.S. policies at home and abroad. In this, dissenting citizenship goes beyond the debate between liberal and conservative appraisals of cosmopolitanism's possibilities (Nussbaum and Cohen 1996) because it raises an issue that is not emphasized enough by these critics: that of cosmopolitanism, and relatedly of globalization, as an *imperial feeling*. I use the term "imperial feeling" to capture an emerging acknowledgment of U.S. policy on the global stage as linked to economic and military dominance, a cautious acknowledgment that is generally expressed not as full-blown critique in the mass media but as an emerging sentiment in the public sphere, a growing "feeling," often an anxiety, that the United States is occupying the role of a new "empire."[6] If the imperial is a feeling, it is also worthwhile to consider dissent as a "feeling," as something that is not simply caught in the binary of resistance and complicity but that is expressed in ambiguous and hard to identify ways, such as Samir's funny pictures. This does not mean giving up on the tangibility of dissent, and the ever pressing need for resistance in the face of state terrorism and violence; on the contrary, thinking of dissenting feelings allows us to acknowledge the continuum of responses of resistance, especially among those who are coerced into silence by repressive state measures.

The dissenting views of Muslim immigrant youth implicitly critique this imperial feeling of U.S. nationalism after 9/11 through their linking of warfare *within* the state to international war. It is this link between the domestic and imperial that makes this an important mode of dissent because the imperial project of the new Cold War, as in earlier times, works by obscuring the links between domestic and foreign policies. The dissent of Muslim immigrant youth is not vanguardist because it does not need to be; they are simply—but not merely—subjects of both the wars on terror *and* the war on immigration, and so their exclusion from processes of being-made as citizens, and their emergent political subject making, highlight the ways in which civic consent is secured by imperial power. The targeting of a population demonized as "Other" and the absorption of previously targeted communities into a unifying nationalism and climate of fear shift attention away from the ways in which the war at home and the war abroad actually work in tandem with each other.

Surveillance and the State

Yet I have also found that over the past two years there has been increasing fear about speaking out about politics among South Asian Muslims in the United States and, understandably, a constant anxiety about surveillance as the racial profiling, detentions, and deportations of South Asian Americans and Arab Americans have continued. Anti-Muslim violence has also not abated, with some particularly vicious hate crimes against young South Asian men in Massachusetts and New Jersey in the summer of 2003, even if the mainstream media has given it less and less coverage after the initial wave of sympathy and condemnation of anti-Muslim incidents after 9/11. Immigrants are forced to respond to new and shifting measures to limit their civil rights, some of which are not publicized widely, creating more uncertainty and terror. Even legal citizens are worried about expressing political critique or dissent, given the sweeping powers of surveillance appropriated by the state with the

PATRIOT Act. Repression works on two levels to silence dissent, as Corey Robin (2003) points out, on a state level but also, as importantly, on the level of civil society where individuals internalize repression and censor themselves. Robin astutely observes that there is a "division of labor" between the state and civil society for "fear does the work—or enhances the work—of repression," arguing that the "effects of "Fear, American Style" are most evident today in immigrant, Middle Eastern, and South Asian communities, as well as in the workplace (2003, 48). Two years after 9/11, when I asked some of the South Asian Muslim immigrant youth from the high school if they would be willing to speak at a community forum about immigrant rights organized by the South Asian Committee on Human Rights (SACH), a group I was involved with, none of them were willing to do so. It was clear that fear had sent a chill throughout the South Asian immigrant community, for no one from the community who was not already involved with immigrant rights organizing attended the forum. Increasingly, there was even hesitation about speaking about the War on Terror at mosques, otherwise considered a relative "safe haven" or at least a private sphere, as it became public knowledge that the FBI had been recruiting imams as informants.

Fear may instill paranoia, but it also evokes strategies to manage anxiety and to respond to the possibility of intrusive state powers in everyday life. On a reflexive level, the responses of youth coexisted with the ways in which I and others in SACH responded to the "Green Scare" climate of Islamophobic suspicion we were all dealing with in the shared environment of the city. There were constant jokes that became "normal" at our meetings, and events I attended sponsored by pro-Palestinian activists, about FBI videotaping and wiretapping, dressing for the camera, and possible informants, a là the COINTELPRO program of infiltration of the civil rights movements in the 1960s (Chang 2002). This humor, I think, was a way to acknowledge the real state powers expanded by the PATRIOT Act and the ways in which we understood state surveillance to be an intimate part of our everyday lives—not unlike the ways in which people have written about the humor employed by those living in police states. These are not simply responses to imagined encounters with the state, for activists in Palestinian rights groups in the Boston area with whom I have worked have indeed been surveilled by law enforcement and intelligence agencies. Members of the New England Committee to Defend Palestine (NECDP), for example, obtained surveillance videotapes of their group recorded by local police agencies working in cooperation with the FBI and have had their phone conversations recorded. Amer Jubran, a well-known Palestinian activist and cofounder of NECDP, who was targeted for deportation on false charges by the INS, learned that twelve FBI agents were working on documenting his political and personal activities. In talking about his case at presentations across the country, Jubran would name the agents, telling people how "Agent John Blake" followed him at rallies and "Agent Sculley" participated in his arrest at his home. This presentation, I realized, has the effect of personifying the state, of letting people know that the secretly enforced powers of state surveillance are embodied by actual persons, by men with names and faces that are not figments of our paranoid imagination. Young people who heard these presentations, at events at college campuses at which I have been present, began to grapple with the real implications of coming of age at a moment in the United States when the state appears both immensely vulnerable and powerful, hypervisible and yet invisible, violent and yet protective. For South Asian Muslim youth, in particular, or for Muslim American youth more generally, the understanding of the state may be no more or less contradictory, but it is increasingly based on a knowledge of the state's reach and powers that is terrifying in its intimacy.

Ethnography of Empire

Thomas Hansen and Finn Steputat propose that an ethnography of the state focus on everyday, local practices that engage with the "languages of stateness" evident in "mythologies of power," the "practical, often nonpolitical routines" or "violent impositions" of the state (2001, 5). Similarly, daily practices of humor and of narrating encounters with the (imperial) state, or its intelligence-gathering officials, are some of the many practices and discourses that become part of an ethnography of empire. The "state of emergency" in empire—this crisis of civil rights and its concomitant mode of dissenting citizenship—is in fact not exceptional in the United States (Ganguly 2001); the post-9/11 moment builds on measures and forms of power already in place; this is a state of everyday life in empire. Contrary to Michael Hardt and Antonio Negri's (2001) amorphous theory of decentered "empire," I argue that it is, in fact, *imperialist* power that is at work, even if it has been transformed by the new logic of global capital and the weakened link between the state and the economy. Similarly, I differ from Mohammed Bamyeh, who has suggested that capital has become decoupled from politics and that the "new imperialism" is a "self-referential system of power" that has "only an irrational attachment to the principle of hegemony," existing in various nations as diverse "local" imperialisms (2000, 12, 15). While it is obvious that imperial power no longer necessarily requires direct governance of colonized states, and the power of the state itself has generally declined (Glick Schiller and Fouron 2002), it is evident that the power of the U.S. state to exercise the globality of violence and globality of economy characterizes this new mode of empire (Joxe 2002). The current moment of empire is situated in a long history of what some call "informal" U.S. empire that has used the framework of "universal rights" to cloak a project of reconstituting social and economic relations into a global capitalist order (Panitch and Gindin 2003). There is also, of course, much work analyzing what Juan Flores (2000) calls "imperialism lite," or the penetration of popular culture, a vigorously debated issue in globalization studies that has important implications for youth culture studies.

I want to conclude by asking the question implied by my introduction: How can we produce an ethnography of everyday life in empire that is not completely complicit with intelligence gathering and surveillance of the target population after 9/11? Are there methods, modes of interpretation, means of dissemination that can allow our research to be used critically rather than complicitly? It seems to me that we need to pay attention to expressions of dissenting citizenship that cannot be integrated into traditional forms of political activism but that contribute to critiques of empire. We also need to consider how our understandings of young people's politics shifted after the events of 9/11, if at all, and how we can connect our own political responses to an international or anti-imperialist analysis. Finally, we need to contemplate how the very intimacy of empire—the everyday encounters with the state evident in the lives of youth—and the feelings of terror, absurdity, dissent, and courage that emerge from the imperial help us understand how far or how close we are willing to go with an ethnography of empire.

Part II
Movements and Outbreaks

Chapter 5
The Amway Connection: How Transnational Ideas of Beauty and Money Affect Northern Thai Girls' Perceptions of Their Future Options

Ida Fadzillah

The examination of women and work in Southeast Asia has a long history in the field of cultural anthropology.[1] In Thailand, much of this literature has focused on farmers and factory workers, and also on work and beauty as it relates to the prostitution industry.[2] Studies of Thai women and beauty have thus tended to present the relationship between women, beauty, and money as merging in only one venue: sex work. While this model is accurate in some respects, it ignores the experiences of the majority of Thai women, creating a scenario in which the only relationship between money and beauty is one that involves the exchange of sex for money, prestige, or power (for example, in the sex trade, in attracting powerful lovers, or in being chosen as a concubine).

This essay explores another relationship between Thai women, beauty, and money that exists at a local intersection of global flows: the door-to-door sales of beauty products produced by national and multinational corporations such as Amway, Avon, and Suprederm (a successful Thai version of Amway) by Northern Thai girls. In Northern Thailand, female beauty has traditionally signified social, economic, and moral status. However, local definitions of beauty are changing owing to several factors, including the increasing exposure of villagers to Western images of attractiveness through television, movies, magazines, and transnational labor migration by the villagers. An active enterprise in the local sale of door-to-door cosmetics has emerged among teenage girls in particular partly because of this change in definitions of beauty, while simultaneously precipitating this change. I argue that these sales—which provide disposable income, financial savvy, and opportunities for travel—offer a means by which Northern Thai girls can disassociate themselves economically, socially, and even geographically from their rural backgrounds and align themselves instead to a more global world. Being an Amway or Avon distributor has taken on the markers (especially for teenage girls) of high-status, or "cosmopolitan," occupations in which cash and a close association with internationally acknowledged beauty and desire have become indicators of female success.

I, like most current social science researchers on youth culture, take adolescence to be a cultural as well as a biological phase of the human life course that is historically shaped and in a state of constant change (Hurrelmann 1989, 3). The adolescent experience is closely linked to economic, political, and cultural changes evoked by the industrialization process and the accompanying establishment of a compulsory school system (Gillis 1974). The experience of globalization is of particular importance to youth, for as Wulff (1995b) explains, "When it comes to globalization or transnational connections youth cultures are in the forefront of theoretical interest; youth, their ideas and commodities move easily across national borders, shaping and being shaped by all kinds of structures and meanings" (Wulff 1995b, 10).

Since the girls of my study are at a stage in their lives when they are confined to the village (owing to family, society, and educational constraints), the influences on these girls can be perceived not simply through their immediate actions, but through their narratives about future possibilities as well. That is, the girls' perceptions of their female identity and expectations are shaped by the influence of globalization, and are expressed through their narratives of desire and of longing. Thus girls have created a way to bring "city life" to the village through their quest to transform themselves into successful and "desirable" women (in their own eyes as well as in the eyes of others). Furthermore, the form globalization has taken has agreed with this task; that is, the model of globalization at the village level encourages the exercise of girls taking more adult and perhaps more mobile roles at an earlier age.

Adolescent girls have developed a keen sense of their place in the world, and of how their status as rural, country folk has distanced them automatically from the desirable images of female identity presented through the international media. To be "successful," that is, to be a "real" woman, in the village girls' eyes, meant to be "cosmopolitan": urban, Western, and modern. To these girls, it is not sufficient to try to attain this by physically moving to an urban center; as girls, their movements are restricted by familial, social, and educational constraints.

I should clarify that my perspective on globalization or cosmopolitanism does not equate these processes only with notions of a unidirectional Westernization, or more specifically, reduce it to an emphasis on the economic imperialism of the West.[3] Rather, my perspective mirrors that of scholars who see globalization as plural manifestations in a variety of locations, and with a multiplicity of results.[4] The model of globalization I use incorporates elements of Harvey's (1989) model of a "time space compression" as well as Appadurai's (1996) concepts of "flows." These flows—cultural, economic, human, and ideological—come together as "scapes" that capture the "fluid, irregular shapes of these landscapes that characterize international capital as deeply as they do international clothing style" (Appadurai 1996, 33). Together the world, city, and village are recast as spaces of ghostly transparency, constantly shifting shapes that are defined by intricate networks that appear and disappear. And like ghosts, they appear to some and not to others, and in different forms to different interests at unexpected moments.

Thus while globalization "from above" is associated with Western financial institutions and media production that have highlighted the material and social inequities between industrialized nations and the "rest" of the world, it is also true that as global flows (of goods, people, images, and ideas) pass through local environments, they are at times discarded, and at other times taken up deliberately. What this article attempts to do is present the reader with a moment in time when global factors seemed of particular salience to some, who then used them to establish their own identities based on local perceptions of age, gender, success, and desire.

The Market Place

When traveling by bus in the Northern Thai province of Chiang Rai, the first sign that one has arrived at Baan Khmer village[5] is the abrupt screeching of the vehicle as it stops in front of a large open-air food market whose perimeters are defined by a wooden roof held up at strategic locations by sturdy beams. The driver shuts off the radio blaring raucous Thai country music and everyone, anthropologist included, emerges from the vehicle to purchase soft drinks, Thai fried chicken, seasonal fruits, sweets, or the ever popular *som tam*.[6] Once the travelers have fortified themselves for the rest of their journey, everyone piles back into the bus, the radio is switched back on, and then all are gone in a cloud of dust and gravel. In its wake the bus leaves the market as it always was, a busy center of village activities catering mainly to the needs of the local community.

At first glance the market seems a female domain: of the approximately forty vendors present from sunrise to sunset daily, only two are men.[7] Upon closer inspection the domain's characteristics become further refined: it is not simply a female space but a space of middle-aged women, for most of the vendors resting behind their goods stacked upon high wooden tables are between the ages of twenty-two and forty, married, and have children. These women have grown, cooked, and assembled their wares themselves. The majority have worked in this market for years, some having inherited their spaces and rickety tables from their mothers who had worked there for thirty years before them, starting when the market was first established as a permanent space for enterprise. The regular buyers at this market are also predominantly women: wives and mothers who buy fresh produce daily for their kitchens, their food stalls, or who buy their ready-made breakfasts and lunches on their way to work. In this space relationships are formed and cemented, gossip is exchanged and local roles and expectations are established. The rhythm of the market is a constant beat of female labor and purchase, of community interaction that has defined female roles and opportunities for generations.

However, this intimate model of "community" and "economic center" with its associated prescriptions of female roles and opportunities is changing with startling rapidity. In 1996, when I began doing ethnographic fieldwork in Baan Khmer focusing on rural adolescent girls' notions of their future possibilities, I expected to find girls' lives revolving around local notions of acceptable behavior as advocated and maintained by the school, family, and Buddhist Church *(Sangha)*, all of which were cited in previous literature as being of paramount importance to rural Thai society.[8] Imagine my surprise when it became clear that the forces that seemed to influence these girls' perceptions of themselves most strongly, and to most motivate their choices and actions, were not grounded in local models of acceptable female identity; rather, the girls were overwhelmingly influenced by increasingly transnational networks of people, money, and ideas. The village setting is thus being experienced by the girls as part of a larger, more cosmopolitan market, a specific point of intersection of multiple, global flows of labor, commodities, and images. I found these village girls to have a keen grasp of the mechanics of national and transnational markets, as well as of the power surrounding modern images of beauty and desire.

About a quarter of the women and girls in Baan Khmer village (out of a population of nearly five hundred people[9]) were involved to some extent in the door-to-door sale of beauty products; according to most, teenage girls were particularly successful at this venture. From my observations, the reasons for this success are numerous: as youth, teenage girls have "free" time to market and sell their products (that is, when they are not in school, girls are not usually constrained by having to perform paid labor, or be in charge of time-consuming chores like cooking, cleaning, and caring for children[10]), they had access to potential and current clients (mainly teachers and other students) on school grounds; they had a relatively consistent disposable income from allowances and no major financial responsibilities (which meant it was possible for them to purchase the initial beauty products required to start such a venture); and they possessed a tangible connection to the "modern" *(thansamay)* image of beauty—based on youthful skin, face, body, and clothes—these products were trying to cultivate, and thus were able to "advertise" the products effectively. Mary Beth Mills defines *thansamay* as "being up to date" (Mills 1999, 5), and I use this term interchangeably with "modern," "urban," and "cosmopolitan" because I believe all these variations are included in the Thai definition (as interpreted by the Northern Thai girls) of being *thansamay.*

Working as beauty distributors for these national and multinational companies provided skills and desires distinct from those provided by the more traditional labor expected of Northern Thai adolescent girls. These companies used a rhetoric of success based on the selling of longings and dreams to their own distributors, a rhetoric that was radically different from models of success supplied through farming or marketing; they emphasized a very different—and for teenage girls, highly successful—system for making and distributing money based on the pyramid system rather than on straightforward buyer-seller relationships; and they created a new definition of ideal womanhood more fitting with the *thansamay* image of beauty. These aspects of cosmetics sales gave girls more competence, and thus more confidence, in participating in what they considered *thansamay* labor options, and affected their abilities and responsibilities in other areas of their lives. In this essay I explore the influence of Amway, Avon, and Suprederm on Northern Thai girls' lives through the examples of two teenage girls: Duan, a fifteen-year-old, who did not distribute beauty products but worked at the market in her free time, and Nim, a sixteen-year-old, who in her free time sold Suprederm. Through the juxtaposition of these girls' stories I attempt to illustrate how the selling of beauty products resulted in different skills, relationships, and attitudes of teenage girls toward their own capabilities, their current lives, and potential future choices. I then explore the appeal of the beauty industry to these girls to understand better why the sale of cosmetics is so successful. Finally, I examine how participation in the beauty industry has instilled in these teenage girls a new definition of "success" that is related closely to their notion of "the good life."

The Place of Labor in Girls' Lives: Duan

In the mornings in Baan Khmer village, the secondary school students who would stop by the market for a breakfast of fruit or fried rice on their way to school would frequently encounter one of their peers, Duan, managing her aunt's vegetable stall. The stall was in a prime location, on the periphery of the market, where it was easily spotted and accessed by potential customers. Duan's aunt had been a market seller for ten years, and hoped to be able to pass on her stall to Duan upon retirement. At the time of my research Duan was fifteen years old and in grade three of the secondary school *(mattyom)* system.[11] When she was twelve, Duan had chosen to leave her family and live with her aunt, who treated her like her own child. Duan had made this move just before starting secondary school because her family lived far enough away from the school that the commute from home would have been inconvenient, and because her parents did not have enough money to support her, as well as her younger siblings, through school. So Duan decided, with the blessing of her parents, to live and work with her more financially stable aunt to earn enough money to support herself through school.

Duan was seen by the local community as an exceptionally hard worker, getting up at five in the morning to help her aunt set up her market stall, where she sold vegetables and fried meats. She would help her aunt unload the vegetables from the back of their motorbike, and organize them on the table. Duan would stay there alone from 6 until 7:30 in the morning, while her aunt gave alms at the temple. If her aunt was busy, then Duan would go to the temple as her family's representative. Her aunt would return after the monks had eaten and Duan would hurry to school to begin class. After school ended she would go back to the market, taking over for any other stall owners who had to leave temporarily.[12] The women in the market trusted Duan implicitly, remarking on her skill at handling and calculating money. I witnessed the other market vendors asking Duan to help them count out change, to manage difficult customers, and to juggle multiple responsibilities (restocking tables, collecting and dispensing money, advertising the goods, handing out merchandise) during peak selling times (the breakfast and dinner hours, for example, or when the buses would stop to allow passengers to disembark). Duan would remain at the market until six o'clock, when her aunt would come and help her close up the stall, and they would go home to cook, eat, and finish the household chores of cleaning and minding the children.

During the day the market women would include Duan in their gossip sessions during the slow hours, and she would frequently join them when they watched the afternoon soap operas on a little battery-operated television. Through such interactions, Duan adopted their pattern of speaking and of interacting when conversing with other adults and took pride in her abilities to handle "adult" responsibilities. This manner and confidence were part of the reason those at school did not see her favorably, for Duan frequently spoke loudly, taunted other school kids, talked back to her teachers, and generally presented a "tough" demeanor. At school she was perceived by her teachers and peers (outside her own circle of friends) as rude and aggressive. She frequently did not finish her assignments and was not considered very intelligent by her teachers. Duan once said she did not want to be a teacher when she grew up. When I asked her why, she replied, "Because I would not like to get students like me."

Duan frequently fell asleep in her classes, exhausted from her long hours. She earned money from her aunt for minding the store, but she often appeared tired and disheveled in school, and the teachers commented on that. Because of her job, she always had money to buy lunch and snacks. She loaned money easily and frequently to her friends, and had taken over the role of the leader of their group of five girls. But because of the responsibility placed on her as co-manager of the stall, Duan did not have the time before or after school or on the weekends to socialize with her friends, who would frequently go to each other's houses or into Chiang Rai City.[13]

Despite Duan's reputation in school and among the students as a rebel, her reputation among the women of the community was glowing. "Why don't you talk to Duan?" one woman asked me when I was looking for a part-time research assistant. "She is hard working and reliable; she will definitely work hard for you." Other women at the market trusted her to watch their stalls, to count out their change, to run their errands, to make purchases on their behalf, to mind their children, and to be otherwise "reliable." She associated easily with these women. What was interpreted as rude or rebellious behavior at the school was seen as acceptable, even normal, behavior among the older women at the market, who were just as loud and raucous as Duan. These interpretations were partly based on Duan's identification with the local, mostly undereducated women whose regional styles of dress, talk, and manner were in distinct contradiction to the more "national" identifications encouraged by the school teachers and administration.

Additionally, Duan's relationship to labor and money was perceived by the community as an accepted way for women (and girls) to earn their income. These jobs connected the girls to their families and their local community, for the girls worked for their neighbors and relatives alongside other women and men from the village. They learned their skills from older family members, and they also supported each other; for example, Duan would regularly help out the other market vendors and vice versa. These were traditional jobs, forms of labor their mothers and grandmothers had also performed. Working at the market earned Duan about 30 baht a day, out of which she would spend 10 baht on lunch at school. There were few expenses to be invested in these jobs, for the clothes worn were country clothes, with no makeup required. In addition, the general community felt a great deal of respect and confidence toward these girls, as did these girls toward their own abilities. The older villagers frequently associated these girls and others who performed similar services with the ideas of "hard working," and "reliable." At the same time, these characteristics were associated by the older community members with religious merit. There was religious merit to be gained for helping parents and working the land and there was a moral quality associated with jobs that required long hours and back-breaking work. Additionally, there was a piety perceived by the rest of the community in girls who "knew their place," helping others rather than trying to succeed on their own. Thus these girls who worked with and within the community were judged by the older villagers as moral and pious, as "good girls" and dutiful daughters.

The teenage girls of the village, however, as a whole did not share these sentiments about more traditional forms of labor. The main issue emphasized by most girls about work like planting and harvesting rice was that it was difficult work with little return. There was little gratification perceived in toiling under the hot sun or having to sit outside for hours selling your wares. The perception of little reward for much effort was a central reason why the thought of staying in the village and becoming farmers like their parents was an option most girls sought to avoid at all costs. Other reasons frequently cited by the girls were that one paid a costly price in terms of getting "black" and leathery skin from exposure to too much sun; having to wear "poor" clothes like the simple farmer shirts, big hats, and high boots of the fields that marked the wearer even from a long distance as being "country folk"; and having no opportunity to display more "feminine" aspects of identity such as stylish clothes, makeup, styled hair, or jewelry. "She's always dirty," one girl commented about Duan, echoing the sentiment of several who pointed out how Duan was disheveled, "did not care how she looked," appeared "rough," and was not "ladylike."

Not all jobs, however, were seen by the younger generation in such negative terms. The commissioned sale of door-to-door beauty products, a relatively new phenomenon in this community, had become immensely popular with the village girls, and illustrates well how girls perceived themselves and their desires. Instead of working in the fields or in other people's homes, many girls opted to earn extra income by selling Amway, Avon, and Suprederm beauty products, thereby succeeding in becoming part of a global network not just through working for a multinational company, but through their participation in defining and exploiting cosmopolitan standards of beauty and desire.

Purchasing Power: Amway, Avon, and Suprederm

Cosmetics provided the cheapest and most accessible means for Baan Khmer women to achieve a cosmopolitan model of attractiveness. While not a traditional beauty enhancer, makeup had become in the last forty years an acceptable way for village women to adorn themselves publicly (see Van Esterik 1996). However, while most women had access to transportation, most simply did not have the time to travel to Chiang Rai City to purchase cosmetics at the department stores. Thus most women, young and old, welcomed the local availability of door-to-door beauty products such as Amway, Avon, and their local equivalents Suprederm, Miss Teen, and Cupid.[14] Amway, Avon, and Suprederm have similar philosophies about what they sell—to their distributors as well as to their clients—and how they sell it. It is not beauty at all that these companies seek to advertise, but success.

According to Kathy Peiss, "beauty is big business, with large scale production, international distribution networks, media saturation advertising, scientific marketing, and sales in the billions of dollars" (Peiss 2001, 7).[15] Companies like Amway are one example of this type of international "big business." Founded in 1959, by 1999 Amway had generated U.S.$5 billion in sales through its global product distribution network. The branch in Thailand was launched May 1987, with twenty-one service centers currently operating. Amway sells personal care products ranging from fragrances and makeup to bar soaps and hair colorants, as well as cookware and cutlery, water and air treatment systems. However, in Baan Khmer it is the personal care line that is most popular.[16]

Avon, formerly known as the California Perfume Company (CPC), was labeled the "depression-proof business strategy" by Katina Marko, who examined how the company was able to thrive during the Great Depression. According to Marko, "Early in the Great Depression, in 1930, more than 25,000 women throughout the nation looked to Avon products to supplement their income. Selling door-to-door, they generated more than 2,500,000 in annual sales. Three years later . . . the representative corps had increased in size by twenty percent to 30,000, and the sales climbed with it. As one California Perfume Company report stated in 1931, 'while most firms were glad to make two-thirds of the profits they enjoyed the year before, our sales were *greater* than the previous year'" (Marko 2001, 142). In terms of the actual process of door-to-door cosmetic sales,

Avon sales women went into homes to teach women about beauty products and how to use them. Unlike selling vacuum cleaners and encyclopedias door-to-door, selling beauty involved a long-tem continuous relationship between seller and buyer. . . . Woven into the "house calls" of the Avon Lady and the wash-and-set beauty parlors was an ongoing conversation about appearances that opened out in many directions. These businesses encouraged a high degree of self-consciousness of the face and body. Operating in a local context, they reinforced yet mediated the barrage of advertising, motion pictures, and national magazines that fostered an external, visual standard for self-assessment (Peiss 2001, 12).

Avon officially explained its success by claiming: "The company's unique market niche in rural America, its devotion to selling a business opportunity to women, and its strong commitment to maintaining its door-to-door sales and service strategy not only helped CPC survive the Great Depression, but made its prosperity possible" (*Avon Outlook* 1931, 2).

In Thailand today, some of the same business strategies seem to be successful with rural Thai female consumers, though in the Thai context they naturally elicit specific local and national concerns. The most financially successful cosmetics brand in the village was Suprederm, a Thai cosmetics company. The Suprederm line of products consisted of skin-care products, makeup, and household articles such as laundry detergent and toothpaste and is based on the Amway model of products and business strategy. Since the company is Thai and thus pays less for the raw materials and production and transportation costs than its American counterparts, the products are substantially cheaper and more affordable to the villagers, making Suprederm the most locally purchased of the brands. Second in popularity among cosmetics brands was Amway, though many people believed Amway to be the superior product. Tuk, a forty-five-year-old woman who sold Suprederm, explained to me, "For example, a tube of Suprederm toothpaste costs 120 baht while the same toothpaste sold by Amway costs 195 baht. Why would you want to buy Amway? And we are Thai, we should buy Thai products right?" Another reason for Suprederm's popularity despite Amway's reputation for better quality was explained rather convincingly to me by another Suprederm distributor. "No," she said patiently, "it's not true that Amway is better quality. Actually their quality is the same, the same! But Thai people think that Amway is better because they think American brands are better than Thai brands. And Thai people think that if something is more expensive then it must be better! But after people try Suprederm then they see that it is just the same quality, that Thai people can make good products too." Thus issues of national identity and the desire to be part of the global market by buying Western goods drives women to associate with certain brands over others.

The Place of Labor in Girls' Lives: Nim

One successful cosmetics distributor was Nim, who also worked at her aunt's house part time. She went to her aunt's home mornings and evenings, helping with the laundry, ironing, sweeping, washing dishes, minding her seven-year-old nephew, and pitching in at her aunt's small restaurant, and for this work Nim made 500 baht a month. Though I observed her working long hours at her aunt's house, the general way Nim's aunt and others described her was as someone who was "lazy" and "didn't like to work."

To understand the difference between older villagers' perceptions of girls like Duan and girls like Nim—who appeared to me to put in the same hours and effort into their labor—one must first understand how Nim's roles and responsibilities were performed. Though Nim was carrying out a traditional form of labor (as house-helper to her aunt), she was also engaging in a form of untraditional labor. Specifically, as a successful distributor of Suprederm products she regularly traveled to Chiang Rai City to deposit money into her savings account, to pick up more makeup supplies, and to collect money from her subsidiary distributors, a geographic mobility not available to her peers in more traditional occupations. Nim was also financially independent: during the time of my research she had 8,000 baht in her savings account.[17] She did not know why she was successful, only saying that in her class there are other people who sell makeup, but "for some reason I'm the one people end up buying from." Her friends, who are not rich, "still want to look good," she explains. According to Nim, it was normal for girls to sell makeup. They regularly received catalogues through the mail, through which they were able to choose what and when they wanted to sell. Several of her acquaintances were cosmetics distributors, and in her school most of the girls she knew were selling makeup at one point or another.

Nim's relationship to the Suprederm line began in 1995 when she met a Suprederm representative for the first time, a man who was invited to her accounting class to lecture on business strategies. The man, a Baan Khmer native, spoke at length about the success of Suprederm. This instance of corporate "sales pitches" is not unusual in the secondary schools. Multiple presentations are arranged as a means to educate the students, both male and female, on extracurricular aspects of life. Thus members of the community are invited to exhibit eyeglasses for sale (along with free eye exams), and to discuss (though not necessarily to promote) certain business ventures. The presentation by the man from Suprederm was not the first by a cosmetics company representative at this school. This direct connection by multinational companies into the village schools is another interesting way the global marketplace has a foothold at the local level.

According to Nim, before the school presentation few villagers were selling Suprederm. But after his talk, several teachers began selling this brand at school, as well as similar products such as Amway, Avon, Miss

Teen, and Cupid. Nim's accounting teacher became involved and recruited Nim as one of her subsidiary distributors. Nim began selling Suprederm mainly to her friends and other school kids, and eventually enlisted her mother, aunt, and grandmother into her Suprederm network. It was interesting to hear Nim and others speak of their teachers in relation to "extra-curricular" relationships such as cosmetics networks. While these relationships did not seem to affect students' grades (Nim, for example, was routinely seen as an "okay" student), they did seem to shape students' relationships with their teachers. Establishing a type of "patron-client" relationship outside of the classroom with a person of authority meant that a student's "cultural capital" was increased, in terms of verbal recommendations for jobs or scholarships in the future.

The commissioned sales worked in such a way that "trees" of people were enlisted who all sold the products and got a percentage of each subsidiary recruitment's "cut." Because Nim was one of the founding members of this network, she kept 25 percent of what she made from selling Suprederm. If she sold over a certain amount of baht, then her 25 percent commission was increased to 35 percent, then to 45 percent. Since Nim recruited her relatives to Suprederm, they had to give her a percentage of their profits monthly. If they had just been starting out and needed a lot of help from their "supervisor," the monthly percentage going to Nim would have been 25 percent of total sales. Once they reached the status of "assistant," and were on their way to forming their own business alliances, Nim's distributors would have to give 10 percent of their sales to her. Since they had been doing this business for a while, and now had their own clients and enlisted distributors, Nim's subsidiary distributors owed her 4 percent of their monthly profits. Nim was currently the group leader of five other Suprederm distributors, who themselves had several distributors under them. But because she was originally recruited by her teacher, she still had to give a percentage of her sales to her. But Nim was doing well financially because both her mother and her aunt were each supervising at least twenty Suprederm sellers. Thus a percentage of all the profits collected by her aunt and mother ultimately went to Nim. In Nim's daily life, her business relationships are thus inextricably intertwined with her family and educational relationships, upsetting and recreating traditional hierarchies of power and prestige.

The Power of Selling Cosmetics

Baan Khmer girls, like most people, are attracted by cosmetics companies' underlying message of the fulfillment of hopes and desires through the use of commodities. They long to be associated with an internationally recognized beauty culture, an association that, in the girls' eyes, would increase the girls' own "cultural capital" by making them part of an international, and thus cosmopolitan, corporate identity. Makeup represents a link in the eyes of cosmetics buyers between village life and cosmopolitan city life, a link exploited by successful Amway and Suprederm distributors. Girls' sales pitches to their peers emphasized how the use of makeup would lead others to view them as women rather than girls; make them desirable like the actresses and models they saw in the media, and especially attractive to members of the opposite sex; and recreate them as active members-consumers in a booming international economy. Girls in particular understood this rhetoric of beauty their products were attempting to sell. They were skilled in phrasing/praising their products in terms of the youthfulness they bring and the Westernized beauty (in terms of creating looks similar to those of Western pop and movie stars) they could create. The exclamation "Wow, you look just like Demi Moore in 'Ghost'!" after a woman had tried on a beauty product, was a highly successful sales pitch I observed more than once. The girls focused their attention on selling youthfulness, emphasizing fairer skin, fewer wrinkles, and clearer complexions. They also linked their products to transnational symbols of beauty, such as Demi Moore, or more local celebrities, most of whom were biracial (half Caucasian and half Thai). Both buyers and sellers understood that there was power in purchasing and using beauty products. They were also aware that there was a market for beautiful Northern Thai girls, especially in the prostitution industry.[18] Girls' "worth" as perceived through their eyes was thus not simply based on cultural definitions, but on active calculations of how their beauty—augmented by cosmetics—could translate into future economic opportunities. The sale of these multinational beauty products thus served to change the communities into which they were placed: transnational beauty products were a *product* of a growing interest in Westernized forms of beauty, and through their presence they also served to *perpetuate* the desire to adopt more Western forms of beauty.[19]

These girls also understood that there was power in being part of the cosmetic distribution network. The successful sales of Suprederm, Amway, and Avon allowed girls to achieve goals they perceived as rewarding, having high returns for relatively little hard work. In Thailand, geographic mobility is perceived as a natural and valued characteristic for men, while women's bodies and their movement are subject to far greater restrictions (Mills 1999, 94). However, through their savings of income earned through their sales, many girls were able to invest in their own modes of transportation, such as motorcycles, or at least pay for their own bus tickets to Chiang Rai City. Additionally, the district headquarters for Suprederm and for Amway were in Chiang Rai City. Most girls who sold these products were required to go to the city regularly to stock up on supplies and to collect commissions. They went sometimes with, sometimes without, their parents' permission. Once in the city they had access to shopping malls, department stores, a movie theater, big restaurants, and numerous flea markets at which to spend their income. Some girls even traveled to Bangkok for the national conventions, courtesy of the local Suprederm branch. Thus their jobs allowed them geographic mobility into the larger world.

The income earned from selling cosmetics, the rhetoric learned of modern *(thansamay)* definitions of beauty, and the increased mobility afforded to these distributors allowed many teenagers to participate actively in the international economic system at a much earlier age than their parents and grandparents. And most perceived that their business venture was indeed global: many girls and women I spoke with had almost mythical stories about Amway and the celebrities (both local and international) who got their start from selling Amway products. These narratives were reported and repeated through conventions, newsletters, and word of mouth from one distributor to another.[20] The girls also recognized that their labor connected to a larger enterprise based in Bangkok or overseas (in the case of Amway and Avon), not their local market or even Chiang Rai City; their jobs thus linked them socially to the outside world. This was the effect the Amway distribution centers wanted to have on their distributors, holding weekly meetings that were more like support groups or religious meetings, emphasizing an international sense of family, and actively trying to be more than just an employer to its workers.

The participation of girls in the cosmetics industry was not always perceived by others as positive. In the area of commissioned sales, and in no other business I knew of, teenage girls did so well financially that an interesting subversion of authority occurred because the teenage daughter was earning more than the parents while still living in the village. In her most profitable month Nim received a commission of 10,000 baht and a necklace as a bonus by Suprederm for reaching her sales goal. With her earnings she bought some clothes for herself, gave her grandparents some money, and in the end deposited 2,000 baht into her savings account. But, she said, everyone found out how much money she made and started teasing her and asking her for loans, even the teachers at her school. Nim's family also thought she was rich; I consistently heard her aunt discuss her in disparaging terms, usually right in front of her, about her "stinginess:"[21] "Oh Nim is so rich, she has her own savings account, but she won't even treat us to a free lunch." Stinginess was the ultimate slight, implying that someone was not a proper member of the society, thinking only of her own good rather than the good of the community.[22] In Baan Khmer it was a powerful means of controlling behavior, redistributing money, and in general emphasizing the traditional rules surrounding (female) roles and responsibilities. "Stinginess" was perceived and portrayed by the general community as akin to amorality, in that it went against Buddhist precepts of generosity to others, and the label was used to align the accused with more "sinful" behavior and attitudes.

When her aunt said Nim was frugal, that is, with a significant amount of money in her savings account, she was not giving praise but voicing criticism. Part of this attitude came from jealousy, but part of it came from the still commonly held notion that wealth was not to be hoarded, but to be dispersed into the family and community: there should be almost no surplus wealth, because income earned by children should be at the disposal of parents for necessary items. Additionally, Nim also consistently loaned money to her family, and now her grandparents and even her mother owed her thousands of baht. Nim's job further subverted the traditionally prescribed community relations: not only did Nim have to teach her older family members the skills required to sell products, but her mother and other members of the family were officially working under her. Nim's commanding role at the top of the Suprederm hierarchy added to her image of being rich. One interesting result of these cosmetics sales was that even if the girls' families were poor and/or in debt, the girls themselves were not. They spent their money on things that accentuated their status as consumers as well as young women living in the modern age: tee shirts, blue jeans, makeup, magazines, and high heels.

This spending reflected one of the biggest areas of contention I encountered, which was in the struggle to control definitions of "children" and "adults." Most of the girls I talked to (even those who did not sell cosmetics) did not see themselves as children when it came to making money, and perceived earning an income as a valued endeavor, one that "buys" them freedom from their obligations as children. "It's my money. I want to save it to buy a new motorbike so I don't have to borrow my parents'," said one girl. "I don't know, I think I want to save the money, and then build a nice house for my parents," said another. In their narratives a central theme is the sense of control, of autonomy; they have earned the money, and they will spend the money as they see fit. This attitude reflects their perception of themselves as adults, rather than as children.

However, the way income is earned is viewed by girls as being of almost equal importance to the amount of income earned. Currently, many of the girls who earned this extra income were contemptuous of the life-styles led by the older women of the village, for whom it was more of a struggle to earn a living. Many girls spoke to me of how the older women did not dress nicely, and got very dark from having to work in the fields. Thus Duan's work in the local market was not considered by her peers to be labor that could lead to "the good life."[23] This image of female success related closely to what these girls wanted in terms of their own futures. Many do not want to live their mothers' lives; they wanted to be fair-skinned, wear Western clothes, and be "beautiful." The desire to acquire beauty—and its link to status and prestige—provided powerful motivation to choose certain jobs over others.

Butterfield, in his exploration of the Amway corporation, explains that "besides a highly successful business concept, Amway represents a value system which has changed the lives of several million people in the United States alone" (Butterfield 1985, 2). He adds, "Amway does something else too. It sells a marketing and motivational system, a cause, a way of life, in a fervid emotional atmosphere of rallies and political-religious revivalism" (Butterfield 1985, 2). This motivational system, based on tweaking the potential distributor's dreams and desires, is a deliberate and highly successful system. As a former Amway distributor, he saw in Amway "a way I could retire in five years with a permanent income that would allow me to make my Dream come true" (Butterfield 1985, 12).

Butterfield captured the material life-style promoted as success by Amway, which is repackaged for the non-Western layperson within ideologies of family and belonging. Suprederm, Avon, and Amway all promoted these models linking desire to social mobility by distributing motivational newsletters and pamphlets,[24] and holding regular rallies and seminars in which people's "personal stories" of success and the attainment of their dreams are narrated. For example, "*Outlook* [Avon's official newsletter] editors employed a variety of rhetorical strategies for making their motivational messages more powerful. . . . Stories from other women who suffered from sickness, the deaths of a spouse, bankruptcy or debt and who had learned to turn hardships into incentives pervaded Avon literature. . . . Many women claimed to have benefited physically, psychologically, and financially from Avon's positive outlook" (Marko 2001, 160).

In Baan Khmer, there were also personal stories expressed about the impact of these companies on women's lives. I was told: "Amway is an investment for my child." "Amway is like a religion, because you must love people, and you must help people. But life is not like that. There are people who lie a lot, so you bring them to the meetings too, and show them another side. They are not successful yet, but they will be successful." La, who is sixteen, said of Amway: "They are really like a family. Sometimes my family does not remember my birthday. But once I went to an Amway convention on my birthday, and they celebrated my birthday! There was a cake and everything for all those who were born on that day. I really cried after that, it made me so happy." Her eyes lit up when she talked about her Amway "family." She said, "I love to go to the Amway meetings because at home there are a lot of problems. And when I am at home my family brings their problems back to the house. But when I go to the office, it is full of happiness and helping. It is so different from home, and it makes me so relaxed that I just love going there. Even when I am just so tired, I still have to get up and go, because it brings me a lot of happiness."

Thus the great draw of Amway is in its potential fulfillment of desires, of the desire for happiness, for family, for acknowledgment. It also fulfills the desire for success. According to La, one of Amway's most desirable qualities was that she perceived it as treating everyone—men and women, young and old—as equals: "No one was higher than anyone else. All the rich, successful Amway sellers came and shook hands with me, and posed for pictures with me, and that made me feel really good. It is so different from the life here in the village." This perception of Amway as an egalitarian organization, though, is misleading, for in actuality this business (as well as Avon and Suprederm) has thrived on developing a pyramid system of profit making and sponsorship. In this scheme, then, no one is truly equal. Additionally, while some Northern Thai girls experience a sense of success selling Amway, Avon, and Suprederm, those who profit most from these girls' labors are the companies headquartered in Michigan, California, and Bangkok. However, because cosmetics companies afforded young women the opportunity to rise above their traditional positions (as children and females) in the local social hierarchy through their sales success, there is a very real feeling among the girls that being involved in these international beauty companies released them from their status as girls, incorporating them (through their successful sales) into the realm of adult womanhood. In these new social positions they perceived themselves as being treated on an equal basis with those of much higher local social status, if not on par with those who held material power in the larger corporate hierarchy, especially beyond the local level.

Conclusion

In Baan Khmer, the girls struggled for a cosmopolitan life-style, though they were not technically rich or actually occupying an urban space. By aligning themselves with a multinational enterprise, complete with geographic mobility and social networks outside of the village circle, these girls were reframing how they perceived notions of success and desire. What they saw available to them extended well beyond the borders of the market square; rather, these girls placed themselves socially (if not physically or economically) within a life where global models of female success (the good life) were not at odds with local models of "the good girl." This *thansamay*, or modern, life-style, which combines elements of global, modern, and urban experiences, has come to signify "success" for these Thai girls. By associating themselves with a global market (the beauty industry), with transnational businesses (such as Amway and Avon), and with a cash flow that extended outside of national borders, these girls were able to align themselves socially and financially with the larger, urban, "cosmopolitan" world. They were thus able to disassociate themselves from a possible future centered on the open-air market in the village center; their center of desire, of community and support, was now Bangkok, California, or Michigan.

This does not mean that the village in turn responded favorably to such redefinitions of female identity; it also does not imply that the girls were able eventually to attain a cosmopolitan life-style in an actual cosmopolitan space by translating their sales successes at home to economic success in the big city. What this essay demonstrates is how the girls' desires and perceptions of their future possibilities were altered by global flows into the local arena; how girls perceived themselves, their skills, and their social connections; and how their connection to money and beauty have all been redefined by the presence of the international cosmetics industry. This redefinition is in part a way by which girls disassociated themselves from their "old" identities (as rural, Northern Thai, young, poor children) and connected themselves to their desired lives (as urban, cosmopolitan, middle-class women) by projecting a persona—combined with the cash flow they had become part of, and mobility they had established—that allowed the girls socially to become part of an international economy.

Chapter 6
Homies Unidos: International Barrio Warriors Waging Peace on Two Fronts

GusTavo Adolfo Guerra Vásquez

The violence, the signals and the "look" come straight from Los Angeles. They are all unique to Salvadoran gangs that, for more than a decade, have run loose on Southern California streets. . . . The country is now fighting a war with gangs . . . the deported gang members have touched off a wave of violence in El Salvador that has now surpassed the murder rate during their civil war. . . . [A halfway house filled with men trying to get out of the gangs] is a place where they come to heal wounds before heading back into battle—while every day, more planes arrive from Los Angeles carrying more troops that again will fill Salvadoran streets with violence. (CBS 2002)

In El Salvador, gangs resembling L.A. gangs, in their use of names, clothing, and other cultural symbols, began to make front-page news during the mid-1990s. The country's two main newspapers published sensationalistic accounts filled with rumor and speculation that did not help the situation on the street and only fed the violence between rival gangs. This type of reporting also fostered the public perception that "U.S. deportees and marginal youth are the principal perpetrators of violent crime" (DeCesare, 1998, 24). Sensationalistic reports regarding gang-involved youth in El Salvador are not only recorded in written form but also emerge in visual popular culture. Ruz, a cartoonist for one of the most popular Salvadoran newspapers, published cartoons depicting gangs, including one entitled "Las Maras: Made in U.S.A.," placing the blame for gangs outside the borders of El Salvador (Ruiz 1995, 53).

The deportation of Southern California youth and the transplanting of U.S. gang cultures to El Salvador intensified after 1996, when the U.S. Immigration and Naturalization Service changed the "Permanent Resident" status of immigrants it deemed "undesirable" because they had been convicted of criminal activity and began deporting them. Many deportees were gang-involved youth who had lived most of their lives in the United States. While sweeping "incorrigible" youth outside the borders of the United States made sense to officials who did not want to deal with these youth's struggles, the reality is that Salvadoran society was not ready to accept them either, given that country's own economic and social crises. The dilemma of youth in El Salvador joining L.A.-type gangs is not something to be taken lightly considering that, as Donna DeCesare writes, "nearly half the country's population is under 18 and three quarters of Salvadoran children live in poverty. . . . How . . . roughly 249,000 youths occupy their time is unknown. But youth gang membership is growing at an alarming pace and some studies suggest that as many as 30,000 youths may belong to street gangs nationwide" (1998, 24–25).

This essay sheds light on the complex relationships involving immigrant youth and gangs in El Salvador and Los Angeles. Homies Unidos, a youth organization composed of gang members, works in response to the needs of at-risk youth in El Salvador and the Pico-Union and Koreatown neighborhoods of Los Angeles using cultural production as well as promoting a "calm" mode of behavior in order to create a "violence-[free] and discrimination-free society" (Homies Unidos 2002). The organization uses the term "calm" to describe members who are not engaging in violent or criminal activity. This concept of a "calm" lifestyle is an important alternative to the traditional arguments recommending that youth simply avoid gangs, which is often unrealistic considering the contexts in which many youth of color live. Rather than preach avoidance, Homies Unidos provides a network for political activities that are critical of injustices as well as training in concrete skills through design and research projects initiated by youth.

The construction of gang-involved youth as "superpredators" renders immigrant gang-involved youth "deportable," literally finalizing their ejection from their societies. Therefore, exploring how national ideologies get grafted onto individual youth in a complex global politics of gang involvement, within and across national borders, is a focus of this essay. Reworking standard academic discussions of gang-involved youth in the United States by introducing a global perspective and highlighting the work of Homies Unidos, this essay problematizes the standard view of gangs as territorial, since both the transnational nature of many of these gangs and the youth involvement in them are not just geographical but ideological. Thus, this essay questions the use of national ideology, by both the United States and El Salvador, as an exclusionary tactic against youth deemed undesirable in order to project the blame for gang involvement outside of their respective borders. Furthermore, since neither the United States nor El Salvador wants to accept the responsibility for youth violence and drug abuse, neither acknowledges that these youth are products of a cycle of violence that has fed upon itself due to U.S. foreign and domestic policy, allowing for a compounding of violence that the deportation of gang-involved youth is also promoting.

Examples of U.S. and Salvadoran mainstream cultures' stereotypes of Salvadoran youth are important because they exemplify the scope of the "superpredator" mythology. I came across these examples while casually attending movies, such as *Training Day,* which deals with police corruption in Los Angeles in heavily immigrant neighborhoods, or reading a recompilation of newspaper comics, which highlights the ease with which the average person in the United States and El Salvador can come away with criminalized impressions of Salvadoran youth. Even within Salvadoran expatriate communities and the literatures they produce, there is disdain toward young gang members (García 1999, 39–42). Lack of understanding by many people raised in El Salvador with regard to youth socialized and racialized in the United States contributes to these negative perceptions.

An example of popular culture that provides a strong contrast to mainstream portrayals of Salvadoran youth is a rap song by Marvin Novoa Escobar, one of the founding members of Homies Unidos who was killed in El Salvador on New Year's Eve 2001, despite having "calmed" down. The rap song, "Fruits of War," written after Novoa Escobar's deportation, deals with issues that Salvadoran youth face as a result of the war and their mass exodus to the United States, as well as the deportations and human rights abuses of young Salvadoran men and women at the hands of Salvadoran society. "Fruits of War" begins with a positive assertion about Novoa Escobar's work as a rapper and the people of his native El Salvador: "With greetings to my country, my native people/ I'll drop this alternative groove/ I'm a Guanaco at heart/ a Pipil from El Salvador/ Backing up my people/ better than an ambassador" (Novoa Escobar 2001). In the first line, Escobar shows an interest in connecting with his Salvadoran English-speaking audience in a polite way, the way Salvadorans teach their children to greet other people. The use of the words "Guanaco" and "Pipil" make reference to Salvadoran identity using the common slang term for Salvadoran and the name of the pre-Columbian indigenous people who inhabited El Salvador, providing cultural affirmation to Salvadoran youth while showing those who consider him and other gang-involved youth un-Salvadoran that he is very much part of the diverse Salvadoran experiences. These lyrics exemplify Homies Unidos's goal of providing not just an "alternative" music to the Salvadoran people but also an "alternative" to gang-involved youth as well as an "alternative" history to the one that has been presented to Salvadorans. It is this type of double duty that Homies Unidos engages in: educating youth about cultural and political alternatives as well as educating the general population about youth at risk.

I first found out about Homies Unidos in 1998 at a conference on Salvadoran identity. I had met some of the members before through youth violence intervention work, but the organization had not yet been formed. During the conference there was a presentation of *Homeland,* an independent film that deals with the subject of deported youth, and members of Homies Unidos addressed the audience afterward. I introduced myself and later asked Alex Sánchez, one of the founders of the L.A. chapter, to come and speak to some of the youth I worked with in the Pico-Union/ Koreatown neighborhoods of Los Angeles. Since then, I keep up to date on Homies Unidos's activities in Los Angeles whenever possible, and on a trip to Central America in 1999 I had the opportunity to visit members of El Salvador's Homies Unidos. I have kept in touch over e-mail and through visits with William Huezo, their president. The members of both chapters defy the stereotypes that people hold of gang-involved youth, both in El Salvador and the United States. They have been very kind and extremely gracious and polite.

While the majority of Salvadoran youth are not gang members, gangs within Salvadoran communities in the United States and in El Salvador have been a reality for quite some time (López and Connell 1996). Also because of their high profile and dangerous behavior, often sensationalized in the media, youth involved in gangs are infamous in immigrant communities in the United States. It is important to note that there were gangs in El Salvador before the Civil War in the 1980s (Cruz and Peña 1998; Homies Unidos 2002). The Civil War altered Salvadoran migration patterns to the United States as thousands of Salvadorans left their country because of the violent situation in their homeland, which is what Novoa Escobar raps about in "Fruits of War:" "Let's start this at the roots/ A history of war that ruined our country/ Twelve years of suffering/ Innocent souls lost their lives/ Innocent people fought without thinking/ Many families had to separate/ In search of a better means of survival/ Obliged to leave their country/ For another, with a different culture/ Completely foreign for our people . . ." (Novoa Escobar 2001).

Marvin Novoa Escobar identifies the "war that ruined" El Salvador as "the roots" of the tree that bore the "fruit of war." Like an oral historian, he tells people about the suffering and fighting that led to the mass exodus of Salvadorans toward the United States and other parts of the world. Novoa Escobar's rap describes how families were separated in order to survive and how those who left their country ended up in the U.S.'s "different" and "foreign" culture. The reference to the difference in cultures has much to do with issues of adaptation and estrangement that many Salvadoran families experience in the United States. However, the use of words like "different" and "foreign" also invoke the anti-immigrant sentiment that peaked in the mid-1990s during Pete Wilson's term as governor of California.

With propositions 187, 227 and 21, there has been a targeting of Latino and Latina immigrant gang-involved youth in order to remove them from the country, even if they are "permanent residents" raised and socialized in the United States. This has been done through the cooperation of local and state law enforcement agencies with federal agencies such as the Immigration and Naturalization Service. Homies Unidos's president in El Salvador, William Huezo, has a story about his own deportation that is typical of this phenomenon: "It was like out of the blue. They took my papers away. Shot me down here to El Salvador . . . they sent me here, to this prison. . . . I thought I was a permanent resident, but not so permanent, you know?" (Banks 2002).

The media has been reviving "the gang myth" in the United States using inaccurate portrayals of youth, reconstructing the "moral panic" about L.A. gangs that flared up in the 1980s (Jankowski 1991, 284). However, this time it was portrayed as "exported" to El Salvador through young deportees. A CBS news report refers to deportees as "L.A.'s dirty export," "troops" in a war between gangs, "running loose" and filling the streets of El Salvador with violence (CBS 2002). This example concurs with the image of the "superpredator" that California and other states have constructed over the past two decades in order to remove youth from society (*Wiretap Magazine* 2002). Draconian anti-youth measures such as California's Proposition 21, which has contributed to the increasing incarceration of minors as adults, are a result of the political climate in which human beings are dehumanized. Furthermore, the "violence," "signals," and "'look'" that the CBS news story claims are unique to Salvadoran gangs are actually part of a youth culture influenced by hip-hop culture with particular affinities to Chicano, African American, and Asian American youth cultures. With language such as "run loose," the story compares young people to vermin. Later in the story, a Salvadoran police chief makes reference to guerrillas and L.A. gang members as the "deadly combination" of groups that has supposedly set off this wave of violence. It is easier to scapegoat deportees and former guerrilla fighters than to expose the roots of the economic and social problems that ravage El Salvador. It is the material and political conditions that led to civil war in El Salvador and to the gang wars in Los Angeles that are responsible for the participation of Salvadoran youth in street gangs both in El Salvador and in Los Angeles. Furthermore, Manuel Castells argues that negative portrayals fail to consider that "gangs, or their functional element are not, by any means, an American graffiti. The *pandillas* in most Latin American cities are a key element of sociability in poor neighborhoods, and so they are in Jakarta, in Bankok, in Manila, in Mantes-la-jolie (Paris), or in Meseta de Orcasitas (Madrid)," proving that the issue of youth membership in gangs has as much to do with class as with national culture (Castells 1997, 64).

Those who claim that U.S. deportees are solely responsible for the current wave of violence ignore the structural problems in Salvadoran society that prevent deported youth from integrating themselves into a country that has been negatively affected by twelve years of civil war. The conditions for young people in El Salvador are so difficult that they alienate youth who act like their Los Angeles counterparts despite having never left El Salvador. In fact, the majority of gang members in El Salvador have never been to the United States, dispelling the myth that the origin of the gang phenomenon is in Los Angeles (Cruz 1998, 51). However, it is not as if influence from L.A. gangs doesn't exist in El Salvador. Although gangs already existed in pre–Civil War El Salvador, U.S. immigration policies and their effects on migration patterns have also contributed to this new phase in Salvadoran gangs (Cruz 1998, 20; Homies Unidos 2002).

Salvadorans in L.A. Gangs

> *Lacking options, they adapted to the system/ Working like mules, no say in the matter/ Ignoring each other and communication/ Leaving their kids without upbringing/ At the start, this was the seed/ Which bore fruit when these kids joined gangs.*
>
> —Novoa Escobar 2001

It is important to understand the gang phenomenon within the context of Salvadoran migration to the United States and to Los Angeles in particular so that we can begin to dispel the image of the ungrateful immigrant teenager who won't take advantage of what "this country has to offer" him or her. What were the lives of Salvadoran immigrant youth like in Los Angeles? Factors that explain why a significant number of youth in Los Angeles join gangs include living in a war zone transplanted from El Salvador, poverty and disadvantage in the receiving communities, and lack of employment opportunities when they reach working age in the United States. As Robin Kelley argues, during the 1990s, "taking advantage of the gaping hole left by the disappearance of a viable local economy, some gangs have become businesses, distributors of illegal and *legal* goods and services and generally define their markets as territory" (Kelley 1997b, 49). Since inner-city neighborhoods in Los Angeles did not have many employment opportunities for young immigrants coming of age, many young Salvadorans joined gangs (Moore 1991, 6), contributing to a "cholo" gang subculture among second-generation immigrant youth because of difficulties they face owing to racism, lack of jobs, and underclass involvement.

The "second-generation problems" that James Vigil describes can also be extended to the 1.5—"knee-high"—generation who arrive in the United States when they're children, since, for the most part, the only home they know and have been socialized in is the United States (Vigil 1988, 32; Pérez Firmat 1994, 4). Deportees are, in many cases, not familiar with any place outside of their neighborhoods in U.S. cities, yet are legally vulnerable because of their immigrant status, a serious reality for many immigrant youth. As Novoa Escobar raps, "We tell you this in all seriousness/ It's senseless but this is reality/ The reality we live is the fruit of a war/ For more than a decade, El Salvador lived/ Hard moments when everything was terrorizing" (Novoa Escobar 2001).

These youth's experiences affected the way gangs function in Los Angeles, combining the violence that they were affected by during the Salvadoran Civil War with that of L.A.'s streets. Added to the psychological stress of having lived through a violent war are all the stresses that come with being in a new country, undergoing the "migration process" of "becoming" Angelenos and "disbecoming" Salvadorans. Tony Waters posits that there is an upsurge in gang activity if two conditions are met: a large cohort of young immigrant boys (and girls) reaches the at-risk age for gang activity and this group of boys (and girls) is rapidly integrated into the host country (Waters 1999, 7). These conditions were met within the neighborhoods to which Salvadorans migrated (Hamilton and Chinchilla 2001, 63). Furthermore, Waters identifies two variables that contribute to an upsurge in crime when the preceding conditions are met: social status and residence in urban areas. If Waters's thesis is combined with the other conditions that Salvadoran families were experiencing in the United States, such as structural disadvantages and in many cases even post-traumatic stress disorder, it is not surprising that there was gang involvement on the part of some Salvadoran youth.

Three Strikes, You're Out!

"Peace arrived and they signed the Accords/ Leaving the past to our memory/ Soon after followed the deportations/ Massive abuse on the part of Immigration/ Obliging "guanacos" to return to their nation/ Making them victims of exploitation."

—*Novoa Escobar 2001*

A change in Salvadoran gang culture occurred when these youth were deported under the new immigration laws, applied to them retroactively (Banks 2002). The U.S. government and California voters, who perceived their problem to be menacing youth of color, figured that the way to get rid of violence was by incarcerating youth under Proposition 21 and the "three strikes law." The situation is even more complicated for immigrants in California because they are already criminalized by nativist politicians and voters: strike one. Young people who make choices that are disadvantageous to them, such as joining gangs, whether because of psychosocial needs, self-defense, or the "immigrant process," are criminalized even further: strike two. "Gang-affiliated" men and women found guilty of criminal activity receive "enhancements" added to their sentences along with their punishments. If they're immigrants, they get a one-way ticket to the country in which they were born, even if they are permanent legal residents: strike three. William Huezo's story illustrates this point.

I got this document right here. It says my full name, and it has a little box right here that is checked. And it says, "deportable. . . . I've been banished from the U.S. you know? Like they used to do in the medieval days. . . . I went to kindergarten in L.A., elementary school, junior high school, high school. I grew up singing, you know, "My Country 'Tis of Thee" . . . "America the Beautiful" . . . pledging allegiance to the flag. I grew up with all that. You know? . . . An INS agent came to visit me. I didn't think nothing of it. . . . So, he interviewed me to prove I was El Salvadorian, right. They said, "What's the national anthem?" I was like, "Man, I don't know." "What's the biggest railroad?" I was like, "What?" I told him, "Look man, I don't know nothing about El Salvador. I've been in this country for over, you know, 20 years man. I don't know nothing about that country. . . ." I didn't know what the biggest river was. I mean, I grew up in L.A. The longest river there is L.A. River, you know? [laughs] Anyways, the bottom line is that they said they've seen a pattern of criminal history and criminal activity. They felt like, you know there was no chance for me. That I couldn't change. And that's why they deported me. (Richman 2002)

William's story highlights many of the issues surrounding the immigration policy of shipping people to an unknown homeland, in some cases to their deaths. As he so eloquently states, he knew far more about life in the United States than in El Salvador, having been socialized in Los Angeles. Once in El Salvador, deported youth like William end up looking for some structure into which they can incorporate themselves (Herbst 2002). Feeling the disdain of a major portion of Salvadoran society, many of these youth find their way into local gangs. The hybrid culture that they take with them from Los Angeles has led to the transformation of gang culture in El Salvador.

L.A. Gang-Involved Youth's Impact on El Salvador

These kids returned to their country with a new style/ People just expected them to reform/ The police abused them and as always searched/ For the quickest way to get them behind bars/ Society tends to fear and doubt/ Not even trying to analyze the situation/ Their approach is extremist/ Living in heartfelt ignorance.

—*Novoa Escobar 2001*

The media blames deportees for the gang wars in El Salvador. While the small number of these deportees in proportion to the total number of gang members does help to dispel the myth of the deported "super-predator," running "loose" on the streets of El Salvador, these expelled youth are looked up to by other youth in El Salvador with recognition and respect. Youth who have been to the United States have an easier time joining a gang and asking for special favors of other gang-involved youth (Cruz and Peña 1998, 52). Considering that the majority of gang members in a Universidad Centroamericana survey stated that they have never been to the United States (83.7 percent) (Cruz and Peña 1998, 52), the transmission of organizational models and cultural traits of L.A. gangs to Salvadoran gangs seems to take on a larger significance than the number of deportees. A multi-clique network gang structure is one of the features that immigrants modified during their gang involvement in Southern California and have introduced to gang-involved youth in El Salvador, since certain L.A. gangs are organized around neighbor-hoods that belong to a bigger network claiming one larger gang.

The already hybrid culture of L.A. gangs blends with Salvadoran culture in order to create yet another mixture of gang culture (Cruz and Peña 1998, 54). A few of the cultural traits of deportees that have been mixed in with gang culture in El Salvador are related to language, signs, and dress. One of those traits is the use of Spanglish, the hybrid mixture of Spanish and English, "caliche" (Central American slang), and "caló" (Chicano slang). Their use of "caló" and other cultural traits are also clear allusions to an evolving U.S. gang culture that they have adopted, in part, as well as hair styles, baggy pants, hand signs, and tattoos. The distinct stylistic elements of this new hybrid gang culture make them the target of Salvadoran society's scorn and violence (Cruz and Peña 1998, 51).

Salvadoran Society's Reception of Deported Youth

Novoa Escobar's rap lyrics allude to the fact that higher levels of crime in El Salvador are not solely because of deportees, and even the director of El Salvador's National Civilian Police admits that deportees are only one factor in the violent crime wave that swept the country after the peace accords were signed (DeCesare 1998). Marvin refers to another factor when he raps about disgruntled former soldiers, "Many of those who'd been involved in combat/ are struggling on the streets now/ Just to obtain their daily bread/ Many of them survive on just cheese and tortillas/ The war killed them and abandoned them" (Novoa Escobar 2001). However, these people don't catch the attention of the media as much as tattooed youth wearing baggy clothes, which is why Marvin provides people with the "alternative" story, reminding his listeners that "we know it's true/ Let's not lie to ourselves" (Novoa Escobar 2001).

Many people point out that El Salvador now has a higher murder rate than it did during the twelve-year civil war. Even though deportees are only a minority within gang activities in El Salvador, they have become the targets of "the pervasive scorn Salvadorans retain towards the tattooed generation." Young people with tattoos often don't get hired and when they do they often get fired by employers (Banks 2002). Tattooed youth are also denied health care, as was the case with Marvin Novoa Escobar. According to Mario Ernesto Maldonado, one misconception that health providers have about tattooed youth is that they may be HIV positive, which is another reason they are not treated when they are assaulted by active gang members or death squads (personal communication, 2003). Ringo, a charismatic Homies Unidos leader, lost his life because he was denied health care after being assaulted by unknown assailants (Banks 2002).

Fear for their lives afflicted many Salvadoran gang-involved youth when they found out they were not only being denied health care but were also being targeted by right-wing paramilitary death squads such as the Sombra Negra (Black Shadow), who kill tattooed youth as a method of "social cleansing" (Banks 2002). "Chino," a young deportee, was one of over thirty youth who became victims of death squad murders in less than two months. "At the time, the Roman Catholic Church's Legal Aid Office, Tutela Legal, charged that the vigilante groups included active members of the newly formed civilian police force" (DeCesare 1998, 223). The saddest aspect of these killings is that because of the Salvadoran media's construction of gang members as incorrigible vermin, coupled with the general population's frustration with social conditions, a radio program and several local newspapers have reported that polls show overwhelming support and even invitations for death squads such as the Black Shadow to come and "clean up" their neighborhoods (DeCesare 1998, 223).

It's a tough situation to be hunted down in an unknown homeland. Furthermore, if these youth don't get killed by paramilitary groups like those funded by the U.S. government during the 1980s, they face a difficult life with limited employment opportunities and scarce resources because Salvadoran society treats them with disdain. If deportees don't have any family, or they don't feel comfortable with their relatives in El Salvador, they revert to the one family structure they know, the gangs.

Creation of Homies Unidos

And they do as they're told/ They have no options, it's the life they're stuck with/ It's something we all have to work to change.
—*Novoa Escobar 2001*

Within this climate of disinformation about youth in gangs and discrimination against deportees, Homies Unidos was born. Magdaleno Rose-Ávila, a Chicano activist who was living in El Salvador when many of these dynamics became evident, decided to solicit help from gang-involved youth with a survey on gang members in the greater San Salvador area (Banks 2002). The survey of over 1000 gang members, coordinated by the Universidad Centroamericana in San Salvador, yet designed and administered by gang members, found that most deported gang members face alienation and lack of educational and job opportunities while most also want a better life for themselves along with respect, friendship, an identity, and a stable family atmosphere. They also identified their biggest problems as getting off drugs, finding jobs, and having a stable family (DeCesare 1998, 225).

The survey showed that most gang-involved youth in El Salvador joined gangs because they liked "hanging out." The majority of these underage youth answered that they were unemployed but wanted jobs and that of all things associated with gangs, they disliked fights, drugs, the high possibility of dying, being harassed by the police, and incarceration. Among the young women, there was a high rate of teenage pregnancy and also a high rate of abortion among minors. The majority wanted to "calm down." However, they wished to retain the friendship, unity, and tattoos that they had gotten while in a gang. They also wanted understanding from other members of society and an end to discrimination (Cruz and Peña 1998, 114).

After conducting the survey and realizing that they had common problems, some of these youth decided to form an organization, called Homeboys Unidos, to address these needs. Female members of the group objected to the word "Homeboys" because of its male specificity and a compromise was reached with "Homies Unidos," keeping in mind the participation of women both in gangs and in the organization. Once the founders were trained in nonviolence and peaceful conflict resolution, "Homies Unidos" was founded on November 2, 1996 in San Salvador, when twenty-two members from two of the largest rival gangs joined together on a shared front: "TO DIMINISH VIOLENCE" (Banks 2002). The organization strives "to provide youth and communities with positive and productive opportunities that will permit the reduction and prevention of violence and allow personal growth." Its vision statement declares: "Homies Unidos recognizes the capacity for positive change in all youth" (Homies Unidos 2001a). This type of language is not what you would expect from presumably "incorrigible" youth.

Sadly, Homies Unidos members weren't taken seriously by other nongovernmental organizations and were harassed by the Salvadoran police. As Rose-Ávila explains, three of the most important structures within El Salvador that youth come in contact with—the nongovernmental organizations, government agencies such as the police, and the gangs—were all very skeptical of Homies Unidos's goals (Herbst 2002). Donna DeCesare echoes Rose-Ávila's comments: "Homies Unidos is unique among the handful of nongovernmental organizations (NGOs). . . . It is also the only organization directed by youths who themselves are involved in gangs. . . . It is clear that the group's eclectic range of activities . . . have enhanced the self-esteem of individual members" (DeCesare 1998, 228). The camaraderie these youth showed toward others was reminiscent of the positive aspects of gang culture. They developed a structure to offer the support provided by gangs, substituting their violent behavior with a nonviolent model. Homies Unidos's programs in El Salvador include deportee assistance, education, job training, and community outreach (Homies Unidos 2002). Health care, leadership development, and jobs are economic and educational alternatives through which Homies Unidos provides support to Salvadoran youth. When hurricanes and earthquakes have hit El Salvador, the organization has helped with emergency relief efforts.

In 1998, youth in Los Angeles started a chapter of Homies Unidos in the Pico-Union/ Koreatown neighborhoods, dealing with issues such as police abuse by the L.A.P.D's Rampart Division. Alex Sánchez, one of the deportees who returned to the United States to reunite with his young son, founded the Los Angeles chapter of the organization. Both chapters focus on diminishing the aspects of gang culture that are most detrimental to themselves and society: violence and drugs. And while they do this, the organization expects its members to remain "calm." According to Magdaleno Rose-Ávila, "The issue is their conduct. As they come under the leadership of Homies Unidos they change into the new and calm life-style. Those who violate the discipline of this new direction lose their good standing until they prove themselves calm" (Herbst 2002).

Aware that gang members are targets of discrimination, both chapters work with cultural products that attract and educate new membership, affirming youth cultures. The strategies for reaching youth and educating the majority of the population about challenges that youth face are in line with their vision statement. The goal of living in a violence-free society may be directed at youth who are involved in gangs, but since there is also a lot of violence directed at youth by the rest of society, in its crudest form represented by death squads and abusive police forces such as L.A.P.D.'s Rampart Division, Homies Unidos seeks to fulfill the second part of its vision: a discrimination-free society. Such a vision seeks to transform neighborhoods in El Salvador and Los Angeles. It is through the education of both youth and society in general that much of the groups' cultural production supports the mission of the organization.

Cultural Productions of Homies Unidos

"That's why we've come here to rap to you."
—*Novoa Escobar 2001*

Rap is only one form of cultural production that Homies Unidos turns young people on to as part of their organizing and outreach efforts. Addressing the need for jobs, Homies Unidos in El Salvador began creating highly stylized buttons to sell to individuals and companies in order to spread their message of peace and unity. "Nobody thought we could do something even as basic as the button's design, and we designed them, we're selling them," says Héctor Pineda, one of the organization's founders. The chapter in El Salvador has plans to produce more cultural products relevant to the new culture of Salvadoran youth in order to produce job opportunities for themselves and their members. With the skills they learned during the youth survey, Homies Unidos organizers plan to conduct more surveys of youth regarding which clothing is popular and to begin producing it (Keefe 2002).

The L.A. chapter of Homies Unidos also provides youth with avenues for cultural expression and sponsors poetry, art, and theater workshops. A product designed by Homies Unidos in Los Angeles that incorporates much of the group's cultural affirmation work is a wall calendar that contains artwork, photographs, and literary pieces that reflect both the realities of gang life in Los Angeles and El Salvador as well as the message of peace and justice. March is recognized as women's month in the calendar, and November, which contains the Days of the Dead from Mesoamerican traditions, features writing and illustrations related and dedicated to those who have died. The 2002 calendar contains photographs, artwork, and poems by members of the group, such as "Thoughts of Prisoner" by Amilcar a.k.a. "Boobee," "Rest in Peace Joker" by Sylvester Tellez, and the lyrics to a rap piece by Mr. Azteca describing Homies Unidos and the transnational struggles of gang-involved youth.

One of the members who wrote a poem about the difficulty of living the "calm" life is Carmen. Her "prayer" represents the struggle that so many of these youth personally engage in on a daily basis while trying to improve their lives:

ORACIÓN

Heavenly father please/ Hear me tonight./ I need so much guidance/ To live my life right/ Sometimes the pressure/ Is so hard to bear./ I often wonder if/ Anyone cares./ How can I wake up/ And face this new day,/ Knowing I have to live/ My life this crazy way/ Heavenly father, forgive/ All my sins./ I want to change,/ But where do I begin?/ Give me the strength to resist/ The wild life I desire,/ Please God bless my/ Family whose eyes silently/ Plead for me not to go out/ As they all watch me leave./ and god bless my mother/ Who cries every night, worrying/ I'll be killed in yet another gang night./ Heavenly father please/ Answer my prayers,/ Please let me know/ That you're listening up there/ When will it end?/ What's it all for?/ To prove to my homies/ Yea I'm down . . . I'm hardcore/ Sometimes I even wonder/ How I will die./ By a bullet wound/ Or a knife in my side/ Heavenly father, Please/ Hear me tonight,/ Give me the courage and/ Strength to live my life right . . . Help give my heart peace/ So I won't have to fight. (Homies Unidos 2001b)

On another page of the calendar, the lyrics of "Fruits of War" by Marvin Novoa Escobar, which is interspersed throughout this essay, describe the plight of the young generation, making the connection between the war and gangs more explicit as well as commenting on the discrimination against youth in El Salvador, both deported and homegrown:

These people feel like outsiders in their society/ It's all a consequence, the fruit of war/ The fruit of war/ I can't imagine how they felt/ In those difficult moments our people endured/ Many people felt humiliated/ And to save themselves many had to seek/ (political) asylum/ I'm not with the left or the right/ I'm just telling you the truth, about what war cultivates/ It's something that people now lament/ They never thought of all the consequences/ War would bring/ All the suffering we see today/ The evil that day to day we see growing/ Human rights have been disrespected/ In fact, as I see it, they're still being violated. (Novoa Escobar 2001)

Novoa Escobar's rap lyrics touch on many of the complex political and historical dynamics that this essay deals with: the humiliation of having to seek political asylum in the same country that has funded the army and death squads that killed thousands of innocent Salvadorans and are nowadays killing those fleeing from the difficulty of living as immigrant youth in the United States with parents who have to work so hard that they don't have time for them. "His lyrics reveal how violent spirits have blossomed from the seeds of war, exile, and neglect, offering a raw account of contemporary Salvadoran history," writes Gabrielle Banks (2002). However, instead of producing lyrics in the genre of "gangsta" rap, "conscious" rappers such as Marvin Novoa Escobar offer a realistic message that young people can relate to while conveying hope. William Hueso, president of the San Salvador chapter of Homies Unidos, was introduced to the group by hearing the Homies Unidos rappers and now, he says, "If it wasn't for Homies Unidos, I'd be lost . . . they're doing positive stuff, and that's what I'm about now, doing positive stuff (Huezo 2002). William's involvement with Homies Unidos started with a chance meeting at a concert in San Salvador and was inspired by the messages that their rappers project through their microphones. The results of Homies Unidos's struggles for nonviolence are small in comparison to the bigger picture, yet significant when we look at individual people's lives. Once a prison inmate that the U.S. government deemed incorrigible, and therefore deportable, William is now the president of Homies Unidos in El Salvador, encouraging change in the "Fruits of war" while also attempting to change the perception that Salvadoran and U.S. societies have of gang-involved youth.

Conclusion: Circuits of Violence and Rays of Hope

> *It's on us to change the world/ I'm not the first or even the second to say so/ We can put a stop to what's bad on Earth/ And bring an end to the fruit of war/ Bring an end to the fruit of war.*
>
> —*Novoa Escobar 2001*

This essay reveals how gangs have changed owing to (im)migration and deportation, dispelling, along the way, misconceptions regarding gang-involved youth. The impact of the deportees wasn't felt in El Salvador so much because of their numbers as because of their cultural practices. The fact that Salvadoran youth recreated deported youth's cultural models while incorporating them into their own life-style says much about the marginalization of youth in El Salvador. For El Salvador the war has come full circle in the form of its migration patterns, creating this "war fruit," which is neither fully Salvadoran nor from the United States but a hybrid layering and blending of the experiences these youth encountered: in El Salvador before they left as young children, in Los Angeles as they were coming of age, and again back in El Salvador where many of them are forced to live, subjected to discrimination because of the way they look. Other youth may not have experienced this circular migration, but the conditions for their participation in the type of violent behavior that gangs engage in exist nonetheless. This circuit of violence may go on as Salvadoran youth continually migrate to Southern California and other points in the Salvadoran diaspora, because the social conditions and lack of basic necessities that exist in El Salvador will force many families to continue to come to the United States, adding yet another cycle to the journey of migrant youth. Hopefully it will not add another layer of violence. But the physical migration may not be necessary to create the conditions for this type of cultural circulation, as MTV and other forms of popular culture that get exported from the United States to Central America contribute to this youth culture.

Homies Unidos is dealing with the plight of many of these immigrant and repatriated youth through a commitment to the positive aspects of youth cultures and a pledge to diminish violence and drugs by living a "calm" life-style. The organization faces the possibility of a backlash from those whose investment in the negative aspects of gang life-style is too strong. Nonetheless, these young men and women have proven the U.S. government wrong about gang-involved youth by changing their lives and making pledges to "calm down" and wage peace. They are an example to other youth facing similar issues owing to globalization. Their determination and energy along with their optimism have shown themselves to be contagious. Can we envision a world that is violence- and discrimination-free and "end the fruit of war?" To quote the positive assertion that Homies Unidos makes in its literature, "Sí se puede, simón que sí."[1]

Chapter 7
Globalizing Child Soldiers in Sierra Leone

Susan Shepler

> [T]he civil war [in Sierra Leone] has shifted our attention to youth in a continent that is demographically the youngest in the world and has made us rethink our benign notions of childhood in the face of atrocities committed by child combatants. At the same time, the war has demonstrated how adept the young can be at organizing themselves amid the collapse of age-based moral hierarchies, which have always been taken for granted in these societies.
> —Mariane Ferme, *The Underneath of Things* (2001, 227)

The war that raged in Sierra Leone throughout the 1990s is often understood as a crisis of youth.[1] Although inequitable access to mineral resources and years of corrupt government must play an important part in any explanation, it was legions of youth with no hopes for education or employment who carried the guns and committed the atrocities that have become the hallmark of this particularly brutal civil war. The stories are similar: children are abducted, forced to commit atrocities, caught between the innocence of youth and the horror of war. A typical characterization of the war in Sierra Leone in the Western media is found in the April 10, 1995 issue of the *New Republic*:

The conflict has all the ingredients of a classic African nightmare: an ineffectual military government whose control extends barely beyond the capital, a band of insurgents fighting for no apparent reason, a traumatized populace and an entire generation of adolescents trained to be soldiers.

Sierra Leone's guerrillas are part of a frightening new phenomenon in Africa: ragtag insurgencies spreading chaos in the countryside and propelling their countries into economic ruin. These new fighters lack ideology, goals or strategy. They tend to be driven by boredom, greed and the thrill of violence, and they see little to be gained by making peace. (Hammer 1995, 10)

On the one hand, youth are portrayed as something to be afraid of— "an entire generation of adolescents trained to be soldiers" who are "driven by boredom, greed and the thrill of violence." On the other hand, these child soldiers are portrayed as victims—innocents who need our help and long to be in school, as an excerpt from the same *New Republic* article shows:

Abdullah Kamala, a scrawny 11-year-old wearing a torn t-shirt, shorts and thongs, sat on the porch of a schoolhouse outside Freetown, clutching a box of crayons and an English language textbook. A month ago, Kamala was trudging through the bush of Sierra Leone as an army private, fighting a rebel insurgency with two pistols and a customized AK-47 assault rifle. Now he's in school for the first time in his life, learning to read and write at a rehabilitation center run by Irish priests. "I'm happy now," he told me. . . . [He] talked excitedly about his plans now that he had been demobilized. "I want to educate myself," he said. "I'm learning to read and write. I'm gonna be a doctor or a teacher." (Hammer 1995, 10)

Child soldiers are right in the middle of a contradiction inherent in the modern construction of youth: innocents versus perpetrators. They are simultaneously feared and cast as innocents who need protection. As individuals they are struggling to find a place in post-war Sierra Leone. In the political imaginary they are vitally important to the future of the nation and to the nation's idea of itself.

Meanwhile, the Sierra Leonean child ex-combatants themselves are struggling in quite different terms to create new post-war identities and, in doing so, they draw on a variety of material and discursive resources, both "local" and "global." There are efforts underway by local and international child protection nongovernmental organizations (NGOs) to rehabilitate and reintegrate young ex-combatants. These programs rely heavily on primarily Western models of youth, such as notions of childhood enshrined in the Convention on the Rights of the Child (CRC).[2] Among the articles of the CRC are the right to an education, the right to self-expression, the right to birth registry, the right to family life, the right to freedom of expression, and many others. Child ex-combatants are also greatly affected by popular culture representations of war (see, for example, Richards 1994 and 1996 on the Hollywood Rambo films and their influence in Sierra Leone and Liberia) as well as by local cultural representations of fighters (for example, the "Kamajoh" Civil Defense Force—a locally organized militia—with its bricolage of secret society signifiers). One aim of my work in understanding the experiences of youth in Sierra Leone today is to map the range of social and cultural influences on them, influences perhaps surprising to a Western audience. I will argue that these children are *globalized* in that they are caught up in sweeping international forces, and they are *globalizing* in that they are strategic users of global discourses and cultural artifacts.

A theory and practice of the rehabilitation and reintegration of child soldiers has emerged in the last ten to fifteen years. This expertise is located in the offices of UNICEF and the various international child protection agencies that have specialized in child soldiers. It also exists in local NGOs around the globe where people are caring for former child soldiers. The model of care moves from veteran post-war countries to newly post-war countries. (For example, program models were taken from Mozambique and tried out in Uganda. They were then tried out in Liberia [David 1998]. Each time, they were improved and made more nuanced in response to on-the-ground problems of implementation.) Within these program models, there is implicitly a model of unilinear transformation from dangerous perpetrator/innocent victim to ordinary young member of society. This model is carried out by moving a child through a system of institutions: UN disarmament teams; local NGOs working on interim care, trauma healing and family tracing; village communities; schools; and peer groups. Young people move through and around these contexts, making use of varying ideologies as they navigate these institutional and cultural circuits. As the well-funded Western interventions come up against local models of healing and forgiveness, new ideologies of youth are formed in social practice. In child soldiers' striving to find a place in post-war society, whether back in their natal villages or on the streets of the capital city, they make use of the ideology of youth innocence central to Western models of childhood, as well as local models of forgiveness. The possibilities for reintegration are built at the intersection of the growing international global discourses on childhood and on local traditions and definitions of youth.

This is a multisited ethnography based on eighteen months of fieldwork in Sierra Leone from October 1999 to October 2001.[3] The focus of my study was a group of young people moving through the rehabilitation and reintegration system at different stages of the process.[4] This required following them across social contexts and also required moving around the country to examine regional differences in discourse and practice. In particular, I compared the experiences of youth across a number of different axes: by region, by gender, by fighting faction, and whether youth demobilized via a formal system or were, in the NGO parlance, "spontaneous reintegrators." I took part in everyday life at interim care centers for child ex-combatants and did ethnographic fieldwork in some of the villages and towns where child ex-combatants were reintegrating into society, meeting with young people, their families, communities, teachers, and social workers. I considered questions such as: Who are these child soldiers? How did they get involved? How are they being "reintegrated"? Who gets to be called a child soldier and how? What emerged from my research was a range of strategies based on maneuvering through and around the different cultural possibilities for youth in the post-war era.

I am not imposing this interest in youth in my research simply from the outside, as it were, or arbitrarily. Sierra Leoneans themselves see youth as perhaps the most important site for reconstructing the nation. Since youth were the primary participants in the war, forgiving youth is seen as paramount to moving the nation toward peace. Furthermore, since it is the problems of youth that are understood to have been the causes of the war, addressing those problems—through education, training, jobs—is seen as a means of assuring that war does not happen again. As a Sierra Leonean student living in Ghana put it: "Every Sierra Leonean craves peace. The war was a result of deficiencies in our politics and general attitudes. We must be thinking of ways to avoiding [sic] war in the future. We must start by drawing up policies for our youths and drawing up programs for them to follow. When all our youths are engaged in meaningful activities they won't just follow any so-called freedom fighters who say they are going to liberate them."[5] Clearly, youth are understood by Sierra Leoneans as the future of the nation, and in the case of post-war Sierra Leone I agree with the editors of this volume that youth are a vital site for understanding nation and globalization.

The War in Brief and Patterns of Child Soldier Participation

Sierra Leone lies on the west coast of Africa, bordered by Liberia and Guinea. It is a former British colony, characterized by years of misrule after independence in 1961. The war started around 1991, as the fighting traveled across the border from Liberia where there was also a civil war. Originally, the fighting was fueled by dissatisfaction with the one-party state of the All People's Congress (APC). Fighting moved from the diamond-rich east of the country, through the south, the north, and eventually into the capital of Freetown. Almost every region of the nation was affected, with at least 80 percent of the population displaced at one point or another. Of course, the war is more complex than what I have outlined here, and there are also tribal aspects, subregional dimensions, and other factors to be taken into account in any full accounting of the causes and effects of the war.

With the participation of the UN and British forces, peace is finally returning to Sierra Leone, combatants have disarmed for the most part, and all parts of the country are open for travel for Sierra Leoneans and foreigners alike. Elections took place peacefully in May 2002, but Sierra Leone now faces many difficult tasks. Most of the infrastructure has been destroyed, refugees are returning from neighboring countries and rebuilding their communities, and ex-combatants need to be rehabilitated and reintegrated into society. There are serious ongoing struggles among Sierra Leoneans about the shape of post-war society, and in particular about the provision of benefits for ex-combatants.

In the West, the war is primarily known for three things: diamonds, amputations carried out as terror tactics, and the use of child soldiers. The course of the war has been very confusing for outsiders and insiders alike, characterized by shifting alliances, coups and counter-coups, and different international actors at different stages. Broadly speaking, three main factions fought the war in Sierra Leone: (1) the Revolutionary United Front (RUF) or "the rebels"; (2) the Sierra Leone Army (SLA), which at certain points was allied with the rebels (these renegades were sometimes called "sobels"—soldiers by day, rebels by night); and (3) the locally organized Civil Defense Forces (CDF), which grew out of local secret societies and are known for their use of magic and medicine. The Kamajohs are the best known and first organized of a set of tribally based Civil Defense Forces. The Kamajohs are a Mende group, Mende being the largest tribe in the south of the country. Each tribe has its own Civil Defense Force group now; for example, the Temne—the largest tribe in the north of the country—have the Gbethis, and so on.

So-called child soldiers took part in the fighting on all sides of the conflict, and it is important not to conflate child soldiers' fighting in very different circumstances. The young people involved in the war as soldiers were mostly boys, but some girls have been involved in fighting as well. Both boys and girls performed various tasks, such as cooking, carrying equipment, sexual slavery, spying, decoying, stealing, front-line fighting, and even commanding battle. Some were abducted by fighting forces, some joined the various factions voluntarily. In addition, the prospects for reintegration or acceptance into their home communities vary considerably, depending on which faction they were involved with and what sort of actions they carried out. Some children were forced to commit atrocities—murdering family members, maiming village elders, and so on—and face an almost impossible task in returning to the lives they knew before the war. Some young people are seen as local heroes for fighting to defend their communities and have very different prospects for post-war life among their communities of origin.

The phenomenon of child soldiers is far from new. In Africa, for example, young men have for generations taken up weapons alongside their fathers to defend their villages, just as they worked in the fields or herded cattle in peacetime.[6] In Sierra Leone during the nineteenth century precolonial era, there was a tradition of "war boys," young men who would attach themselves to local warlords for material benefit and training opportunities. The occupation of warrior was clearly institution-alized and many young boys were given special training under appren-ticeship to older, experienced men. Frequently, important men would send their sons to famous warriors for training (Wylie 1977, 60; see also Howard and Skinner 1984). The patterns of recruitment in the recent civil war demonstrate both continuities and shifts in this tradition.

With regard to recruitment, the RUF is mostly known for abducting fighters—both children and adults. However, there are a fair number of fighters who joined voluntarily, especially in the early days of the fight-ing. Not unexpectedly, some children joined the rebels as a means of assuring their own survival.[7] The SLA's use of child soldiers started with the participation of children in some way related to army members. A soldier's family might be involved in helping him with domestic duties, and his children might even be responsible for carrying weapons onto the battlefield. This falls within the Sierra Leonean cultural patterns of young men learning their fathers' (or other male relatives') occupations through what Lave and Wenger (1991) call "legitimate peripheral par-ticipation." As the SLA changed to the AFRC and became RUF allies, they adopted more of an RUF style of recruitment through abduction. In my work with child ex-combatants I saw many boys and girls with the initials "RUF" or "AFRC" carved into their chests as a kind of marking.

The CDF are groups of locally organized militias, emerging from and reconstituting hunting secret societies. They reference their traditional-ness and local-ness in explaining their power. The clothes they wear (at least for journalists) are local *ronkos* made of native cloth that are cov-ered with charms, and they claim to have the power to repel bullets among other supernatural powers. In truth, most of the time CDF mem-bers dress like anyone else, and have become a modern political force. Some of the guns they used during the war were paid for by Sierra Leoneans living in the diaspora in Britain and the United States, orga-nized over e-mail lists. Although they are part of a transnational political movement, they explain their power as part of local and traditional forces.

Recruitment by the CDF depended on existing local networks, for chiefs and other "big men" enlisted their own children. This is an inter-esting point because it contravenes the conventional wisdom that sepa-rated children are more likely to take part in war. On the contrary, these children took part precisely because of their connections. I did see some variation in the pattern of child participation between the RUF and the CDF. With the RUF, child fighters were often on the front lines as a kind

of human shield or first line of defense. With the Kamajohs, child fighters often followed at the rear, their task to kill the wounded enemy with
machetes. The CDF also used children as seers of a sort, claiming that
some of the youngest and most innocent had more magical powers and
could see through the enemies' supernatural protection.

Krijn Peters and Paul Richards (1998) conducted interviews with
young rank-and-file combatants from all three main factions. Their analysis shows that in one crucial respect it hardly matters to which faction a
combatant belongs; "all tend to share membership in an excluded and
educationally-disadvantaged youth underclass" (Richards 1996, 174).
My research confirms their findings, for people all over the country
would say to me that they are all the same boys: they acted the same at
checkpoints, they dressed the same, and they took the same drugs. I also
found several examples of boys who had been through formal demobilization from the RUF or AFRC who upon returning to their home villages immediately joined the local CDF, completely undoing their
pledge not to pick up guns. Essentially, the CDF rank and file was made
up of the same sorts of young men as the RUF and AFRC. This explains,
for example, why Kamajohs eventually started using some of the same
tactics at checkpoints—shaking down drivers for money and goods—
that their rebel adversaries used. Exhausted civilians told me often "soja-
man no good—once he de carry gun, he no good."[8] In practice, faction
often mattered little in the everyday lives of Sierra Leoneans, and indeed
any young man with a gun was a man to be feared. The point here is
that understanding the war as a crisis of youth does not mean just understanding the RUF rebels and their reasons for revolt. We must strive to
understand the situation of a whole generation defined by political and
economic disenfranchisement.

Crisis of Youth in Sierra Leone

In Africa in particular, Jean-Francois Bayart and others have theorized
youth almost as a political class for themselves owing to the geronto-
cratic nature of many African societies (Murphy 1980; O'Brien 1996;
Bayart et al. 1999). Paul Richards says in his conclusions to *Fighting for
the Rain Forest* (1996): "I am more than ever convinced that the RUF
must be understood against a background of region-wide dilemmas concerning social exclusion of the young. . . . [T]he increasing resort to
violence stems from past corrupt patrimonial manipulation of educational and employment opportunities" (174). Drawing on Mahmood
Mamdani's famous formulation of the problem of political belonging in
South Africa (Mamdani 1996), that one of colonialism's effects was to
divide the public into citizens (the elite who have access to political

power) and subjects (the rest of the people who are the target of state power), Fanthorpe (2001) goes even further and argues that this class of youth in Sierra Leone is "neither citizen nor subject" and that "the only moral communities available to these agents may be those of their own desperate making" (385). Is the situation really that bleak, or can we find evidence of something that might be called youth power or agency or even vernacular citizenship?

Historically, youth power in Sierra Leone was defined, actualized, and understood through violence, especially political violence. The long ruling APC party was kept in power in part through legions of young thugs, recruited from the *poht* (a recreational place for youth where the smoking of marijuana is prevalent) and other hangouts. Many Sierra Leonean scholars believe that an understanding of the violent youth cultures of the past is vital to understanding the outbreak of war (Abdullah et al. 1997). These youth groups are still active, since the culture is formed in response to a lack of economic opportunity and the economic opportunities are even fewer in post-war Sierra Leone than they were before. Young men still call themselves *dregman* (hustler), *savisman* (street smart person), *san san boy* (diamond digger), etc.[9] The Sierra Leoneans contributing to the special issue of *Africa Development* (Abdullah 1997) on the civil war agreed that understanding the various youth cultures of Sierra Leone is crucial to understanding the genesis of the war, and they spend a fair amount of time outlining the regional and class differences in the various youth cultures and discussing how the youth of Sierra Leone are required to "negotiate" their identities. In my own fieldwork, I spent a good deal of time in some of these youth hangouts. I met with some young men—the name of their social club was Bone Suffer—organizing for peaceful elections in their community in one of the poorest sections of Freetown. I also spent time with some demobilized CDF boys in Freetown who explained to me that they had been used by the system and that they did not trust their own leaders anymore. The young men in various *pohts*—many of them ex-combatants—explained to me that they are the new generation, the "conscious generation," taking an explicitly political posture.

Sierra Leone youth navigate many cultural forces. In the next section I will describe some of the—perhaps surprising—cultural influences on youth in Sierra Leone today.[10] I think of identity as a kind of bricolage, a process in which people use various resources in making their identities, and in which identities change as people move through contexts. Young ex-combatants are drawing on "traditional" notions of youth even as they rework global popular culture, and are also drawing on ideas about how youth should behave and what rights are due to youth. This means that on the one hand they are constructing an identity that requires deference to elders, and on the other producing a certain kind of power, the power of the powerless.

Sources of Meaning: Traditional and Modern

Paul Richards (1994, 1996) has written about the importance of Rambo films to front-line fighters, for learning fighting tactics and style. He details the traveling video parlors that bring images of the world to the smallest African villages. I would add to that list of circulating cultural products in Sierra Leone: Indian musicals, Hong Kong action films, rap and hip-hop from the United States, Nigerian films with their emphasis on the supernatural, and Celine Dion in concert. Music and clothing styles for Sierra Leonean youth are also international: clothes and hair-styles from the Ivory Coast, reggae from Jamaica and Africa, soukous and other Congolese styles. Some young men have started "planting" or braiding their hair, and even wearing earrings in the style of western hip-hop. These fashions are shocking to most elders as something previously only women would do.

Rap music is an import with powerful influence on youth in Sierra Leone. I regularly saw pictures of the biggest U.S. hip-hop stars, repro-duced on Nigerian-made posters, and for sale in the streets. These post-ers are displayed all over the country, from police offices to farm house doors. There is a large mural painted on a cement wall in Freetown hon-oring the Notorious B.I.G., an American rapper killed in a drive-by shooting. During an informal interview with a child ex-combatant, we were comparing our two countries. He jokingly asked me to take him back to the United States with me so he could *jia-jia* (shake people down for loot) in America since he'd become so expert at it in Sierra Leone. He told me "When I go to America, I want to be a 'G.'" Although gang-ster rap may be on its way out in the United States, it is still powerful in Sierra Leone. Many of the child ex-combatants asked me whether Tupac (Shakur, the famous rapper shot down in his prime) was really dead. I would always say yes, and they would always ask "Are you sure? Did you ever see the body?" These kind of conspiracy theories echoed the kind of theories one would hear about famous rebel commanders like Colo-nel Blood, and Maskita: Are they really dead? Or are they hiding and ready to attack again?[11]

Another modern import is the commercialized culture of war. There is an international style associated with armed resistance that is popular with young men in various youth subcultures around the world: think of the ubiquitous fatigues of someone like Fidel Castro. Certainly many of the young male combatants and even commanders modeled themselves on well-known rebel leaders, in style of dress and speech. Jalloh (2000) complains in the *BBC Focus on Africa* magazine that proper Krio—the Sierra Leone lingua franca—is being overtaken by *savisman* Krio, a motley collection of underworld and military terminologies. In my fieldwork, I would hear school children asking their companions in the schoolyard, "*Us class you deploy?*" (Which class are you deployed in?) To leave someplace is to "pull out." When a student takes another's pencil, for example, he will say, "I've disarmed you." Also circulating are rebel names such as Cobras, Ninjas, and "Operation No Living Thing." They are a part of this culture of war, and they are spreading around Africa wherever wars are fought.

Another important context for the production of youth identities is formal schooling. In addition to being a trajectory for a lucky few to the elusive paying job, school is also a style. Students in Sierra Leone wear uniforms, and the uniform is the site of a great deal of anxiety. Children who perhaps have only one other set of clothing religiously clean and iron their uniforms. Many of the children I worked with took great care of their uniforms, ironing them meticulously with a coal iron every night for school the next morning, sometimes with intricate patterns ironed into them. Post-war economic difficulties mean that many school-going children can't afford a uniform. The importance of uniforms became more clear to me in talking with communities struggling to rebuild after the war: one of the first things they wanted was help rebuilding their destroyed schools. My initial thought was that they would need help with books and supplies, but almost universally people were calling for uniforms. It almost seemed that the appearance of school-going children, walking through the village in uniforms, was more symbolically important than the details of what took place in class.

Around the world, there is growing interest in the rights of children. Starting with the 1989 UN Convention on the Rights of the Child, there has spread a particularly Western notion of childhood as a "special time." The UN is pushing for eighteen years as the cut-off for the end of childhood, but clearly different cultures have different notions of how and when childhood ends and adulthood begins. Within this growth of interest, the problem of child soldiers has also gained recognition. Probably the most influential study on children and war was Graça Machel's 1996 study on the problems of children affected by warfare under the auspices of the UN (Machel 1996). This interest follows on the heels of the rise of other discourses on children in trouble: street kids, "children in especially difficult circumstances," "at-risk youth," and so on.

Often, scholars of youth culture have focused on clothes, music, or dance: in short, style. Others have interpreted culture more broadly and have looked at youth at work, in political activism, and with respect to education. I think we can also understand the often well-funded efforts of UNICEF and other NGOs as having an impact on youth culture. In Sierra Leone, among other places, NGOs produce radio programs, local drama, songs, tee shirts, and so on to promote a global standard of human rights. There is increasing "sensitization" in Sierra Leone to the Convention on the Rights of the Child (CRC), and more and more children and young people are invoking their rights *as children*. In a 2002 study on human rights in Sierra Leone, Abdalla et al. discovered that the Convention on the Rights of the Child was the most familiar of any human rights instrument in Sierra Leone, scoring higher than even the constitution of Sierra Leone for popular recognition (Abdalla et al. 2002).

I believe we need to include international NGO/UN discourse in our understanding of global cultural forces, for NGO culture is important and neglected in the literature on youth. The discourse of the Rights of the Child might be more along the lines of what Appadurai calls ideoscapes: "*Ideoscapes* are . . . concatenations of images, but they are often directly political and frequently have to do with the ideologies of states and the counterideologies of movements explicitly oriented to capturing state power or a piece of it. These ideoscapes are composed of elements of the Enlightenment worldview, which consists of a chain of ideas, terms, and images, including freedom, welfare, rights, sovereignty, representation, and the master term democracy" (1996, 36). Put another way, Sierra Leone is at the forefront of working out a new global governmentality that takes childhood as its object (Foucault 1991).

Frederick Cooper (2001), in his article "What Is the Concept of Globalization Good For? An African Historian's Perspective," makes the argument that Africa has always been global and certainly more so at times in the past than today. Does it make sense to take up globalization as something new? One answer, in the spirit of ethnography, is that it is a vital native category. The people I worked with used it in important, meaning-making ways in their everyday lives and practices, just as distinctions between modern and traditional are still powerful, despite their muddy reality. Malkki (1994) says about the refugees she worked with in Tanzania: "The spatial and social isolation of this refugee camp from what I thought of as 'the world at large' seemed so obvious and defining a fact about these persons' circumstances that it was very surprising to discover the prominent, even intimate place of the 'international community' as a figure in their everyday lives" (45). The global and the local are always in tension in the practices of NGO workers and in communities and I argue this is a *productive* tension. I want to point to how talking about the global or the international is a powerful force in people's lives.

I found that child soldiers have become adept at manipulating their image, for several excellent reasons. They must learn quickly how to tell people what they want to hear and what will bring the best results for them. They have a wide variety of scripts to draw on in their own remaking: rebel fighter, unfortunate victim, school child, and so on. In the course of an afternoon I have seen a young former rebel fighter ask about homework from geography class, threaten a passing vendor with violence, and explain to a visiting NGO worker that he was "traumatized." Naturally, this poses some difficulties for ethnographic methodology. How do I know which self-presentation—or if perhaps all of them—are correct? My solution is to analyze under which circumstances they tell which stories, and thereby get at their strategic uses of various discourses of youth.

What Is Youth Power?

Scholars of the Centre for Contemporary Cultural Studies (CCCS) and others working in their tradition, focusing primarily on Britain, might say youth power is realized through youth reinventing themselves through consumption (for example, Hebdige 1979a). Lave et al. (1992), in discussing the many contributions of the CCCS, praise it for "produc-(ing) work that, at its best, allows discussion of the creation of persons in terms that are variously dialectical, mediated, social-historical, and practice based" (258), but the problem with much of the CCCS work is that it often erred by going too far in its emphasis on style and consumption as markers of youth identity. I think the CCCS approach is partly useful for my research, but its focus on consumption needs to be reworked, as it has been by others since its early work in the 1970s.

The most recent Human Development Report by the United National Development Program listed Sierra Leone as having the lowest quality of life in the world (2003, 334). How can we theorize youth power in Sierra Leone, where money and items to consume are rare? I submit that one can see a kind of power in the shift from carrying a gun to claiming the helplessness of a child. Child ex-combatants can claim helplessness as a political stance, the ironic power of powerlessness. In her work on the Mende, one of the main tribal groups of Sierra Leone, Ferme claims that "Mende representations of childhood are fraught with ambivalence. Given that power is inscribed within an order of concealment, people who are most manifestly devoid of it, like children, might in fact conceal it in unexpected ways" (Ferme 2001, 197). Furthermore, she states, "It is precisely when children are regarded as insignificant—as liminal beings between the world of animality and madness—that they are perceived as potentially most dangerous" (198). What is the difference between the power of holding a gun, and other types of power? Children are moving from a blunt kind of power to a power legitimated through international structures; one that requires them to take on certain (other) identities. Herein lies a story of globalization and its articulations. My work shows how some child soldiers access what I have called "discourses of abdicated responsibility" to allow their communities to forgive them and reintegrate them. I see them as perhaps paradoxically exercising agency through their claims of no agency. This contradiction comes back to the insistence that youth be seen not just as cultural dupes, but as the active creators of their own lives.

Youth in this context are strategic, and skillful, users of these different discourses as they move through different contexts. For example, I have often seen ex-child combatants manipulate their image for the media; they run and put on their rebel sunglasses and bandanna (or Kamajoh traditional garb.) Or they will adopt the posture of the innocent victim in a way they never do in their everyday interactions.

This process happens in relations to institutions such as Interim Care Centres, schools, and village-level governance structures. These young people become the conduit through which a certain amount of aid and rehabilitation help is funneled: money from UNICEF to rebuild schools that register child ex-combatants, micro-credit loans from the Catholic Church for families fostering child ex-combatants, and so forth. Clearly, communities are also invested in refashioning former child soldiers in this way. Struggles over youth are political struggles over *futures*, and especially about national futures. Many discussions in Sierra Leone on the radio and in the public sphere that revolve around what to do with this population of child ex-combatants (and related groups of war-affected youth such as street children and young prostitutes) are cast in a national rhetoric: these children are the future, they will be the leaders tomorrow, support children for a better tomorrow. This rhetoric of nation-building through the image of children takes on an added urgency in the post-war context where the emphasis is not just on making a better future, but on rebuilding a shattered past.

My research ties together ideas about youth, forgiveness, and the nation. National discourses suggest that forgiving youth is vital to post-war reconstruction; I claim that Western notions of youth, circulating globally, make this task much easier. In essence, the notion of youth innocence at the base of Western constructions of youth makes it easier for Sierra Leoneans to forgive children for their crimes during wartime. Although there exists Sierra Leonean judicial thought on the lesser culpability of children, the Western version of the innocence of the child is much stronger in its iconography, and sets clear age guidelines for the categorization of youth (and thus also for the rights denied to children in the West). The Sierra Leonean version of youth innocence is much more pliable and contingent. The idea that anyone under eighteen years is a child and therefore not to be held accountable allows whole groups of young people to be forgiven by their communities in what I claim is a new way. This obviously helps the young people who are struggling to reintegrate; it also helps the communities into which they are moving. Finally, it helps the nation move toward peace.

I am not saying that discourses about children are only about the future. We must acknowledge that these discourses are present and potent, but that they coexist with the social reality of children as social agents. A wide range of scholars of childhood have insisted on taking into account children's agency and theorizing them as complete social actors in themselves (James and Prout 1997; Scheper-Hughes and Sargent 1998; Stephens 1995). The construction of children as innocent makes them silent and apolitical, and about potential rather than actuality. I am also not arguing for the wholesale acceptance of Western definitions of youth in the Sierra Leonean context. Elsewhere I have pointed to some of the ways that too strict an adherence to Western models by NGOs and governments can be problematic. Rather, I am making clear the way Sierra Leonean actors take up globally circulating discourses for their own strategic ends, in sometimes unexpected ways.

Conclusion

The definition of "child soldier" is being made in practice as a result of struggles over material resources (what kind of child protection programs get funded) and discursive resources (who claims the identity of child soldier, and what that implies). These struggles go right to the heart of national ideologies for, as the editors of this volume point out, "Youth personify a given society's deepest anxieties and hopes about its own transformation." In Sierra Leone, "youth" is understood as an important site by various observers, but what is youth and who constitutes youth is contested and affected by unexpected influences. In particular, I have argued that NGO and human rights community discourse about child rights or about child soldiers is used pragmatically and even transformed by youth in practice.

The importance of this work on child soldiers is twofold. First, it is clear that one cannot hope to understand rehabilitation and reintegration programs for child soldiers outside of the social, cultural, and political contexts in which they are embedded and the many conflicting cultural traditions surrounding youth. Second, the Sierra Leone case forces us to understand youth more broadly, since it has a very different meaning and is used differently than in the West.

I believe one of the goals of critical ethnographies of youth should be understanding the tropes of youth and "globalized youth culture" and how they get used politically and globally. An interlocking set of assumptions about war, nation, development, education, and youth function in our common representations of Africa, and I claim that the separation of these topics in standard discourse is an effect of power and needs to be interrogated. In other words, we need to question the "obvious" separations between transnational political realities and the liberal urge to help individual young people through schooling. We need research on how global discourses such as "rights of the child" are worked out locally, in practice. Too much that happens in the aid community is ahistorical, asocial, and is most political precisely when it claims to be apolitical.

Part III
Icons and Retakes

Chapter 8
"Jackie Chan Is Nobody, and So Am I": Juvenile Fan Culture and the Construction of Transnational Male Identity in the Tamil Diaspora

Alexandra Schneider

Upon leaving school at age sixteen, Mani (a pseudonym), the Tamil foster child of my neighbors in Zurich, Switzerland, was asked to write a twenty-five-page graduation paper. The topic of his choice was Jackie Chan, the Hong Kong movie star. I remember well how some years earlier, Mani, who was then still living in a foster home three hours away by car from his foster parents, first began to tell us about Jackie Chan. Previously, his idol had been Jean-Claude van Damme, and we—Mani's foster parents and their friends—were secretly relieved by this switch of allegiance. Compared with the outrageously violent van Damme, Jackie Chan seemed positively less offensive. The weekends after Mani's discovery were spent with communal watching of Jackie Chan films by him and varying combinations of grown-ups from his surroundings. Incidentally, the first Jackie Chan movie I ever watched together with him was *Twin Dragon* (1992). In this film, Chan appears in a double role as a pair of twins separated at birth but reunited with their mother at the end of the movie. One of the twins is a penniless mechanic working in a garage, the other one is an internationally successful concert pianist, a combination spanning the entire set of social status options and class dynamics characteristic of Hong Kong (Gallagher 1997, 32).

At first, my own interest in *Twin Dragon* was mostly that of a film studies scholar. I was intrigued by how the film's style of narration differed from what I was used to in classical Hollywood cinema. But then I also recognized that the film's plot mirrored some important aspects of Mani's own biography. Mani's father had arrived in Switzerland in 1985 in the course of the first phase of Sri Lankan Tamil migration to Europe in the mid-1980s.[1] Like most Tamils living in Switzerland, he found a job as a kitchen hand in a restaurant in Zurich. In 1989, Mani's mother joined his father with their almost five-year-old son, leaving Mani's sister in Sri Lanka. In 1993, Mani's mother returned to Sri Lanka. Mani, then eight years old, remained in Switzerland with his father, where he spent the weekdays in a foster home. Eventually, his former schoolteacher and her partner took him into their care. At first, they had looked after him on weekends when he was in Zurich while his father was at work. Mani's Swiss foster parents do not have children of their own. They both work full time; she is a schoolteacher, he an independent filmmaker. They are comparatively well off, but their life-style does not correspond to the model of the nuclear family still largely dominant in Switzerland, where the husband earns the family income while the wife concentrates on what Americans like to call homemaking. At the time the foster parents took Mani into their care, Mani's father was in a difficult situation. The fact that his wife had left him—that is, that he had apparently not been able to hold his family together—was perceived as a stigma by many members of the Sri Lankan Tamil community who distanced themselves from him.

Like so many Tamil refugees of the 1980s, Mani's family was spread all over the world and the local social network proved too weak to support him and his father; hence Swiss authorities had made the decision to send Mani to a foster home. On the one hand, his father did not oppose the decision, which he could have, apparently not least because the foster home reminded him of an English boarding school. On the other hand, Mani's father was dealing with alcohol problems. In the eyes of the Swiss authorities these problems made him unfit as a parent, and allowing his son to be sent to a foster home permitted him to hold on to his parental authority over the child. Mani, then, spent his formative childhood years as a member of a diaspora subculture outside the cultural, economic, and psychological frames of reference of that particular subculture. While his biographical trajectory is highly specific, his family situation was also fairly typical of Sri Lankan Tamils living in Switzerland, and thus his story is still indicative of the Tamil diaspora in a Western country. Much of the recent debate about diaspora and juvenile subcultures has been focused on the communal aspects of these subcultures. A story like Mani's draws our attention to a different type of diaspora: a diaspora outside the diaspora, if you will, which is located at a crossroads of cultures within cultures.

In this essay, I would like to propose an approach to diaspora and youth culture based on an individual case study of Mani's reception of Jackie Chan films. Working from within the theoretical frameworks developed in the recent debates in film studies and film theory, but going beyond the approaches proposed by some students of the historical reception of films, I would like to argue that individual reception histories, far from being merely anecdotal accounts of personal fandom, allow us not only to improve our understanding of the role films play in the formation of youth culture and other subcultures, but also shed new light on the processes involved in the symbolic construction of diaspora identities.

If one is to understand Mani's situation more fully, one has to remember that Switzerland is already a cluster of overlapping communities. Switzerland, a country of seven million in central-western Europe, is a confederation of minorities: German-, French-, Italian-, and Romantsch[2]-speaking communities, both Catholic and Protestant, plus a small Jewish community, make up modern Switzerland as it was created in the mid-nineteenth century. Although the earliest country on the continent to be industrialized, Switzerland in the mid-nineteenth century was still a country on which impoverished rural workers turned their back and emigrated, particularly to the Midwestern United States. But over the last 150 years, since the foundation of the Swiss federal state, the development of the Swiss economy has been decisively influenced by the immigration of foreign workers (Golder and Straubhaar 1999, 1). In fact, "foreigners constitute a third of Switzerland's total working population" (McDowell 1996, 55). The history of migration to Switzerland developed in three main periods. The first "lasted until 1963 and was characterized by a liberal admission policy, with the exception of the time from 1914 until 1945. The second period started in 1963 when the Swiss government introduced restrictions on the admission of immigrants" (Golder and Straubhaar 1999, 1).[3] In the post-war economic boom years, Switzerland acquired an important population of foreign labor that was recruited mostly from southern European countries. The third period "began in 1991 when the Swiss government introduced an admission policy which was based on country of origin considerations" (Golder and Straubhaar 1999, 1), also known as the three-circles model. Under the three-circles model, immigration candidates are sorted into three different groups. The "inner circle" consists of people from the European Union and EFTA states, the middle circle is comprised of people from the United States, Canada, and East European countries, whereas the "outer circle" contains the citizens of all other countries, who should only be admitted in exceptional cases. This new policy can be understood as a reaction against certain changes in the political and discursive context of immigration policy during the 1980s. In this period, migration issues became more emotional and politicized, partly as a response to the increase in the number of refugees from so-called third world countries applying for asylum in the West. Since the 1980s, fears of migration in Western countries have been centered on the "third world," even though migration along the south-north axis had grown by only 2 percent in the 1990s, while migration along the east-west axis into Europe and the West had grown by 20 percent in the same period (Bade 2001, 24, 25).[4] The Swiss "three-circles" admission policy was actually not a new policy, however. The old recruitment policy had always been directed toward specific countries, and had been based on ethnic-cultural stereotypes from the outset; with the three circles model these criteria simply became formal policy (Mahnig and Piguet 2003, 97).

Crucial among the factors that had an influence on Swiss immigration policy is the EU. Although located in the midst of EU countries, Switzerland is not a member. In the debates about the three-circles model, Swiss politicians defended the policy with the argument that this model would be compatible with the policies of EU member states.[5] Interestingly enough, however, the member states of the EU still have not yet achieved a common migration concept. In terms of migration policy, the nation-state members still maintain their sovereign status even after the introduction of the Schengen treaty, and a number of European states are not yet willing to acknowledge their status as migration countries.[6]

Generally speaking, as McDowell points out, "successive [Swiss] governments did not . . . pursue a general immigration programme but instead recruited temporary . . . workers" (McDowell 1996, 54). For a long time, there was no integration policy to speak of on a federal level. Integration efforts were mainly undertaken by nongovernment bodies and lower-level local administrations. Accordingly, some scholars speak of the "integrationist federalism" in Switzerland (Cattacin 1996). In 1998, an amendment to the Aliens Act defined integration mainly in terms of a "mutual understanding" between people with and without Swiss nationality, but also in terms of "shared values," a "will to integrate" of noncitizens, and an "openness" of the Swiss toward the resident foreigners.[7] Naturalization laws remain highly restrictive, however, which keeps the tally of non-naturalized residents of Switzerland at 20 percent, by far the largest number of foreign residents in any western European country.[8] The greater part of these immigrants—as I already mentioned—are from southern Europe, particularly from Italy, Spain, Portugal, the former Yugoslavia, and Turkey. In addition, compared with other European countries, Switzerland hosts a relatively large population of asylum seekers and officially recognized political refugees. The Tamil residents are part of this group.[9] They represent the largest Asian refugee community in Switzerland.[10]

Tamils in Switzerland generally live in culturally homogeneous circles. Outside of their professional activities, they remain mostly within their community, which consists not only of political refugees from Sri Lanka, but also of Tamil immigrants from India, Singapore, and other Asian countries. Their relative seclusion is due to the fact that they are first-generation immigrants with strong ties to their country of origin, and also to their legal status. Many of them have only been granted a temporary right to stay, and they have to be constantly prepared to leave the country and return to Sri Lanka.[11] While initially faced with overt and very public racism in the form of xenophobic campaigns in the tabloid press and even occasional physical attacks, Tamils had at least on the face of things become more accepted into Swiss society in the mid-1990s. Tamils have proven particularly apt at learning the language(s) and ways of the country. Furthermore, the cheap labor they provide has virtually made them the backbone of the Swiss restaurant industry, assuring them the support of at least one important economic pressure group in relation to the government. In some cases, however, their wages are so low that even families with two working parents depend on welfare. In a way, the Tamil immigrants continue in the footsteps of the Italian immigrants of the 1960s, who also started out at the lower end of the social strata in Switzerland, and for much of the 1960s and 1970s provided most of the cheap labor that was at the base of the prosperity of the Swiss economy in the last forty years.[12]

A Film Studies Perspective

While classical film theory mostly produced philosophical accounts of film as art, post-classical semiotic and semio-psychoanalytic film theory, as it emerged in the 1960s and 1970s, mainly focused on understanding how films are interpreted. Since the mid-1980s, cultural studies and cognitive film theory have shown in different ways that textual analysis alone cannot account for all the ways in which films are viewed and understood. It has become increasingly obvious that next to the implied spectator construed by the text, actual or empiric spectators and their viewing activities need to be taken into account as well. While both cognitive film theory and cultural studies can be understood as responses to semio-psychoanalytic film theory's passive conception of the spectator as a mere aftereffect of the text's symbolic operations and ideological positioning strategies, these theoretical approaches vary significantly with regard to their accounts of the cultural specificity of reception processes. While cognitive theory tends to be rationalist and universalist, cultural studies tend to produce culturalist and relativist accounts of how spectators make sense of films. Hence, psychoanalytical, cognitive, and cultural studies approaches might at first seem to be completely at odds with each other. Adopting a *piecemeal approach* to theory, in the sense suggested by Noël Caroll (1996), I would nonetheless like to propose the individual case history as a model of analysis that integrates both psychological concepts and observational modes of research.

The case history method as developed by Freud remains to this day the most widely used form of communication of empirical, clinical knowledge within the psychoanalytical community. "Histories," that is, narratives based on personal observation, are used to communicate experiences with patients, which the author deems to be of exemplary interest, to colleagues or nonpsychoanalytical audiences (Leuzinger-Bohleber 2000, 184). For the purposes of this essay, I am interested in the case history as a way of representing the creative potential of the psychological processes involved in the establishment of a juvenile fan's personal bond with his idol. Hence, my use of the case history will not primarily be interpretive in the psychoanalytical sense. While I am certainly interested in the meanings of Mani's fandom—in what it means to him and what cultural meanings it produces—my primary interest is not in its hidden truth and in what it reveals about the human psyche, but rather in how it works on a social level and what it does in a specific biographical situation. In other words, I would like to use the case history as a way of representing the social aspects of Mani's psychological investment in Jackie Chan, the star.

My point is that far from simply offering psychological explanations for what are after all primarily social phenomena, the reception case history paves the way for a more fully complex understanding of the media appropriation processes of juvenile audiences. Media appropriation not only implies the consumption of popular culture in everyday life, as it was first described by John Fiske (1989). It also means appropriating the texts of popular culture by way of one's own cultural production, which can be described in terms of a process of negotiation between specific media texts, their consumption, and one's own biographical situation. Appropriating popular culture artifacts in one's own productions is a process addressed in concepts such as Willis's (1990b) notion of popular texts as "symbolic resources," or in Henry Jenkins's (1992) notion of "textual poaching", which he borrows from Michel de Certeau (1988) to describe the media appropriation strategies typical of fan culture. The fan-as-poacher, both in de Certeau's and Jenkins's sense, operates at the margins of culture and has no direct access to the means of commercial cultural production. While de Certeau clearly distinguishes between producers and recipients, Jenkins focuses on the recipient-as-producer. Someone like Mani qualifies as a poacher in Jenkins's sense because, while clearly not in the economic position to produce cultural artifacts for mass consumption, he is still a producer in the sense that he appropriates popular media for his own productions. Like most students of youth culture, however, Jenkins is primarily interested in the peer group dynamics of youth subculture and on the formation of collective group identities rather than on the individual trajectories that I would like to address in this essay. It is precisely in this respect that the case history method departs from traditional cultural studies approaches, which it might at first resemble. While by no means rendering studies of media appropriation processes on a group level superfluous, the reception case history can more fully account for the individual conditions of reception and negotiation than group level analysis, which it actually complements. This is particularly true of the reception case history method if combined with the methods of film studies, which account for the role film's formal aspects and the viewer's interaction with the film play in the process of media appropriation.

The approach to youth media consumption I would like to propose here is inspired by Janet Staiger's work on film reception (1992, 2000). Staiger's work represents an important step toward an integration of psychoanalytical film theory and cultural studies within the field of film studies. She uses case studies of what she calls reception events: an event is "a set of interpretations or effective experiences produced by individuals from an encounter with a text or set of texts within a social situation." The focus of analysis is on the various (material) traces left by a particular event, be they of the textual, visual, or oral variety (Staiger 2000, 163). Staiger's model of analysis is directed, on the one hand, against a certain tendency in cultural studies that focuses on individual reception activities. According to Staiger, such research yields "at best, lists of what readers do in creating alternative texts or identifying with stars." That is, it merely produces protocols of individual reception attitudes. Against this tendency, but in tune with one of cultural studies' original impulses, Staiger stresses the importance of contextual factors over textual ones in the analysis of film and television viewers' everyday experience of media programs (2000, 1). On the other hand, Staiger's model of analysis implies a critique of cognitive film theory. Against this model, as well as against conventional approaches to the interpretation of filmic texts, Staiger claims that the text itself has no inherent meaning, and that there is no "free reader" either. Instead, there are "contexts of social formations and constructed identities of the self in relation to historical conditions [that] explain the interpretative strategies and affective responses of readers" (2000, 162). Accordingly, there is no possibility of a "unifying reading" of a media text because the discursive formations produced at a particular historical moment are necessarily "contradictory and heterogeneous." In order to analyze cultural meanings, then, Staiger argues for a historical-materialist approach to reception studies, which is based on post-structuralist textual analysis of films and other texts such as reviews, which together form the basis of what is Staiger's actual object of analysis, the event.

Drawing on Staiger's notion of event, but going beyond her approach in two important respects, I would like to discuss Mani's fandom in terms of an individual, highly specific reception event. On the one hand, I would like to move away from Staiger's focus on textual analysis and textual traces, such as promotional material, film reviews, and letters to the editors, in order to include other kinds of traces and other methods of tracing the *event,* such as interviews and participant observation. On the other hand, I would like to extend the temporal delimitation of the event to several years but focus on that period in one individual viewer's life, thereby attaining a degree of relevance for individual case histories that is indeed often missing from synchronic, short-term studies of individual viewers' activities. In reconstructing the history of Mani's reception of the Jackie Chan films and star persona, I eventually will try to develop a reading that can explain why this particular encounter took place in its specific way, place, and time. More specifically, I will try to understand what makes Jackie Chan so attractive as a role model for a teenage and late adolescent immigrant from Sri Lanka living in Switzerland in the mid- to late 1990s.

The Event: Mani's Fandom

My analysis is based on two sets of data. On the one hand, there are the data that I personally generated from film analyses, as well as from personal observations made during conversations and shared activities with Mani, such as watching movies, and mutual personal computer support. On the other hand, and more importantly, there is the set of data generated by Mani himself. Over a period of roughly five years, his encounter with Jackie Chan led him to produce a series of texts of different types. His "initiation" into Chan's filmic world took place in the foster home, where he saw his first Chan movie on TV. His fandom started out with watching movies, and in a first phase, Mani developed classical fan activities such as clipping, collecting, and archiving newspaper articles and promotional materials in fan albums, creating collages from printed materials, making film lists, and imitating the star's poses in personal photographs. Later, Mani started making short movies of his own, such as Jackie Chan trailers and video clips. Furthermore, he expressed his passion for Chan movies in works such as the paper mentioned at the beginning of this essay. Using semi-professional digital video cameras and video editing software, Mani currently uses his spare time to produce so-called "Schlegli" films (which roughly translates from Swiss German as "beat'em-up movies") in a style reminiscent of Jackie Chan's work.

At first sight, Mani's activities seem to be triggered by, and expressive of, the very set of fan emotions Jackie Stacey (1994) describes in her study of movie star fandom. These emotions include devotion, adoration, worship, transcendence, aspiration, and inspiration. Mani's extra-filmic activities also include the typical fan's behavioral patterns of pretending to be the star, trying to resemble the star, and imitating and copying the star. In several photo series and short films Mani can be seen imitating Chan's various roles. However, a closer look at Mani's fan practices and their social and psychological conditions reveals that they are more than just examples of what any fan would typically do according to the protocols of cultural studies. Rather, one can discern a set of characteristic fields of conflict on which specific correspondences between textual offerings and Mani's juvenile everyday life occur. The predominant theme of these correspondences is that of identity. That is, they all contribute to the symbolic construction of cultural/ethnic, social, and sexual, or rather gender, identities. I will analyze the two main characteristic fields of conflict or negotiation more closely, which together constitute much of what you might call the imaginary field of interaction between fan and star. They are the fields of a) language, expression, and cultural skills; and b) local and global belonging, displacement, and male subjectivity.

Language, Expression, and Cultural Skills versus Body Skills

While growing up, Mani was facing complex language problems. Although a native Tamil speaker, Mani became confused about his Tamil language skills while he was living in a foster home and, later, with his foster parents. Apparently, his command of Tamil deteriorated to a point where, according to his own statements, he now often has problems understanding his father or his mother when she calls him from Sri Lanka. Tamil relatives and friends in turn have problems understanding Mani when he expresses himself in his native language. Neither is his command of his adopted language without problems; although being an average to good student in most subjects, Mani has difficulties in reading and writing as well as in speaking German.[13] Also, most Tamil children in Switzerland attend language lessons in both German and their native Tamil language. Because Mani was showing strong reading and writing impediments, his teachers decided he should receive additional training in German instead of attending the Tamil lessons, thus further alienating him from his native language.

Jackie Chan's characters often face similar problems. In *Nobody* (*Who Am I*) (1998), Chan's character is lost in the South African desert and is saved by a group of "natives" who speak a language unknown to him. The Chan character first responds to them in a highly comical pseudo-language, but then starts to learn their language. He is suffering from amnesia due to an accident and can't remember his name. Having learned the basics of the natives' language, he starts shouting "Who-am-I," which his hosts take to be his name. "Who-am-I" is adopted into the natives' community and quickly becomes a kind of medicine man. Later, he decides to leave the community and go in search of "civilization," in a satiric retelling of the classic, colonial explorer narrative in Africa, recast with an Asian protagonist. On his way, he meets two rally drivers who have also lost their way in the desert. One of the drivers is wounded, and the Chan character treats him according to the lessons of his newly acquired medical knowledge. Suddenly, "Who-am-I" loses the ability to talk. He chews some herbs, which were meant to heal his patient and which instead paralyze his tongue. For several minutes of the film, the Chan character is deprived of language and has to communicate non-verbally, via facial expressions and body gestures, which returns him to the more typical image of the Asian male as foreigner with strange expressions.

"Who-am-I'"s language difficulties are no accident. Language impediments are in fact part of Jackie Chan's star persona and star image. Chan characters are on the whole more proficient in body skills than in language skills, their primary means of expression being punches and kicks rather than the linguistic apparatus. It comes as no surprise then, that in *Rush Hour* (1998), Chan's first successful Hollywood film, he is teamed with Chris Tucker to play an odd couple of cops who excel in body skills and verbal language respectively. Drawing on ethnic and racial stereotypes, Chan incarnates Asian martial arts and fighting skills, while Tucker represents African American musicality and fast-talk comedy at its most hysterical.

On the occasion of Mani's fourteenth birthday, his foster parents gave him a computer, partly because they hoped that the use of the computer would help improve his language skills. Mani's first interest in the computer, however, was in the graphic programs that he used to create collages of film promotion materials, such as one for *Rush Hour,* which is made up of materials found on-line and of additional elements he designed himself. Most of the writing is taken from preexisting materials, but he typed out the tag line himself ("The fastest hands in the east meet the biggest mouth in the west"). One of the first uses Mani made of the color options of the Photoshop program was for lightening the skin colors of his Asian and African American idols; it seems that an underlying ambivalence about ethnic identity and skin color are issues in Mani's fandom. *Rush Hour*'s odd couple of Chan and Tucker may indeed be particularly attractive to Mani because of the fact that Tucker is black. In talking about movie stars and in creating his artifacts, Mani keeps on referring to a twofold experience of ethnic and racial difference. On the one hand, he sees himself as part of a genealogy of Asian martial arts stars such as Bruce Lee and Jackie Chan. He likes to quote a line commonly attributed to Jackie Chan: "I hope that after I die people will say: First there was Bruce Lee, and then there was Jackie Chan," only to add "and then came Mani." On the other hand, he is also a big fan of Eddie Murphy, whom he idolizes, not least because of his skin color. Mani sees himself primarily as Asian, but also as black, and generally identifies with people of color. Although an ethnically highly diverse country, Switzerland is home to a relatively small number of people with dark skin tones, particularly if compared with other western nations such as the United States. Most native Swiss people are not very knowledgeable about the ethnic and cultural backgrounds of the country's nonwhite inhabitants, and Tamils are quite often perceived as black and not Asian. Mani's schoolmates have actually developed a habit of teasing him with the racist epithet, "Limmatneger" ("Limmat-Nigger," "Limmat" being both the name of the river running through the city of Zurich and an anagram of "Tamil"). Children are of course no strangers to cruelty anywhere in the world, but it is no coincidence that Mani's schoolmates should choose a combination of a racist slur and a term borrowed from the local geography to mark out his particular position in the group. The "Limmatneger" label goes to show, among other things, that Tamils in Switzerland are still very much perceived as different along the lines of a racial divide.

However, Mani's attraction to the *Rush Hour* star couple could be rooted in more than just the fact that the actors represent something like the twin dragon of his experience of difference, of not being white and not being recognized as Asian. It is highly probable that the decision to go ahead with the production of *Rush Hour* was preceded by market research evaluating the popularity of Jackie Chan with young African American audiences for the casting of Chris Tucker was clearly geared to this audience. While it could be argued that the film reinforces racial stereotypes of African Americans and Asians, it seems equally obvious that the film may well be used as a symbolic resource by youth in a different way. Compensating for each other's weaknesses, the Chan-Tucker duo successfully brave all the dangers they face. Merging into a kind of two-bodied super hero, Chan helps Tucker out with his body skills, while the fast-talking Tucker makes up for Chan's linguistic inadequacies. In the process, Chan moves from a state of prelinguistic stupor to fluent English with Tucker's help, while Chan's bodily antics help Tucker overcome what might be called the stigmatization of his black body. This is not to say that the Chan and Tucker characters necessarily overcome the stereotypical representations of African American and Asian men as being inherently socially deficient or marginal. However, if one agrees that no film ever allows for a single, unified reading, then one can assume that the Chan/Tucker body-language double bind may give rise to a certain effect of empowerment. This at least seems to be the case for Mani, who derives pleasure from imagining himself as Chan and Tucker and, in a way, as both at the same time.

Local/Global Belonging, Displacement, and Male Subjectivity

Mani uses his computer almost exclusively for his fan activities, and one of his computer files lists all the films in which Jackie Chan has ever appeared. The list is over seventy titles long, and Mani has seen more than half of these films. Another file carefully lists Mani's visits to movie theaters over a period of almost two years, quite an achievement for someone who is not exactly an avid writer in school. The file lists the dates of more than eighty visits, the original English and also German titles, the actors and the country of origin of the films, as well as the names of the movie theaters. Nearly ten of these eighty films feature Jackie Chan. Furthermore, the file includes ratings for the films, ranging from one to six stars. The file also lists the names of the people who went to the movies with Mani, and in some cases even the name of the person who chose the film. These last two categories seem particularly important because they stress the communal aspect of Mani's movie going. Watching movies in theaters or in the home is still a family or peer group activity for most audiences. For Tamil emigrant families in Switzerland in the 1980s and 1990s, movie watching in the living room was an important family activity, and it was an important feature of Mani's early youth. Hardly any Tamil or South Indian movies are shown in theaters in Switzerland. Thus, watching them at home on video is not only cheaper but in most cases the only chance to see the films at all (see Luethi 2002). The last two categories on Mani's file indicate that moviegoing is still primarily a communal activity for him, and he once said that he would have liked to see each film on the list with as many friends and family members as possible.

Movie consumption, then, offers a sense of belonging that emerges in yet another of Mani's fandom-related artifacts. On the occasion of the sixty-fifth birthday of his foster father's mother, Mani was asked to create a greeting card as well as a title sequence for a birthday video. Using Photoshop, Mani created an entire alphabet from cutouts of promotional material for Jackie Chan films he found on the Internet. He used the letters of this Chan alphabet to "write" the greeting card and the credit sequence for the birthday video. Much like the bricoleur described by French anthropologist Claude Lévi-Strauss, who invents his own tools and building materials to create something new out of familiar objects, Mani used objects from his everyday surroundings to creatively reinvent an activity he had practically loathed—writing. His technique was rather time-consuming, but it helped to obliterate the onerous aspects of the activity of writing. Mani's creation of the Chan alphabet and his enjoyment of creating visual products and pursuing his fan activities represent a productive way of dealing with a potentially difficult or disagreeable situation, of turning a weakness into a strength, into a source of self-fulfillment. But by creating the Chan alphabet he also reaffirmed his own identity. One could argue that by creating and using the Chan alphabet Mani managed to write himself into the family history of his foster father without forsaking his own background. The Chan alphabet marks his difference in belonging. While his foster grandparents always perceived him as one of their family, Mani's position was by no means entirely clear to him; at the very least it has remained ambiguous. Self-made visual representations thus contribute to a complex sense of local-global belonging, a point that can be made similarly for Mani's collages, in which he likes to insert pictures of his friends and himself into preexisting movie posters and lobby cards.

In addition to the role played by language, multiple or split identities are an important element of the Jackie Chan star persona, as Chan's role in *Twin Dragon* already indicates. Through his extra-filmic statements, Chan carefully inscribes himself into the mythology and tradition of the Asian martial art film. Chan sees himself as the direct successor to Bruce Lee, as apparent in the statement Mani likes to quote from him, and not without justification. If the American-born Lee was the first Asian martial arts performer to become a box-office film star in the United States and in Europe, Jackie Chan was the next Asian male star to cross over into Western mainstream popular culture.

In his paper on Jackie Chan, mentioned at the beginning of this article, Mani devotes an entire chapter to "Jackie Chan's experiences in America." His summary of Jackie Chan's autobiographical narrative is as follows: "Even though Jackie Chan enjoys greater luxury when working in America, he prefers the way they make movies in Hong Kong. The work at home is less complicated. The people have more fun at work. Everybody helps everybody. The atmosphere at work is just like in a family. . . . If you have fun [on the set], and if you want to shoot an action scene, [in America] an insurance agent shows up. He tells you that you can't do it that way, that you have to install mats and security nets first. It's all much more complicated" (Mani 2001, 11). The entire passage is built on a dichotomy between Hollywood and Hong Kong: Hong Kong represents a family atmosphere, Hollywood stands for a more complicated and hostile outside world. One could argue that this passage represents another articulation of Mani's complex sense of belonging. The Hong Kong situation, "where everybody sleeps in the same room and eats from the same plate" (as Mani recounts from Jackie Chan's autobiography), might remind Mani of his childhood in a Tamil family, while Chan's problems with the Hollywood way of doing things perhaps reflect Mani's own difficulties in accommodating to the rules and regulations imposed by his Swiss educators.

In his analysis of Jackie Chan, David Bordwell writes of the movie actor's intra-filmic star image—the star image as constructed in the films—in terms of a "calculated cosmopolitanism" (Bordwell 2000, 58). Many Chan films are indeed set outside of Hong Kong, and they are often shot in multiple locations in different countries. Thus, *Thunderbolt* (1995) was filmed in Japan, *First Strike* (1996) in Russia and Australia, *Rumble in the Bronx* (1995) in Canada, *Who Am I* (1998) in South Africa and the Netherlands, and *Operation Condor* (1991) in the Sahara desert and various places in Europe. In a way, then, the Chan heroes are polyglot, they are at home everywhere and nowhere. According to Bordwell, the multiple and international settings of the Chan movies are part of an economic strategy of the Hong Kong film industry to appeal to international audiences. But there are also cultural reasons for setting these films in more than one location. Since the early 1990s, popular films from India, particularly the so-called Bollywood (mainstream Hindi) films, regularly feature non-Indian and transnational settings (Mishra 2002). Again, this is a case of a national film industry trying to appeal to international audiences. But the transnationalization of Indian cinema similarly reflects the growing importance of the Indian diaspora communities in both cultural and economic terms and it attests to the impact of media globalization in a post-colonial age. While the Hong Kong film industry is in many ways different from Bollywood, the international locations in Jackie Chan films can similarly be seen as linked to the contemporary processes of media globalization. It is not just Western audiences these films are targeting, but rather a new kind of diaspora audience.[14]

Perhaps most migrants never quite leave their home countries, which often accompany them in their cultural imagination, in the form of reminiscences or sometimes a desire to return (Appadurai 1996, 6).

Migrants often have a way of searching for "windows to home" (Luethi 2002, 154). For Mani's family, as for most Tamil families living in Switzerland, television and home video were such "windows to home," media vehicles of the social imaginary.[15] Just like Indians watching Bollywood films in their diaspora homes, South Asian migrant families mediate "the cleavages between an estranged diasporic culture and an 'integrative' home culture" by their film viewing (Mishra 2002, 247). Mani's media socialization began, as I pointed out, with the communal watching of South Indian movies in the family living room. Marie Gillespie has shown in the case of young British Indians' relationship to Hindi cinema that for diasporic youth, watching films from their ancestral nation is vital for their emotional and psychological well-being (Gillespie 1995, 87). When Mani went to live in his foster home, he stopped watching South Asian films on video and thus lost what was probably his primary cultural window into his native culture. Mani never went back to watching South Indian films, but instead shifted his communal movie-watching activities to Jackie Chan films.

Given the importance he attributes to communal movie going, Mani's Jackie Chan fandom thus could be understood in terms of a cultural negotiation between his Tamil and his Swiss families. The fact that Mani could not watch South Indian films with his Swiss foster family may have been due to the fact that until very recently, popular Indian films had no visibility in Europe whatsoever, and therefore lacked any form of cultural legitimacy outside South Asian migrant communities. Jackie Chan films, in contrast, may have never received the kind of critical acclaim bestowed upon Asian auteurist films but are certainly visible in the United States and Europe; their success with Western audiences guarantees them an important degree of (pop-)cultural legitimacy, if not cult status (Teo 1997). Also, switching over to Jackie Chan films allowed Mani to stay true to a distinctly Asian tradition of cinematic narration, in effect, because many of the elements characteristic of Chan films can also be found in South Indian films. Hollywood films tend to represent the action as if it took place by and of itself, while Chan films constantly refer to their own conditions of production. The end title sequence always features outtakes and other behind-the-scenes material, and early Chan films use montage techniques such as repetition in action scenes that are quite at odds with traditional Hollywood editing, which emphasizes temporal and spatial continuity of action. These signature elements can also be found in Chan's Hollywood movies—you can't forsake your initial fanbase, even if you're moving into new territory.

Seen in an Asian context, however, these elements are anything but idiosyncratic. There, they appear less as signature devices of Chan's personal style than of a different tradition of filmmaking. Commercial

Hong Kong cinema, just like popular Indian cinema, has in the course of time similarly "indigenized" the conventions of Hollywood's supposedly universal mode of cinematic narration. In both Hong Kong and Indian cinemas, the indigenization of the Hollywood mode was accomplished through the fusion of the adopted cinematic idiom with traditional, vernacular forms of dramatic art. Hollywood's economic pressure was only a minor factor in this oblique way of adopting Hollywood conventions, particularly in the case of the Indian film industries. To this date, Hollywood controls only 5 percent of the Indian movie market. Partly, this is due to the exceedingly low level of ticket prices, which dents the profitability of big blockbuster releases. In western Europe, where ticket prices are much higher and box-office revenues more significant, Hollywood's market share ranges between 50 and 90 percent, depending on the country. As a result of the indigenization of Hollywood conventions, both Hong Kong and Indian popular cinemas favor narrative structures that subordinate the linear progression of the action to spectacle and give way to song and dance or martial arts numbers and fantasy segments at every turn. In a way then, Mani's choice of Jackie Chan as the object of his fandom can be understood in terms of a replay of the origins of his media socialization through South Indian popular films. This reading is further substantiated by the fact that Jackie Chan, unlike most action or martial arts film stars, is also a comedian. His star persona integrates several genres, a trait also characteristic of most contemporary Indian mainstream films. More so than even the most broadly aimed Hollywood blockbusters, popular Indian films transcend genre differentiation and bring together love stories, action and fight scenes, and comedic interludes in one big all-family spectacle that offers something for everyone. Therefore, the fact that Mani values Jackie Chan over all other action and martial arts stars may again be seen as an echo of his South Indian film socialization. In this sense, Mani's fandom for Jackie Chan articulates his complex sense of belonging in difference as well as his sense of difference in belonging.

This brings us to another field of interaction between fan and star: next to the question of ethnic and cultural belonging, the question of male identity is central to what you might call Mani's imaginary convergence with his idol. In his analysis of the Chan persona, Mark Gallagher speaks about "masculinity in translation" and characterizes Chan's star image as a "transcultural star text" (Gallagher 1997, 23). Chan's heroes differ from classical Hollywood action heroes in several important respects. Chan's characters are comical as well as action heroes, and they are closer to slapstick-burlesque figures than to action heroes in the sense familiar to most Western audiences. Chan heroes do use physical violence to fight evil and pursue their goals, but where the typical American action hero foregrounds his efficiency in reaching his goals, Chan's heroes highlight their physical versatility and celebrate their acrobatic skills and Asian martial artistry. Characteristically, these male heroes also expose a certain vulnerability, which is quite relevant in terms of the construction of their gender identity. One of the staples of Chan's films is outtakes of stunts gone wrong shown over the final credits. According to Gallagher, Chan "displays an excess of activity" and "an unwilling-ness to police the 'reasonable' boundaries of human aspiration" through his inevitable accidents during stunt performances. Compared to Hollywood action heroes, who may do their own stunts but never get hurt in the process, Chan is an aberration. His ability to "overreach the screen, to perform beyond the requirements of a conventional narra-tive" occurs "outside the social order, particularly the order that Holly-wood action films impose." His body's "continuous, antic motion, feminized through its implied vulnerability, calls into question concep-tions of the ideal male body," and thus Chan's persona as a whole "does not ascribe to dominant cinematic models of male identity" (Gallagher 1997, 39). While Gallagher's implicit claim that Chan's masculinity is "feminized" reiterates the stereotypical view of Asian masculinity (and of all femininity) as somehow deficient, Chan's brand of masculinity cer-tainly does come with an unusual degree of self-consciousness with regard to its own weaknesses. While Hollywood action stars stand for a kind of unbreakable superiority, Chan's masculinity is of a much more ambivalent variety; it is a shrewd masculinity that reaffirms itself not only by turning adversity into advantage, but also by turning weaknesses into strengths. It is a masculinity that speaks of an altogether different idea of what it means to be a rounded and powerful human being, an idea that may be closer to a diasporic youth's biographical situation than that represented by Hollywood action heroes.

Conclusion

With regard to Mani's situation as a youth belonging to the Tamil dias-pora, I agree with Mike O'Donnel and Sue Sharpe that it would be sim-plistic to characterize the situation of diasporic youth as being "'caught' between two cultures" (O'Donnel and Sharpe 2000, 78). The authors of *Uncertain Masculinities* propose the term negotiation of cultures instead, since "'negotiation' is a better and more neutral descriptor of the process by which individual youth work out their cultural identities and relation-ships than one which implies constant angst and struggle" (O'Donnel and Sharpe 2000, 79). However, in comparison with the Asian youth studied by O'Donnel and Sharpe in Britain, Mani's ties to his diasporic community are more distant. Furthermore, compared with the Pakistani or Indian diaspora in Britain, the Tamil community in Switzerland is much smaller. Rather than belonging to a minority in the classroom, a Tamil child in Switzerland is usually the only one in his class; this isolation is even more so in foster homes, where Mani spent part of his elementary school years. For someone like him, it becomes virtually impossible to find an idol among members of his own community and, in fact, he is faced with the general lack of visibility of his culture of origin in his everyday experience. It is no coincidence that on the occasion of the opening of a recent exhibition on the representation of Switzerland in contemporary popular Indian cinema, Mani remarked with pride and satisfaction that "the nice thing about this exhibition is that it will show people how many good things my culture has to offer."

Because Mani is faced with a general lack of potential idols from his own specific cultural background, Jackie Chan, the highly visible superstar of Asian cinema, cannot fail to appear to Mani as the ersatz Asian male par excellence. Rather than being just "an international ambassador for a reevaluation of Asian masculinity" (Gallagher 1997, 23), Chan to him serves as a model for Asian masculinity's reinsertion into a Western context. From Mani's perspective, the Jackie Chan persona offers a privileged example of successful cosmopolitanism, a cosmopolitanism that is global in its reach and yet remains anchored in certain local traditions and fields of socialization and might relate to what Stuart Hall calls a "vernacular cosmopolitanism" (Hall 2002, 35). In that sense, the Hong Kong action star and his films represent to Mani a necessary symbolic resource for the negotiation of questions of belonging and diaspora identity, and of the conflicts that come with them.

In *Nobody*, Jackie Chan plays a hero called "Who-am-I." Unlike Ulysses, who just pretends to be *oudeis* (nobody), in order to fool the Cyclops, "Who-am-I" has actually lost his memory in an accident and cannot even remember his name. At least temporarily, he doesn't know where he's from, and he doesn't know where he belongs. Nonetheless, Chan's character brilliantly masters all the difficult and dangerous situations he is faced with in his life as a special agent. Even without an identity, then, or rather with an identity he makes up as he goes along, he can hold his own in a hostile world. For Ulysses, the loss of identity is a clever trick. For Who-am-I, it is fate, albeit a temporary one. Successful action heroes they are both.

Chapter 9
Authenticating Practices: Producing Realness, Performing Youth

Nicole R. Fleetwood

We were at the center—the hub—of the digital revolution, but, at times, our presence alone acknowledged our marginalization from the digital economy that had taken over the San Francisco Bay Area. Our small group of youth and adult educators, organized by the Media Education Center (MEC), a community-based media production organization located in the San Francisco Bay Area, was embarking on an intensive project that would result in a short narrative video about youth life in San Francisco's Mission District. The Mission District, a historically working-class Latino neighborhood, has been reshaped in recent years by an influx of primarily white artists and young professionals. We were working in a space that reflected these new shifts in the district, a state-of-the-art nonprofit media center on the edge of the community. The whirring of computers from the production suites surrounding us hummed throughout the room as we brainstormed the plot. It was 1999, MEC's second year of operation. The organization's co-founder, Sarah, had made arrangements for classes to be held at the West Coast Video Foundation (WCVF), one of the nation's premiere nonprofit media production centers. One wall of our workshop space was floor-to-ceiling windows that faced a long hallway that led to other media suites; and because of this we worked under constant observation. During one of our meetings, Sarah exclaimed, "We're in a fishbowl!" We all agreed. The very stylish media savvy employees, clients, and consultants of WCVF passed along the corridor looking in at us in utter curiosity.

The video was decidedly about youth and was to be shot from youth's perspectives. Yet, framing the project in such a way raised a host of issues about the creation and representation of identity categories, specifically those of racialized youth, through visual media.[1] As significantly, the project highlighted the complexities of community collaboration through video. This essay explores the relationship between representations of racialized youth in U.S. popular culture, local cultural practices, and ideologies of race and authenticity through an examination of the MEC summer workshop.[2] I argue that similar to mass media and popular culture in the United States youth-based media arts organizations share a common goal—a drive, that is—to document an authentic urban experience from the perspective of racialized youth. The pursuit of the real governing this collaborative relationship relies on cinematic realism and invokes an anthropological search for essence or authenticity. My analysis also considers the specificity of video that makes it the exemplary medium for exploring the real in everyday culture, particularly for representing a racialized version of authenticity called "realness." In the context of U.S. popular media, realness as a normative discursive strategy manifests itself commonly through the performance of blackness and the visual rendering of subjects marked as black. The tendency to use video to represent the realness of racialized youth grows out of a broader cultural practice in contemporary U.S. visual culture to frame racialized subjects through discourses of authenticity and essentialism. Moreover, as this essay considers, cultural narratives based on representations of an authentic youthful subject who is more often racialized as darkly other and gendered as masculine reify U.S. ideologies that consistently mark racialized youth as outside of normative white adult society, yet "indigenous" to U.S. urban ghettos, and as responsible for their own marginalized conditions. It is important to note that the popularity of these authenticating practices in contemporary U.S. popular media and advertising has direct material effects. The discourse of realness positions racialized youth as deviant and aberrant, while also serving as the vehicle of consumption of a particular racialized youthful identity through its association with a range of commodities (Gray 1995, Kelley 1997b, Rose 1994, Watkins 1998).

Influenced by Lacanian psychoanalytic theory, my use of the real, on one level, refers to "that which remains unsymbolized" (Soler 1996, 58); and because of its inaccessibility, the real drives our desires and simultaneously leads to anxiety and feelings of loss at one's incompletion (Ragland 1996, 194). At the same time, I adopt performance theorist Peggy Phelan's critique of how the concept within psychoanalysis and other systems of knowledge relies on the visible as "an unmarked conspirator" and who argues for an exposure of "the ways in which the visible real is employed as a truth-effect for the establishment of these discursive and representational notions of the real" (1993, 3). Further complicating my use of the real is Baudrillard's assessment of how the search for authenticity and "the proliferation of myths of origin and signs of reality" are the result of anxieties over the loss of the real (1988). With this as a theoretical framework, the study argues that the pursuit of the real governs the collaboration between video artists and youth video producers and unwittingly reinforces normative power relations through representation. The study considers, for example, the tendency of youth participants to use video as an opportunity to show audiences their "real" experiences as authentic and distinct from white adult cultural practices.[3] The essay suggests that community arts organizations that strive to challenge non-normative representations of youth are often complicit in the construction of racialized youth as exuding authenticity through visual markings. By examining the major production phases in the MEC summer project—pre-production, production, post-production, and distribution—the analysis elucidates the process of creating narratives and tropes of youth authenticity through local media and their relationship to U.S. mass popular culture. While my research is heavily influenced by and indebted to Stuart Hall's work on representation, this study attempts to make a critical intervention into scholarship on representation by focusing on the process of production (Hall, 1996).

The complexities that arise in the adult-youth collaboration of the MEC summer workshop are in large part due to what Jane Gaines calls "a crisis in representation stemming from the very problem of who represents and who is represented" in contemporary scholarship, particularly anthropology and visual media (1999, 6). Recent critical studies have questioned the positionality of the "framed" and the "framer" in cultural production and the pursuit of "authenticity" (Trinh 1992; Renov 1993; Pratt 1992). In the context of youth-based media projects, video presumably represents the ideal medium for accessing an unmediated relationship with the real, while youth come to represent unmediated "authenticity" in contemporary visual and material culture. Anthropologist Vincanne Adams argues that the stability of the category of authentic is an illusion, because "authenticity is always a product of the relationship between observer and observed—a consequence of the desire for the authenticity that always slips out of our grasp in transient relationships, which are never fixed for long over time or in space" (1996, 37). In contemporary culture, youth—this transitory identity—is the site of mythic experience of both pleasure and deviance. Through video, media organizations attempt to connect with and document the temporally fleeting, but discursively repetitive and static, authenticity of a racialized youth experience.

MEC is one of several youth-based media arts organizations in the United States that developed over the past decade. Other well-known organizations include Code 33 (Oakland, Calif.), Educational Video

Center (New York), and Street-Level Youth Media (Chicago). Responding to the predominance of visual media in contemporary popular culture, most organizations base their practices on concepts of media literacy to educate young people to read and analyze the symbols of media construction. In the 1990s, many media organizations benefited from the rise in high-technology industries, specifically the development and proliferation of moderately priced digital video cameras and editing systems. Using new digital technologies and teaching the principles of media literacy, youth-based media organizations attempt to bridge "the digital divide" (a condition at least partly attributed to the excessive greed and social irresponsibility of high-technology companies) by equipping underrepresented groups with the tools of media production.[4] The organizations' overriding goal is to provide individuals, particularly youth, with access to visual technology and to aid youth in creating visual media from the perspective of (almost always racialized and impoverished) youth.

Youth-based media arts organizations grow out of a history of community outreach, public art initiatives, and video activism. (For more on the development of video art and activism, see Hall and Fifer 1990; Juhasz 1995; and Boyle 1997.) Collaborative projects such as white media artist and activist DeeDee Halleck's film workshops with black and Puerto Rican youth in New York during the 1960s and 1970s set the stage for the birth of these organizations and the range of projects that they produce (Halleck 2002). They are also influenced by the practices and goals of indigenous media movements (Ginsburg 1995). Similar to the video collectives of the early 1970s, based primarily in New York and San Francisco, youth-based centers believe in the democratization of society through media access. According to media theorists Martha Rosler and Dierdre Boyle, groups such as Videofreex, Downtown Community Television Center, and Global Village pooled resources and equipment, provided artists with access to video technology, and explored the possibilities of artistic practice and political commentary through the medium itself. These groups saw their work as alternatives to the growing power and reach of mass-mediated popular culture, specifically television, in the United States. Video, as an accessible and portable technology, developed in the midst of the civil rights, student, and antiwar movements of the mid- and late 1960s. Martha Rosler analyzes how the history of video art commingles with 1960s radical political movements and a growing skepticism of mass media and corporatized cultural production. Rosler writes that pioneering artists saw video as a revolutionary medium artistically and socially: "Not only a systemic but also a utopian critique was implicit in video's early use, for the effort was not to enter the system but to transform every aspect of it and—legacy of the revolutionary avant-garde project—to redefine the system out of existence by merging art with social life and making audience and producer interchangeable" (1990, 31). These sometimes competing goals have remained in constant tension in community video practices throughout the late twentieth century and the early twenty-first.

Scripting Youth

We were working together and it was a difficult "together" that we very self-consciously discussed. During the first two weeks of the MEC video project, the group size shifted from session to session. In the end, the group settled at five: Anita, Michelle, and Kathleen (three teenage girls), Sarah (the instructor), and me (assistant instructor and observer). Surrounded by audiovisual devices and in the throes of an awkward but exciting collaboration, the youth producers seemed not to notice my tape recorder that sat in the center of the table.[5] At times, we felt as if we were on the verge of making the next *Do the Right Thing.* We radiated with excitement and possibility. At other times, it felt as if our tenuous collaborative relationship would collapse before the production was completed. What brought us there varied greatly. We were all paid for our involvement through private grants and city funding. Kathleen, whose father is Algerian and whose mother is Native American and white, was the oldest of the youth producers. Having just graduated from high school and with an interest in visual art and theater, she wanted to gain video production skills that would translate into future employment. Anita, whose mother is white and whose father is black, lived with her aunt in Valencia Gardens, a housing project in the center of the Mission that became one of our primary locations for the video shoot. She was the least vocal in the group. Michelle, a fifteen-year-old black girl, learned about MEC through Anita and knew the least about video production. Michelle had spent most of her life in the predominantly black neighborhoods of Potrero Hill and Lakeside and was also the only youth who was not from the Mission District; she resented that the project focused almost exclusively on this district. "Why can't we include HP [Hunter's Point] or Potrero Hill?" she asked frequently. Driven by her vision of media education, Sarah, a middle-aged white woman, poured a great deal of energy and excitement into this young organization that she co-founded. She was also working hard to turn a talent and passion into something financially sustainable. I was there in search of something as a researcher and a participant—an exploration of youth subjectivity and localized cultural production. I was also there out of friendship; Sarah had asked me to be involved with the project, knowing that I had grown interested in youth-produced media and had worked with youth professionally for several years. I sensed that Sarah thought that my black skin would help mediate the relationship between white instructor and racialized student producers in the project.

Through the process of working together, the polemics of collaboration and production in youth-based media organizations and the peculiarity of video as a medium for documenting the subject's "real" experience of the world surfaced as crucial issues for me. For media arts organizations, video is an effective tool for attracting and securing funding because it demonstrates to funders quite tangibly the process of youth learning and expressing themselves visually. Collaborative video projects produce for the organizations, funders, and participants alike a visual document—a product—that outlives the process of temporary collaborations. This visual document stands in not only for the process itself, but also for the lived experiences of youth represented. Thus, the product acquires value as an object that captures the realness of youth's experiences as authentic and distinct from mass-mediated representations. Similar to MEC, many youth media organizations are entrenched in the production of culture and the promotion of visual media as community-based practices. On a fundamental level, the artists/educators and youth producers work to produce "community" visually through the projects. The implications of production with regard to these organizations' work are rich. To produce means to give something form and shape; to make an idea into a product; to create a relationship through the product. Production implies both a performance and labor process. It has material ramifications. Media arts organizations' work with youth demonstrates that youth can produce, that they are productive in the face of anti-youth legislation in the United States and a public discourse of youth as terror.[6] To provide a highly structured and planned format for cultural production is at the most basic level what youth media organizations do routinely.

Understanding how the projects begin is crucial to understanding their role in cultural production and their engagement with representation. Most of the projects originate long before youth are recruited as producers and/or laborers. They take shape through the process of fundraising. During fundraising and developing community collaborations, the organizations, for the purpose of acquiring funds, begin to sculpt a narrative about the "youth producers" and the community with which it proposes to work. The grant narrative then produces and articulates the community in particular ways that, in many cases, frame the project as a combination of charity, community work, and art outreach. Ron Burnett, in his analysis of community video, problematizes the representation of "community" in these localized practices: "The often-expressed desire of video activists to bring the people in the communi-

ties they work with together for the purposes of change and social cohesion is situated in a concept of community that is both naïve and
untheorized. Aside from the difficulties of gaining access to the rather
complex and multilayered aspects of community life, the very notion of
community is based on a denial of difference and on a vague concept of
conflict resolution" (1996, 299). The notion of community within the
context of localized media practices often simplifies or denies differences among constituents of a neighborhood or group; in other words,
youth are often homogenized as either "the community" or its off-
spring, whereas in most instances, the artist often has no connection to
the community.[7] In the case of MEC, Sarah had been approached by
local Bay Area foundations with funds to work specifically with youth
from Mission District housing projects, which is why the project could
not adequately address Michelle's frustration about focusing solely on
this district. The participants who are brought in much later in the process typically do not have access to the grant narrative and the language
that produces the collaboration or the community. In essence, the par-
ticipant-producers rarely inform the structure that shapes the project's
narrative or have the ability to make significant changes to this structure.

While Sarah worked to create a workshop space where all voices were
heard and considered, the grant narrative had already laid the ground-
work for the project—a video that addressed the real issues that youth
in the Mission District face. Once the group size had settled we immediately moved into scripting a narrative about a racially mixed group of
youth who reflected the producers' backgrounds. Although the project
was intended for both young females and males and a few young men
attended the first two meetings, the youth who decided to participate
were all females. Sarah walked us through the stages of video production
(pre-production, production, post-production, distribution). After the
first two weeks of general introduction to the equipment, concepts of
production, and the principles of media literacy, we began to map out
the subject and structure of the project. The youth producers brainstormed several topics that interested them and eventually limited them
to four: juvenile justice, teen pregnancy, racism, and welfare/families in
poverty.[8] They chose these topics because they believed that these are
the most pressing issues for youth whom they knew.

After agreeing that each topic would receive a storyline in the video,
Sarah led the group in a series of exercises to turn their ideas into a
script. For example, each youth producer wrote a scenario for the four
topics. Once they completed the writing assignment and shared their
initial stories, Sarah and I facilitated a discussion about how to bring the
scenarios together into one story. The selection process and honing of
a preliminary script went on for several days amidst heated discussions.

In fighting for the legitimacy of a subplot, Michelle and Kathleen argued back and forth about how "real" the idea was. For example, Michelle wanted to include a confrontation in a corner store between a black youth and an immigrant store owner because, she argued, "That really happened." In the end, her scenario was incorporated into the script. The issue of realness continued to be a hotly contested topic for the producers throughout every phase of the project. Though selecting or more significantly abandoning plot ideas was a contentious issue for the group, the producers were in agreement about the style and structure of the project. They wanted the events to happen in "real time" and for the story to unfold in one cinematic day. The group agreed that the final piece should appear as one ordinary day in the lives of San Francisco teens. To underscore this purpose, the group agreed on a title suggested by Kathleen, *Mission Tales*.

Theorizing the Real

One week after the youth producers began crafting the final script, the conflict about representing the real climaxed. Working to create a subplot about racism and teen dating, Kathleen devised a story about an Asian American teenage girl who dates a young black male. The conflict centers on the teen and her mother, a first-generation immigrant who does not approve of her daughter dating interracially. Kathleen suggested that the daughter also have an African American female friend to reflect the diversity of San Francisco. Michelle, who felt uncomfortable with the story from its premise, argued that an Asian girl would not interact with a black one. The rest of the group tried to convince Michelle that her opinion did not represent that of everyone else. Michelle became angry and asserted, "You wouldn't see a Filipino hanging with a black and white girl and getting into a car with a nigga." The argument got louder and more emotional. Sarah and I threw nervous glances at each other about whether we should intervene. Finally, I said to Michelle that her experience did not speak for all youth in San Francisco. Exasperated, Michelle conceded to the inclusion but was angry and withdrew from the discussion temporarily. Her investment in her viewing position, her sense of narrative authority, and the politics of realness made it difficult to accept the other producers' visions and experiences of the city in which they all lived. For Michelle, her narrative of what is "true" and "real," therefore valuable, was more authentic than the narratives of the other group members; she struggled to claim solely the position from which the narrative is authorized. Michelle believed that anything that did not reflect her experience of racial politics cheapened the realist aesthetics of the group project, thereby undermining the reality represented in their video. Her comments also have a particular resonance in California where racial and ethnic demographics are drastically shifting. As black populations tend to shrink throughout the state, the number of Latinos, Asian Americans, and immigrants continues to grow. This transformation plays out in community practices in San Francisco where neighborhoods like the Mission District and the Tenderloin, heavily populated by Southeast Asian youth, tend to be targeted with programs and funds.

The drive to document the real or authentic experience of racially coded youth is complicated by the advent of new digital technologies and image manipulation software. At an important moment in digital technology's expansion of image-making possibility and visual manipulation, realness as a set of discursive practices to mark and identify certain marginalized bodies thrives within the practices of media arts organizations and within contemporary visual culture at large. Realness is a discursive strategy that attempts to collapse the distinction between the material world, visuality, and representation; in so doing, it attempts to mask its relationship with the real, by standing in as the real. It desires to reproduce an authentic experience of racial subjectivity, and in so doing it aims to abandon representation and mediation altogether.

Realness operates in relationship to representations of racialized youth on multiple levels: as a concept alluding to that which is the essence of reality; as an aesthetic style in black popular cultural production, namely hip-hop music and film; and as a set of visual tropes that constitute a particular racialized and gendered subject position. Realness has a troublesome history within the realm of black cultural theory and artistic practices. Black cultural scholars have critiqued the concepts of realness and authenticity within black popular culture as a reification of an essentialist notion of masculine black subjectivity that is both misogynistic and anti-gay (see Smith 1992; Hall 1996; and Harper 1996). Along these lines, critical race theorist Kendall Thomas problematizes the popularity of the discourse of realness in African American popular culture when he writes: "The discourse of authentic black identity has been increasingly accompanied by an authoritarian effort to impose its normative vision. The proponents of authenticity have fashioned a crude racialist litmus test to establish true 'blackness,' which African Americans for whom the organicist idea of a unitary racial identity is neither a necessary nor desirable predicate for progressive antiracist politics predictably fail to pass" (1997, 129). The limitations that Thomas sees in such a quest for authenticity are relevant to youth cultural practices, as well as the struggles of other minoritized groups. Thomas writes further that "the jargon of racial authenticity does not repudiate but instead reveals its reliance on the white supremacist logic from which it purports to declare its independence" (1997, 131). While racial authenticity has been used to call for collectivism among minoritized groups, the discourse ultimately supports normative power systems, specifically white male heterosexual power in the context of the United States.[9] Even more troubling, the reliance on realness and authenticity reduces racialized youth's capacity for cultural engagement to a "telling of their own stories."[10]

Paul Gilroy offers a reading of realness that places the concept within theories of performativity and ethnicity. He argues that, with regard to black expressive culture, "to be real" is not simply about the shortsidedness of essentialist narratives of the self. Instead, he sees it as a performative maneuver in the face of white oppression. Invoking the contingency of identity categories, Gilroy writes, "To be inauthentic is sometimes the best way to be real" (1995, 29). The fetish of the real in black culture has been appropriated by various nonblack youth cultures, primarily through the vehicle of hip-hop culture and music. Whereas "keeping it real," at one moment, referred to an identification with a particular shared (whether mythic or actual) black experience, it now also refers to a style that reacts against adult norms and codes of conduct in the United States. "To be real" or "to keep it real" within certain U.S. youth cultures serves as a validation of an experience outside of mainstream, white adult value systems. At the same time, the concept remains bound by the pursuit of an essence or aura of a specific identity category that is racialized and gendered in which blackness represents the ultimate referent of realness.

While realness as a discourse operates on symbolic, psychic, and material levels, it relies heavily on the conventions of realism to construct tropes in visual culture. Post-structuralist theorists have widely attacked realism as the dominant style of Western representation, arguing that its aesthetics, specifically through optical technologies, reinforce dominant power relations and mask the production process of representation (see MacCabe 1986). In the context of race and cinematic representation, Wahneema Lubiano writes, "Realism poses a fundamental, long-standing challenge for counter-hegemonic discourses, since realism, as a narrative form, enforces an authoritative perspective" (1996, 181). While realism purports a totalizing narrative, Lubiano theorizes that in its attempt at totality lies the tools for realism's undoing: "Realism establishes a claim to truth, but it also presents the ground for its own deconstruction" (1996, 182). Although realism is employed to represent dominant interests, it is not a closed representational system. Thus, space exists for subjects to disidentify with normative realist narratives. (For more on disidentification, see Munoz 1999; Juhasz 1995.)

The purpose of the MEC narrative was to disidentify with mass-mediated realist representations of racialized youth by re-presenting a realist narrative of youth produced by racialized youth. A combination of dramatic and documentary realism was the style that our group chose to create *Mission Tales*. The producers desired to create fictional youth characters who had to face "real" decisions familiar to other youth. With that in mind, the debate about realness in the MEC production workshops intensified during scene rehearsals, as the group prepared to shoot the project. Kathleen's mother, who is a theatrical facilitator and an educator, came in to help the producers through this process. In one scene from the script, there is a fight between two girls that takes place in a neighborhood housing project. Anita and Michelle, who were close friends and had spent much time outside of the workshop space planning the fight scene, were excited to rehearse it. The scene begins with Anita's character exchanging money with a neighbor for food stamps at her aunt's request. She then sees Michelle's character at the park. Having heard that Michelle's character has been talking "mess" about her, Anita's character confronts her and they fight in front of a group of youth.

During the rehearsal, Michelle attempted to direct and choreograph Anita's character. For example, she repeatedly told her to back up and to be more aggressive. Kathleen's mother tried to intervene and told Michelle to let the scene play out spontaneously. The rehearsal began to mirror the friendship between Anita and Michelle in which Michelle is the more outspoken one and makes decisions for both of them. They ran the scene several times with increased interruption and heightened frustration. Their fight rehearsal grew more heated during each run-through. Finally, as the rehearsal of a fight turned into an actual physical fight, play and reality were blurred. After a moment when everyone, except for Michelle and Anita, stood frozen—not quite sure of their level of engagement (wondering were they "really" fighting or just acting well)—Sarah, Kathleen, and I separated the two. Anita's face was bleeding and tears were in her eyes. She left the room with her head down, and Sarah asked Michelle what happened. Michelle breathed heavily and paced the room. She said that she could see Anita aiming to make contact with her and so she decided to hit her "for real." The seamless transition from a rehearsed, scripted fight to an actual fight underscores the operation of competing versions of what is "real" in the production process that questions the fixed discourse of realness. The fight between Michelle and Anita was the climax in the youth producers' struggle over the narrative about youth identity and whose experience is considered more valuable and authentic. Michelle's sense of disenfranchisement continued to brew and ultimately led to the confrontation. After the fight, her attendance and participation grew sporadic; by the time we reached post-production, she was no longer involved.

(Re)Producing Youth Narratives

Attention to personal experience often becomes the pedagogical method by which artistic practice merges with activism and tropes of "real" youth in many media arts collaborations. Youth participants, also embedded in the discourse of realness as a method of framing youth, consider the collaborative project as an opportunity to render their "real" experiences for an audience. Very often, youth media projects are interested in visually exploring what is perceived to be the extraordinary and everyday experience of racialized youth. Events based on one's personal experiences (particularly experiences that racialize and sexualize participants as outside normative, white adult culture) serve as potential scenes and storylines. Along with the incorporation of personal experience, youth media projects authenticate narratives by setting stories in sites considered to be places where youth gather or "hang out." The central milieu for representing racialized youth in visual culture is the post-industrial urban street. From fashion advertisement to news media to large budget films, youth are most familiar, most at home, on city streets (Hebdige 1979a; Kelley 1997b; Hall and Jefferson 1976; Willis 1990a, 1977). They are therefore naturalized as residents, or even possessors, of the streets. The location choices of *Mission Tales* underscored the street as the primary site for authenticating (racialized and working-class) youth.

The development of the corner store subplot in MEC's project is an example of the role of personal experience and setting in creating youth narratives. Early in the workshops, Michelle and Anita worked on a storyline about two black youth who experience discrimination as customers in a neighborhood corner store. The producers were interested in addressing the tensions in many ghettoized urban communities in the United States between Asian and Arab store owners and black residents. They based this plot on an actual experience, but were initially vague about whether they had experienced the discrimination or their friends had. Their reasoning for including this subplot was that it was based on an actual experience and that black youth commonly face such discrimination as consumers.

In mass-produced and community-based visual representations of urban youth, the corner store functions as an extension of the street—urban public space. Contemporary visual culture, particularly film and music videos, reproduces images of immigrant shop owners who are uncomfortable with or antagonistic toward black youth. The corner store often recurs as a contested zone where marginalized cultures clash. The Hughes brothers' critically acclaimed urban drama, *Menace II Society* (1993), most notably demonstrates the significance of the corner store as a symbol of tensions between different constituents of post-industrial urban communities in the United States.[11] In the film, O-Dog, a young black menace, kills two Korean immigrant store owners after the owners insult him. The recurrence of the corner store as a site to locate black youths' "real" experiences as one of conflict with older immigrant adults displaces the role of normative white power relations in marking both groups as Other through economic, geographic, educational, and other restrictions. In so doing, normative power relations remain unchallenged. Instead, racialization and the process of othering are located outside of whiteness and relocated within the contested zones of the "domestic other" and "immigrant other."[12] Michelle and Anita's storyline plays into the tropes of hostile immigrant store owner and unruly but victimized black youth; again, they justified their reliance on these tropes with the argument that the story was based on actual experience.

In *Mission Tales*, Taquan, a black youth, enters a corner store with his friend Darryl (who was scripted as black, but because of the difficulty finding someone to play this role, Kathleen's brother, also of Native American and North African descent, played the character). Taquan loiters around the store counter aimlessly looking at product displays, while his friend Darryl goes to the malt liquor cases at the back of the store. The actual owner of the store, Sal (who agreed both to let MEC use his store and to play a racist owner), watches Taquan suspiciously and seemingly ignores Darryl in the back of the store. Sal tells Taquan to get out of the store, "I'm sick and tired of you god-damn punks trying to steal." Darryl senses that trouble is brewing in the front of the store, and he runs to the front counter just as Taquan points a gun at Sal's head. (The story unfolds similarly in *Menace II Society*.) The frame then freezes and we are exposed to Taquan's thoughts through voice-over narration: "This punk ass Arab disrespecting me in front of my friend. I'm going to squash it because I don't want to go to jail. It ain't even worth it."

Though the youth producers of MEC did not make mention of films like *Menace II Society* explicitly in shaping their script, the familiar interactions and dialogue between Sal and Taquan refer to visual tropes of deviant black youth and racist immigrant owner. Even more significantly, the lines between Sal and Taquan are unscripted and unrehearsed. Instead, the nonactors playing Taquan and Sal were both aware of the opposition between the subject positions that they portrayed and the language that represented each position.[13] Sal refers to the trope of criminal blackness when he tells Taquan to leave his store. Taquan's deliberate racialization of Sal as an Arab (he pronounces it "Aye Rab") implies that racial groups exist in opposition to each other. In the scene from *Menace II Society*, O-Dog marks the shop owners as Other when he declares, "I hate ya'll." *Mission Tales,* in its unscripted scene, is more explicit in racializing minorities who are not black as "the Other" and as in opposition to the othered black youth. In both scenes, the store owners through posturing and language make it known that O-Dog and Taquan respectively are not welcome in these spaces and that the economic exchange is strictly out of necessity. The interactions in both cases set up a contest between who has relative economic power and property ownership and who has cultural and legal citizenship in contested racialized spaces of U.S. cities.[14] Yet, at the same time, the MEC producers attempt to disrupt the trope by allowing the spectator access to Taquan's thoughts and, most importantly, by stopping Taquan from enacting racial and xenophobic violence against the owner.

In developing the scene, Anita and Michelle made a very conscious choice to have Taquan walk away from the conflict. Michelle explained their reasoning during pre-production when Sarah, hesitant about the story line, warned the youth producers about playing into stereotypes unwittingly.

Sarah: We need to really be aware of the kind of images that we are creating, that doesn't play into stereotypes that we don't support.

Michelle: If I was going to keep it real, cause I know what you saying that we should have it positive, but if I was going to keep it real, in that story the dude, he would have stole something. [laughing] But we left that little stealing part out. He didn't shoot him, but we left the stealing part out. But I mean, I'm just telling you the truth. That would have happened.

Sarah: . . . We have to think already about what the audience is going to think about this stuff.

Their exchange demonstrates the ambivalence between portraying the "real" experience of youth and of local racial politics and constructing narratives that do not reify racialized youth as deviant and xenophobic and immigrants in the United States as racist toward black Americans. Most significantly, Michelle's response alludes to the blurring of the material real and representational real through an invocation of the discourse of realness. Michelle's statement that if she was going to "keep it real," then she would show some type of asocial or criminal act appears at odds with her earlier statement that the story should be included because it really happened and that it was based on real experience of youth as targets of discrimination. Although Michelle's use of "real" refers to actual lived experience in this case, it is steeped nonetheless in the privilege of authenticity. In other words, Michelle subjugates the actuality of experience to the realness of youth as victims of discrimination to further the producers' narrative. Anita, who agreed with Michelle's reasoning, exposed the basis of the storyline by telling the group about the actual experience that motivated the producers. Anita stated that Michelle and her friend were targeted by immigrant store owners because Michelle's friend attempted to steal from the store. In the final script, this level of complexity was not included in the plot. Furthermore, the producers changed the gender of the characters, so that the conflict would take place between a black male youth and a non-black store owner, as is commonly portrayed in popular media representations. Michelle's experience was altered for the script to match a narrative of black youth's experiences as one of perpetual discrimination and victimization.

Each of the story lines in *Mission Tales* moves toward a level of intervention by presenting voice-over narrations of their characters' thoughts at critical moments of decision making. The MEC producers, in trying to reflect the realness of youth's experience as closely as possible, decided to include statistics about youth violence, poverty, and teen pregnancy. The statistics, taken from official governmental sources, are presented at the end of the narrative over the faces of characters who represented the respective topic. For example, over Taquan's face, there is a gloomy statistic about the abuse of youth who are incarcerated in adult prisons. The youth producers unanimously chose statistics that framed youth as victims of violence, poverty, and oppression. The incorporation of statistics as factual evidence works to blur the boundary even more so between material reality and representation. While the video is quite consciously a docu-drama with fictional narratives, the use of statistics and ethnographic footage allude to a truth that is distinct from reality. Though the audience is aware that the characters are fictional and that the producers have constructed the situations, the ethnographic stylized footage and "scientific" facts express a certainty about the conditions of urban, racialized youth. Thus, the statistics in the final video evoke a disembodied and objective authority on the status of racialized youth, juxtaposed with the subjective nature of the youth narratives presented in *Mission Tales*.

Circulating the Authentic

During the editing process, the youth producers paired with adult technicians or supervisors and worked in shifts, using an AVID Media Composer, a broadcast standard digital editing system, in a suite at the West Coast Video Foundation. The goal in editing *Mission Tales* was to give each producer a level of autonomy in shaping scenes for the final video. In actuality, Kathleen was the most consistent about showing up for these tedious, and often boring, sessions. Thus, the final video reflected more closely her vision. The relationship between the youth producers and adult instructors/facilitators also changed during this phase. Most significantly, Sarah had to leave town during post-production and had no hand in shaping the editing; another MEC instructor stepped into Sarah's position and I continued as an assistant and observer.

When the MEC summer collaboration was over and the final edits had been made on the video, the youth producers organized a large community screening that attracted hundreds of people, primarily youth and adults from other community organizations in the San Francisco Bay Area. The team of adult and youth volunteers who worked with the youth producers as cast and crew was also present. Kathleen made a speech about the process and presented flowers to Sarah and me. Though much of *Mission Tales* delves into intergenerational and interracial strife, the community screening, in which all participants were acknowledged, demonstrated how the project was a meaningful collaboration between various constituents of the Mission District and other San Francisco neighborhoods (from Sal, the corner store owner, to WCVF employees who agreed to play characters in the production, to Valencia Gardens, which allowed much of the project to be shot there).

In many instances, the circulation of youth media ceases with this type of community premiere and celebration. Yet, when videos do circulate beyond these screenings, the context of their distribution typically contributes to their authenticity as portraits of "real" experiences of urban youth. During the mid-1990s, youth-produced videos gained increasing circulation in museums, major film festivals, and other adult-oriented cultural events. Often, though, the videos' circulation within sanctioned spaces of art presentation reifies notions of realness, as the value of work is based on the authenticity of experience represented and the lack of sophistication of the production. Using John Fiske's concept of "video high" (highly produced, mass distributed) and "video low" (little technical expertise, considered more authentic), youth-produced videos circulate as "video low," or as unmediated access to the mind and experiences of racialized youth (1996). Unlike adult media productions, youth videos are not promoted by advertising the names of the producers but by advertising the realness of the production, the authenticity of experience represented, and the fetish of the category "youth." For example, recent exhibitions of youth-produced videos at the San Francisco Museum of Modern Art and at the Yerba Buena Center for the Arts had titles like *Keepin' It Reel* and *Extreme Teens* respectively.

The lack of attention and resources that are put into circulation and distribution complicates the fetishization of the product, that is, the video within the collaborative process of youth-adult art making. Once the product has been realized, it both gains and loses value. The final video stands to funders and publicity venues as proof of the success of the collaborative model and yet it may never be seen again in public circles. In some ways, the product experiences a death after its completion. While it often goes unstated that the future of the video project is a shelf life, the youth producers may have expectations that their tape will have the type of visibility of an MTV show or mass-produced film. Throughout the production of *Mission Tales*, Kathleen glowed with possibility about the life of the final video. When I interviewed her during the editing phase about her hopes for the project, she stated: "We're about to take the 1999 Sundance Festival. I'm not joking; they accept video . . . I'm planning on hopefully taking one of the awards for the Stockholm or the Amsterdam or the France Festival. No seriously, this video is about to lead into a career for me as a director slash actress. . . . The main reason why I did this project is cause I'm out of high school. I'm trying to find something to do as a career and I really think that this is going to lead me somewhere." While the video did not go nearly as far as Kathleen expected, she did, on her own accord, enter the project into several festivals. The Mill Valley Film Festival, located in the very wealthy and predominantly white region of Marin County in Northern California, accepted and screened *Mission Tales* in their youth shorts program. The video, however, became a source of controversy at the festival. *Mission Tales* was grouped in the children and youth media section of the festival, and therefore many parents brought their young children to the screening. The language, crime, and sexual references in the narrative offended several people in the audience who stated that it was inappropriate and should be removed from the lineup. Kathleen and the other producers interpreted the response as proof of the realness and effectiveness of their project. Given that the audience of the festival is primarily white, upper class, and suburban, for the youth producers, the parents' responses demonstrated how out of touch this audience was with the experiences of urban, working-class, racialized youth.

Due to the premature death of most of these videos, the product, the video resulting from the collaboration, is not the most lasting or successful component of media arts organizations. The power of such organizations rests in the possibilities that production creates. The process of making a video project *produces* relationships with others and the public sphere. The organizations ultimately underscore the necessity of youth being active and engaged in larger public discourses. On the one hand, youth media production offers an alternative to globalized, corporatized popular visual culture by emphasizing the significance and dynamism of localized cultural practices. The work of the organizations defies notions of youth as merely consumers or recipients of popular culture. On the other hand, producing videos in media arts collaborations in no way resolves the problem of realness in representations of racialized youth. In fact, the process of collaboration for our MEC group demonstrates how the struggle over resources and representational control is not simply resolved by giving tools of media production to minoritized groups.

The complexities of producing and distributing *Mission Tales* highlight the limitations of the discourse of realness in representing racialized youth on localized and transnational levels, for the two are inseparable. With regard to representations of racialized youth, the discourse of realness is at the center of ideologies of race and ethnicity in the United States. In the context of multiethnic, multi-linguistic U.S. urban centers, realness masks the systemic and structural forces that maintain social, economic, and political imbalances. It also limits the expressive possibilities of racialized youth and the cultural practices of other minoritized groups. Just as significantly, the discourse of realness with its overemphasis on "authentic blackness" simplifies the complexity of social groupings and interactions among youth and adults in the multiracial settings of the United States. By focusing on the hypervisibility of blackness as aesthetic, commercial, and rhetorical devices, realness makes invisible the social and economic forces, controlled by white, male transnational conglomerates, that simultaneously turn U.S. black youth into globalized marketing products (most notably through popular music, sports, and fashion) while systematically continuing the disenfranchisement of blacks and other racialized groups in the United States.

Chapter 10
Making Hard-Core Masculinity: Teenage Boys Playing House

Elisabeth Soep

The first thing you might notice in Aaron's mom's basement is an impressive collection of sports trophies displaying shiny figures frozen in athletic gestures. The poses on those pedestals are somehow both manly and delicate. On a Thursday night in the summer of 1998, Aaron and four buddies gathered amid the trophies while waiting for some pizza to arrive. World Wrestling Federation blared from the TV, and occasionally the guys interrupted what they were doing to comment on the match. "Hey, Mom, how was work?" Aaron asked, greeting his mom warmly when she showed up around eight o'clock. Mrs. Davis stuck around for a while and then headed upstairs to a chorus of "Thank you!" called after her by the guys; Aaron wasn't the only one who called her "Mom." At one point Johnnie started pulling unloaded pistols, toy rifles, and fake vampire blood out of his backpack. Everyone oohed and aahed. They poured iced tea into glasses to simulate whiskey and debated whether bread sticks would make believable cigars. Johnnie tried on various outfits, worrying for a moment that he might look stupid, and asking his friends what they thought, since there was no mirror in the basement. Keith borrowed one of my elastic hair bands and fastened his hair into a ponytail, teasing JR about how much he ate. Meanwhile, the whole group sucked down the powdery contents of pixie sticks as they prepared to make a movie.

The boys were African American (Aaron and Jason), Filipino American (JR and Keith), and Chinese American (Johnnie), and they occupied different locations within the American middle class.[1] These were close friends who attended an urban Bay Area parochial school, where they were juniors and seniors. The school accepted boys of "varying abilities" and promoted the "Christian values" of loving God, oneself, and others among a student population that was about 75 percent boys of color.[2] Catholic school students and drama club members by day, this particular group of boys spent many of their nights in Aaron's basement, shooting camcorder videos. Even when they didn't have money to buy tape stock, they would "keep [their] thinking going" by brainstorming ambitious plots and scenes they could never actually execute. "We were sober, basically," JR told me, recalling his high school years. "I felt really strongly back then about not drinking, not smoking. That was another thing we had together, another notch in our belt. . . . I think that's why we had time on our hands." Staying clean was a way these friends "stuck together" as well as a personal choice for JR. "Me, in this area, it's not commonly known for a Filipino to be acting," he said, "You're hanging around, being hard, drinking beer or whatever . . . Everyone else was drinking. And I was here, sober, doing what I love to do."

If JR describes his crowd as relatively unusual within his immediate context, a review of academic youth culture literature makes this scene seem like an absolute aberration. Predominant in that literature are images of young, urban, racialized males engaged in spectacular resistance, apathy, and risk (Kelly 2000). The "hearth and home" is usually described as a girls' space, where young females paint their nails, read magazines, and gossip their hearts out in bedrooms, kitchens, and other protected places (Griffin 1993). Masculinity, by contrast, is often depicted as "mobile" as well as magnified through performances that are publicly delinquent, or at least disruptive—boys acting out in class, partying at clubs and concerts, cruising streets in tricked-out cars, or loitering around street corners causing trouble. The idea that public and private spheres are clearly demarcated and gender coded has, of course, been widely critiqued in both cultural studies and sociolinguistic literature. Feminist theory rejects the traditional emphasis on "masculine public discourse," which obscures the extent to which men and boys, like and with their female counterparts, live, labor, and play within the domestic arena (Valentine, Skelton, and Chambers 1998, 16). Drawing on the work of Judith Butler, Debra Morris (2000, 310) contends that "gender eludes—slips over and through—somatic barriers, not to mention flimsy theoretical ones like the public-private distinction," and she argues that the shifting and overlapping relationship between "public culture and private fantasy" is powerful precisely because it makes "clear and univocal meaning" impossible (2000, 329). Feminist language scholars as well as those interested in masculinity in particular also regard with suspicion any suggestion that women and men are homogenous groups that occupy separate social geographies and display distinct discourse patterns. In recent years, there has been a growing body of work that considers the ways in which personal, intimate conversational styles, which in the past may have been associated with private relations, have entered the public domain, among and between female and male speakers (Fairclough 1989; Johnson and Finlay 1997).

Despite these important critiques of essentialist classifications of private and public domains as divided and clearly gendered, rarely do academic accounts reveal scenes of male youth of color reconfiguring private spaces, in particular through aesthetic labor (for example, see Cintron 1997 chapter 4 as exception). Where young men do appear in relation to aesthetics, they are often already publicly iconized—for example, as hip-hop artists—or engaged in the consumption or creative use of public culture—as protagonists within mass audiences, life-style trends, and market niches. Aaron and his crowd, by contrast, gathered inside his basement, bathroom, and garage to produce a no-budget movie, with an anticipated audience composed of the actors themselves, selected family members, friends, and potential love interests. Because their movie involved several shoot-outs, the confines of private space were necessary. It was nearing the end of what JR called the "era of gangster season" in major cities across the United States in the late 1990s. Youth homicides dominated the news, police were notoriously misrecognizing gang activity, and these boys were smart enough not to run around outside shooting at each other, even if some of their guns were toys, and the real ones were locked and unloaded. The realities of the risks faced, especially by young males of color, in public space drove these boys into private rooms. Besides, Aaron's mom gave them no choice: "Guns all stay in the house" was her parting instruction. Their movie-making itself, then, convoluted public and private domains of practice in some interesting ways. The process took place behind closed doors, outside official institutional purview, and yet the product was a public artifact, developed out of social relations and for an audience release.

The guys called themselves Hard-Core Productions, and they used the word "arsenal" to describe the collection of features and shorts they inserted into VCRs at parties when the conversation lagged. This particular movie was originally supposed to be a vampire film, but at the last minute, the group decided to create a narrative, called *The Gamble*, about a high-stakes card game. They brainstormed an overarching plotline, mapped out scenes, assigned character motivations, shot, edited, and titled the movie, all in the space of one night and early morning. The scenes they produced, and the characters they portrayed, while hyperbolic, were more in line with the literature that describes adolescent boy-culture than were the "real lives" of these young men engaged in creative play.

The Gamble: A Synopsis

Four smoking, swearing, hard-drinking, deep-voiced, mean, damaged, womanizing, criminal young men are playing the last poker game of their lives. One is a down-and-out Latino gambler in debt to a homicidal loan shark. There is a Rastafarian cocaine-user with a dangerous habit of embezzling cash from his supplier. The guy in the Chinese mafia needs money to bring his family to the United States, and the IRA-implicated escaped convict breaks out of jail by feigning illness and fleeing the prison's critical care unit. These stories emerge in the movie through flashbacks that insert themselves into the unfolding scene of the poker game, which serves as an organizing narrative device. The flashbacks are shot through with gory gun battles, fist and knife fights, car chases, and shouting matches. The poker game escalates with hostile intensity until it is revealed that one of the guys is wearing an FBI wire. How does it all end? In Aaron's words: "Big old shoot out. Has to be." That's how all the Hard-Core Productions end.

Imagined Scripts

The making of *The Gamble* was an exercise in imagination as a social practice—a process Arjun Appadurai (1996) characterizes as a way of experimenting with self-making. Appadurai argues that imagination is a driving force in globalization, contributing to the broader and growing body of work (compare, Cheah and Robbins 1998; Jameson and Miyoshi 1998; Ong 1999a) that emphasizes the cultural and emotional dimensions of globalization alongside and enmeshed within political-economic factors. Through encounters with media and experiences of migration, individuals can "re-script" their lives, Appadurai says, in relationship to opulent film stories, realist twenty-four-hour news programing, as well as the "ideoscapes" materializing within social circles and institutions; the media are a "prism" of possible lives through which people's lived experiences pass (Appadurai 1996). Appadurai's notion of "script," used metaphorically in his analysis, takes on concrete utility here as a way to understand episodes of interaction in the making of *The Gamble.* I use this notion of "scripting" to avoid speculating about the underlying unconscious desires driving individual actions and fantasies. National *imaginaries* and globalized *sensibilities* emerge in fleeting face-to-face encounters inside intimate spaces. Even "local happenings," like the all-night Hard-Core production analyzed here, are shaped by transnational media products, processes, and technologies (Gupta and Ferguson 1997b, 10, see also Clifford 1992). Aaron and his friends used relatively cheap media equipment (camcorders and VCRs) to introduce into their domestic space global narratives—about immigration, world politics, organized crime across national borders—to portray on screen. They also played out "real life" dreams of someday working in the entertainment industry and moving from basement to theater or cineplex. In the end, the fate of these dreams raises questions that echo critiques in the literature on cultural globalization, which suggest that the emancipatory potential of imagination as a liberated free space can be easily overstated in light of the processes that differentiate and limit the power and mobility of youth subjects (Cheah 1998; Ong 1999b, 11).

Youth culture constitutes an especially important site for analyzing the social practice of imagination. A persistent theme in popular and academic discourse about youth suggests that young people are the next generation on the vanguard of a more modernized, cosmopolitan future. Adults, in everyday life and as scholars, seem curious about the technological and interactive innovations of youth—their navigation of on-line friendship, command of popular culture repertoires, and new forms of political organizing that blend music, visual art, and activism. Yet very often, young people are seen as media consumers or literal migrants, leaving less accounted for those youth who experience globalization through cultural production as well as consumption, and not only in travel but also by staying home (Tomlinson 1999, 119).

Cultural studies scholarship offers an important tradition of describing and theorizing youth as *producers*. My argument integrates insights from these two fields of inquiry—globalization and youth culture studies—by considering the cultural production of gender, as it relates to race and labor, through the micro-analysis of face-to-face interaction, a focus that is often neglected in both bodies of literature. This analysis draws on sociolinguistic techniques, particularly those applied to the study of learning, style, gender, and race as interactive performance (Cameron 1998; Eckert 1998; Gutierrez 1994; Gutierrez, Rymes, and Larson 1995; Lee 2001; Tannock 1998, 1999), to analyze not abstract networks for information flows but unfolding face-to-face interactions among co-participants in joint production.[3] Young people use language literally to articulate their private play into symbolic realms of national and global ideologies and activities (Morley 2000). These articulations also link the contexts examined here to prospects for youth participation in aesthetic labor—a topic to which I turn in the final section of the chapter.

The Collaborative Production of Hard-Core Masculinity

In the content of their movie, the Hard-Core producers experimented with various gendered mass media tropes—especially those associated with action-movie blockblusters and legends, including Jet Li, Bruce Lee, and Francis Ford Coppola (all mentioned, among others, during *The Gamble* shoot). These scripts resonated with familiar references to sensationalized heterosexual masculinity, scenarios potentially both enabled and handicapped by the absence of real-life girls and out-queer boys in this homosocial arena for play and production. In my presence at least, no one challenged the group's reliance on film-making traditions based in dramatic masculine spectacle. And there were no females to play the forbidden lover, hardened wife, or sexy partner in crime. While *The Gamble* script did not call for female characters, in other Hard-Core Productions, the guys cross-dressed to play women's parts. Neither girl friends nor girls who were friends joined this "circle," this "brotherhood," in JR's words. It was strictly "fellas hanging around."

But there was also another kind of imaginary script at work within Hard-Core Productions. While the content of the producers' story displayed the kind of magnified masculinity familiar in both popular discourse and academic treatments of young male heterosexuality, their moment-to-moment interactions revealed a very different ideology— one coded in everyday life and scholarship as "feminine," characterized by intimacy, propriety, and intense collaboration (Cameron 1998; Eckert and McConnell-Ginet 1998; Eckert 1998; Goodwin 1998). This dimension of hard-core masculinity reveals the layering of scripts at work when boys (close friends who bond in real life over their pact to avoid drugs and alcohol) act like girls (modeling femininity produced within academic literature and popular ideology) in order to portray men (who swear, drink, and intimidate until they shoot each other to death).

Boys Only?

There were no girls in Hard-Core Productions. That does not mean females had no place in this group. I have already described how Mrs. Davis, Aaron's mom, moved in and out of the scene. JR called his girlfriend of eight months repeatedly throughout the night, talking to her in hushed, gentle tones. Johnnie mentioned that he and his girlfriend had just broken up, and Jason talked about wanting to borrow one movie from the "arsenal" to show his mom. Female characters made fleeting appearances through (often derogatory) references in *The Gamble*, for example, when one character is called a "pussy" for always talking about his "woman," or through the insult that Keith's ponytail made him look like a girl.

And then there was me, a twenty-eight-year-old (at the time) white woman with a tape recorder. My introduction to Hard-Core Productions grew out of a multiyear study of language and learning I had been conducting in nonschool sites for youth arts production.[4] That research included in-depth ethnographic fieldwork and discourse analysis within a community-based youth video project in which JR was a participant. He happened to mention at one point in my fieldwork that he and his friends made camcorder movies in their spare time, and I asked if I could join them to tape-record the next time they shot a film, as well as interview members of the group. *The Gamble* was the last film Hard-Core Productions made before the crew dispersed after graduating from high school.

My work with Hard-Core Productions was motivated, on some level, by a personal fascination with creative play among older children and teens, in part because of my own memories of afternoons spent performing beauty-product infomercials in front of the mirror with my girl friends well into high school. There was also probably a desire on my part to find acceptance within this group of talented young men of color at play. Nowhere was that desire more evident than in the transcript itself, where practically every time I opened my mouth I was trying to belong—laughing extra-heartily at their youth culture references and exaggerated impersonations of stiff white male characters; and offering my red pen (to draw a ghastly scar on JR's neck), my hair elastics (for Keith's ponytail), the forty-six dollars in my wallet (on loan for the poker pot), and one of my tape-machine wires (for the FBI tap, although I'm not sure how I would have recorded their discourse if they had said yes). When Aaron finally turned to me and said, "You know, I'm gonna need for you to cue the music," I felt enormously honored. I offered one plot suggestion that actually made its way into the final movie. And no more than forty-five minutes had passed before I asked if they wanted to use my *car* for a chase scene—a proposition the group was wise enough to decline.

As an adult researcher, I was animating my own gendered, racialized script, trying to be helpful, sounding a bit giggly, and acting not overly impressed—a strategy I had probably honed during my own teenage years. I was acting like a teenage girl to move among these teenage boys who acted like girls to portray men. None of these categories consolidated as essentialized identities; rather they operated as clusters of actions and encounters that get classified and coded, in academic literature and in everyday life, as gendered, sexualized, raced, and aged. The Hard-Core producers mostly ignored me, but then they occasionally shifted into a chivalrous, gentlemanly register—apologizing for swearing in my presence, repeatedly asking if I was okay, offering me a comfortable place to sit or a "nice cold refreshing beverage." My presence provided material for them to construct a masculinity that was, in real life, more "old school" than "hard-core."

The Soft Side of Hard-Core

Excerpt 1: Hella Hard-Core

Aaron: So check it out. I'm thinking it's gonna be like four dudes, just like hella hard-core. See what I'm saying?

JR: Okay. That's original. /Hard-core (laughing).
Jason: /Hard-core poker game (laughing).
JR: Hard-core!
Jason: Hard-core gangsters play poker.
JR: Ha ha! Hard-core gangsters playing poker (laughing).
Aaron: No no, check it out dude. They're gonna be like from all opposites ends of, you know what I'm saying?
JR: Oh, different gangsters, like different ethnicities.
Aaron: Maybe, maybe—Oh! /that's a good idea!
JR: /that's good, dude.
Aaron: That's a good, cuz then they could be like =
JR: =Yeah, exactly, you guys are playing together, like, I can play=
Aaron: =Awe, you could have Italian, /Latino
JR: /Yeah, exactly, Latino, Filipino, we gotta have Asian Islanders, yup=
Aaron: =Cool dude. There you go. And then what we'll do is, what I'm thinking is, the opening scene will be like chips, throwing it in or whatever. It'll be in that room over there, with that one light, see what I'm saying, so it'll be like hella dark=
JR: =Yeah, oh I feel you=
Aaron: =And then we'll have somebody zoom in on that one shot, and then we'll do like around of each face, hella serious, like (demonstrates stoic expression) and then I was thinking, we could have flash backs of each dude, see what I'm saying?
Jason: What will the flashbacks be about?
Aaron: I don't know. Like of them doing /some bad deed.
Jason: /Like why they're there?
Aaron: Yeah, or like why they're there=
JR: =How they got there.
Aaron: Why they need the money! How bout that?
JR: Boom!

Research on the relationship between gender and communication suggests that language contains stereotyped arrays of features and practices conventionally associated with gendered identities. Discourse styles marked by "nurturance, emotional expressivity, connectedness, sensitivity to others, and solidarity" are taken to index feminine stances, while so-called men's talk is conventionally associated with "toughness, lack of affect, competitiveness, independence, competence, hierarchy, control" (Eckert and McConnell-Ginet 1998, 485). Put crudely, a focus on maintaining relationships and "face" is seen as a female preoccupation, while using language to report and accomplish tasks is taken to index more masculine concerns. Specific discourse features mark these differences. For example, latching—indicated in the above transcript by the " = " sign, which signals no audible pause between conversational turns—reveals evidence of close attention and cooperation; latching is often most associated with communication among girls and women (Coates 1989, 1996). Simultaneous speech, marked in the transcript by a "/" at the point where two or more people start talking at once, is a second feature conventionally linked with a highly collaborative conversational style often attributed to female discourse (Coates 1997; Tannock 1998; see James and Clarke 1992 for critical review). Finally, format tying and "story-chaining," where speakers repeat and build on one another's contributions (both structural and substantive), create an environment where "ideas are felt to be group property rather than the property of a single speaker" (Cameron 1998, 277). Language scholars have clearly established that no simple or essential correspondence binds identity to communicative style (Johnson and Meinhof 1997, Ochs 1992). There is some indication in the sociolinguistic literature that young people in general, as compared to adults, are more likely to normalize overlapping, interruptive speech as an unmarked and unproblematic way to communicate among peers (Eder 1998), although the basic argument has prevailed, despite critiques (compare Goodwin 1998; Hewitt 1997), that boys pursue hierarchy and conflict, girls intimacy and solidarity.[5]

The high frequency of latching, simultaneous speech, and story-chaining characterizing the above excerpt and throughout the making of *The Gamble* unsettles that argument. Within the first six turns, speakers repeated "hard-core" six times, in a sense collectively ratifying Aaron's plot proposal while laughing at him and themselves for the predictability of this particular theme for a Hard-Core production. Excerpt 1 (*Hella Hard-Core*) tracked the elaboration of Aaron's vague idea, that the gangsters would come from "opposite ends of" somewhere, into a more specific premise of keying each character to an ethnicity and motivation inspired by a "bad deed." Questions ("What will the flashbacks be about?"), proposals ("like different ethnicities"), evaluations ("Oh, that's a good idea" and "Yeah, oh I feel you") came at rapid pace and propelled ideas across speakers and conversational turns. The interaction was highly collaborative in the sense that simultaneous talk was smoothly incorporated rather than regarded as interruption. Ideas migrated and evolved through interaction, and affectionate support emerged through explicit compliments and the more subtle affirmation of unmarked uptake. Throughout the night the producers jointly monitored just how hard-core each character was, insisting that the cop got to "beat up everybody," the Irish guy got to shoot the cop, the Latino guy didn't "go out like a sucker," and every flashback had a brutal fight scene. Hard-core-ness was a property of individual characters maintained by vigilant collaborative monitoring and the systematic elimination of weakness. Members of this group needed and supported one another by not allowing anyone's *character* to come off looking needy for support.

Comic Book Cells

The final line in this transcript excerpt—JR's "Boom!"—holds particular significance. The Hard-Core producers used expressions like "Boom!" "Swa Swa Swa!" and "Pow!" throughout the transcript, bursting into a sound-movement performance that looked like a live-action version of a comic book cell. Picture one of those graphic squares that barely contain clenched fists, colliding bodies, zig-zagged lines suggesting movement, capitalized words, and exclamation points. These moments of loud, energetic, overlapping talk usually came in response to a breakthrough in the group's scripting process—a solution that solved a problem in plot or character development. When an unpopular idea was proposed, silence and stillness, or else comments like "That's whack, dude!" or "Hell no!" replaced the comic book cells come-to-life (although in some cases these animated eruptions functioned as ridicule instead of ratification). Through high-volume, overlapping speech and improvised performance—episodes that were in many cases nearly impossible for me to transcribe—the boys acted out the scene under discussion, incorporating the new proposal. Because that scene typically involved some kind of physical or verbal assault, the explosion sounds seemed both to ratify an idea and to provide a platform for experimenting with possible lines and gestures for *The Gamble*'s main characters.

At one point in the scripting process, the group had to decide how to introduce some tension. JR suggested that one of the gamblers should find a wire-tap in a soda bottle. Before he could finish his thought, the others immediately started affirming and elaborating on this idea, talking loudly and all at once. Without any observable explicit direction, JR, Aaron, and Jason then simultaneously and energetically began acting out the scene when the card players discovered that someone among them was "in cahoots," making gunshot sounds, calling out bits of improvised dialogue, and falling to the floor in mock injury. Just a few minutes later, another "comic book cell" moment manifested itself when JR complained that having his character, Alessandro Lopez, defined by his gambling problem wasn't "hard-core" enough. "Ever owed a loan shark money?" Jason countered, and when JR admitted that you did have to be pretty hard-core to have a loan shark in your life, the group spontaneously erupted into a possible "flashback" scene showing

Lopez narrowly escaping his menacing bookie. "You know what, dude, you'll lose a finger, or something!" Aaron proposed, apparently providing further physical evidence for Lopez's hard-core status, and again they all burst into exaggerated enactments filled with sound effects and laughter. "All right, so that's cool," Aaron suddenly said in the midst of the flurry, and then they were serious again and resumed neat turn-taking sequences: "So the Latino's set, the Chinese guy's set. Um, who's the other guy?" Jason asked, and they moved on to the "Irish guy's" flashback narrative.

Excerpt 2: Screech!

Jason:	Okay, so for everybody we got the flashbacks. Except, okay, for the Irish guy, we gotta get from a prison, to a hospital, and then to an escape.
Aaron:	How does he fake the condition that he has? Does he take a pill or something?
Jason:	I know. Why don't we just cut to the hospital, we have a scene where the doctor's walking in /and that's
JR:	/And he's about to do surgery
Jason:	Yeah.
JR:	And then he =
Aaron:	= That'd be good! The doctor'd be like, okay "This ex-con is this this and that," no not "this ex-con," "this convict" or whatever =
Jason:	= "Convict 85342 is in for" = (said in deeper voice, acting out doctor)
JR:	= oh, "352 Stat!" (also acting out doctor line)
Jason:	"XXX[6] and he has a small problem and /he has a small problem that's" (still acting out the doctor line) =
Aaron:	/XXX whatever, "We're gonna have to cut" (speaking as the doctor)
Jason:	= "gonna require surgery" = (still in doctor character)
Aaron:	= Whatever, what happens is, "We're gonna have to cut" and be like, "I know we do. /Bah!" (shifts from the doctor role to acting out the convict jumping up from the gurney)
JR:	/(laughing, acting out) Oh, that's tight!
Jason:	/There you go!
Aaron:	/Be like, "Oh, no!" (acting out the doctor)
Jason:	/Like, "Why you have to be so XXX" (acting out the convict role)
JR:	"That means we have to do some surgery." Be like /"Ahhh!" (shifting from doctor to convict lunging at the doctor)

Aaron: /That might be where we use the cars, dude. See what I'm saying?

JR: Yeah. Oh, yeah, yeah!

Aaron: Screech! (very high pitched, like a sound effect) . . . Okay so let's go back to the Chinese one. What do we got?

Stuart Tannock (1998) noticed episodes of noisy, overlapping talk similar to these in his analysis of a group of youths collaboratively composing a brochure for a community-based organization. He used the term "swarming" to describe these instances, which are easy to dismiss as disruptive and off-task, or at best as benefiting primarily group cohesion, without contributing to the collaborative task at hand. But Tannock contended that these moments contained some of the most important substantive work accomplished by the young people coauthoring their agency's brochure. However, because heavily latched, jointly produced simultaneous speech has most commonly been associated with interactions among girls and women, and because Tannock's group of nine youths included seven girls, he hypothesized that gender might have been a factor in the frequency of swarming in his study. My analysis of Hard-Core Productions illustrates that girls are not the only ones who spontaneously swarm. In this case, young men generated cooperative talk genres by animating the boyish trope of the comic book cell, while producing manly themes of physical violence and other sundry "bad deeds" among hard-core criminals. Moments of swarming during the making of *The Gamble* contained the contradiction of hypermasculinized performances used to accomplish creative consensus—a principle conventionally associated with female styles of work and play, according to research literature and popular "language ideologies" (Schieffelin, Woolard, and Kroskrity 1998).

The layering of these scripts—one evident in the surface characters of *The Gamble*'s brutal gangsters, one apparent in the "comic book cells" punctuated by energetic gestures and sounds of explosion and violent contact, and one embedded in the structure of the guys' intimate collaborative interactions—creates an interpretive puzzle. I have argued that this group of clean-cut close friends used speech structures associated with girls to play hard-core men. There is something romantic about this finding that boys actually act more like (stereotypical) girls than one might think, based on the surface level of their creative products and processes. But there are ways that their mode of interaction might in fact be more, rather than less, conventionally gendering. Analyzing adolescent boys chatting while watching a basketball game, Deborah Cameron (1998) argued that young men used "feminine" discourse strategies, including collaborative speech and gossip, to reinforce a group's heterosexual solidarity in contrast to homosexual others. It is likewise possible to argue about Hard-Core Productions that these boys portrayed hard-core men to sustain sober friendships and creative activities without raising the specter of homoeroticism. Their roles as hardened criminals prone to violence created a convincing counterscript to their moment-to-moment interactions as boys immersed within intimate same-sex relationships and engaged in collaborative tasks that involved disclosure, vulnerability, and feeling. Hard-core among *The Gamble* characters derived from the card players' bad deeds. But for the makers of this movie, achieving hard-core was ultimately about sharing an emotional mood:

Excerpt 3: Don't you feel it?

JR:	Man, I got this intensity in me. For real.
Johnnie:	Don't you feel it? Isn't that cool?
JR:	I feel it.
Johnnie:	I feel it.
Jason:	Hella pumped, huh? It's all them pixie sticks.
JR:	No, I'm serious.

Racializing Hard-Core Imaginaries

The hard-core status of the criminal characters in *The Gamble* was revealed not only in their "bad deeds," but also in their down-and-out desperate circumstances—conditions quite different from the relative comfort of the lower-middle- and middle-class, college-bound boys producing the script, who wore neat uniforms to school and participated in student government. These criminal characters were also specifically racialized, linked with elaborate ethnic and national histories inscribed in *The Gamble* narrative through explicit collaborative planning and improvisation.

Excerpt 4: You're a Latino with a Gambling Problem

Aaron:	No, you're not a pimp (to JR, who has just proposed that story line for his character—laughter)
JR:	Drugs, then. Am I in a drug cartel, or something?
Jason:	No, you're a Latino with a gambling problem, trying to fix it by gambling.
JR:	Am I in a drug cartel, or do I have a problem with gambling?
Aaron:	What's he doing? What is he doing?
Jason:	He's a Latino with a gambling problem who's trying to fix it by gambling.

JR:	Because, think about it. Drugs and Latinos. Movies=
Jason:	=Don't even say it. /Don't even say it.
JR:	/Every single time.
Aaron:	So no drugs then.
JR:	No /drugs.
Jason:	/No drugs.
JR:	All right, you want me to be a gambler? An overexcessive gambler.
Jason:	/Yeah.
Aaron:	/There you go, and you owe a loan shark some money.
Jason:	You owe a loan shark some money, it's the only way you can get the money.
JR:	All right, I'll play a dorky Latino, like
Aaron:	/Nah nah
Jason:	/No no no.
Aaron:	Everybody's hard-core. Hard-core=
Jason:	=Hard-core=
JR:	=Hard-core . . .

Excerpt 5: He's an Asian Dude, Not a Retarded Person

Keith:	Where's my gun? Why don't I get a gun?
Jason:	Cuz you're Asian. You can't afford to get a gun.
Johnnie:	You don't get a gun.
Aaron:	What are you talking about, he don't get a gun? (all laughing, inaudible overlapping talk)
JR:	You get a sword, you get a sword. Yeah, you get a sword cuz he's Asian (all laughing). He'll come out with a sword during a gun fight, I'm telling you (all laughing and talking at once, acting out the scene).
Jason:	He's an Asian dude, not a retarded person . . .
Aaron:	He can have both, bro (all laughing). Aw, in his flashback, saucing up people—swa, swa, swa (demonstrating cutting through the air with an imaginary sword).

In the previous section, I showed how Hard-Core producers scripted hyperbolic masculinity, using speech marked by stereotyped features conventionally taken to index female discourse patterns, even as these young men acted out sounds and gestures that at times looked like boy-fantasy comic book cells come-to-life. There is a related point to be made here with respect to race. The boys created spectacular racialized characters within friendships that, in many ways, defied stereotypes and criss-crossed ethnic histories. *The Gamble* was populated by predictable and problematic characters—the Rastafarian drug addict, the down-and-out Latino, the stiff white guy. These perspectives were hardly critical or particularly nuanced. And yet Aaron vehemently rejected JR's suggestion that the character of Han Lee, the "Chinese guy," should speak with an extra-exaggerated Asian accent on the basis that, "Uh uh, dude . . . Ain't no stereotype stuff up in here dude. Come on now." JR balked: "Oh, you're tripping!" he exclaimed, laughing, and pointing to Keith's hairstyle and sword: "How can you say no stereotyping!"

To some extent this entire analysis, and the interactions cited throughout, center on the contradictory and ambivalent status of stereotyping embodied in this kind of exchange. Evident in the prior two excerpts is a certain degree of reflexivity on the subject of race— particularly around the character whose race was not actually represented among members of the group. In Excerpt 4 (*You're a Latino with a Gambling Problem*), the conversation surrounding "Alessandro Lopez's" possible connection to drugs is interesting in the degree of truncation marking the key moment where a decision is made: "Think about it. Drugs and Latinos. Movies/Don't even say it./Every single time./So no drugs then." The boys did not need to spell out to one another their concern. A kind of critical, partially tacit mode of communication enabled them to arrive upon a course of action that avoided the predictable images they see in the movies. But that is not to say they rejected stereotyping altogether, whether it was the Chinese guy pulling out a sword in the middle of a gunfight, or the white cop (but notably *not* the more explicitly nationalized and "foreign" Irish escaped convict) playing something of a buffoon—although of course that cop was the kind of buffoon who got to bust someone up in every single flashback scene, and in this sense a generalized male hard-core-ness trumped race as a guiding imaginative principle.

Race in these scenes was considerably more hyperbolic, whether through serious narrative or "comic relief," than were the interactions among the actual young men producing this "Rainbow Coalition poker game," as Johnnie called the movie at one point during the night. In describing his group of friends, JR told me that when they were just hanging around, or shooting footage that would be "for our eyes only," they would "do anything"—Jason would give him a hard time about "Filipino things," and JR would start prancing around saying, "Yeah, I'm a hard-core gangster, walking around the 'hood . . ." To some extent cartoonish racialized images made their way into the Hard-Core scripts as well, although in the editing phase they would cut out passages that they thought might cause offense. While race was a site of humor among these young men as friends and producers, then, these same categories were also sources of a kind of heroism that amplified the script's hard-core masculinity. It is not surprising, given taken-for-granted U.S. ideolo-

gies, that a narrative structure based on four parallel racialized histories—where the short-hand for individual characters was to call them
"the Irish guy," "the Rasta guy," "the Latino guy," and so on—would
lend itself so easily, so naturally, to this particular experiment in self-
and movie-making. Members of this group had resources within their
own relationships and experiences to tell more complex, overlapping
racialized narratives, where characters might be connected in ways that
went beyond a single, life-and-death poker game. However, it would be
highly problematic to look to these movies for some kind of sociological
"truth effect," as is so often the case in criticism directed toward visual
culture produced by artists of color (K. Jones 2002). Glimpses of reflexivity were evident in their scripting processes—when they poked fun of
themselves for the lengths to which they would go to make every character indisputably hard-core, or when they explicitly countered mainstream media treatments of racialized individuals and groups. These
moments contained the seeds for a critique of biased representations
and structural inequalities with respect to gender and race (although
there was no indication, in my presence, of a specific critique of class).[7]
Yet the blockbuster movie industry (led largely by white, male heads of
multinational corporations) also entered this basement space, by providing a vocabulary for hyper-masculine accomplishments and spectacular
racialized tropes (see Fleetwood, this volume). In this sense, the boys'
camcorder-mediated imaginaries were "glocalized," drawing on local,
national, and international information, beliefs, and rituals (García
Canclini 2001, 59). And perhaps it was this particular meeting of transnational industries and intimate interactions that inflected the boys'
moment-to-moment discourse with a kind of "official language," which
laid down a "dividing line between the thinkable and the unthinkable,
thereby contributing towards the maintenance of the symbolic order
from which it draws its authority . . . through which the group teaches
itself and conceals from itself its own truth" (Bourdieu 1972, 21–22).
Analyzing collaborative youth cultural production in a different context,
that of graffiti, Cintron (1997 and this volume) argues that nationalistic
themes provide a "topos" for story-making, lending a heroic narrative
to graffiti writers and artists. Here race intersected with gender and class
to provide a "topos" for narrating hard-core gangsters on screen, while
the actual relationships and moment-to-moment interactions that generated those screen images in many ways contradicted the content contained in the group's finished product.

Implications for Youth Culture Studies and Aesthetic Economies

While young people do not figure centrally in Appadurai's analysis of
the cultural dimensions of globalization, he does consider their active

media consumption practices when he suggests that cinematic genres such as martial arts films are "reformulated to meet the fantasies of contemporary . . . youth populations" who "create new cultures of masculinity and violence, which are in turn the fuel for increased violence in national and international politics" (1996, 41). Appadurai's notion of imagination as social practice has been useful in this study of collaborative cultural production among youth, as it provides a context for looking "sub-locally," at the level of micro-analysis, to reveal ideologies that are massive in scale. But his statement about youth media consumption, with its familiar linking of youth culture and deviant masculinity, falls short of accounting for the activities of groups such as Hard-Core Productions. These boys certainly reformulated film genres including martial arts (or what JR called "kung fu"). They experimented with cultures of masculinity and violence. But the political significance of their activities is more nuanced than a simple promotion of increased national and international violence. National and global narratives as "topos" for heroic storytelling factored in *The Gamble* script, and to some extent in the lives of the writers/actors/producers. But these young people experimented with tropes of sensationalized masculinity and violence—through scripted narratives and comic book enactments—while animating scenes of intimacy, collaboration, and heightened emotion. These scenes are often taken to index female language ideologies and located within the so-called feminine spaces of privacy and home. And yet the analysis offered here erodes the imaginary walls that in fact fail to "protect" private spaces as sanctuaries from national ideologies and media industries, even when youth are producing their "own" visual cultures.

Textual analyses of mass media products have found a similar mixing of male- and female-coded performance. In her study of formal dimensions within John Woo's Hong Kong films, Gates (2002) argues that Woo's films are widely regarded as action movies—a genre associated with male audiences. Yet reviews of the films evoke melodrama—a genre associated with female audiences. Gates says reading melodrama into the action of Woo's films is possible because of the pathos and intense emotionality of his stories, which feature "moments of excess in mis-en-scene, emotion, music, and gesture" (2002, 61). This is not a matter of emotion alongside or in spite of the violent action, says Gates, but rather melodrama through "defiantly unrealistic" or hyperbolic brutality: "In each film there is a juxtaposition of the apparent hypermasculinity at the surface of the text and the suggestions of vulnerability, emasculation, and homoeroticism revealed through moments of melodramatic excess" (2002, 62). Melodrama is deployed in the "unreality" of the action and violence, and through the "exploration into male emotionality beyond heterosexual coupling" (2002, 71). Like Woo's body of work,

Hard-Core productions contain layers of gendered juxtapositions. But here the excess comes not only in the formal features of *The Gamble* as a movie, but especially in the interactive dimensions of this *context for making*. While scholars interested in cultural studies and globalization tend to posit youth as media consumers or study the textualities of products aimed at teen markets, here the actual networks of moment-to-moment communication behind youth-produced media come into focus. This concrete interactive work produces its own spaces of excess, as evident in the vulnerability, emotionality, and spirit of collaboration marking the boys' communication, operating against the grain of the highly stereotyped performances surfacing in their script. While Gates reads emasculation into Woo's movies, it is also possible to argue that the young men in Aaron's basement were simply "masculating" in a way that depended on feminine excess as well as homosocial practice, where any overt indicators of eroticism were suppressed behind the spectacle of hard-core performance.

While the boys of Hard-Core Productions describe their movie-making marathons as "high jinks" and "hanging around," they also took this work seriously, as a way to practice the kind of aesthetic labor they someday hoped to do for real, and for pay. New academic insights within cultural studies coupled with changing economic realities make it no longer viable to frame leisure simply as an escape from labor (Ball, Maguire, and MacRae 2000). It is increasingly common for community-based youth projects to frame their goals not only in terms of "positive recreation" or "youth development" but also by offering themselves up as sites for social entrepreneurship and neighborhood economic revitalization (see Heath 2000). Robin Kelley (1997a, 45) shows how some youth, not always working within official organizations, see athletics and hip-hop as possible ways to turn aesthetic labor into "cold hard cash." These arenas provide young people "with a wider range of options for survival, space for creative expression, and at least a modicum of control over their own labor," says Kelley, as they frame profit not only in terms of monetary gain but also through "the visceral pleasures of the form, the aesthetic quality of the product, the victory, the praise" (1997a, 75).

The potential conflation of leisure and labor is hardly new, nor is it necessarily radical or countercapitalist. What is striking is how this possibility can take shape through relatively inexpensive technologies, within private spaces, and embedded within often contradictory scripts related to gender, race, and labor. On the streets, a movie producer might punch out e-mails on a PDA and talk into a microphone dangling from an ear-plug on a thin chord. This is one kind of aesthetic labor in motion. And yet labor is also happening around a makeshift table the producer might pass on the street, where a seventeen-year-old girl might be selling hand-sewn skull caps or imported toe-rings. And labor is happening behind closed doors, where kids are designing videogames online at family computers, or perfecting makeup application techniques in bathrooms, or making movies in the basement. "Subcultures stand at one end of the culture industry spectrum and the glamorous world of the star system and the entertainment business at the other," says McRobbie (1994, 162), in her discussion of the possibility for youth cultures to commercialize their activities without necessarily "selling out" in the old-school sense of the term.

It seems that JR and his crowd plotted their own activities somewhere within that spectrum. JR told me he saw Hard-Core Productions not only as a way to "kick it together," but also as an "environment" for learning, since none of the boys had experience working on "real films." And in this sense their basement studio was more than a subterranean private room or "space of belonging" (Morley 2000, 4). It was also a place of just plain longing for a future in the entertainment industry with public recognition. The longing was not, according to JR, to be more like the hard-core gamblers the boys portrayed: "It's a character. I mean, it's not something that I want to do," he told me, rolling his eyes and asking with a smile if I'd ever heard of *method acting* when I suggested that some people might say the boys made these hyperbolic movies as an excuse to act tough and hard. The longing was, rather, based in the inaccessibility of *realistic* roles in the movie business. Every other bagger and checker and cashier in low-paid jobs where youth dominate the labor force wants to find work as a music producer or actor or some other sexy occupation (Tannock 2002). And yet the reality is that few will land well-compensated, emotionally rewarding, and nonexploitative (on some level) positions in any field, let alone the global entertainment industry. When I interviewed JR four years after he and his friends made *The Gamble,* he was attending a state university and working as a production assistant and emcee for on-campus performances. At the same time he was looking for office work to pay bills and tuition. Aaron was going to college in New York: "Last I heard," JR said, "he was about to get a show, a one-man show on Broadway. Yeah, this guy is crazy . . . The last e-mail I received, he goes, 'Someone wants to take my show.' He wrote a show. This man is either gonna be on Broadway or on film," JR told me, "and I'm gonna be able to say, 'that's my friend.'" So long as opportunities to translate aesthetic labor into "cold hard cash" are as limited and unevenly distributed as they are, Aaron just might get to play the hero in this unfolding script, but most young people will be in the audience with JR, already nostalgic for trusted collaborators, and still plotting pathways to the stage.

Chapter 11
Bad Boys: Abstractions of Difference and the Politics of Youth "Deviance"

Todd R. Ramlow

As in common homophobic discourse, the object of devaluation and intolerance in discourses of disability is seemingly erased in the phobic utterance. Phrases like "That's so gay" and "That's retarded" are used colloquially to indicate that an object or event is senseless or silly. These speech acts become so routinely abstracted that those who perform and witness them lose sight of the real gay and disabled people whose very lives are overcoded with negative social and individual value by such idiomatic usage. There is, then, a metaphorics to the discourses and social processes of both "erotophobia" and "stigmaphobia" in which word and meaning become abstracted from or divested of the object to which they originally adhered (Patton 1985; Goffman 1986).[1]

The most obvious recent example of the abstraction of erotophobia is found in the lyrics of the rapper Eminem, who has been assailed for his repeated use of the term faggot and the often vicious misogyny of his music. Eminem has attempted to defend and distance himself from overt hatred of gays by claiming that for him, fag or faggot does not necessarily mean "gay" or even "homosexual" but is a term of disempowerment, used to refute the masculinity of an adversary.[2] Eminem's defense, however, fails to acknowledge that his sense of the term as demasculinizing precisely reinforces the stereotype of the "effeminate" gay man. Of course, this is nothing new, and the disciplinary connections among gender "inappropriateness" in men, homosexuality, and social exclusion have a rich history.

Speaking about his youth in Harlem and his own constellation of race, gender, and sexuality, James Baldwin (2001) remarks: "The condition that is now called gay was then called queer. The operative word was faggot and, later, pussy, but those epithets really had nothing to do with the question of sexual preference: You were being told simply that you had no balls" (211). Baldwin is a little disingenuous; certainly, he understood how these emasculating epithets connect to structural racism and sexism, which often cast black and/or homosexual males as "boys," or "quasi-women," that is, as passive and less than men. Baldwin's remark, however, attests to the persistence of discursive investments in erotophobia that mask or displace the object of social scorn and shame. Being called a "faggot," a "pussy," or "gay," then, is not always or overtly about the material fact of sexual difference or same-sex relations; it is about the failures of heteronormative masculinity. Or so dominant cultural logic (and self-justification) would have us believe.

But there is another displacement in the debates and scandals surrounding Eminem. When "we" criticize him for his misogyny and homophobia, what is less directly expressed are dominant cultural anxieties over perceived crises of racial and class mobility, which are displaced onto concerns over a seemingly pathological white masculinity. Still more displacements are made in the accusation that Eminem contributes to the corruption of American youth; common cultural concerns over the state of today's youngsters are rarely about real teens and their problems but, rather, are about perceived threats to a normative social order. Jonah Goldberg's (1995, 55) assertion that "among the few things that Americans seem to agree on these days is that our children are in trouble" indexes these displacements without specifying who this "we" is, or how and why we agree on the troubled nature of our youth, and demonstrates how naturalized these discursive investments have become.

In this essay I examine precisely these sorts of displacements, but I add the dimension of disability to questions of physical, racial, and sexual difference and demonstrate how disability complements and complicates discursive investments in structural segregation. Focusing my analysis on youth as the site of specific cultural panics and crises over masculinity and race suggests, further, how discursive abstractions of queerness and disability intersect with gender, race, and class to compose a hegemonic formation of cultural aberrancy and social exclusion. The crises of youth deviance that I examine here, and that are expressed in the debates about Eminem, in the wake of the shootings at Columbine High School in Littleton, Colorado, and in popular culture in *Boyz N the Hood* (1991) and *Kids* (1995), circulate metaphors of disability and queerness to manage the "threat" of a non-normative heterosexual masculinity that is tied to questions of racial and class mobility.

It is odd that as a culture we have been so enraged by Eminem, a white-boy rapper, when his genre of popular music has been consistently homophobic and misogynist for years. While there has been plenty of cultural criticism about gangsta rap and specific black rappers in the past, few of the controversies caused by them have reached the level of national panic that Eminem has created. This is a situation of which Eminem himself is keenly aware and which he addresses in the song "White America," off his most recent album, *The Eminem Show*. To attack black rappers for "inappropriate" lyrical content or for sexism and homophobia, I suggest, not only would be "culturally insensitive" but would require both a much broader analysis of the structural inequalities that have produced these prejudices in America and an open admission of white America's continuing complicity in racial oppression.

This is an analysis to which as a nation we remain most resistant. We can attack Eminem, however, for on some level, if only on the surface level of his skin, he is "white," even if his status as such is complicated by his own upbringing and class. Yet the controversy over Eminem is not merely sustained by our cultural reluctance to consider our own role in systemic injustice; it is driven by anxieties about shifting social relations and increasing racial and class mobility. While gangsta rap threatened mainstream America from the cultural margins for years, it was not until it had moved from the margins to the center of popular culture, as the immense popularity of Eminem shows, that it directly concerned white America. Once gangsta rap had moved from the inner cities to the suburbs, to white middle-class teenagers' bedrooms, the genre, embodied in the spectacular whiteness of Eminem, became the site of national panic and ideological concern.

So the crisis signaled by Eminem is not so much about vulgar language, homophobia, and sexism as it is about the increasing prevalence of black cultural forms in U.S. mass media and the economic and social mobility of black America. To attack P. Diddy or Jay-Z or Lil' Kim for flossin' their ice or "not knowing their place" would be overtly racist, so instead we attack Eminem for his "inappropriate" language and behavior and for "corrupting" the (white) youth of America.

The displacement of racial and class anxieties into the policing of Eminem's homophobia and misogyny is further complicated by his performance of a normatively understood pathological masculinity. In his performances Eminem strikes the gangsta pose that is, Brent Staples (1994) argues, a unique manifestation of masculinity in response to the ongoing history of racism and oppression in America. In this case, the social and historical devaluation of black men has worked to produce a comportment of masculinity in opposition to the traditional infantilization and emasculation of racism.[3] This pose has produced a panic in the dominant culture precisely because it exceeds (or perhaps points up what we all already knew to be) traditional, heteronormative associations of masculinity with aggressiveness and the potential for violence.

So in the controversies over Eminem we find a number of displacements, all of them filtered through discursive investments in erotophobia. When we talk about Eminem's homophobia and misogyny, what we really express are cultural anxieties about the increasing social, economic, and political mobility of racial minorities. Furthermore, this threat is not confined to the material realm but verges on entering the more abstract realm of identity. As Eminem's gangsta pose and performance demonstrate, on some level blackness is contagious and threatens the normative coherence of white masculinity.

These metaphoric abstractions of difference in dominant social and ideological discourses have come under criticism by scholars and activists in disability studies and queer theory. My focus on these abstractions is in no way meant to ignore this politically important work; rather, it suggests that we need to consider more carefully how these erasures of identity and materiality constitute the very limits of social inclusion. Recognizing that disability and queerness have metaphoric lives in excess of "real" physical and/or sexual difference does not mean that those abstractions cease to organize social life. The analysis of the "use of disability [and queerness] as a metaphor for social conflict" is of real urgency for disability studies and queer theory if we are to understand how our bodies and identities are made to do social and political work that seems to have little or nothing to do with us (Snyder and Mitchell 2001). While "scholars and activists have demonstrated that disability is socially constructed to serve certain ends," which is equally true of queerness, it still "behooves us to demonstrate how knowledge about disability [and queerness] is socially produced to uphold existing practices" (Linton 1998). What concerns me here, then, is how knowledge about disability and queerness as marks of cultural disqualification is (re)produced in and around the cultural category of youth and in moral panics over contemporary youth and its deviance. This knowledge has little to do with the real lives or sociopolitical status of youth today, just as it has little to do with the materiality of disability or queerness; instead, it seeks to "uphold existing practices" of social segregation and the organization of U.S. culture according to dominant racial and gender regimes.[4]

When I refer to "disabled" and "disabling" youth in this essay, I use the terms in their dominant cultural and ideological senses. While I refrain from placing them in scare quotes, they should always be read in the context of this exclusionary logic. Disabling youth, for example, has nothing to do with Simi Linton's deft "claiming disability," which is a destabilization of dominant understandings of and paranoia over what it means to claim disability and, at the same time, a resignification of the term disability as a site of critical intervention into ableist discourse.

Similar to the queering of queer, the claiming of disability redefines a term of social exclusion, staking a claim to community, identity, and the reorganization of social life.[5] Instead, disabled and disabling, as I use them in and around the category of youth, reflect only dominant cultural logics of disqualification and exclusion, which perceive disability as having only negative social value and as something to be pitied, policed, or overcome (Clare 2001).[6] My use of the terms disabled and disabling draws attention to their function in the normative organization of society and their circumscribed usage by dominant ideologies; it does not uncritically and unselfconsciously reassert the "natural" understanding of the terms as having negative, exclusionary power.

Similar rhetorical strategies animate my use of erotophobia and stigmaphobia, although perhaps in the opposite direction. Rather than confine the discursive investments of social normativity in physical and sexual difference to homophobia and ableism, I expand those terms to erotophobia and stigmaphobia to draw attention to the many markers of identity that social exclusion comprises. The terms are deliberately wide-ranging, suggesting the many ways that individuals, identities, and communities can "find themselves at odds with straight culture" (which I would reterm dominant culture) (Warner 2000, 38).

Cindy Patton (1985, 103) defines erotophobia as "the terrifying, irrational reaction to the erotic which makes individuals and society vulnerable to psychological and social control in cultures where pleasure is strictly categorized and regulated." Erotophobia is a disciplinary regime that manages and sorts individuals and identity by regulating pleasure and sexuality; it is not limited to the usual associations of homophobia with same-sex desire, identity, and pleasure.[7]

Similarly, stigmaphobia extends the reach and disciplinarity of ableism, so that the marks of physical difference on which social exclusion is based, while often filtered through the representation and materiality of physical disability, are not limited to them. The terms of social and political disqualification register simultaneously across multiple boundaries of identity. Queer theorists and disability studies scholars alike have noted how injunctions to normativity through race, class, ethnicity, sexuality, gender, and physical ability share modes of discursive investment and practices of exclusion (see Warner 2000, 28; Snyder and Mitchell 2000, 2; Garland-Thomson 1997, 6). Stigmaphobia draws attention to the various ways in which bodies, individuals, and identities can be marked as different and to how various stigmas associated in dominant logic with race, class, sexuality, gender, and physical ability operate simultaneously to reconstruct a normative social order.

In what follows I first consider how discourses of race, disability, and queerness function together in regimes of power to determine bases of social and cultural disqualification. Next I consider how the culturally constructed category of youth is a particularly impacted site on which these social anxieties and crises are played out. Finally, through an analysis of specific youth crises and controversies (post-Columbine media coverage and the films *Boyz N the Hood* and *Kids*), I demonstrate how this system of disqualification circulates in popular culture and around youth over time and how social and political metaphors of exclusion are caught up in dominant discourses of queerness and disability.

Social Isolation and the Erasure of Material Differences

In my example of the cultural crises surrounding Eminem, what I hope to have highlighted is how dominant discourses displace their own objects of concern, so when we appear to be talking about one thing, we are really talking about something else. In caviling over Eminem's misogyny, homophobia, and corruption of youth, we really express cultural anxieties about racial mobility and masculinity. This discursive sleight of hand is accomplished first and foremost by paving over, masking, or displacing the materiality of difference (whether physical, racial, or sexual) so that, metaphorically, the category becomes dissociated from identity and specific words or terms are "naturally" presumed to resonate across social and political boundaries.[8]

Just so, disability studies scholars have demonstrated how dominant discourses of disability have functioned historically to sort human beings and physical differences for social and political purposes. In *Claiming Disability* Linton (1998, 6) points out "the mechanisms by which disability is covered over, layered with meaning and rendered invisible." The materiality of disability is often erased to justify the heteronormative, racist, and ableist organization of society. Dominant discourses of disability have functioned in excess of the physical embodiment and experience of disability and, as master tropes of social exclusion, have "rationalized cultural segregation."[9]

Far from limited to the discursive regime of disability, this "metaphoric vitality" is common in various (if not all) discourses of social exclusion and difference. These abstractions are carried out not only through the radical dissociation of category or identity from embodiment but through an individuation and isolation that rejects anything but singularity and specificity. Marks of social difference or "deviance" are isolated so they may make no appeal to community or belonging; their very singularity is the basis of their abstraction.

This individuation and isolation of physical, racial, and sexual difference has been experienced historically by people with disabilities, queers, and racial minorities in America as the disavowal of the dominant culture's responsibility for the disciplining of difference. In the past this individuation justified the confinement of disability to the purview of institutional medicine and had wide-ranging social repercussions. It attempted to "keep [disability] a personal matter and 'treat' the condition and the person with the condition rather than 'treating' the social processes and policies that constrict disabled people's lives" (Linton 1998, 11). This reliance on the individual as the site of difference and deviance has a similar history in racist discourse, which habitually imagines black men, women, and communities as distinct and separate from a normative America. "The idea that there are discrete black communities, beset by black problems, which can and should be solved exclusively by black people taking responsibility for themselves, is precisely the logic of segregation, no matter how empowered individual black people may feel in the process of its articulation" (Reid-Pharr 2001, 264). Specific differences, whether racial, physical, or sexual, are idiosyncratic problems that must be dealt with by the individual or subculture—an imperative that attempts to cover over the dominant culture's involvement in the processes and policies that segregate social life.

Thus various cultural discourses of difference and intolerance abstract those differences, make their status as social disqualifiers seem natural, and, at the same time, individuate those differences so that the dominant culture can remain blissfully (or willfully) ignorant of its own role in social segregation. These discourses do not operate in isolation but intersect with and influence each other and continually redefine the bases of cultural exclusion. The "metaphoric vitality" of queerness and disability, in particular, functions in and around the cultural categories of youth and youth "deviance" to manage, through displacement, certain cultural anxieties about the future of the social and certain perceived crises of masculinity and racial mobility.

How race, class, gender, and various sexual and physical embodiments intermingle with and complicate the truth claims of queer theory and disability studies has been carefully considered by each discipline; the part that age plays, however, has not. Age is, of course, a numerical fact; it is a matter of lived years. But it is also a cultural construction, with meanings and politics that change over time. This is nowhere more obvious, perhaps, or more socially and politically urgent than with regard to youth, whose social and political enfranchisements are circumscribed by an arbitrary age of majority and whose basic civil rights are repeatedly violated in America until that magical number of years has been lived. As contemporary debates about youth in America demonstrate, when metaphoric abstractions of difference circulate around a specific site of cultural concern, their normative functioning becomes increasingly naturalized and difficult to resist or undo. Goldberg's all-encompassing "we" who agree on the trouble of contemporary youth ("Our children are in trouble") is an excellent example.

The Freak Show of Youth

In multiple media, contemporary youth are marked by the rhetorics of disability and queerness as objects both of discipline (they are the physical embodiment of a deviance in the body politic that must be controlled) and of pity and social concern (they, and by extension American culture, are increasingly disabled by violence). These representations of youth are often not directly concerned with or reflective of real physical difference, disability, or queerness, although the "threat" of all three factors is a regular part of the parables we tell about the perils of youth. Disability and queerness circulate around youth more often as metaphoric abstractions through which the dominant culture seeks to understand (or at least to manage or discipline) the lives, experiences, and social and political import of one of its constituencies. These abstractions might be more clearly understood if we reconsidered the category of youth within the history and politics of the American freak show.

In her introduction to the anthology *Freakery* Rosemarie Garland-Thomson (1996, 3) remarks on the changing significances of the "extraordinary body": "The trajectory of historical change in the ways the anomalous body is framed within the cultural imagination . . . can be characterized simply as a movement from a narrative of the marvelous to a narrative of the deviant."[10] Garland-Thomson (1996, 30) locates the shift in perception by which what once inspired wonder "becomes error" within the complex social, political, and cultural changes engendered by modernity.

In short, Garland-Thomson locates the change from a discourse of wonder to a discourse of deviance in the radical transformations of modern social life, which produced a host of uncertainties about the continued relevance of traditional norms and forms of social and physical life. Similarly, shifting notions of the politics and problems of youth today are indicators of anxieties about the continuity of a dominant social, political, and cultural order and about "upholding" standing social practices.

Garland-Thomson (1996) remarks that "in response to the tensions of modernity, the ancient practice of interpreting extraordinary bodies not only shifted toward the secular and the rational, but it flourished as never before within the expanding marketplace, institutionalized under the banner of the freak show" (4). Furthermore, the freak show reemerged "in almost unrecognizable forms in the late twentieth century" (11). One such form can be found in the treatment and representation of youth in America and in the cultural norms and imperatives to normativity that circulate around this often deeply conflicted social category. Indeed, the conflation of youth with the freak show, or with the metaphors of freakishness, has been the basis of a common cultural discourse at least since the social and political rhetoric of the hippies, yippies, and counterculture (Fiedler 1993). More recently, scholars have demonstrated the continuity of the youth-freak connection with regard to the rise of tabloid television as a youth cultural form and the resurgence of postmodern freak shows and sideshows, like the Jim Rose Circus (which headlined the side stage during the first few years of the alternative rock festival and youth cultural spectacle Lollapalooza), the Bindlestiff Family Cirkus, and Circus Amok (see Adams 2001; Gamson 1998).

Garland-Thomson (1996) also notes that the freak show "fashioned . . . the self-governed, iterable subject of democracy—the American cultural self" (10) and "bonded a sundering polity together in the collective act of looking" (4). This function of the freak show, I suggest, is performed by contemporary media(ted) spectacles of youth. In a multivoiced, diversified, multicultural environment, youth is one of the last unmarked categories, with little or no claim to individual rights or to specific cultural and political consideration. Discourses of disability and queerness circulate around the category of youth to reunify a polity fractured by multiculturalism and diversity, as well as by violence and uncertainties about the future.

Whether on television or in movies, music, magazines, or the news, America is perpetually caught in the "collective act of looking" at the freak show of youth. From the idealized celebration of youth's crazy styles and behavior in a commercial that declares "being young . . . priceless," while "for everything else, there's MasterCard," to our carefully mediated horror at killing sprees in our schools, American culture is perpetually fascinated and repelled by the spectacle of youth.

Charles Acland's (1995) theorizing of the category of youth helps us see that the crises of youth, disability, and queerness are similar (if not ideologically the same) in that all of them express anxieties about the future of the social. Acland, who attempts to show "the way in which youth in crisis corresponds to an anxiety concerning the reproduction of social order" (12), claims that the category of youth has "no fundamental essence except as a problem; as a crisis of value, of economics, or of resources" (24). The crisis of youth as one of value and resources is similar to the one that Garland-Thomson posits for the extraordinary body, which came to express a crisis of economic and labor value in the expanding marketplace of industrial capitalism.

Historically, youth and people with disabilities have been perceived to threaten the reproduction of labor and economic systems of value, as well as the political and ideological norms of bodily and national life with which these systems are aligned. The crisis of labor and value posed by people with disabilities is that their "special needs" interrupt the Fordist rhythms of capitalist America. People with disabilities are often perceived as nonproductive members of society or, worse, as unnecessary burdens on industry, which must accommodate their needs. At times, of course, capitalism is directly responsible for the production of disability (whether through work-related accidents, unsafe working conditions, repetitive-motion or stress-related injuries, or environmental toxins that affect reproduction) and indeed relies on the differences it constructs between able-bodied worker and disabled burden.

The threat that youth apparently poses to capitalist systems of labor is that, because youth is a time of instruction and indoctrination between childhood and adulthood, it might come to reject or fail to learn or conform to traditional patterns of labor or of socioeconomic and political value. This economic crisis created by youth was most clearly elaborated in the late 1980s and early 1990s in the cultural panics and debates over "Gen-Xers" and "slacker" youth, who were perceived as listless and, most important, unproductive.[11]

To defuse such a threat to the social order, the cultural other (whether the person with disability, the queer, the racialized, or the young—or rather, all of these separately and at once) must be visible. A primary function of the freak show, then, is to make physical difference and disability spectacularly visible and therefore manageable. This is also a function of cultural stereotypes about queer bodies and mannerisms (butch dykes, femme fags) and about dominant (that is, adult) cultural preoccupations with racial and youth styles and performance (mohawks, dreadlocks, safety pins as fashion accessories, hip-hop baggy trousers, 40s, blunts). Garland-Thomson (1996, 8) makes the spectacular visibility of all these others clear: "Invested with meanings that far outstrip their biological bases, figures such as the cripple, the quadroon, the queer, the outsider, the whore are taxonomical, ideological products marked by socially determined stigmata, defined through representation, and excluded from social power and status." Add "youth" to the mix, consider how all these categories are mutually constitutive of cultural normativity and social disqualification, and you arrive at what I mean. The multiple positioning, intersections, and visibility of "deviance" of all sorts are integral factors in the construction of social order; they prescribe the very limits of the social.

Columbine, Queerness, and Pathological White Masculinity

The visibility of deviance, youth, queerness, and disability contributes to the metaphoric abstractions of erotophobia and stigmaphobia as they circulate around youth and as they gesture toward an understanding of contemporary social and political life in America through various figures of disabled youth. Consider the following image reported in the *Washington Post* a year after Columbine:

> Outwardly, Littleton has recovered a sense of normalcy. . . . The police tape was removed long ago from the school, a sprawling beige brick structure near the entrance to a quiet residential neighborhood. But there are reminders and frailties, still. The student who walks into class and tells a teacher he had a flashback and ended up crashing a car. The unfailing shivers from the sound of a helicopter whirring overhead. The sight of a few students still propelling themselves down the school's corridors in wheelchairs. (Goldstein 2000, A2)

The scene was reported in florid prose in newspapers and given visual representation on local and national television news programs on the first anniversary of the shootings: innocent teens physically and psychologically disabled by school violence.

The flashbacks, the shivers, the physical and emotional "frailties" of these post-trauma students are all a part of the abstractions of disability and stigmaphobia that routinely surround our culture's narration of the stories of youth violence. These disabling effects directly contrast with some fantasy ideal of normality. In the same *Washington Post* article Sergio Gonzales, a witness of the shootings, remarks that the aftereffects and the lingering sadness in Columbine students are not "the regular life of a teenager" (Goldstein 2000, A2). Of course, what was everywhere implicit but nowhere stated in the ongoing national coverage of Columbine was that this was not "the regular life" of suburban, middle- to upper-class teenagers. Underclass and inner-city teens have faced quotidian school violence for decades, but as long as it stayed confined to those other neighborhoods, middle- to upper-class America felt safe.

In the face of the disabling effects of school violence, the students at Columbine, their parents, the local residents of Littleton, and citizens across the country tried to restore some notion of "normalcy" and "regular" youth life. Such an attempt to reclaim an impossible normality is subtended by the visible presence of disabled teenagers. But how are we to argue against normality when these youth have been so dramatically altered, psychologically and physically, by the eruption of deviance and violence in school? Seeing images of or reading about teenage survivors "still propelling themselves down the school's corridors in wheelchairs," we are somehow to conclude that these youth, precisely because of the visible presence of their wheelchairs, are owed and deserve only our pity, such is their tragedy. That they are "still propelling themselves" in wheelchairs, moreover, suggests that their disability is something that they will eventually overcome or forget about, just as we as a nation must move beyond the disabling effects of violence.[12]

In the context of post-Columbine understandings of the crisis of youth, the visible presence of disability becomes a marker of how the physical and mental integrity of the normate is always threatened with disability by unrestrained deviance. Normality is always already subject to its own disability by the presence of deviance.[13] Of course, in the wake of Columbine and other school shootings, nontraditional youth, of whatever size and stripe, have come under increasingly strict surveillance and discipline across the country.

Just as we have been encouraged to understand the effects of deviance on the dominant culture through disability, or through the susceptibility of the normate to disabling deviance at any moment, we have been encouraged to consider the motives behind Eric Harris and Dylan Klebold's act of violence through an abstraction of erotophobic discourse and a heteronormative logic of queerness. Immediately after the Columbine shootings the media seized on the moniker "the Trenchcoat Mafia" for the school subculture to which the teens belonged. It was as if the Trenchcoat Mafia were the name of an organized paramilitary group rather than a nickname given to a group of somber teens who dressed in dark colors by their normate counterparts in jockdom. The *Washington Post* neatly summed up the Trenchcoat Mafia as "mostly . . . seniors who wore black clothing and black trench coats to school and sounded doomsday warnings about the end of the millennium. Some of their classmates described them as white supremacists absorbed by Gothic fantasies" (Kenworthy 1999). Other Columbine students were not as sophisticated in their day-to-day dealings with these high school misfits. As one student reported, the Trenchcoat Mafia "were called 'faggots' and school jocks 'threw rocks and bottles at them'" (Von Drehle 1999). One cultural discussion that has emerged from the Columbine shootings is increased attention to school bullying as a major contributing factor in youth violence, and recent studies have focused on verbal harassment as the primary form of bullying. The most common example of verbal harassment among teenage boys is the epithet faggot (which further complicates Eminem's self-defense), a slur launched regularly not only at Harris and Klebold but at Andy Williams, who opened fire at Santana High School in Santee, California, two years later (Sessions Stepp 2001; Okie 2001; Strauss 2001).

Nevertheless, the language used by the *Washington Post* and by newspapers across the country immediately circumscribed the shooters with a rhetoric of deviance rather than considering how institutional bullying and the microcosmic violence, intolerance, and erotophobia of Columbine High School produced the very act of violence that cultural commentators were trying to understand. It is worth recalling Linton's suggestion that dominant disability discourse ignores or elides the "social processes and policies" that delimit disabled people's lives in favor of an individualized conception of physical difference. The same phenomenon can be seen at work in the demonization of Harris, Klebold, and other deviant youth: ignore the social and political processes and inequalities that produce youth violence in favor of a simplified understanding of individual pathology. Hey, they were outcasts, misfits, queers. It is no surprise that they acted out so violently. We, so the logic goes, should have seen it coming, if only because of their clothes.

It was not just their sartorial style that got Harris and Klebold labeled queers. The books they read, the movies they liked, the music they listened to, and the statements they posted on their websites were all used as evidence of the boys' outsider status. The *Washington Post* reported that "they hated jocks, admired Nazis and scorned normalcy," "loved explosives and guns," and quoted lyrics from the German industrial-metal band KMFDM (Kenworthy 1999). In its desperation to explain and to assign blame for this explosion of youth violence, the *Washington Post* and media outlets across the country failed to acknowledge that morbid fascination with mortality, guns, and violence is common among youth, especially nontraditional, unpopular, perpetually bullied young boys.

Just so, Kevin Merida (1999) sought out answers to the question "Why?" in the pervasive violence of American entertainment. Merida blamed Marilyn Manson and KMFDM; the films *The Basketball Diaries* (1995), *Apt Pupil* (1998), and *American History X* (1998), even though this third film is explicitly antiracist and antiviolence; the video games *Doom* and *Wolfenstein 3D*; and even the fashion designs of Alexander McQueen, Anna Sui, and Helmut Lang, which Merida deems "pessimistic urban armor." The incessant blaming of shock rock "Antichrist Superstar" Manson is telling, considering the gender trouble (or "crisis of masculinity") Manson has posed for American culture. Characterizing Harris and Klebold as Manson fans set up a seemingly natural connection in the public mind between the boys' act of violence and the genderfuck amorality of Manson. Indeed, following Columbine, Manson's concerts were canceled throughout the United States, and the performer was continually put on the defensive by national media that attempted to locate blame for the Colorado teens' actions in Manson's influence. All of these popular cultural products were enlisted to prove exactly how and why Harris and Klebold were different from "normal"

American youth. The subtext, of course, was instruction for parents who did not want their children to become deviants: Don't expose them or let them be exposed to any of these things.

Part and parcel of the demonizing and making queer of Harris and Klebold was their characterization as un-American. That they "admired Nazis" was the most common motif establishing their disavowal of American normality. This characterization was (and continues to be) the most difficult to resist, since Nazi Germany has been cast as the antithesis of everything America presumably stands for, regardless of the reality of certain fascistic strains of conformity in U.S. culture.[14] Indeed, much consideration was given in the news to whether the boys had planned their assault for Adolf Hitler's birthday (April 20) or whether this was a coincidence, although most reports assumed that they had set the date because of its neo-Nazi significance.

Attention was also given to the fact that Harris had applied for enlistment in the marines but had been rejected because he had been prescribed the antidepressant Luvox. Harris, it was reported, had been deemed unfit to serve his country. Furthermore, this unfitness was based on a mental deficiency, and thus metaphors of disability were reintroduced into coverage of the event: not only was Harris a queer social outcast, but he was psychologically disabled. In the end, every attempt was made to distance normal Americans from Harris and Klebold. As Colorado governor Bill Owens summed it up: "These are children who don't have the same moral background as the rest of us" (Kenworthy 1999). In other words, these boys were different; one of them was depressed, and they were both queer.

In the aftermath of the Columbine shootings, a whole disciplinary arsenal was deployed through the media to distance "us" from "them"—normal youth, normal Americans, from these deviant teens. An attempt was made to quell perceived threats to a normative social order through abstractions of queerness, as in the "truths" applied to Harris and Klebold in terms of gender and national identification, and through the visible presence of disability, as in the imagery of disabled students still propelling their wheelchairs down school hallways. Yet the debates and concerns surrounding Columbine had little to do with either queerness or disability as material reality; they had everything to do with a perceived crisis in the presentation of heterosexual masculinity as it is connected to questions of cultural violence. This crisis of masculinity was tied to the dominant culture's paranoid fantasies about the effects of popular culture and mediated violence on youth, and the future of a normative social order.

Ensuring the reproduction of prevalent social, cultural, and political processes well after the fact, the image of real disabled youth on the first anniversary of Columbine served as a metaphor for the threat posed by youth deviance to the physical, psychological, and cultural integrity of the normate subject (and nation) and as a call for the increased surveillance and discipline of all types of non-normative youth.

Boyz and *Kids:* Disability, Blackness, and Social Mobility

It is not only in the news, in the wake of youth violence and/or deviance, that queerness and disability become useful, mobile metaphors through which we are to make sense of the crisis of youth and which express anxieties over the continuity of a normative social order. In popular film, as Snyder and Mitchell (2000, 16) relate, the visible mark of physical difference conveys an "overheated symbolic imagery" and plays host to a multitude of metaphoric abstractions. Physical difference in film becomes reflective of, for instance, internal/psychological/moral corruption, political regimes and power relations, and social change. The visible mark of race in film often performs a similar social and political duty and dovetails with Linton's assertion that representations of disability work to uphold certain cultural practices. Richard Delgado and Jean Stefancic (1995) observe that racial stereotypes in film are not "accidental, but functional." In white-dominated media, they assert, "racist depiction, far from being a social evil, is a social good that enables society to accomplish goals that vary from era to era but always include the subordination or marginalization of minority men" (212). As dominant cultural responses to John Singleton's *Boyz N the Hood* and Larry Clark's *Kids* demonstrate, when abstractions or stereotypes of disability and race circulate together in popular film, their politics become all the more difficult to unpack and resist.

Boyz and *Kids* are, arguably, the most controversial American movies of the 1990s. Both films provoked public outcry and cultural debate about the state of American youth, youth violence and deviance, and the future of a normative social order.[15] Singleton's filmic critique of racism and institutionalized structures of social and economic oppression and exploitation, and his antiviolence message (at the end of the film, before the credits roll, the message "Increase the Peace" flashes across the darkened screen), were largely ignored or overlooked by audiences and cultural commentators. The film's release was met with acts of violence across the United States. *Newsweek* reported that the film's opening weekend "triggered a spree of largely gang-related violence that left at least one dead and more than 30 wounded" (Kroll 1991, 57). The violence surrounding *Boyz* was largely taken as proof that black men really are, as the stereotypes imply, violent and criminal. Furthermore, the film's release produced a contentious, often one-sided debate over representations of violence and acts of violence and about gangs, drugs, and inner-city life at a time when public anxiety over the threat of inner-city black youth to national life was at its peak.

Four years later, when the site of cultural panic had shifted from the threat of inner-city black youth to the moral decay and deviant behavior of relatively privileged, middle-class white youth, *Kids* was released. Clark envisioned his film, in contrast to the host of other youth-oriented films that have attempted and (he claims) failed to portray youth authentically, as a "real" representation of kids growing up in New York in the late 1990s. Accordingly, the film's stylistics of representation—from its documentary, cinéma vérité filming and editing to its use of unknown, young actors and a supporting cast of "real" street kids—and its scripting by nineteen-year-old Harmony Korine contribute to a feeling of authenticity. Belief in the realness of the film was picked up on across America by the public and by critics and cultural commentators, who whipped up another national panic about the state of today's youth.

Despite the vast differences of race, class, social location, support structures, education, opportunity, and even enactments of deviance between the populations of youth represented in *Boyz* and *Kids*, both films became emblems of youth in/as crisis, and they provoked similar, if not identical, cultural panics about youth and the future of the social. It was in his *Commentary* review of *Kids* that Goldberg (1995, 55) stated, "Among the few things that Americans seem to agree on these days is that our children are in trouble; the causes and cures may be debated, but the diagnosis has reached a point of consensus."

What these films also share is a representational intersection of youth deviance and disability in which the visible presence of disability becomes a natural(ized) correlate to the social, moral, and political disabling of youth lamented in the films' receptions. This is due partly to the films' stereotypical vision of urban life in America, particularly as connected to racialized and underclass subcultures. Valerie Smith (1992, 57) notes that "certain narrative films construct themselves as part of a widely shared and widely recognizable reality" and that cultural critics, film reviewers, and specific (read: dominant, white, privileged) audiences participate in the continual reconstruction of the reality effects of films like *Boyz* and *Kids*.

Boyz is the story of how two sets of young black men—the ambitious Tre Styles and his high school football-star best friend, Ricky Baker, in contrast to their apathetic, gangsta counterparts Doughboy, Mad Dog, and Little Chris—try to cope with the violence of 'hood life and racist America. This binary structuring of heterosexual black masculinity is one of the most basic characteristics of racial and gender stereotyping in American culture. The Doughboy-Mad Dog-Little Chris axis is probably the most familiar, for it plays into the "overwhelming media mythology of black men as lazy, criminal, undeserving, and drug-addicted" (Williams 1995, 241). However, the Tre Styles-Ricky Baker axis of black masculinity is equally phantasmatic. Michele Wallace (1995) cautions that "they are flip sides of the same coin, and neither of them has anything to do with who black people—black men or black women—really are" (302). Both ends of this binary of heterosexual black masculinity demonstrate the racist fetishization of blackness: "Black men on welfare, homeless, with AIDS, in jail, and so forth are seen as disproportionately villainous, just as famous blacks are seen as extraordinary freaks of nature. In both cases, blackness is fetishized. There is no middle ground" (Wallace 1995, 305). While one may hesitate to say that the young black men at the "positive" end of this spectrum are "famous," especially considering that Ricky is dead by the end of the film, Tre at least represents a fetishization of black masculinity insofar as he is offered, or extended as a consolation prize, some success in life and is able to escape the disabling of 'hood life.

Because *Boyz* is specifically a tale of heterosexual black masculinity, it has come under criticism from black feminist scholars. Jacquie Jones (1992), Lisa Kennedy (1992), and Michele Wallace (1992) call attention to the abjection of black femininity in the persons of the film's welfare-queen and crack-addicted single mothers. Wallace (1995, 125) declares that the real issue in the film is the reassertion of patriarchal authority and heterosexual masculine prerogative; for her, the film and its success confirm hegemonic cultural values. Feminist critics rightly point out the gender inequalities that *Boyz* reinscribes, but what their analyses often elide is how severely limited the film's binary vision of black masculinity is.

There is a (tentative) third possibility in *Boyz*, however, a nonpathological or nonfetishized black maleness, and that is modeled by Tre's father, Furious Styles. A veteran of the Black Power movement and the consciousness-raising, counterculture era, Furious might be taken to represent self-empowered, righteous black masculinity. Smith (1992, 59) makes a pitch for Tre—"Our protagonist rises above the conditions of his peers because he alone has a strong, present, and neonationalist black father"—or at least she claims that this is the logic of the film. But the film itself undoes this possibility by showing that Furious's mode of black masculinity is not available as a model for any of the film's young black men, not even his own son. This is made clear in father's and son's differing relationships to institutionalized authority as represented by the police. After Tre moves in with Furious, who is to teach him "how to be a man," and after the house is broken into, Furious stares down the black police officer who is dismissive of his desire for justice and who complains about the "niggers" like Furious who give black men like him a bad name. Later, when Tre and Ricky are pulled over for no apparent reason by the same self-hating black cop, Tre remains silent and passive, capitulating to the cop's invective and his bending of Tre backward over the hood of his cruiser with the barrel of his gun. Where Furious stands up to institutional authority, Tre can only break down in the face of it and of racism, and his masculinity is further compromised when it is finally his tears that win his and Ricky's freedom.

The fetishizing and pathologizing performances of black masculinity in *Boyz*, and the cultural politics behind them, can be seen more clearly when the social disqualifier of disability is added to the film's characterizations. In a scene in which Doughboy, Mad Dog, and Little Chris struggle with the existence of God, social and racial justice, and gender relations and come to a point of disagreement, Doughboy tells Little Chris that if he does not like Doughboy's opinion, they will "see [Little Chris] walk his crippled ass all the way home." Little Chris's disability, visible everywhere in *Boyz* but alluded to only a few times, is the result of a spinal injury suffered, we are told, in a drive-by shooting. Here black youth violence is literally, physically, and visibly disabling.

Little Chris's disability is an obvious way for Singleton to comment not only on the disabling violence that infects inner-city black communities but, more abstractly, on the social and political disenfranchisement of blacks and the oppression and exploitation visited on them by a racist dominant American culture. Moreover, Little Chris's disability is a commentary on the greatly compromised access to social, economic, and political mobility in America's inner cities and on the near impossibility of making it out of the 'hood.

More insidiously, Little Chris's disability plays a role in the hierarchy that operates among the characters in the film. Little Chris and Doughboy, with their shuttling back and forth from the streets to juvie and prison, their 40-oz.-swigging, trash-talking, violence-ridden, gangsta lifestyles, represent one of the film's two visions of young black American masculinity. Doughboy's football-star brother, Ricky, and their book-smart friend Tre, who are frustrated with inner-city life and desire to get out of the 'hood, represent the other. The quotidian struggles of these young men represent a cultural situation in which one can either be disabled by 'hood life or work to escape it. While the film forecloses that possibility for Ricky, who is murdered in a senseless act of gang violence, it celebrates Tre's resistance to violence and gang life and suggests that he, at least, will make it out.

Of course, Tre's moral and ethical conviction, his respect for his elders and authority, his monogamous and relatively chaste relationship with his girlfriend, and his narrative of pulling himself up by his bootstraps mimic a stereotypical script of American individualism in no way threatening to a normative social order. The young men who do pose a threat to it, Little Chris and Doughboy, are physically, psychologically, and socially unable to escape 'hood life. Little Chris's disability becomes not only a visible marker that comments on the physical and social effects of inner-city life but a marker through which we can more easily identify the threat or crisis embodied in these youth (that is, violence somehow equals disability). Finally, his disability assuages dominant cultural anxieties about racial and class mobility by showing that threat to be literally disabled: there is no way out of the 'hood for these youths. The violent threat of race and pathological black masculinity has been immobilized.

Although the intersections of youth, deviance, and disability in *Kids* at first glance seem very different from those in *Boyz*, the two representations are strikingly similar, and both use notions of youth and disability to express cultural anxieties about social, racial, and sexual mobility. *Kids* chronicles a single summer day in the lives of two working-class high school-aged white boys in New York City. The film wastes no time in establishing their deviance; it rather infamously opens with the main character, Telly, pressuring a fourteen-year-old girl into intercourse with promises of his devotion and of how much she is going to "love it." Meanwhile, Telly's friend Casper waits outside on the girl's front stoop, swigging from a 40-oz.

Shortly afterward we see the two boys riding the subway, where they encounter a legless panhandler who rides his skateboard through the train, rattling a cup of change and chanting, "I have no legs."[16] As he passes the two boys, Casper puts what little money he has in the man's cup—the only gesture of empathy or sentiment of any kind expressed by either boy in the film. Elsewhere their faces are completely affectless as they steal, smoke pot, harass queers, beat a man nearly to death, vandalize property, trespass, and sexually abuse their female peers. This sentimental gesture on the train is therefore striking and is significant because it sets up a strange equivalence in which the panhandler's disability becomes the visible counterpart to Casper and Telly's moral and psychological disability and deviant behavior.

Garland-Thomson (2000) has suggested that this scene may actually reassert a hierarchy between normate people and people with disabilities, so that Casper's gesture is one of pity, full of the understanding that as bad as he and Telly may be, they are at least better off than the panhandler. While the suggestion is compelling, I find it hard to read the gesture as one merely of pity, if only because of the boys' obvious connection to working-class, black, and Latino urban subcultures. In this gesture they recognize a fellow outcast trying to make it from day to day.

Additionally, Telly's voice-over throughout the film comments on what it is like to be young and to have (or so he believes) nothing to lose, and yet nothing to live for, and Casper's gesture seems to acknowledge the panhandler's limited resources and opportunity as the boys' own.

Significantly, the panhandler is black, and in many ways *Kids* contributes to a racialization of deviance and disability that, at the same time, intersects questions of class relations and a pathological heterosexual masculinity. Throughout the film the threat posed by these two youths comprises their sexual irresponsibility and their connections to underclass or working-class economies and racialized urban subcultures. James Bowman (1995), in the *American Spectator* (a questionable source, although Bowman's racially biased rhetoric is illustrative), remarks that "the real-life Beavis and Butthead are Telly and Casper, who, though white, talk in the foul-mouthed accents of black street lingo, full of yos and bros and wassups, with the all-purpose s-word a frequent signifier for the entire range of the comprehended but unexpressed" (40). Bowman's comment, and his indexing of those other youth culture pariahs Beavis and Butthead, makes clear how *Kids* further abstracts the connections forged among youth, deviance, race, and disability by Singleton. For all their visible whiteness, Telly and Casper are, through their lingo and behavior, black (and furthermore, "foul-mouthed" black); this is again underscored by their self-identification with the panhandler. Where in *Boyz* disability functions to confine the threat of inner-city black youth to the 'hood, in *Kids* this threat is nothing if not mobile, entering even the sanctified space of the middle-class, white father's house and daughter's bedroom.

In his self-professed occupation as "virgin surgeon," Telly represents a threat to the social order carried out through his exploitation and violation of young girls, who in turn represent a stable, heteronormative, family-oriented order threatened by racial, class, and sexual deviance. Cultural critics such as bell hooks (1996) and film critics such as Terrence Rafferty (1995, 80) and John Simon (1995, 47) have remarked on the racial politics of the film, in which Jennie, who is infected with HIV by Telly and on whom misery is heaped, is emblematic of a normative social order that must be protected. Through HIV and AIDS *Kids* expresses its own, or at least the dominant culture's, erotophobia. That kids this young should be sexually active and promiscuous is inappropriate, even queer, but the film's real scandal is that, though they all engage in heterosexual sex, they fall victim to and themselves spread HIV, which continues to be largely, if erroneously, thought a consequence of queer sex and deviant life-styles.

Jennie's sexual inexperience (she has had sex only with Telly, and then only once) contrasts with the promiscuity of the other girls, most of them Latina or black girls who talk freely about oral sex and proclaim that "nothing beats fucking!" Of course, none of these girls is infected with HIV; they are, in many ways, immaterial to the film's cautionary tale. Rather, it is Jennie's transgression of sexual morals and of racial and class boundaries that must be punished. Her class and economic privilege, represented by the traditional family life she enjoys, is underscored when, after learning of her HIV infection, she attempts to call home to talk to her mother but reaches only her little brother; while searching for Telly, she also can afford to take taxis all over Manhattan, whereas the other characters walk. Jennie clearly comes from a relatively affluent, stable family. The difference in characterization between Jennie and her racialized girl friends is not surprising, considering how the bodies of white women have been shielded by an ideology that has often excused the most oppressive, exploitative, racist social movements and policies. Ironically, however, Jennie herself cannot be protected. Unable to reach her mother or to return home, she finally finds Telly but cannot stop his sexual abandon, and in the last scene Casper rapes her while she is unconscious. In *Kids* youth embody the triple threat of the disabling influences of race, class, and sexuality, all figured in Telly and Casper, with their working-class roots, their connections to urban black and Latino subcultures, and their sexual promiscuity. It is a disabling of youth and a threat to social order made explicit in the subway scene that connects a physically disabled, homeless, black panhandler to "foul-mouthed," working-class, black-acting, white boys.

Conclusion

In the recent cultural debates over Eminem, school violence as witnessed in Littleton, Colorado, and the reality effects of films like *Boyz* and *Kids*, race, class, sexuality, and youth are repeatedly cast as disabilities that preclude social and political enfranchisement and that express cultural anxieties about the social mobility of America's internal others. In all of these crises of deviance and violence, disability and queerness as material facts are metaphorically abstracted into commentaries on the state of youth and by extension the normative future of the social in America. Queerness and disability in these media become mobile metaphors that circulate around the culturally constructed category of youth and that define the very limits of the social in the naturalization of dominant tropes of cultural and political disqualification. Through these visual and rhetorical abstractions, queers, people with disabilities, youth, and racial minorities are produced as sites of social anxiety that require increasing surveillance and discipline. If the one thing "we" can all agree on today is that "our children are in trouble," then it behooves us to consider not only the rhetorical strategies of the media(ted) stories we tell about these troubled youth but also the ways that these representations, and minority life in America generally, are circumscribed and defined at every turn by the discursive abstractions of erotophobia and stigmaphobia.

Contributors

Ralph Cintron is associate professor in the department of English at the University of Illinois at Chicago. He is currently working on a book tentatively titled *Work Fields in the New Economy*, based on fieldwork that will cut across social classes, from CEOs to members of marginalized Latino communities. Cintron is interested in the languages of the rich and powerful as they organize their lives in the "new economy" as opposed to the languages of the poor and marginalized.

Ida Fadzillah received her Ph.D. from the University of Illinois, Urbana-Champaign, in 2003. She is an assistant professor of Anthropology at Middle Tennessee State University. Fadzillah was born in Kedah, Malaysia. She deals with several feminist issues in her work, including how history and society shape female identity; what labor and education options exist for girls; and how the concept of "beauty" is a defining force in pushing girls in one direction or another in regard to their future.

Nicole R. Fleetwood is assistant professor of American Studies at the University of California, Davis. She has worked as an art education director, artist in residence, and consultant for several arts organizations and youth programs. She has written on black visual and performing arts, youth culture, and race and technology issues. Currently she is conducting research for a manuscript on visuality, blackness, and everyday cultural practices.

Murray Forman is assistant professor of Communication Studies at Northeastern University. His publications on popular music, media, and youth include *The 'Hood Comes First: Race, Space, and Place in Rap and Hip Hop* (Wesleyan University Press, 2002). He edited *That's the Joint! The Hip-Hop Studies Reader* (Routledge, 2004) with Mark Anthony Neal and is co-editor of the *Journal of Popular Music Studies*.

GusTavo Adolfo Guerra Vásquez is a Guatemalangelino (born in Guatemala and raised in Guatemala City and Los Angeles) multidisciplinary artist. GusTavo has worked as a youth and family counselor and elementary school teacher serving predominantly Latino(a) youth in Watsonville, California and the Pico-Union and North Hollywood Districts of Los Angeles. His work focuses on U.S.–Central American identity formations and their relationship to cultural productions and social movements in the Central American diasporas. He is a doctoral candidate in the University of California, Berkeley's Comparative Ethnic Studies Graduate Program with a designated emphasis in Women, Gender, and Sexuality, focusing on Latino Cultural Studies.

George Lipsitz teaches American Studies at the University of California, Santa Cruz. He has worked extensively with K-12 teachers, students, and parents on programs designed to promote active learning, to encourage the development of teacher leaders, and to connect classroom issues to community concerns. He is the author of several books, including *American Studies in a Moment of Danger* (University of Minnesota Press, 2001) and *The Possessive Investment in Whiteness* (Temple University Press, 1998).

Sunaina Maira is associate professor in Asian American Studies at the University of California, Davis. She is the author of *Desis in the House: Indian American Youth Culture in New York* (Temple University Press, 2002) and the co-editor, with Rajini Srikanth, of *Contours of the Heart: South Asians Map North America* (Asian American Writers' Workshop, 1996), which won the American Book Award in 1997. She was one of the founding organizers of Youth Solidarity Summer, a progressive program for South Asian youth from the United States and Canada, and the South Asian Committee on Human Rights, a grassroots organization working on immigrant and civil rights in the Boston area.

Mica Pollock is an assistant professor at the Harvard Graduate School of Education, where she teaches anthropological courses on youth cultures, U.S. racial inequality, and ethnographic methodology. Her work uncovers the everyday inequality and diversity struggles of youth and adults, in both school and community settings. She is the author of *Colormute: Race Talk Dilemmas in an American School* (Princeton University Press, 2004), in which she explores six central dilemmas of U.S. race talk that play out particularly explicitly in schools. Mica has worked as a high school teacher and civil rights analyst, and she is embarking on a study of transnational youth activism entitled "Global Youth/Global Justice."

Todd R. Ramlow is adjunct professor of English at George Washington University and associate film and television editor of *PopMatters*.

Alexandra Schneider holds a Ph.D. in Film Studies from the University of Zurich. Her current research is about Bollywood cinema's relationship with the West, particularly about the representation of Switzerland in recent Bollywood films. She has directed a research project, co-curated an exhibition, and edited an anthology on the subject. She is currently a lecturer at the Film Studies Department of the Freie University of Berlin. Her publications include *Bollywood: The Indian Cinema and Switzerland* (Edition Museum für Gestaltung Zurich 2002), as well as two anthologies on film and culture in Switzerland. Her book on home movies, *Die Stars sind wir*, is forthcoming from Schueren Verlag, Marburg, in 2004.

Susan Shepler is a doctoral candidate in Social and Cultural Studies in Education at the University of California, Berkeley. She worked as a secondary school math teacher in rural Sierra Leone with the Peace Corps in the late 1980s. She has worked on short-term research projects for Children at Risk, UNICEF, and Search for Common Ground. Her interests include youth and violence, identity, and reintegration of child ex-combatants.

Elisabeth Soep is a lecturer in urban education at the School of Education at the University of California, Berkeley. Her academic research, featured in various journals and books, centers on youth discourse and media practices in nonschool settings, and on artistically grounded approaches to research. She is also the education director and a producer at Youth Radio, where she collaborates with youth on stories for national and local public radio outlets. Youth Radio's honors include the George Foster Peabody, the Edward R. Murrow, and the National Association of Black Journalists awards.

Notes

Foreword

1. I thank Kathy Glass for calling this quote to my attention.
2. Environmental justice case study: West County Toxics Coalition and the Chevron refinery. Richmond Justice Page, www.umich.edu/~snre492/sherman .html.
3. Asian Pacific Environmental Network, Children's Environmental Health Activities, www.igc.org g/envjustice/training/apen.html 4.
4. Although the county promised this system in 1999, it has still not been put in place (Nguyen 2001, 32).

Chapter 1. Straight Outta Mogadishu

Chapter 1 was reprinted from an earlier version of "Straight outta Mogadishu," *Topia: A Canadian Journal of Cultural Studies* 5 (May 2001). Reprinted with permission of Murray Forman.

I am indebted to my colleagues at the Office of Research on Educational Policy, McGill University—especially Lynn Butler-Kisber—for their insights and support throughout the research stages of this study. I also thank the administration, staff, and students who granted me access to their schools and their daily lives.

1. This study is based on observational and ethnographic research among Somali students in two schools—one in the northeastern United States and one in central Canada—conducted between 1995 and 1998. The primary youth respondents, numbering approximately twenty, were between the ages of fifteen and twenty-one during the research period and were engaged in both formal focus groups and informal field interviews. Members of the schools' wider student populations and members of both staff and administration were also interviewed in multiple formal and informal contexts. In neither instance is the student body predominantly white in composition, although in the Canadian case the teaching staff consisted entirely of white men and women. In the U.S. school, the Somali students accounted for only a very small percentage of the total school population, which was 97 percent black or Latino; in the Canadian school, they comprised as much as half.
2. Somalia's civil unrest gradually intensified through the late 1980s, erupting into full-scale civil war by 1991. The period between roughly 1988 and 1995 saw the highest volume of Somali emigration. In 2000, Somalia's warring fac-

tions arrived at a general agreement leading first to a cease-fire and later to discussions on reforming a national government. In January 2001, for the first time since the early 1990s, Somalia sent an ambassadorial delegation to the United Nations. Despite these successes, internecine clan violence continues to hobble the nation. For a fascinating and detailed examination of the U.S. military misadventures in the streets of Mogadishu that led to the deaths of eighteen American soldiers and up to five hundred Somali civilians and militia men, see Bowden 1999.

3. The issue of intentionally channeling immigrant and refugee students and of facilitating exit transfers among native-born students was cited by school administrators as well as parent members of the school council in individual and group interviews.

4. Clarke makes an important distinction between Canadian and U.S. racial politics, writing that "Canadian identity, such as it is, defines itself primarily in opposition to the United States. Canada is pristine, unpolluted wilderness; the U.S. is decaying urban centers. . . . The most significant difference between Canada and the U.S. is, finally, that America has a race problem. In Canada, the party line goes, there are no racists save those who watch too much American television" (1998, 100–101).

5. Hip-hop is generally understood as a series of specific practices including B-boying (break dancing) and graffiti spray art, as well as the musical innovations of DJ turntable artists and rappers.

6. In the U.S. school, bilingual Somali-English education programs sustain a linguistic barrier and students often remain slightly more isolated from the general student population, resulting in an extended and deepened marginality within school society. In the Canadian school where immigrant students are immediately channeled into an ESL immersion curriculum, Somalis are more rapidly integrated into the English language and the school community where they experience a greater level of intercultural interaction and have a much more prominent profile in student government, clubs, and other extracurricular activities. This suggests that the different educational systems and the methods of educating foreign language students provide valuable information in assessing the pace of cultural adaptation and the rate at which Somali youths absorb and communicate the norms and values associated with North American black youth subcultures.

Chapter 2. Gangs and Their Walls

Chapter 2 was reprinted from *Angels' town: Chero ways, gang life, and rhetorics of the everyday.* Copyright 1997 by Ralph Cintron. Reprinted with permission of Beacon Press, Boston.

1. Street gangs have been studied by social scientists for a considerable amount of time. The perspective, as one might expect, has been that of social science realism. For instance, the amount of fieldwork behind Jankowski's *Islands in the Street* (1991) has been far more wide ranging than my own. But the work of Conquergood (1992) in Chicago has been more relevant to my text because it has dealt with street gangs aligned to those in Angelstown and, more importantly, because his approach to culture as performative and my own as rhetorical have been very similar and sharply different from the goals of traditional

social science. The work of Padilla (1993) has also been relevant because of its Chicago focus.

2. These quotations come from a variety of conversations and other sources.

3. One weekend someone associated with the Insane Deuces was visiting me in Iowa City, which is about a four-hour drive from Angelstown and the home of the Iowa Hawkeyes. Black and gold are prominent in the city, particularly on a football weekend. We drove through one area of the town in which different *coronas* were the logos of different businesses, including a motel chain. He jokingly remarked that the whole city was owned by the Latin Kings. To be immersed in a specialized language is to translate automatically the world into that system—sometimes jokingly, sometimes seriously.

4. The marketing of beer, gangster rap, certain movies, and clothing apparel rely on the imagery of street gangs. Such examples reinforce the notion that the mainstream or dominant society is economically enmeshed in its "antisociety" and can utilize it as a source of legal profit.

5. Traditionally, in the Chicago area the Insane Deuces and the Latin Kings have belonged to the same confederation, the People. In the late 1980s, however, a war broke out between the Kings and Deuces. Rather quickly, Angelstown became known as a rogue city whose gangs had broken traditional alliances and forged new ones. One result of this realignment was a steady increase in gang-related homicides despite a "no tolerance" police campaign during the 1990s. For more, see Cintron 1997.

6. Thumpers and Too Low Flows are cars that have been refitted and somewhat resemble the better-known Low Riders.

7. For de Certeau, a tactic is mobile; it makes use of the cracks that appear within the "surveillance of the proprietary powers. It poaches in them. . . . It can be where it is least expected. It is a guileful ruse . . . an art of the weak." In short, de Certeau's interest in quotidian practices acknowledged the power to act in everyone, regardless of his or her place in the hierarchy and despite the fact that tactical actions are always framed by the dominant power. This observation, as well as terms such as "subjectivity," "narratives of graffiti," and important concepts, such as the relationship between graffiti and the public sphere, were developed in conjunction with Dan Anderson.

8. See also Anderson 1991.

9. Other important *topoi* cycled through the names that gangs had chosen for themselves—specifically, images of royalty, and evocations of madness/disorder. I explore these themes fully elsewhere (Cintron 1997).

10. A week or so before the printing of the letter, it was reported in the same newspaper that Mothers Against Gangs had lost its backing from the county's Juvenile Court Services because of long-standing differences between the letter writer (the president of the group, who was in the process of resigning) and Court Services as well as the mayor of Angelstown. To the best of my knowledge, the arguments in the letter were not related to these political disputes.

11. I do not know whether the following observation is significant, but the writer's name was distinctly of Spanish origin.

12. The letters that I have selected were actually published *after* the newspaper's response.

13. The paraphrases and quotations for this paragraph have been taken primarily from two front-page articles, dated August 24, 1991 and September 9, 1991. I continue not to name the paper in order to mask the identity of the city.

Chapter 3. Race Bending

Chapter 3 was reprinted from Mica Pollock, "Race bending: 'Mixed' youth practicing strategic racialization in California," *Anthropology and Educational Quarterly* 35(1) (2004): 30–52. Reprinted with permission of *AEQ.*

1. See Montagu 1942; see Pollock 2004 for additional bibliography.

2. Data excerpts in this article, along with several paragraphs of description and data analysis, also appear in Pollock 2004, introduction and chapter 1.

3. For ethnographic evidence of how children start reproducing racial categories and orders in U.S. preschools with the help of adults, see Van Ausdale and Feagin 2001; on high schools, see Fine et al. 1997; Fordham 1996; Perry 2002; Peshkin 1991; Pollock 2004. On the racialized distribution of school resources, see Oakes et al. 1990; Orfield and Eaton 1996.

4. Ironically, in his autobiographical novella, Thomas describes his own youthful dilemmas of racial self-classification, particularly regarding the U.S. category "black."

Chapter 4. The Intimate and the Imperial

1. For example: Agosin and Craige 2002; Benson and Kayal 2002; Burbach and Clarke 2002; Etzioni and Marsh 2003; Kim, Jee, et al., eds. 2002; Leone and Anrig 2003; Lincoln 2003; Mailer 2003; Schulhofer 2002; Silberstein 2002; Sorkin and Zukin, eds. 2002.

2. This research was funded by a grant from the Russell Sage Foundation and the Institute of Asian American Studies, University of Massachusetts, Boston.

3. The high school has approximately two thousand students, of whom about 40 percent are white and 60 percent are students of color. African Americans are the largest group of students of color (about 25 percent), followed by Latino(a)s (15 percent), and Asian Americans (about 7 percent). In 2000–2002, 33 percent of students had a first language other than English and 14 percent were in the bilingual program.

4. The 2000 Census reported 2,720 Indian immigrants (2.7 percent of the population), 125 Pakistanis, and 120 Bangladeshis in Cambridge, a city that is 68.1 percent white American, 11.9 percent African American, 11.9 percent Asian American, and 7.4 percent Latino (U.S. Census Bureau, 2000). This, of course, does not include undocumented immigrants. The "native" population is 74.1 percent and foreign born is 25.9 percent; 17.7 percent are not citizens and 31.2 percent speak a language other than English. Cambridge is of course skewed by the presence of the academic community; while 8.2 percent (3,108) of those enrolled in schools are in high school, fully 70.5 percent are in college or graduate school, and 38.5 percent of the population over twenty-five years of age have graduate or professional degrees.

5. The re-registration component of the program was officially ended by the Department of Homeland Security in December 2003 after protests by immigrant/civil rights and grassroots community organizations. Other aspects of the program have remained in place, and the detentions and deportations put in place by the program continue.

6. For example, Michael Ignatieff's cover article, The burden, *New York Times Magazine,* January 5, 2003, and the pro-empire historian Niall Ferguson's, The empire slinks back, *New York Times Magazine,* April 27, 2003. Among other arti-

cles in the liberal mass media, a recent issue of a widely distributed Boston arts and entertainment newspaper—alternative in its cultural reportage but fairly conservative on foreign policy—featured at least three commentaries that referred to the United States within the framwork of "colonial powers," "imperial powers," and "empire-building" (Dan Kennedy, Waging post-warfare, *Boston Phoenix*, April 25–May 1, 2003: 16–18). See also the cover story of *Harper's Magazine*, titled The economic of empire, (William Finnegan, May 2003: 41–54).

Chapter 5. The Amway Connection

1. For example, the study of market women in Indonesia (Brenner 1995; Blackwood 1995), and female factory workers in Penang (Ong 1987), Manila (Margold 1995), Java (Wolf 1992), and Bangkok (Mills 1995).

2. See Montgomery 1998, Bishop and Robinson 1998, Tannenbaum 1999, Van Esterik 1999, and Watanabe 1998 for the most recent work on the subject of Thai women and prostitution.

3. For example, ethnographies by Freeman 2000, Kelsky 2001, and Tsing 1993 provide concrete examples of the multiple directions and shapes taken by globalization.

4. See Inda and Rosaldo 2002b for a comprehensive explanation of this model of globalization; see also the works of scholars of China (Rofel 1999) and the Chinese diaspora (Ong 1999b; Yang 1997).

5. A pseudonym. All personal names in this article have also been changed to protect the identities of the informants.

6. *Som tam* is Thai fresh papaya salad.

7. The numbers rise and fall according to the harvest: there are fewer vendors at the market during the planting and harvesting seasons for most of them are off tending to their fields at that time.

8. See Potter 1977, Wijeyewardene 1981, Van Esterik 1982, 1988, Keyes 1984, Kirsch 1982, and Tambiah 1970, for example.

9. The numbers rise and fall according to numbers of people working abroad or working seasonal jobs (conducted during the off-season for crop planting and harvesting) in other parts of Thailand. The numbers also change during the day when children from nearby villages come to attend the secondary school in Baan Khmer, which increases the population by about another five hundred individuals.

10. This does not imply that the girls do not have chores; while most do engage in cleaning and childcare activities, these duties are mainly conducted as helping the older women (the mothers or other relatives) whose principal role is to provide the majority of childcare, cooking, cleaning, and other household duties.

11. *Mattyom* 3 is the Thai equivalent of grade 9 in the Western system of education. The primary school (*phratom*) ends at grade 6 (age twelve), and *mattyom* ends at grade 6 (age eighteen).

12. Usually they were checking up on their children who were returning from school, or to getting more produce/food to sell at their stalls.

13. Chiang Rai City is the nearest big city to Baan Khmer, with shopping centers, a movie theater, large-scale restaurants, and convenience stores such as 7-Elevens.

14. When I refer to such brands I want to make clear that while these compa-

nies also manufacture several other items, such as cleaning products, vitamins and food supplements, jewelry, water purifying systems, smoke detectors, and burglar alarms, to name a few, in Baan Khmer their best-selling products were cosmetics. The term "cosmetics" in this essay is used to include such items as makeup, powders, lotions, blemish cream, "whitening" cream (a mild bleaching agent immensely popular in Asia), and masques.

15. According to Peiss, part of the reason for its success in the West was that nineteenth-century beauty ideals spurred a growth in the women's market in publishing, which "began a long-term process of educating the eye, channeling desires, and creating an identification between representation and viewer that would serve the sale of goods and foster new perceptions of beauty in the culture at large" (2001, 11).

16. All statistics are from www.amway.com, the official Amway website.

17. This amount was worth approximately U.S.$350 dollars at the time of my research.

18. This was not ever discussed explicitly in the context of selling or buying cosmetics; it was something that was linked to the girls' understandings of their future possibilities. For example, girls frequently discussed beauty in regard to beauty pageants as a means of achieving fame, fortune, and a rich boyfriend; they also mentioned that they were well aware that beauty pageants are often indirect conduits into the prostitution industry.

19. For an in-depth essay on how the invention of modern cleaning products introduced and further perpetuated a new way of life for the 1950s American housewife, see R. Cohen 1985.

20. This is the case with most commissioned beauty products. See Marko 2001 for more examples of inspirational materials as created and used by Avon.

21. According to Nim, she actually was not rich at all because she had "to pay for everything in [her] life" herself: her school fees, her school uniform, her books, and her school meals.

22. See more on the controlling role of accusations of "stinginess" in J. Scott 1985.

23. Interestingly, the image of local market women is one of the most frequent images used in international brochures to promote Northern Thailand as a tourist destination. In this way Duan's labor too is connected to a multinational business enterprise.

24. Avon relied heavily on newsletters and pamphlets: "Motivational literature became key to CPC's strategy for it served instructional purposes and conveyed a sense of business ownership and responsibility. CPC encouraged women to set goals for themselves—a logical consequence of not being able to assign them specific tasks or enforce strict objectives" (Marko 2001, 158).

Chapter 6. Homies Unidos

Dedicated to Marvin Novoa Escobar (R.I.P.), Weasel, and the rest of the Homies struggling in this transnational madness.

1. Literally translates as "it can be done, of course it can."

Chapter 7. Globalizing Child Soldiers in Sierra Leone

1. See Richards 1995, 1996; Riley 1996; Abdullah et al. 1997; Opala 1994.

2. The field of childhood studies takes as its starting point the notion that

modern childhood grew out of a specific history in Europe. Ariès is the best known and first proponent of the field (Ariès 1962). In her groundbreaking work on children and the politics of culture, Sharon Stephens says, "The crucial task for researchers now . . . is to develop more powerful understandings of the role of the child in structures of modernity. The historical processes by which these once localized western constructions have been exported around the world and the global political, economic, and cultural transformations that are currently rendering childhood so dangerous, contested, and pivotal in the formation of new sorts of social persons, groups, and institutions" (1995, 13).

3. Fieldwork was generously supported by a grant from the Center for African Studies at the University of California, Berkeley. Write-up has been funded by the American Association of University Women, the Institute on Global Conflict and Cooperation, and the Harry Frank Guggenheim Foundation.

4. Of course, this system was also in flux before, during, and after the period of my fieldwork. Policies were revised, populations moved, certain agencies gained or lost funding.

5. From a letter to *BBC Focus on Africa,* November 14, 2001.

6. In Europe and the United States, too, child recruits were common. Emmy Werner, in her excellent study of children involved in the U.S. Civil War, writes: "Historians estimate that anywhere between 250,000 and 420,000 boy soldiers, many in their early teens or even younger, served in the armies of the Union and the Confederacy between 1861 and 1865. Their experience in battle, seen from their vantage point, bears a striking resemblance to the eyewitness reports of contemporary child soldiers in Angola, Ethiopia, Liberia, Mozambique, Central America, and the Middle East" (1998, 2).

7. Cohn and Goodwin-Gill (1994), in their review of the child soldiers around the world, found that children separated from their families were especially likely to join fighting forces as a means of survival.

8. "Soldiers are no good. As long as they are carrying guns, they are no good."

9. In Abdullah et al. 1997. Patrick Muana uses the Mende term *njiahungbia ngorgeisia* to mean the smart, sharp, and alert young men.

10. Another influence, one that I didn't spend much time researching and therefore cannot really comment on, is an international culture of Islamic youth militancy.

11. Maskita, after rumors of his death on the BBC, resurfaced in Liberia and was involved in the civil war there and then in the Ivory Coast.

Chapter 8. "Jackie Chan Is Nobody, and So Am I"

1. McDowell (1996) distinguishes between three phases of Sri Lankan Tamil emigration: an early phase between 1983 and 1985, a middle phase between 1986 and 1988, and a late phase from 1998 to 1991. In terms of the numbers of emigrees, the late phase is the most significant. In the following, I use "Tamil diaspora" to refer exclusively to the Sri Lankan Tamil community.

2. Romantsch is an alpine Latin dialect.

3. According to Mahnig and Piguet, the Swiss immigration policy of restricted admissions or quota policy is singular in Europe, as no other European country practices a similar policy (Mahnig and Piguet 2003, 65).

4. Data for Switzerland: "[O]nly 7.8 percent [of these foreigners] are non-European" (McDowell 1996, 55).

5. The three circles roughly correspond to the immigration zones defined by the Schengen Agreement (Solioz 1996, 41).

6. Cf. Sassen 1996, 171. Further readings and details on EU immigration policy can be found in Sassen 1996; Bade 2001, and Koslowski 1998.

7. For more information see: www.admin.ch/ch/d/sr/142_205/index.html.

8. In 1995, the three European countries with the highest rate of foreign residents were Liechtenstein (38.1 percent), Luxemburg (33.4 percent) and Switzerland (18.9 percent). Naturalization laws and practices still differ very much among European nations: Sweden and the Netherlands are the countries with the highest naturalization rates; Germany remains the country with the lowest rate (for the period 1986–1994, according to Bade 2001, 20).

9. "The diversification of the countries of origin from labor-migrants—the former Yugoslavia, Portugal, and Turkey got increasingly important during the 1980s—as well as from asylum-seekers—who come mainly from Sri Lanka, the former Yugoslavia, and Turkey—led in the last years to an increasing heterogeneity of the cultural background of migrants. However, in 1997 the most important foreign groups were still the Italians (25.8 percent), followed by the people from the former Yugoslavia (23.2 percent), the Portuguese (10.2 percent), and the Spaniards (7.1 percent). So the "traditional recruitment countries' are still the most important countries of origin of migrants in Switzerland" (Mahnig and Wimmer 1998).

10. Between 1983 and 1991, roughly two hundred thousand Tamils fled the strife of civil war between the Tamil and Singhalese populations in Sri Lanka and emigrated to Europe. Switzerland hosts the largest Tamil population in Europe, currently counting thirty thousand people (McDowell 1996).

11. "Tamils became the first target group for Europe's most significant country-specific return programme for refugees, being sent home to a country in which a conflict still continued" (McDowell 1996, 59). This status applies mostly to Tamils who arrived in Switzerland after 1989.

12. The Italian immigrants suffered from a similiar racism at the time in the 1960s (as shown, for example, in Alexander J. Seiler's documentary, *Siamo Italiani,* from 1964).

13. Children growing up in the German part of Switzerland usually speak Swiss German, a German dialect different in grammar and vocabulary from written German. They only learn written, or "High" German, in school, while continuing to speak Swiss German among their family and friends. While this technically makes written German the first foreign language for Swiss children, children with a foreign language background, whose first contact with German is with other children's Swiss German, face additional problems in learning the adopted language properly.

14. See Hing-Yuk Wong (1999).

15. Tamils in Switzerland mostly watch South Indian films produced in Madras, India, as they did in their ancestral homes. South Indian films share many of the characteristics of Hindi mainstream films in terms of narration, which does not mean that they are identical.

Chapter 9. Authenticating Practices

I would like to thank Vassar College for support through the Andrew W. Mellon Post-Doctoral Fellowship that facilitated the writing of this article. My appreciation also goes out to the MEC collaborative team, Harry Elam Jr., Robin D. G. Kelley, Paulla Ebron, Elisabeth Soep, Sunaina Maira, Lisa Arellano, Shirley Brice Heath, Raul Coronado Jr., Yael Ben-zvi, Cynthia Tolentino, Lisa Thompson, and Colleen Cohen for invaluable feedback and critical engagement at different stages of writing this essay.

1. I adopt the term "racialized" from Michael Omi and Howard Winant's influential study of race (1994). "Racialized" refers to the marking of subjects as racial beings through historical and social processes. The authors base the term in what they describe as "racial formation," or "the sociohistorical process by which racial categories are created, inhabited, transformed, and destroyed" (1994, 55).

2. This is part of a much larger study of collaboration and representation in youth-based media arts organizations. In addition to MEC, the larger study looks at four other media arts organizations in urban centers in the United States.

3. I use "real" (in quotation marks) to designate what is considered actual or lived experiences of reality.

4. "The digital divide," referring to the disparity between those who have technological access and skills and those who lack resources and exposure in an increasingly globalized technocracy, is a concept that I find problematic because it does not fully address issues of inequality and representations of inequality with regard to race and technology. At the same time, the concept has gained a great deal of cultural cache in American public discourse and public policy circles. A recent anthology, *Technicolor: Race, Technology, and Everyday Life* (Nelson, Tu, and Hines 2001), attempts to address critically issues of race and technology that move beyond the remedial debates currently taking place regarding "the digital divide."

5. Prior to the start of the workshop, I had arranged with Sarah to spend half of my time during the project as her teaching assistant and half of my time taking research notes. I worked with her on an administrative level to recruit participants and to secure a workshop site before the project began. Once the workshops began, all sessions were recorded. Recording during production and post-production was logistically impossible. The youth producers were aware of my role; I explained to them that I was doing research for my dissertation at Stanford University and that I was interested in community media practices and representations of youth through media. During the first couple of sessions, Anita enjoyed the novelty of the tape recorder and would point the microphone at individuals when talking. She also often prompted me when the tape needed changing. This curiosity soon died as we moved into developing the narrative. Occasionally, I felt conflicted by my dual position, particularly during pre-production meetings when shaping the narrative. As a participant, I felt responsible to be present and involved; yet, I was also concerned about my influence in shaping the project and the power dynamics between the youth producers, Sarah, and myself. In the end, I recognized that there was no clear division between my different roles in the project and that my search to document and represent the workshop process and the politics of representation involved in the program contributes to the reliance on realness in representational practices.

6. During the mid-1990s, a politicized youth movement emerged in California as a response to growing anti-youth sentiment and legislation. This movement often overlapped and collaborated with youth-adult artistic collaborations. One of the most oppressive measures targeted at youth was Proposition 21: The Juvenile Crime Initiative. The measure, approved by voters in 2000, lowered the

age at which youth could be tried as adults for felonies to fourteen. The representations of youth as terror ran throughout American news media in the 1990s, from images of blacks and Latinos as gang members to disaffected, white young males on shooting rampages at schools. For more on representations of youth crime and violence, see Giroux 1996; Acland 1995; and Kelley 1994.

7. Sarah actually has lived in the Mission District for several years, though she is not a member of the various "communities" to which the youth belonged. At the time, I lived in Oakland and was not involved in the "community" represented through the grant or the collaborative project.

8. These topics are typical of the youth-based media projects that I researched. Many of the final pieces often serve as public service announcements on the dangers of drugs, violence, or unprotected sex.

9. Kendall Thomas and a host of other scholars (including Gayatri Spivak and Stuart Hall) have argued for the necessity of a new form of collectivism across differences, often called "strategic essentialism." Seeing racial identification as "a contingent situated strategy" (Thomas 1997, 132) allows for collective political engagement to challenge white, heterosexual, adult normative systems, while also recognizing the contradictory and conflictual variables that constitute this identity. In the context of youth community art practices, strategic employment of identity is used to call forth participants. My critique here is how this collectivism among youth in American urban centers often relies on the rhetoric of racial authenticity associated with heteronormative black political and artistic movements in the United States.

10. I am indebted to Elisabeth Soep for my formulation of the problem here.

11. For an analysis of authenticity, racial masculinity, and "the ghetto" in *Menace II Society*, see Farred 1995.

12. Endemic of the polarization between minoritized groups is the representation in news and popular media of tensions between black communities and Korean shopkeepers. These tensions and their portrayals have intensified since the Los Angeles riots (April 1992). The reiteration of these groups as diametrically opposed and divided by unbridgeable cultural gaps overshadows the material struggles for limited resources and the ways in which normative white power marginalizes and divides minoritized groups. George Lipsitz's recent study is a compelling analysis of these divisive political practices and the ways in which they have negative effects on struggles of minoritized groups (2001).

13. It is important to note that during the set-up for the corner store scene and between "takes," Sal and the youth playing Taquan joked and talked uninhibitedly with each other. The two had not met prior to the MEC shoot. Their ease at performing tropes of opposing identity groups was based on what I interpret as an unspoken awareness and trust that the words were iterative and not targeted at the being to whom they were addressed.

14. For more on discourses of race, citizenship, and immigration in the United States, see Lowe 1996.

Chapter 10. Making Hard-Core Masculinity

I would like to thank Shirley Brice Heath, Jabari Mahiri, Leisy Wyman, Stuart Tannock, Rachel Sherman, and Sunaina Maira for thoughtful feedback on earlier versions of this chapter.

1. All individuals named in this essay have been given pseudonyms. I have changed the title of the movie and production company described here, doing

my best to maintain the spirit of the original names, including their gendered quality. JR had, in another context, described himself as "low income" and worked to help support himself and get through school. Some of the other boys lived in comfortable one-family homes and planned to attend private universities.

2. The school's website lists these demographics for students: approximately 32 percent Asian (majority Filipino), 25 percent White, 23 percent Latino, 11 percent multiracial, 8 percent African American, and the remaining less-than-1 percent Native American.

3. Communication is a major preoccupation among globalization scholars who analyze how information flows through new economic, technological, and cultural orders (Beck, Giddens, and Lash 1994; Burawoy 2000; Jameson 1998; Ong 1999b). The notion of "networks" offers one way to examine how individuals and groups experience asymmetrical access to privileged forms of knowledge through work and leisure (de Certeau 1997). Consumption is seen as a driving force within those networks through which young people and adults exercise citizenship (García Canclini 2001). In this analysis, I am especially indebted to Cameron's 1998 study of how young males in everyday communication produce "red blooded heterosexuality" by using speech patterns normally associated with girls to distance themselves from queer guys. See also Gaudio 1997.

4. My focus in that study, which has now extended over an eight-year period, is a particular linguistic practice that emerges in settings where young people jointly produce original work. That practice is critique, and it manifests in moments of collaborative judgment or mutual assessment among peers. Through observation, audio and video recording, and participation, I have studied critique among college art students, high-school-aged cartoonists, teenage girls shopping together in urban malls, on-line videogame designers, and most extensively youths participating in community-based multimedia arts projects (Soep 2000, 2002 and 2003). My own study of critique built on the foundation of a ten-year national study of the nonschool lives of youth (Heath 2001; Heath and McLaughlin 1994a and b; Heath and Soep 1998; Tannock 1998 and 1999).

5. One way to avoid these abstract binaries is to locate language use within complex "communities of practice" defined by joint social engagement (Eckert and McConnell-Ginet 1998, 490). Youth-initiated activities like Hard-Core Productions, which are devoid of adult or institutional sponsorship, are among the least-examined communities of practice (Austin and Willard 1998), despite a burgeoning interest within youth culture studies in producing a "theory of cultural learning" (Cohen and Ainley 2000) that accounts for how young people produce social categories such as gender and race through situated performance and practice (Wyn and White 1997).

6. XXX in this transcript signifies brief passages of indecipherable speech.

7. This absence of an explicit class analysis is interesting but perhaps not surprising given how silent class analysis tends to be in the United States, and the extent to which class is often spoken of through the proxy of race.

Chapter 11. Bad Boys

Chapter 11 was reprinted from Todd Ramlow, "Bad boys: Abstractions of difference and the politics of youth 'deviance,'" *GLQ* 9 (2003): 1–2, 107–32. Reprinted with permission of *GLQ*.

1. Throughout this essay I prefer to use Cindy Patton's (1985) term "eroto-phobia" and Erving Goffman's (1986) "stigmaphobia" rather than the some-times limiting "homophobia" and "ableism" (although these words do appear from time to time) to suggest that the abstractions of social disqualification, while in many ways based on the material fact of sexual and physical difference, rely not on the presence of such difference but on its availability for metaphoric erasure.

2. The May–June 2001 issue of the *Gay and Lesbian Review,* which takes on the Eminem analysis in the wake of the rapper's duet with Elton John at the 2001 Grammy Awards, offers careful analysis from lesbian and gay intellectuals who both criticize and defend Em's "freedom of artistic expression."

3. At this end of the continuum of racist stereotypes and disqualification, the black race is disempowered through devaluation, while at the other end black men, in particular, are subjected to increased surveillance and policing precisely because of their unrestrained (hetero)sexuality and aggressive masculinity.

4. In reference to social discourses of disability, Sharon L. Snyder and David T. Mitchell (2000, 7) note: "It is important to state at the outset that this argu-ment does not deny the reality of physical incapacity or cognitive difference. Rather, we set out the coordinates of the social reception and . . . representation of those labeled deviant on ideological as well as physical planes." Similarly, Rosemarie Garland-Thomson (1997, 6) remarks that "disability . . . is the attribu-tion of corporeal deviance—not so much a property of bodies as a product of cultural rules about what bodies should be or do." That some of the youthful bodies I consider here are queer and/or disabled, then, is perhaps less impor-tant than that all of them are marked abstractly as queer and/or disabled by dominant discourses insofar as they exceed or break cultural rules about what young bodies and subjectivities should be or do.

5. Various scholars besides Linton have promoted the resignification of dis-ability. Robert McRuer (2002, 88–99) offers the neologism compulsory able-bodiedness, Carol A. Breckenridge and Candace Vogler (2001, 349–57) theorize "the willed production of disability," Eli Clare (2001, 359–65) considers the figure of "irrevocable difference," and Snyder and Mitchell (2001) offer the phrase reclaiming disability, to list only a few.

6. Clare (2001, 360) delimits the dominant cultural models of disability as follows: "The medical model insists on disability as a disease or condition that is curable and/or treatable. The charity model declares disability to be a tragedy, a misfortune, that must be tempered or erased by generous giving. The super-crip model frames disability as a challenge to overcome and disabled people as superheroes just for living our daily lives. The moral model transforms disability into a sign of moral weakness."

7. Warner (2000, 38), recognizing the limitations of the term homophobia, remarks that "it suggests that the stigma and oppression directed against this entire range of people can be explained simply as a phobic reaction to same-sex love. In fact, sexual stigmas are more shifty than we think."

8. Linton (1998, 16) characterizes this function as the "metaphoric vitality" of "nasty words." She offers the following hypothetical example: "The exposé in the newspaper crippled the politician's campaign." Here the term crippled, divested of its connection to real physical disability, takes on a metaphoric life of its own.

9. Snyder and Mitchell (2001, 375) make this function even clearer: "Disabil-ity translates into a common denominator of cultural fascination (if not down-

right obsession)—one that infiltrates thinking across discursive registers as a shared reference point in deciding matters of human value and communal belonging."

10. Rachel Adams (2001) also analyzes how freak shows have functioned in American cultural history and how U.S. culture attempted to "frame" the anomalous body during the twentieth century.

11. Richard Linklater's *Slacker* (1991) and Ben Stiller's *Reality Bites* (1994) are the most succinct visual representations of the Gen-X debates and of cultural anxieties over "nonproductive" youth.

12. This figuration of disability deploys at least two of Clare's (2001) normative models of disability discourse: the "charity" and "supercrip" models. In the case of Columbine, however, these models are deployed not to say anything about disability in itself but to delineate the disabling effects of youth violence and deviance on normative American culture.

13. This stigmaphobic response to violence and youth deviance has an erotophobic correlate in the stereotype of homosexual predation on the young, particularly the notion that gay men tend or seek to "corrupt" straight men and young boys, and that homosexuality is somehow contagious and heterosexuality is always already susceptible to infection.

14. These connections between Nazi Germany and American fascism have been clearest, perhaps, in relation to the AIDS epidemic. For excellent commentary on these trends from both American and German perspectives see Wojnarowicz 1991; Scholder 1999; Zingler 1989.

15. Both Singleton and Clark continue to be attuned to shifts in the cultural perception and enfranchisement of black and working-class youth cultures in America. Clark's most recent film, *Bully* (2001), is based on Jim Schutze's (1998) book *Bully: Does Anyone Deserve to Die?*, in which a group of picked-on high school kids murder the school bully. While Singleton moves away from visible disability as commentary on 'hood life in *Baby Boy* (2001), his characterization of a generation of young black men as infantilized by the 'hood and by a racist dominant culture echoes the stories that people with disabilities tell of their own sexual and psychological infantilization at the hands of institutional authority. See Shakespeare, Gillespie-Sells, and Davies 1996.

16. That this man is one of the film's "real" people, a recognizable figure in the New York City subway system, adds to the authenticity of the film, at least for those of us in the know. Yet the man's obvious exploitation by Clark for shock value or pity and his metaphoric identification with Telly and Casper further attest to the spectacle of youth in/as crisis as the modern-day equivalent of the freak show.

References

Abdalla, A., et al. 2002. Human Rights in Sierra Leone: A Research Report to Search for Common Ground. Washington, D.C.: Search for Common Ground.

Abdullah, I., et al. 1997. Lumpen youth culture and political violence: Sierra Leoneans debate the RUF and the Civil War. *Africa Development* 22(3/4):171–215.

Acland, Charles. 1995. *Youth, murder, spectacle: The cultural politics of "youth in crisis."* Boulder, Colo.: Westview.

Adams, Rachel. 2001. *Sideshow U.S.A.: Freaks and the American cultural imagination.* Chicago: University of Chicago Press.

Adams, Vincanne. 1996. *Tigers of the snow and other virtual sherpas.* Princeton, N.J.: Princeton University Press.

Affi, Ladan. 1997. The Somali crisis in Canada: The single mother phenomenon. In *Mending the rips in the sky: Options for Somali communities in the twenty-first century,* edited by Hussein Adam and Richard Ford. Lawrenceville, N.J.: Red Sea Press.

Agosin, Marjorie, and Betty Jean Craige. 2002. *To mend the world: Women reflect on 9/11.* Buffalo, N.Y.: White Pine Press.

Air salta: Taking a stand for clean air through community organizing. 2000. *Toxinformer* 19(2) (April).

American Anthropological Association. 1998. AAA Statement on "Race." *Anthropology Newsletter,* May 17, 1.

American Civil Rights Coalition. 2002. April 5 editorial: Undermining identity politics. Electronic document, http://www.acrc1.org/editorial.htm (accessed October 9, 2003).

Amit-Talai, Vered, and Helena Wulff, eds. 1995. *Youth cultures: A cross-cultural perspective.* London: Routledge.

Amway. 2002. www.amway.com. Official Amway website.

Anderson, Benedict. 1991. *Imagined communities: Reflections on the origin and spread of nationalism.* London: Verso.

Appadurai, Arjun. 1996. *Modernity at large: Cultural dimensions of globalization.* Minneapolis: University of Minnesota Press.

Ariès, P. 1962. *Centuries of childhood.* New York: Knopf.

Austin, Joe, and Michael Nevin Willard. 1998a. *Generations of youth: Youth cultures and history in twentieth-century America.* New York: New York University Press.

———, eds. 1998b. Introduction: Angels of history, demons of culture. In *Generations of youth: Youth cultures and history in twentieth-century America,* edited by Joe Austin and Michael Nevin Willard, 1–20. New York: New York University Press.

Avon Outlook newsletter. 1931. February edition.

Bade, Klaus J. 2001. Einwanderungskontinent Europa: Migration und Integration am Ende des 20. Jahrhunderts. In *Einwanderungskontinent Europa: Migration und Integration am Beginn des 21. Jahrhunderts,* edited by Klaus J. Bade, 19–47. Osnabrück: Universitätsverlag Rasch, 2001.

Bailey, Benjamin. 2000. Language and negotiation of ethnic/racial identity among Dominican Americans. In *Language and Society* 29:555–82.

Baker, Lee. 2000. Profit, power, and privilege: The racial politics of ancestry. Paper presented at the Annual Meeting of the American Educational Research Association, April 25, New Orleans, La.

Baldwin, James. 2001. Here be dragons. In *Traps: African American men on gender and sexuality,* edited by Rudolph P. Byrd and Beverly Guy-Sheftall. Bloomington: Indiana University Press.

Ball, Stephen, Meg Maguire, and Sheila MacRae. 2000. Space, work and the "new urban economies." *Journal of Youth Studies* 3(3):279–300.

Bamyeh, Mohammed A. 2000. "The new imperialism: Six theses." *Social Text* 62, 18(1):1–29.

Banks, Gabrielle. 2002. The tattooed generation: Salvadoran children bring home American gang culture. [online] *Dissent Magazine* 47(1) (winter 2000), http://www.dissentmagazine.org/archive/wi00/banks.html (accessed October 26, 2002).

Basch, Linda, Nina Glick Schiller, and Cristina Szanton Blanc, eds. 1994. *Nations unbound: Transnational projects, postcolonial predicaments, and deterritorialized nation-states.* Amsterdam: Gordon and Breach.

Baudrillard, Jean. 1988. *Selected writings.* Edited by Mark Poster. Stanford, Calif.: Stanford University Press.

Bayart, J.-F., et al. 1999. *The criminalization of the state in Africa.* Oxford: James Currey.

Beck, Ulrich, Anthony Giddens, and Scott Lash. 1994. *Reflexive modernization: Politics, tradition, and aesthetics in the modern social order.* Stanford, Calif.: Stanford University Press.

Benson, Kathleen, and Philip M. Kayal. 2002. *A community of many worlds: Arab Americans in New York City.* New York: Museum of the City of New York.

Beynon, John, and Dunkerley, David, eds. 2000. *Globalization: The reader.* New York: Routledge.

Bhabha, Homi. 1991. Introduction: Narrating the nation. In *Nation and narration,* edited by Homi Bhabha, 1–7. London and New York: Routledge.

———.1994. *The location of culture.* London: Routledge.

———.1995. Freedom's basis in the indeterminate. In *The identity in question,* edited by John Rajchman. New York: Routledge.

Bhavnani, Kum-Kum. 1991. *Talking politics: A psychological framing for views from youth in Britain.* Cambridge: Cambridge University Press.

Bishop, Ryan, and Lillian S. Robinson. 1998. *Night market: Sexual cultures and the Thai economic miracle.* New York: Routledge.

Blackwood, Evelyn. 1995. Senior Women, Model Mothers, and Dutiful Wives: Managing Gender Contradictions in a Minangkabau Village. In *Bewitching Women, Pious Men: Gender and Body Politics in Southeast Asia,* ed. Aihwa Ong and Michael G. Peletz, 124–58. Berkeley: University of California Press.

Bordwell, David. 2000. *Planet Hong Kong: Popular cinema and the art of entertainment.* Cambridge, Mass.: Harvard University Press.

Bourdieu, Pierre. 1972. *Outline of a theory of practice.* Cambridge: Cambridge University Press.

Bowden, Mark. 1999. *Black hawk down: A story of modern war.* New York: Atlantic Monthly Press.

Bowman, James. 1995. Clueless Kids at the Apollo. *American Spectator,* November, 28(9):60+.

Boyd, Todd. 1997. *Am I black enough for you?: Popular culture from the 'hood and beyond.* Bloomington: University of Indiana Press.

Boyle, Dierdre. 1997. *Subject to change: Guerrilla television revisited.* New York: Oxford University Press.

Breckenridge, Carol, and Candace Vogler. 2001. The critical limits of embodiment: Disability's criticism. *Public Culture* 13:349–57.

Brenner, Suzanne. 1995. Why Women Rule the Roost: Rethinking Javanese Ideologies of Gender and Self-Control. In *Bewitching Women, Pious Men: Gender and Body Politics in Southeast Asia,* ed. Aihwa Ong and Michael G. Peletz, 19–50. Berkeley: University of California Press.

Buckingham, David. 2000. *The making of citizens: Young people, news, and politics.* London and New York: Routledge.

Buff, Rachel. 2001. *Immigration and the political economy of home: West Indian Brooklyn and American Indian Minneapolis, 1945–1992.* Berkeley: University of California Press.

Burawoy, Michael. Introduction: Reaching for the Global. In *Global ethnography: Forces, connections, and imaginations in a postmodern world,* edited by Michael Burawoy, Joseph Blum, Sheba George, Zsuzsa Gille, Teresa Gowen, Lynne Haney, Maren Klawiter, Steven H. Lopez, Seán Ó Riain, and Millie Thayer, 1–40. Berkeley: University of California Press.

———. 2000. Reaching for the global. In *Global ethnography: Forces, connections, and imagination in a postmodern world,* edited by Michael Burawoy, Joseph Blum, Sheba George, Zsuzsa Gille, Teresa Gowen, Lynne Haney, Maren Klawiter, Steven Lopez, Sean Riain, and Millie Thayer, 1–40. Berkeley: University of California Press.

Burbach, Roger, and Ben Clarke. 2002. *September 11 and the U.S. war: Beyond the curtain of smoke.* San Francisco: City Lights.

Burnett, Ron. 1996. "Video: The Politics of Culture and Community." In *Resolutions: Contemporary video practices,* edited by Michael Renov and Erika Suderburg, 283–303. Minneapolis: University of Minnesota Press.

Butler-Kisber, Lynn, and Murray Forman. 1998. ON2 Case Study. In *Student engagement in learning and school life: School case reports,* edited by W. Smith, H. Donahue, and A. Vibert. Montreal: Office of Research on Educational Policy, McGill University.

Butterfield, Steve. 1985. *Amway: The cult of free enterprise.* Boston: South End Press.

Cameron, Deborah. 1998. Performing gender identity: Young men's talk and the construction of heterosexual masculinity. In *Language and gender: A reader,* edited by Jennifer Coates, 270–84. Oxford: Blackwell.

Carroll, Noël. 1996. Prospects for Film Theory: A Personal Assessment. In *Post-Theory: Reconstructing Film Studies,* edited by David Bordwell and Noël Carroll, 37–68. Madison: University of Wisconsin Press.

Castells, Manuel. 1997. *The power of identity.* Malden, Mass.: Blackwell.

Cattacin, Sandro. 1996. Il federalismo integrativo: Qualche considerazione sulle modalità di integrazione degli immigrati in Svizzera. In *I come identità, integrazione, interculturalità,* edited by Vittoria Lusso Cesari, Sandro Cattacin, and Cristina Allemann-Ghionda, 67–82. Zurich: Federazione Colonie Libere Italiane in Svizzera.

CBS. 2002. L.A.'s dirty export. In CBS News Special Assignment, CBSNews.org, http://earthops.org/immigration/marasalvatrucha.html (accessed October 26, 2002).

Chambers, Iain. 1994. *Migrancy, culture, identity.* New York: Routledge.

Chang, Nancy. 2002. *Silencing political dissent: How post-September 11 anti-terrorism measures threaten our civil liberties.* New York: Seven Stories/Open Media.

Cheah, Pheng. 1998. The cosmopolitical—today. In *Cosmopolitics: Thinking and feeling beyond the nation,* edited by Pheng Cheah and Bruce Robbins, 20–40. Minneapolis: University of Minnesota Press.

Cheah, Pheng, and Bruce Robbins, eds. 1998. *Cosmopolitics: Thinking and feeling beyond the nation.* Minneapolis: University of Minnesota Press.

Cintron, Ralph. 1997. *Angels' Town: Chero ways, gang life, and rhetorics of the everyday.* Boston: Beacon Press.

Clare, Eli. 2001. Stolen bodies, reclaimed bodies: Disability and queerness. *Public Culture* 13:359–65.

Clarke, George Elliott. 1998. White like Canada. *Transition,* issue 73, 7:1.

Clarke, John, et al. 1976. Subcultures, cultures and class: A theoretical overview. In *Resistance through rituals: Youth subcultures in post-war Britain,* edited by Stuart Hall and Tony Jefferson, 9–79. London: Routledge.

Clarke, Paul A. 1996. *Deep citizenship.* East Haven, Conn.: Pluto Press.

Clifford, James. 1992. Traveling cultures. In *Cultural studies,* edited by Lawrence Grossberg, Cary Nelson, and Paula Treichler, 96–111. New York: Routledge.

———. 1997. Diasporas. In *The ethnicity reader: Nationalism, multiculturalism, and migration,* edited by Montserrat Guiberneau and John Rex, 283–90. Cambridge: Polity Press.

———. 1998. Mixed Feelings. In *Cosmopolitics: Thinking and feeling beyond the nation,* edited by Pheng Cheah and Bruce Robbins, 362–70. Minneapolis: University of Minnesota.

Coates, Jennifer. 1989. Gossip revisited: Language in all-female groups. In *Women in their speech communities,* edited by Jennifer Coates and Deborah Cameron, 94–122. New York: Longman.

———. 1996. *Women talk: Conversation between women friends.* Oxford: Blackwell.

———. 1997. One-at-a-time: The organization of men's talk. In *Language and masculinity,* edited by Sally Johnson and Ulrike Hanna Meinhof, 107–29. Oxford: Blackwell.

Cohen, Jody. 1993. Constructing race at an urban high school: In their minds, their mouths, their hearts. In *Beyond silenced voices: Class, race, and gender in United States schools,* edited by Lois Weis and Michelle Fine. Albany: State University of New York Press.

Cohen, Phil. 1997. *Rethinking the youth question: Education, labour, and cultural studies.* Durham, N.C.: Duke University Press.

Cohen, Phil, and Pat Ainley. 2000. In the country of the blind? Youth studies and cultural studies in Britain. *Journal of Youth Studies* 3(1):79–95.

Cohen, Ruth Schwartz. 1985. The Industrial Revolution in the home. In *The Changing Shape of Technology,* edited by Donald MacKenzie and Judy Wajcman, 181–201. Philadelphia: Open University Press.

Cohen, Stanley. 1972. *Folk devils and moral panics: The creation of the mods and rockers.* Oxford: Basil Blackwell.

———. 1997. Symbols of trouble. In *The subcultures reader,* edited by Ken Gelder and Sarah Thornton, 149–62. London: Routledge.

Cohn, I., and G. Goodwin-Gill. 1994. *Child soldiers: The role of children in armed conflict.* Oxford: Clarendon Press.

Connell, Rich, and Robert J. López. 1996. Special report: An inside look at 18th Street's menace. *Los Angeles Times Sunday,* November 17.

Conquergood, Dwight. 1992. On reppin' and rhetoric: Gang representations. Unpublished manuscript.

Cooper, F. 2001. What is the concept of globalization good for? An African historian's perspective. *African Affairs* 100(399):189–213.

Cose, Ellis. 1997. *Colorblind: Seeing beyond race in a race-obsessed world.* New York: HarperCollins.

Cruz, José Miguel, and Nelson Portillo Peña. 1998. Solidaridad y violencia en las pandillas del gran San Salvador: Más allá de la vida loca. San Salvador, El Salvador: U.C.A.

Dannin, Robert. 2002. *Black pilgrimage to Islam.* New York: Oxford University Press.

David, Kelly. 1998. The disarmament, demobilization, and reintegration of child soldiers in Liberia: 1994–1997: The process and lessons learned. New York: UNICEF—Liberia and the U.S. National Committee for UNICEF.

Davis, F. James. 1997. *Who is black? One nation's definition.* University Park: Pennsylvania State University Press.

de Certeau, Michel. 1988. *The practice of everyday life.* Translated by Steven Rendell. Berkeley: University of California Press.

———. 1997. *The capture of speech and other political writings.* Minneapolis: University of Minnesota Press.

DeCesare, Donna. 1998. The children of war: Street gangs in El Salvador. *NACLA Report on the Americas* 32 (July-August):21–29.

Delgado, Richard, and Jean Stefancic. 1995. Minority men, misery, and the marketplace of ideas. In *Constructing masculinity,* edited by Maurice Berger, Brian Wallis, and Simon Watson. New York: Routledge.

Diawara, Manthia. 1993. Black studies, cultural studies: Performance acts. In *Border/lines: Canada's magazine of cultural studies* 29(30): 21–26.

Dirlik, Arif. 2001/2002. Colonialism, globalization, and culture: Reflections on September 11. *Amerasia Journal* 27(3)/28(1): 81–92.

Downs, Peter. 1997. Tax abatements don't work. *St. Louis Journalism Review,* February, 5.

DuBois, W. E. B. 1903. *The souls of black folk.* Chicago: A.C. McClurg and Co.

Duncombe, Stephen, ed. 2002. *Cultural resistance reader.* London: Verso.

Duranti, Alessandro, and Charles Goodwin, eds. 1992. *Rethinking context: Language as an interactive phenomenon.* Cambridge: Cambridge University Press.

Dyson, Michael Eric. 1994. "The politics of black masculinity and the ghetto in black film." In *Subversive imagination: Artists, society, and social responsibility,* edited by Carol Becker, 154–67. New York: Routledge.

———. 1996. *Between God and gangsta rap: Bearing witness to black culture.* New York: Oxford University Press.

Eckert, Penelope. 1998. Vowels and nail polish: The emergence of linguistic style in the preadolescent heterosexual marketplace. Proceedings of the 1996 Berkeley Women and Language Conference. Berkeley: Berkeley Women and Language Group.

Eckert, Penelope, and Sally McConnell-Ginet. 1998. Communities of practice: Where language, gender, and power all live. In *Language and gender: A reader,* edited by Jennifer Coates, 484–94. Oxford: Blackwell.

Edelman, Marian Wright. 2001. A healthy start on the act to leave no child behind. *Chicago Defender,* June 20, 11.

Eder, Donna. 1998. Developing adolescent peer culture through collaborative narration. In *Kids talk: Strategic language use in later childhood,* edited by Susan Hoyle and Carolyn Temple Adger, 82–94. New York: Oxford University Press.

Environmental racism. 2000. *Toxinformer* 19(1) (January).

Epstein, Jonathon, ed. 1998. *Youth culture: Identity in a postmodern world.* Malden, Mass.: Blackwell.

Erikson, Erik H. 1968. *Identity: Youth and crisis.* New York and London: W. W. Norton. 1994 edition.

Etzioni, Amitai, and Jason H. Marsh. 2003. *Rights vs. public safety: America in the age of terrorism.* Lanham, Md.: Rowman and Littlefield.

Fabian, Johannes. 1998. *Moments of freedom: Anthropology and popular culture.* Charlottesville and London: University Press of Virginia.

Fairclough, Norman. 1989. *Language and power.* London: Longman.

Fanthorpe, R. 2001. Neither citizen nor subject? "Lumpen" agency and the legacy of native administration in Sierra Leone." *African Affairs* 100:363–86.

Farred, Grant. 1995. "No way out of the *Menaced Society:* Loyalty within the boundedness of race." *Camera Obscura* 35 (May):7–23.

Ferguson, James. 2002. Global disconnect: Abjection and the aftermath of modernism. In *The anthropology of globalization: A reader,* edited by Jonathan X. Inda and Renato Rosaldo, 136–53. Malden, Mass.: Blackwell.

Ferme, M. 2001. *The underneath of things: Violence, history, and the everyday in Sierra Leone.* Berkeley: University of California Press.

Fiedler, Leslie. 1993. *Freaks: Myths and images of the secret self.* New York: Anchor.

Fine, Michelle. 1997. Witnessing Whiteness. In *Off-white: Readings on race, power, and society,* edited by Michelle Fine, Lois Weis, Linda C. Powell, and L. Mun Wong, 57–65. New York: Routledge.

Fine, Michelle, Lois Weis, Linda C. Powell, and L. Mun Wong, eds. 1997. *Off-white: Readings on race, power, and society.* New York: Routledge.

Fiske, John. 1989. *Understanding popular culture.* Boston: Unwin Hyman.

———. 1996. *Media matters: Race and gender in U.S. politics.* Minneapolis: University of Minnesota Press.

Flores, Juan. 2000. *From bomba to hip hop: Puerto Rican culture and Latino identity.* New York: Columbia University Press.

Flores, William V., and Rina Benmayor, eds. 1997. *Latino cultural citizenship: Claiming identity, space, and rights.* Boston: Beacon Press.

Fordham, Signithia. 1996. *Blacked out: Dilemmas of race, identity, and success at Capital.* Chicago: University of Chicago Press.

Forman, Murray. 2002. *The 'hood comes first: Race, space, and place in rap and hip hop.* Middletown, Conn.: Wesleyan University Press.

Foucault, M. 1991. Governmentality. In *The Foucault effect: Studies in governmentality,* edited by G. Burchell, C. Gordon, and P. Miller, 87–104. Chicago: University of Chicago Press.

Frake, Charles. 1980. *Language and cultural description.* Stanford, Calif.: Stanford University Press.

Fraser, Nancy. 1993. Rethinking the public sphere: A contribution to the critique of actually existing democracy. In *The phantom public sphere,* edited by Bruce Robbins, 1–32. Minneapolis: University of Minnesota Press.

Freeman, Carla. 2000. *High tech and high heels in the global economy: Women, work, and pink-collar identities in the Caribbean.* Durham, N.C.: Duke University Press.

Gaines, Donna. 1990. *Teenage wasteland: Suburbia's dead end kids.* New York: Pantheon.

Gaines, Jane M. 1999. Introduction: "The real returns." In *Collecting visible evidence,* edited by Jane Gaines and Michael Renov, 1–18. Minneapolis: University of Minnesota Press.

Gallagher, Mark. 1997. Masculinity in translation: Jackie Chan's transcultural star text. *The Velvet Light Trap* 39:23–41.

Gamson, Joshua. 1998. *Freaks talk back: Tabloid talk shows and sexual nonconformity.* Chicago: University of Chicago Press.

Ganguly, Keya. 2001. *States of exception: Everyday life and postcolonial identity.* Minneapolis: University of Minnesota Press.

García, Raúl. 1999. *El vómito: Carta a H.C. Moya.* Los Angeles: Editorial Patria Perdida.

García Canclini, Néstor. 2001. *Consumers and citizens: Globalization and multicultural conflicts.* Minneapolis: University of Minnesota Press.

Garland-Thomson, Rosemarie. 1996. From wonder to error—a genealogy of freak discourse in modernity. In *Freakery: Cultural spectacles of the extraordinary body,* edited by Rosemarie Garland-Thomson, 1–22. New York: New York University Press.

———. 1997. *Extraordinary bodies: Figuring physical disability in American culture and literature.* New York: Columbia University Press.

———. 2000. Personal communication, October.

Gates, Philippa. 2002. The man's film: Woo and the pleasures of male melodrama. *Journal of Popular Culture* 35(1):59–79.

Gaudio, Rudolf. 1997. Men who talk like women: Language, gender, and sexuality in Hausa Muslim society. Ph.D. diss., Stanford University.

Geertz, Clifford. 1973 *The interpretation of cultures.* New York: Basic Books.

Gelder, Ken. 1997. Introduction to part 3. In *The subcultures reader,* edited by Ken Gelder and Sarah Thornton, 145–48. London: Routledge.

Gillespie, Marie. 1995. *Television, ethnicity and cultural change.* London: Routledge.

Gillis, John R. 1974. *Youth and history: Tradition and change in European age relations, 1770–present.* New York: Academic Press.

Gilroy, Paul. 1987. *There ain't no black in the Union Jack: The cultural politics of race and nation.* Chicago: University of Chicago Press.

———. 1993a. Between Afro-centrism and Eurocentrism: Youth culture and the problem of hybridity. In *Young* 1(2), electronic document, http://www.alli.fi/nyri/young/1993-2/y932gilr.htm (accessed October 6, 2003).

———. 1993b. *The black Atlantic.* Cambridge, Mass.: Harvard University Press.

———. 1995. ". . . To be real": The dissident forms of black expressive culture. In *Let's get it on: The politics of black performance,* edited by Catherine Ugwu, 12–33. Seattle: Bay.

Ginsburg, Faye. 1995. "Mediating culture: Indigenous media, ethnographic film, and the production of identity." In *Fields of vision: Essays in film studies, visual anthropology, and photography,* edited by Leslie Devereaux and Roger Hillman, 256–91. Berkeley: University of California Press.

Ginsburg, Faye, Lila Abu-Lughod, and Brian Larkin, eds. 2002. *Media worlds: Anthropology on new terrain.* Berkeley: University of California Press.

Giroux, Henry. 1996. *Fugitive cultures: Race, violence, and youth.* New York: Routledge.

———. 2000. *Impure acts: The practical politics of cultural studies.* New York: Routledge.

Glick Schiller, Nina, and Georges Fouron. 2001. *Georges woke up laughing: Long-*

distance nationalism and the search for home. Durham, N.C.: Duke University Press.

Goffman, Erving. 1986. *Stigma: Notes on the management of spoiled identity.* New York: Simon and Schuster.

Goldberg, Jonah. 1995. Grownups and 'Kids.' *Commentary* 100(6):55–57.

Golder, Stefan M. and Thomas Straubhaar. 1999. *Empirical findings in the Swiss migration experience.* Bonn: 12A.

Goldstein, Amy. 2000. At Columbine, reflections on a painful past: Community apprehensive as anniversary nears. *Washington Post,* April 6, A2.

Gonzales, Nancy A., and Ana Mari Cauce. 1995. Ethnic identity and multicultural competence: Dilemmas and challenges for minority youth. In *Toward a common destiny: Improving race and ethnic relations in America,* edited by Willis D. Hawley and Anthony W. Jackson, 131–62. San Francisco: Jossey-Bass.

Goodwin, Marjorie H. 1998. Games of stance: Conflict and footing in hopscotch. In *Kids talk: Strategic language use in later childhood,* edited by Susan Hoyle and Carolyn Temple Adger, 23–46. New York: Oxford University Press.

Gray, Herman. 1995. *Watching race: Television and the struggle for "blackness."* Minneapolis: University of Minnesota Press.

Green, Jordan. 2003. Silencing dissent. *ColorLines* 6(2):17–20.

Griffin, Christine. 1993. *Representations of youth: The study of youth and adolescence in Britain and America.* Cambridge: Polity Press.

Gross, Joan, David McMurray, and Ted Swedenburg. 2002. Arab noise and Ramadan nights: Rai, rap, and Franco-Maghrebi identities. In *The anthropology of globalization: A reader,* edited by Jonathan X. Inda and Renato Rosaldo, 198–230. Malden, Mass.: Blackwell.

Grossberg, Lawrence. 1992. *We gotta get out of this place: Popular conservatism and postmodern culture.* New York: Routledge.

———. 1996. Toward a genealogy of the state of cultural studies: The discipline of communication and the reception of cultural studies in the United States. In *Disciplinarity and dissent in cultural studies,* edited by Cary Nelson and Dilip Gaonkar, 131–69. New York: Routledge.

Guinier, Lani, and Gerald Torres. 2002. *The miner's canary: Enlisting race, resisting power, transforming democracy.* Cambridge, Mass.: Harvard University Press.

Gupta, Akhil, and James Ferguson. 1997a. After "peoples and cultures." In *Culture, power, place: Explorations in critical anthropology,* edited by Akhil Gupta and James Ferguson, 1–29. Durham, N.C.: Duke University Press.

———, eds. 1997b. *Culture, power, place.* Durham, N.C.: Duke University Press.

Gutierrez, Kris. 1994. How talk, context, and script shape contexts for learning: A cross-case comparison of journal sharing. *Linguistics and Education* 5:335–65.

Gutierrez, Kris, B. Rymes, and J. Larson. 1995. Script, counterscript, and underlife in the classroom: James Brown versus Brown v. Board of Education. *Harvard Educational Review* 65(3):445–71.

Hall, Doug, and Sally Jo Fifer, eds. 1990. Illuminating video: An essential guide to video art. San Francisco: Aperture.

Hall, Stuart. 1996. What is this "black" in black popular culture? In *Stuart Hall: Critical dialogue in cultural studies,* edited by David Morley and Kuan-Hsing Chen, 465–75. London: Routledge.

———. 1997. The local and the global: Globalization and ethnicity. In *Dangerous liaisons: Gender, nation, and postcolonial perspectives,* edited by Anne McClintock, Aamir Mufti, and Ella Shohat. Minneapolis: University of Minnesota Press.

———. 2002. Democracy, globalization, and difference. In *Democracy unrealized: Documenta11_Platform1*, edited by Okwui Enwezor, et al., 21–36. Ostfildern-Ruit: Hatje Cantz.

Hall, Stuart, and Tony Jefferson, eds. 1976. *Resistance through rituals: Youth subcultures in post-war Britain*. London: Hutchinson and Co.

Hall, Stuart, Chas Critcher, Tony Jefferson, John Clarke, and Brian Roberts, eds. 1978. *Policing the crisis: Mugging, the state, and law and order*. New York: Holmes and Meier.

Halleck, DeeDee. 2002. *Handheld visions: The impossible possibilities of community media*. New York: Fordham University Press.

Halliday, M. A. K. 1978. *Language as social semiotic: The social interpretation of language and meaning*. Baltimore: University Park Press.

Hamilton, Nora, and Norma S. Chinchilla. 2001. *Seeking community in a global city: Guatemalans and Salvadorans in Los Angeles*. Philadelphia: Temple University Press.

Hammer, J. 1995. "Teenage wasteland: Freetown—postcard." *New Republic* 212(15):10.

Haney, Lynne, and Lisa Pollard, eds. 2003. *Families of a new world: Gender, politics, and state development in a global context*. New York: Routledge.

Haney Lopez, Ian F. 1996. *White by law: The legal construction of race*. New York: New York University Press.

Hannerz, Ulf. 1996. Transnational connections: Culture, people, places. London and New York: Routledge.

Hansen, Thomas B., and Finn Steputat. 2001. Introduction: States of imagination. In *States of imagination: Ethnographic explorations of the postcolonial state*, edited by Thomas B. Hansen and Finn Steputat, 1–38. Durham, N.C.: Duke University Press.

Hardt, Michael, and Antonio Negri. 2001. *Empire*. Cambridge, Mass.: Harvard University Press.

Harper, Phillip Brian. 1996. *Are we not men? Masculine anxiety and the problem of African-American identity*. New York: Oxford University Press.

Harvey, David. 1989. *The condition of postmodernity*. Oxford: Blackwell.

———. 1990. *The condition of postmodernity*. Cambridge, Mass.: Blackwell; London: Routledge.

Heath, Shirley B. 1995. Race, ethnicity, and the defiance of categories. In *Toward a common destiny: Improving race and ethnic relations in America*, edited by Willis D. Hawley and Anthony W. Jackson, 39–70. San Francisco: Jossey-Bass.

———. 2000. Making learning work. *Afterschool Matters* 1(1):33–45.

———. 2001. Three's not a crowd: Plans, roles, and focus in the arts. *Educational Researcher* 30(7):10–17.

Heath, Shirley B., and Milbrey McLaughlin. 1994a. The best of both worlds: Connecting schools and community youth organizations for all-day, all-year learning. *Educational Administration Quarterly* 30(3):278–300.

———. 1994b. Learning for anything everyday. *Journal of Curriculum Studies* 26(5):549–67.

Heath, Shirley B., and Elisabeth Soep. 1998. Youth development and the arts in the non-school hours. *Grantmakers for the Arts* 9(1):9–32.

Hebdige, D. 1979a. *Subculture: The meaning of style*. London, Methuen.

———. 1979b. *Subculture: The meaning of style*. London: Routledge.

———. 1981. *Subculture: The meaning of style*. London and New York: Routledge.

Herbst, Kris. 2002. Magdaleno Rose-Ávila and Homies Unidos. Interview tran-

script in Changemakers.net 1998, http://www.changemakers.net/studio/
avila/avilatr.cfm (accessed October 26, 2002).

Hewitt, Roger. 1997. "Box-out" and "taxing." In *Language and masculinity,*
edited by Sally Johnson and Ulrike Hanna Meinhof, 27–46. Oxford: Blackwell.

Higgins, Laura. 2000. The lead menace. *Riverfront Times,* April 12–18, 17.

Hing, Bill O. 2002. Vigilante racism: The de-Americanization of immigrant
America. *Michigan Journal of Race and Law* 7(2):441–56.

Hing-Yuk Wong, Cindy. 1999. Cities, cultures, and cassettes: Hong Kong cinema
and transnational audiences. *Post Script* 1:87–106.

Homeland. 1999–2000. Directed by Doug Scott. 30 min. Huevos indios produc-
tions/bluestocking films.

Homies Unidos. 2001a. *Homies Unidos 2001 calendar.* Los Angeles: Homies
Unidos.

———. 2001b. *Homies Unidos 2002 calendar.* Los Angeles: Color World Graphics.

———. 2002. Homies El Salvador, http://www.homiesunidos.org/about/about
uselsalvador.htm (cited October 26, 2002).

hooks, bell. 1996. *Reel to real: Race, sex, and class at the movies.* New York:
Routledge.

Howard, A. M., and D. E. Skinner. 1984. "Network building and political power
in northwestern Sierra Leone, 1800–65." *Africa* 54(2):2–28.

Huezo, José William "Weasel." 2002. Former gang members speak. In Radio
Netherlands 1998, http://www.rnw.nl/humanrights/html/stories2.html
(cited October 26, 2002).

Huntington, Samuel P. 1996. *The clash of civilizations and the remaking of world
order.* New York: Simon and Schuster.

Hurrelmann, Klaus. 1989. *Social world of adolescents: International perspectives.*
Amsterdam: Walter de Gruyter.

Hutnyk, John. 2000. In *The right to difference is a fundamental human right: Stephen
Corry and Iris Jean-Klein vs. Richard Wilson and John Hutnyk (GDAT debate no.
10),* edited by Peter Wade, 40–52. Manchester: Group for Debates in Anthropological Theory, University of Manchester.

Inda, Jonathan Xavier, and Renato Rosaldo. 2002a. *The anthropology of globalization: A reader.* London: Blackwell.

———. 2002b. Introduction: A World in Motion. In *The anthropology of globalization: A reader,* ed. Jonathan Xavier Inda and Renato Rosaldo, 1–34. London:
Blackwell.

Jackson, John L., Jr. 2001. *Harlemworld: Doing race and class in contemporary black
America.* Chicago: University of Chicago Press.

Jalloh, A. R. 2000. Sierra Leone: The language of violence. *BBC Focus on Africa*
11:45.

James, A., and A. Prout, eds. 1997. *Constructing and reconstructing childhood: Contemporary issues in the sociological study of childhood.* London and Washington,
D.C.: Falmer Press.

James, Deborah, and Sandra Clarke. 1992. Women, men, and interruptions: A
critical review. In *Gender and conversational interaction,* edited by Deborah Tan-
nen, 281–312. New York: Oxford University Press.

Jameson, Frederic. 1998. Notes on globalization as a philosophical issue. In *The
cultures of globalization,* edited by Frederic Jameson and Masao Miyoshi, 54–77.
Durham, N.C.: Duke University Press.

Jameson, Frederic, and Masao Miyoshi, eds. 1998. *The cultures of globalization.*
Durham, N.C.: Duke University Press.

Jankowski, Martín Sánchez. 1991. *Islands in the street: Gangs and American urban society*. Berkeley: University of California Press.

Jenkins, Henry. 1992. *Textual poachers: Television fans and participatory culture*. London: Routledge.

Johnson, Sally, and Frank Finlay. 1997. Do men gossip? An analysis of football talk on television. In *Language and masculinity*, edited by Sally Johnson and Ulrike Hanna Meinhof, 130–43. Oxford: Blackwell.

Johnson, Sally, and Ulrike Hanna Meinhof, eds. 1997. *Language and masculinity*. Oxford: Blackwell.

Jones, Jacquie. 1992. The accusatory space. In *Black popular culture*, edited by Gina Dent, 95–98. Seattle: Bay.

Jones, Kellie. 2002. *Lorna Simpson*. London: Phaidon Press.

Joxe, Alain. 2002. *Empire of disorder*. Los Angeles and New York: Semiotext(e).

Juhasz, Alexandra. 1995. *AIDSTV: Identity, community, and alternative video*. Durham, N.C.: Duke University Press.

Keefe, Beverly. 2002. Gang members speak up. *Peace Magazine* 13(6) (November–December 1997), http://www.peacemagazine.org (cited October 26, 2002).

Kelley, Robin D. G. 1994. *Race rebels: Culture, politics, and the black working class*. New York: Free Press.

———. 1997a. Looking to get paid: How some black youth put culture to work. In *Yo' mama's disFUNKtional! Fighting the culture wars in urban America*, 43–77. Boston: Beacon Press.

———. 1997b. *Yo' mama's disFUNKtional! Fighting the culture wars in urban America*. Boston: Beacon Press.

Kelly, Peter. 2000. Youth as an artefact of expertise: Problematizing the practice of youth studies in an age of uncertainty. *Journal of Youth Studies* 3(3):301–15.

Kelsky, Karen. 2001. *Women on the verge: Japanese women, western dreams*. Durham, N.C.: Duke University Press.

Kempadoo, Kemala, ed. 1999. *Sun, sex, and gold: Tourism and sex work in the Caribbean*. Lanham, Md.: Rowman and Littlefield.

Kennedy, Lisa. 1992. The body question. In *Black popular culture*, edited by Gina Dent, 106–11. Seattle: Bay.

Kenworthy, Tom. 1999. Up to twenty-five die in Colorado school shooting, two gunmen are found dead. *Washington Post*, April 21, A.01 + .

Kernaghen, Charles. 1999. Sweatshop blues: Companies love misery. *Dollars and Sense* 22:18.

Keyes, Charles. 1984. Mother or mistress but never a monk: Buddhist notions of female gender in rural Thailand. *American Ethnologist* 11(2):223–41.

Kim, Jee, et al., eds. 2002. *Another world is possible: Conversations in a time of terror*. 2d ed. New Orleans: Subway and Elevated Press.

King, Martin Luther, Jr. 1981. *Strength to love*. Philadelphia: Fortress Press.

Kirsch, Thomas. 1982. Buddhism, sex-roles, and the Thai economy. In *Women of Southeast Asia*, edited by Penny Van Esterik, 6–41. Dekalb: Northern Illinois University Press.

Kitwana, Bakari. 2002. *The hip hop generation: Young blacks and the crisis in African American culture*. New York: Basic Civitas Books.

Koslowski, Ray. 1998. European migration regimes: Emerging, enlarging, and deteriorating. *Journal of Ethnic and Migration Studies* 24:735–49.

Kroll, Jack. 1991. The "boyz" of bloodshed. *Newsweek*, July 22, 57.

Lave, J., et al. 1992. Coming of age in Birmingham: Cultural studies and conceptions of subjectivity. *Annual Review of Anthropology* 21:257–82.

Lave, J., and E. Wenger. 1991. *Situated learning: Legitimate peripheral participation.* Cambridge: Cambridge University Press.

Leblanc, Lauraine. 1999. *Pretty in punk: Girls' gender resistance in a boys' subculture.* New Brunswick, N.J.: Rutgers University Press.

Lee, Carol. 2001. Signifying in the zone of proximal development. In *Vygotskian perspectives on literacy research: Constructing meaning through collaborative inquiry,* edited by Carol Lee and Peter Smagorinsky, 191–225. Cambridge: Cambridge University Press.

Leone, Richard, and Greg Anrig Jr. 2003. *The war on our freedoms: Civil liberties in an age of terrorism.* New York: Century Foundation.

Leuzinger-Bohleber, Marianne. 2000. Fallgeschichte. In *Handbuch der psychoanalytischen Grundbegriffe,* edited by Wolfgang Mertens and Bruno Waldvogel, 184–85. Stuttgart: Kohlhammer.

Levinson, Bradley A. 2001. *We are all equal: Student culture and identity at a Mexican secondary school, 1988–1998.* Durham, N.C.: Duke University Press.

Lincoln, Bruce. 2003. *Holy terrors: Thinking about religion after September 11.* Chicago: University of Chicago Press.

Linton, Simi. 1998. *Claiming disability: Knowledge and identity.* New York: New York University Press.

Lipsitz, George. 1994. *Dangerous crossroads: Popular music, postmodernism, and the poetics of place.* London: Verso.

———. 1998. *The possessive investment in whiteness: How white people profit from identity politics.* Philadelphia: Temple University Press.

———. 2001. *American studies in a moment of danger.* Minneapolis: University of Minnesota Press.

López, Robert J., and Rich Connell. 1996. Special report: Gang turns hope to fear, lives to ashes. *Los Angeles Times,* November 18, sec. A, p. 1.

Lowe, Lisa. 1996. *Immigrant acts: On Asian American cultural politics.* Durham, N.C.: Duke University Press.

Lubiano, Wahneema. 1996. "But compared to what?": Reading realism, representation, and essentialism in *School Daze, Do the Right Thing,* and the Spike Lee discourse." In *Representing black men,* edited by Marcellus Blount and George P. Cunningham, 173–204. New York: Routledge.

Luethi, Damaris. 2002. The media window on home: Sri Lankan Tamils in Swiss exile and Indian film. In *Bollywood: The Indian Cinema and Switzerland,* edited by Alexandra Schneider, 42–44. Zuerich: Edition Museum für Gestaltung Zuerich.

Luttrell, Wendy. 2002. *Pregnant bodies, fertile minds: Gender, race, and the schooling of pregnant teens.* New York: Routledge.

Luykx, Aurolyn. 1999. *The citizen factory: Schooling and cultural production in Bolivia.* Albany: State University of New York Press.

MacCabe, Colin. 1986. Theory and film: Principles of realism and pleasure. In *Narrative, Aparatus, ideology: A film theory reader,* edited by Philip Rosen, 179–97. New York: Columbia University Press.

Machel, Graça. 1996. Impact of armed conflict on children. New York: United Nations.

Mahnig, Hans, and Etienne Piguet. 2003. "Die Immigrationspolitik in der Schweiz von 1948 bis 1998: Entwicklung und Auswirkungen." In *Migration und die Schweiz: Ergebnisse des Nationalen Forschungsprogramms "Migration und interkulturelle Beziehungen,"* edited by Hans-Rudolf Wicker, Rosita Fibbi, and Werner Haug, 65–108. Zurich: Seismo.

Mahnig, Hans, and Andreas Wimmer. 1998. Zurich: Political participation and exclusion of immigrants in a direct democracy. Third International Metropolis Conference, Israel. Unpublished paper.

Mailer, Norman. 2003. *Why are we at war?* New York: Random House.

Maira, Sunaina Marr. 2002. *Desis in the house: Indian American youth culture in New York City.* Philadelphia: Temple University Press.

———. Forthcoming. "Planet youth: Asian American youth cultures, citizenship, and globalization." In *New directions for Asian American studies,* edited by Kent Ono. Malden, Mass: Blackwell.

Males, Mike A. 1996. *The scapegoat generation: America's war on adolescents.* Monroe, Maine: Common Courage Press.

Malkki, L. 1994. Citizens of humanity: Internationalism and the imagined community of nations. *Diaspora* 3(1):41–68.

Mamdani, Mahmood. 1996. *Citizen and subject: Contemporary Africa and the legacy of late colonialism.* Princeton, N.J.: Princeton University Press.

Mani. 2001. Film und Jackie Chan. Unpublished paper.

Marable, Manning. 2003. 9/11: Racism in a time of terror. In *Implicating empire: Globalization and resistance in the 21st-century world order,* edited by Stanley Aronowitz and Heather Gautney, 3–14. New York: Basic Books.

Marcus, George. 1998. *Ethnography through thick and thin.* Princeton, N.J.: Princeton University Press.

Margold, Jane A. 1995. From the assembly line to the front lines: Filipina workers in multinational factories. Working Paper No. 3. Department of Anthropology, Chinese University of Hong Kong.

Marko, Katina L. 2001. *Beauty and business: Commerce, gender, and culture in modern America.* New York: Routledge.

Massey, Doreen. 1994. *Space, place, and gender.* Minneapolis: University of Minnesota Press.

Maxted, Julia. 2003. Children and armed conflict in Africa. *Social Identities* 9(3) (March):56.

McAlister, Melani. 2001. *Epic encounters: Culture, media, and U.S. interests in the Middle East, 1945–2000.* Berkeley: University of California Press.

McCarthy, Cameron. 1998. *The uses of culture: Education and the limits of ethnic affiliation.* New York: Routledge.

McDermott, Ray. 1987. Achieving school failure: An anthropological approach to literacy and social stratification. In *Education and cultural process: Anthropological approaches.* 2d ed. Edited by George Spindler, 82–118. Prospect Heights, Ill.: Waveland.

McDowell, Christopher. 1996. *A Tamil asylum diaspora: Sri Lankan migration, settlement, and politics in Switzerland.* Oxford: Berghahn Books.

McLaren, Peter, and Henry Giroux. 1997. Writing from the margins: Geographies of identity, pedagogy, and power. In *Revolutionary multiculturalism: Pedagogies of dissent for the new millennium,* edited by Peter McLaren. Boulder, Colo.: Westview.

McRobbie, Angela. 1994. *Postmodernism and popular culture.* London: Routledge.

———. 1999. *In the culture society: Art, fashion, and popular music.* London: Routledge.

———. 2000. *Feminism and youth culture.* Basingstoke, Hampshire: Macmillan.

McRuer, Robert. 2002. Compulsory able-bodiedness and queer/disabled existence. In *Disability studies: Enabling the humanities,* edited by Sharon Snyder, Brenda Jo Brueggemann, and Rosemarie Garland-Thomson, 88–99. New York: Modern Language Association of America.

MEE Foundation. 1993. Teaching the hip hop generation. In *The MEE Symposium Final Report*. Philadelphia: MEE, Inc.

Mehan, Hugh. 1996. Beneath the skin and between the ears: A case study in the politics of representation. In *Understanding practice: Perspectives on activity and context*, edited by Jean Lave and Seth Chaiklin, 241–68. Cambridge: Cambridge University Press.

Menace II society. 1993. Directed by Albert Hughes and Allen Hughes. 97 min. New Line Home Video. Videocassette.

Merida, Kevin. 1999. When death imitates art: Before teenagers commit violence, they witness it in American culture. *Washington Post*, April 22, C.01+.

Millen, Joyce V., Alex Irwin, and Jim Yong Kim. 2000. Introduction: What is growing? Who is dying? In *Dying for growth: Global inequality and the health of the poor*, edited by Jim Yong Kim, Joyce V. Millen, Alec Irwin, and John Gershman. Monroe, Maine: Common Courage Press.

Miller, Toby. 1993. *The well-tempered subject: Citizenship, culture, and the postmodern subject*. Baltimore: Johns Hopkins University Press.

Mills, Mary Beth. 1999. *Thai women in the global labor force*. New Brunswick, N.J.: Rutgers University Press.

Minow, Martha. 1990. *Making all the difference: Inclusion, exclusion, and American law*. Ithaca, N.Y.: Cornell University Press.

Mishra, Vijay. 2002. *Bollywood cinema: Temples of desire*. New York: Routledge.

Mission tales. 1999. Produced and directed by Kathleen "Butta-Fly" El Beze, Anita Fabio, and Michelle Davis. 26 min. MEC Production. Videocassette.

Mizen, Philip. 2002. Putting the politics back into youth studies: Keynesianism, monetarism and the changing state of youth. *Journal of Youth Studies* 5(1):5–20.

Moerman, Michael. 1968. Being Lue: Uses and abuses of ethnic identification. In *Essays on the problem of tribe*, edited by Jane Helm, 153–69. Seattle: University of Washington Press.

Montagu, Ashley. 1942. *Man's most dangerous myth: The fallacy of race*. 1997 edition. Walnut Creek, Calif.: Altamira Press.

Montgomery, Heather. 1998. Children, prostitution, and identity: A case study from a tourist resort in Thailand. In *Global sex workers: Rights, resistance, and redefinition*, edited by Kamala Kempadoo and Jo Doezema, 139–50. New York: Routledge.

Moore, Joan W. 1991. *Going down to the barrio: Homeboys and homegirls in change*. Philadelphia: Temple University Press.

Moore, Kathleen. 1999. A closer look at anti-terrorism law: American Arab Anti-Discrimination Committee v. Reno and the construction of aliens' rights. In *Arabs in America: Building a new future*, edited by Michael Suleiman, 84–99. Philadelphia: Temple University Press.

Morley, David. 2000. *Home territories: Media, mobility, and identity*. London and New York: Routledge.

Morris, Debra. 2000. Privacy, privation, perversity: Toward new representations of the personal. *Signs: Journal of Women in Culture and Society* 25(2):323–51.

Munoz, Jose Estaban. 1999. *Disidentifications: Queers of color and the performance of politics*. Minneapolis: University of Minnesota Press.

Murphy, W. P. 1980. Secret knowledge as property and power in Kpelle society: Elders versus youth. *Africa* 50:193–207.

Nelson, Alondra, Thuy Linh N. Tu, and Alicia Headlam Hines, eds. 2001. *Technicolor: Race, technology, and everyday life*. New York: New York University Press.

Newsweek. 2000. Special issue: Redefining race in America. September 18.

Nguyen, Tram. 2001. Unsettled refugees. *Color Lines* 4(3) (Fall):31.

Nieto, Sonia. 2000. *Affirming diversity: The sociopolitical context of multicultural education*. New York: Addison Wesley Longman, Inc.

Novoa Escobar, Marvin. 2001. Fruits of war. In *Homies Unidos 2002 Calendar*. Los Angeles: Color World Graphics.

Nussbaum, Martha C., and Joshua Cohen, eds. 1996. *For love of country*. 2002 edition. Boston: Beacon Press.

Oakes, Jeannie, with T. Ormseth, R. Bell, and P. Camp. 1990. *Multiplying inequalities: The effects of race, social class, and tracking on opportunities to learn mathematics and science*. Santa Monica, Calif.: Rand Corporation.

O'Brien, D. C. 1996. A lost generation? Youth identity and state decay in West Africa. In *Postcolonial identities in Africa*, edited by R. Werbner and T. Ranger, 55–74. London: Zed Books Ltd.

Ochs, Elinor. 1992. Indexing gender. In *Rethinking context: Language as an interactive phenomenon*, edited by Allesandro Duranti and Charles Goodwin, 335–58. New York: Cambridge University Press.

O'Donnel, Mike, and Sue Sharpe. 2000. *Uncertain masculinities: Youth, ethnicity, and class in contemporary Britain*. London: Routledge.

Okie, Susan. 2001. Survey: Thirty percent of U.S. schoolchildren involved in bullying. *Washington Post*, April 25.

Olneck, Michael. 1995. Immigrants and education. In *Handbook of research on multicultural education*, edited by J. Banks and C. McGee Banks. New York: Macmillan.

Olsen, Laurie. 1997. *Made in America: Immigrant students in our public schools*. New York: The New Press.

Omi, Michael, and Howard Winant. 1994. *Racial formation in the United States from the 1960s to the 1990s*. 2d ed. New York: Routledge.

Ong, Aihwa. 1987. *Spirits of resistance and capitalist discipline: Factory women in Malaysia*. Albany: State University of New York Press.

———. 1995. State versus Islam: Malay families, women's bodies, and the body politic in Malaysia. In *Bewitching women, pious men: Gender and body politics in Southeast Asia*, edited by Aihwa Ong and Michael G. Peletz, 159–94. Berkeley: University of California Press.

———. 1999a. Cultural citizenship as subject making: Immigrants negotiate racial and cultural boundaries in the United States. In *Race, identity, and citizenship: A reader,* edited by R. D. Torres, L. F. Miron, and J. X. Inda. Malden, Mass.: Blackwell.

———. 1999b. *Flexible citizenship: The cultural logics of transnationality*. Durham, N.C.: Duke University Press.

———. 2002. The Pacific shuttle: Family, citizenship, and capital circuits. In *The anthropology of globalization: A reader,* edited by Jonathan X. Inda and Renato Rosaldo, 172–97. Malden, Mass.: Blackwell.

Opala, J. 1994. "Ecstatic renovation!": Street art celebrating Sierra Leone's 1992 revolution. *African Affairs* 93:195–218.

Orfield, Gary, and Susan Eaton. 1996. *Dismantling desegregation: The quiet reversal of Brown v. Board of Education*. New York: The New Press.

Ortner, Sherry. 1996. Making gender: The politics and erotics of culture. Boston: Beacon Press.

Padilla, Felix M. 1993. *The gang as an American enterprise*. New Brunswick, N.J.: Rutgers University Press.

Panitch, Leo, and Sam Gindin. 2003. Global capitalism and American empire. In *The new imperial challenge,* edited by Leo Panitch and Colin Leys, 1–42. London: Merlin Press.

Parr, Josh. 1999, Young Laotian women build a bridge in Richmond. *Shades of Power* 1(4).

Parreñas, Rhacel Salazar. 2001. *Servants of globalization: Women, migration, and domestic work.* Stanford, Calif.: Stanford University Press.

Patton, Cindy. 1985. *Sex and germs: The politics of AIDS.* Boston: South End.

Peiss, Kathy. 2001. On beauty . . . and the history of business. In *Beauty and business: Commerce, gender, and culture in modern America,* edited by Philip Scranton, 7–23. New York: Routledge.

Pérez Firmat, Gustavo. 1994. *Life on the hyphen: The Cuban-American way.* Austin: University of Texas Press.

Perry, Pamela. 2002. *Shades of white: White kids and racial identities in high school.* Durham, N.C.: Duke University Press.

Peshkin, Alan. 1991. *The color of strangers, the color of friends: The play of ethnicity in school and community.* Chicago: University of Chicago Press.

Peters, K., and P. Richards. 1998. "Why we fight": Voices of youth combatants in Sierra Leone. *Africa* 68(2):183.

Phelan, Peggy. 1993. *Unmarked: The politics of performance.* New York: Routledge.

Pollock, Mica. 2001. How the question we ask most about race in education is the very question we most suppress. In *Educational Researcher* 30(9):2–12.

———. 2004. *Colormute: Race talk dilemmas in an American school.* Princeton, N.J.: Princeton University Press.

Portz, John, Lana Stein, and Robin Rones. 1999. *Institutions and leadership in Pittsburgh, Boston, and St. Louis.* Lawrence: University Press of Kansas.

Potter, Sulamith Heins. 1977. *Family life in a northern Thai village: A study in the structural significance of women.* Berkeley: University of California Press.

Prashad, Vijay. 2003. The green menace: McCarthyism after 9/11. *The Subcontinental: A Journal of South Asian American Political Identity* 1(1):65–75.

Pratt, Mary Louise. 1992. *Imperial eyes.* New York: Routledge.

Rafferty, Terrence. 1995. Growing pains. *New Yorker,* July 31, 80–82.

Ragland, Ellie. 1996. An overview of the real, with examples from Seminar I. In *Reading seminars I and II: Lacan's return to Freud,* edited by Richard Feldstein, Bruce Fink, and Maire Jaanus, 192–211. Albany, N.Y.: State University of New York Press.

Reid-Pharr, Robert. 2001. It's raining men: Notes on the Million Man March. In *Traps: African American men on gender and sexuality,* edited by Rudolph P. Byrd and Beverly Guy-Sheftall. Bloomington: Indiana University Press.

Renan, Ernest. 1991. What is a nation? Translated by Martin Thom. In *Nation and narration,* edited by Homi Bhabha, 8–22. London: Routledge.

Renov, Michael, ed. 1993. *Theorizing documentary.* New York: Routledge.

Richards, Paul. 1994. Videos and violence on the periphery: Rambo and war in the forests of the Sierra Leone-Liberia border. *Knowledge is power? The use and abuse of information in development,* edited by Susanna Davies. *IDS Bulletin,* special issue 25(2):88–93.

———. 1995. Rebellion in Liberia and Sierra Leone: A crisis of youth? In *Conflict in Africa,* edited by O. Furley, 134–74. London: Tauris.

———. 1996. *Fighting for the rain forest: War, youth, and resources in Sierra Leone.* Oxford: James Currey.

Richman, Joe. 2002. Deported: Weasel's diary. Broadcast on "This American

Life," 1999, http://www.radiodiaries.org/transcripts/otherdocs/weasel.html (accessed October 26, 2002).

Riley, S. 1996. *Liberia and Sierra Leone: Anarchy or peace in West Africa?* London: Research Institute for the Study of Conflict and Terrorism.

Robbins, Bruce. 1998. Introduction part 1: Actually existing cosmopolitanism. In *Cosmopolitics: Thinking and feeling beyond the nation,* edited by Pheng Cheah and Bruce Robbins, 1–19. Minneapolis: University of Minnesota.

Robin, Corey. 2003. Fear, American style: Civil liberty after 9/11. In *Implicating empire: Globalization and resistance in the twenty-first century,* edited by Stanley Aronowitz and Heather Gautney, 47–64. New York: Basic Books.

Robins, Kevin. 1991. Tradition and translation: National culture in its global context. In *Enterprise and heritage: Crosscurrents of national culture,* edited by John Corner and Sylvia Harvey. New York: Routledge.

Rodriguez, Luis J. 1993. *Always running, la vida loca: Gang days in L.A.* Millimantic, Conn.: Curbstone Press.

Roediger, David R. 1991. *The wages of whiteness: Race and the making of the American working class.* London: Verso.

———. 1998. What to make of Wiggers: A work in progress. In *Generations of youth: Youth cultures and history in twentieth-century America,* edited by Joe Austin and Michael N. Willard, 358–66. New York: New York University Press.

Rofel, Lisa. 1999. *Other modernities: Gendered yearnings in China after socialism.* Berkeley: University of California Press.

Root, Maria P. P., ed. 1996. *The multiracial experience: Racial borders as the new frontier.* Thousand Oaks, Calif.: Sage.

Rosaldo, Renato. 1997. Cultural citizenship, inequality, and multiculturalism. In *Latino cultural citizenship: Claiming identity, space, and rights,* edited by William F. Flores and Rina Benmayor, 27–38. Boston: Beacon Press.

———. 1999. Cultural citizenship, inequality, and multiculturalism. In *Race, identity, and citizenship: A reader,* edited by R. D. Torres, L. F Miron, and J. X. Inda. Malden, Mass.: Blackwell.

Rose, Tricia. 1994. *Black noise: Rap music and black culture in contemporary America.* Hanover, N.H.: Wesleyan University Press University Press of New England.

———. 1997. Cultural survivalisms and marketplace subversions: Black popular culture and politics into the twenty-first century. In *Language, rhythm, and sound: Black popular cultures into the twenty-first century,* edited by Joseph Adjaye and Adrianne Andrews. Pittsburgh: University of Pittsburgh Press.

Rosler, Martha. 1990. Video: Shedding the utopian potential. In *Illuminating video: An essential guide to video art,* edited by Doug Hall and Sally Jo Fifer, 31–50. San Francisco: Aperture.

Ruiz, Carlos Alfredo "Ruz." 1995. *100 caricaturas sin gracia.* San Salvador, El Salvador: CONCULTURA.

Rumbaut, Rubén. In press. Sites of belonging: Acculturation, discrimination, and ethnic identity among children of immigrants. In *Discovering successful pathways in children's development: New methods in the study of childhood and family life,* edited by Thomas S. Weisner. Chicago: University of Chicago Press.

Saechao, Fam Linh. 2003. From war to welfare. In *InvAsian: Asian sisters represent,* edited by Marjorie Beggs, 65–66. San Francisco: Asian Women United of California.

Sanjek, Roger. 1996. The enduring inequalities of race. In *Race,* edited by Steven Gregory and Roger Sanjek, 1–17. New Brunswick, N.J.: Rutgers University Press.

Sansone, Livio. 1995. The making of a black youth culture: Lower class young men of Surinamese Origin in Amsterdam. In *Youth cultures: A cross-cultural perspective*, edited by Veret Amit-Talai and Helena Wulff, 114–43. London: Routledge.

Sassen, Saskia. 1996. *Migranten, Siedler, Flüchtlinge: Von der Massenwanderung zur Festung Europa*. Frankfurt am Main: Fischer.

Scheper-Hughes, N., and C. Sargent, eds. 1998. *Small wars: The cultural politics of childhood*. Berkeley: University of California Press.

Schieffelin, Bambi, Kathryn Woolard, and Paul Kroskrity. 1998. *Language ideologies: Theory and practice*. New York: Oxford University Press.

Schlesinger, Arthur M., Jr. 1998. *The disuniting of America: Reflections on a multicultural society*. New York: W. W. Norton.

Scholder, Amy, ed. 1999. *In the shadow of the American dream: The diaries of David Wojnarowicz*. New York: Grove.

Schulhofer, Stephen J. 2002. *The enemy within: Intelligence gathering, law enforcement, and civil liberties in the wake of September 11*. New York: Century Foundation.

Schutze, Jim. 1998. *Bully: Does anyone deserve to die?* New York: Avon.

Scott, James C. 1985. *Weapons of the weak: Everyday forms of peasant resistance*. New Haven, Conn.: Yale University Press.

Sessions Stepp, Laura. 2001. A lesson in cruelty: Anti-gay slurs common at school. *Washington Post*, June 19, A.01+.

Shaheen, Jack G. 1999. Hollywood's reel Arabs and Muslims. In *Muslims and Islamization in North America: Problems and prospects*, edited by Ambreen Haque, 179–202. Beltsville, Md.: Amana Publications.

Shakespeare, Tom, Kath Gillespie-Sells, and Dominic Davies. 1996. *The sexual politics of disability: Untold desires*. London: Cassell.

Shakur, Sanyika (Kody Scott). 1993. *Monster: The autobiography of an L.A. gang member*. New York: Atlantic Monthly Press.

Sharma, Sanjay. 1996. Noisy Asians or "Asian noise"? In *Dis-orienting rhythms: The politics of the new Asian dance music*, edited by Sanjay Sharma, John Hutnyk, and Ashwani Sharma, 32–57. London: Zed Books.

Shepherd, Benjamin, and Ronald Hayduk, eds. 2002. *From Act Up to the WTO: Urban protest and community building in the era of globalization*. London: Verso.

Shepherd, John. 1993. Difference and power in music. In *Musicology and difference: Gender and sexuality in music scholarship*, edited by R. A. Solie. Berkeley: University of California Press.

Shields, David L. L. 1996. What color is hunger? In *The color of hunger*, edited by David L. L. Shields. Lanham, Md.: Rowman and Littlefield.

Silberstein, Sandra. 2002. *War of words: Language, politics, and 9/11*. New York: Routledge.

Simon, John. 1995. Spaced out. *National Review*, August 25.

Siu, Lok. 2001. Diasporic cultural citizenship: Chineseness and belonging in Central America and Panama. *Social Text* 69, (19)4:7–28.

Skelton, Tracey, and Gill Valentine, eds. 1998. *Cool places: Geographies of youth cultures*. London: Routledge.

Smith, Valerie. 1992. The documentary impulse in contemporary African-American film. In *Black popular culture*, edited by Gina Dent, 56–64. Seattle: Bay.

Snyder, Sharon, and David Mitchell. 2000. *Narrative prosthesis: Disability and the dependences of discourse*. Ann Arbor: University of Michigan Press.

———. 2001. Re-engaging the body: Disability studies and the resistance to embodiment. *Public Culture* (13):369.

Soep, Elisabeth. 2000. To make things with words: Critique and the production of learning. Ph.D. diss., Stanford University.

──────. 2002. Art in the city beyond school. *Kappa Delta Pi.*

──────. 2003. Learning about research from youth media artists. *Perspectives on Urban Education* 1(2).

Soja, Edward. 1989. *Postmodern geographies: The reassertion of space in critical social theory.* London and New York: Verso.

Soler, Colette. 1996. Transference. In *Reading seminars I and II: Lacan's return to Freud,* edited by Richard Feldstein, Bruce Fink, and Maire Jaanus, 56–60. Albany, N.Y.: State University of New York Press.

Solioz, Christophe. 1996. Overcoming the paradox of the Swiss policy on integrating immigrants. *HCA Quarterly* 17: 41–42.

Sollors, Werner. 2000. *Interracialism: Black-white intermarriage in American history, literature, and law.* New York: Oxford University Press.

Sorkin, Michael, and Sharon Zukin, eds. 2002. *After the World Trade Center: Rethinking New York City.* New York: Routledge.

Spivak, Gayatri Chakravorty. 1987. *In other worlds: Essays in cultural politics.* New York: Routledge.

Stacey, Jackie. 1994. *Star gazing: Hollywood cinema and female spectatorship.* London: Routledge.

Staiger, Janet. 1992. *Interpreting films: Studies in the historical reception of American cinema.* Princeton, N.J.: Princeton University Press.

──────. 2000. *Perverse spectators: The practices of film reception.* New York and London: New York University Press.

Staples, Brent. 1994. Into the white ivory tower. *New York Times Magazine,* February 6.

Stephens, Sharon., ed. 1995. *Children and the politics of culture.* Princeton, N.J.: Princeton University Press.

Strauss, Valerie. 2001. No beating the problem of bullies. *Washington Post,* May 8, A11.

Suárez-Orozco, Carola, and Marcelo Suárez-Orozco. 2001. *Children of immigrants.* Cambridge, Mass.: Harvard University Press.

Suárez-Orozco, Marcelo. 2001. Globalization, immigration, and education: The research agenda. *Harvard Educational Review* 71(3):345–65.

Surinamese origin in Amsterdam. 1995. In *Youth cultures: A cross-cultural perspective,* edited by Vered Amit-Talai and Helena Wulff, 114–43. London: Routledge.

Taco Shop Poets, and Stephanie de la Torre. 2000. *Chorizo tonguefire: Taco Shop Poets anthology.* San Diego: Chorizo Tonguefire Press.

Tambiah, Stanley. 1970. *Buddhism and the spirit cults in northeast Thailand.* Cambridge: Cambridge University Press.

Tannenbaum, Nicola. 1999. Buddhism, prostitution, and sex: Limits on the academic discourse on gender in Thailand. In *Genders and sexualities in modern Thailand,* edited by Peter A. Jackson and Nerida M. Cook, 243–60. Chiang Mai: Silkworm Books.

Tannock, Stuart. 1998. Noisy talk: Conversation and collaboration in a youth writing group. In *Kids talk: Strategic language use in later childhood,* edited by Susan Hoyle and Carolyn Temple Adger, 241–66. New York: Oxford University Press.

──────. 1999. Working with insults: Discourse and difference in an inner city youth organization. *Discourse and Society* 10(3), 31:7–50.

————. 2002. Personal communication.

————. 2000. Youth at work: The unionized fast-food and grocery workplace. Philadelphia: Temple University Press.

Taylor, Charles, K. Anthony Appiah, Jürgen Habermas, Steven C. Rockefeller, Michael Walzer, and Susan Wolf. 1994. *multiculturalism: Examining the politics of recognition.* Edited by Amy Gutmann. Princeton, N.J.: Princeton University Press.

Tedlock, Dennis, and Bruce Mannheim, eds. 1995. *The dialogic emergence of culture.* Urbana: University of Illinois Press.

Teo, Stephen. 1997. *Hong Kong: The extra dimensions.* London: British Film Institute.

Thomas, Kendall. 1997. "Ain't nothin' like the real thing": Black masculinity, gay sexuality, and the jargon of authenticity. In *The house that race built: Black Americans, U.S. terrain,* edited by Wahneema Lubiano, 116–35. New York: Pantheon.

Thomas, Piri. 1973. *Down these mean streets.* New York: Knopf.

Thornton, Sarah. 1996. *Club cultures.* Cambridge: Polity Press.

————. 1997. Introduction to part one: The "Chicago school" and the sociological tradition. In *The subcultures reader,* edited by Ken Gelder and Sarah Thornton, 11–15. New York: Routledge.

Tomlinson, John. 1999. *Globalisation and culture.* Cambridge: Polity Press.

Training day. 2001. Directed by Antoine Fuena. 122 min. Warner Bros. Pictures.

Trinh, T. Minh-Ha. 1992. *Framer framed.* New York: Routledge.

Truth, Sojourner. 1962. Speech at New York City convention. In *The Heath anthology of American literature.* 1994 ed. Edited by Paul Lauter et al. Lexington: D. C. Heath.

Tsing, Anna Lowenhaupt. 1993. *In the realm of the diamond queen.* Princeton, N.J.: Princeton University Press.

Turner, Graeme. 1996. *British cultural studies: An introduction.* 2d ed. London: Routledge.

United Nations Development Program. 2003. Human development report 2003. Millennium development goals: A compact among nations to end human poverty. New York: UNDP.

Valentine, Gill, Tracey Skelton, and Deborah Chambers. 1998. Cool places: An introduction to youth and youth cultures. In *Cool places: Geographies of youth cultures,* edited by Tracey Skelton and Gill Valentine, 1–32. London: Routledge.

Van Ausdale, Debra, and Joe R. Feagin. 2001. *The first R: How children learn race and racism.* Lanham, Md.: Rowman and Littlefield.

Van Esterik, Penny. 1982. Laywomen in Theravada Buddhism. In *Women of Southeast Asia,* edited by Penny Van Esterik, 55–78. Dekalb: Northern Illinois University, Center for Southeast Asian Studies.

————. 1988. *Gender and development in Thailand: Deconstructing display.* Toronto: York University, Department of Anthropology, Thai Studies Project.

————. 1996. The politics of beauty in Thailand. In *Beauty queens on the global stage: Gender, contests, and power,* edited by Colleen Ballerino Cohen, Richard Wilk, Beverly Stoeltje, 203–16. New York: Routledge.

————. 1999. Repositioning gender, sexuality, and power in Thai studies. In *Genders and sexualities in modern Thailand,* edited by Peter A. Jackson and Nerida M. Cook, 275–89. Chiang Mai, Thailand: Silkworm Books.

Varenne, Herve, and Ray McDermott. 1998. *Successful failure: The school America builds.* Boulder, Colo.: Westview.

————. 1999. *Successful failure: The school America builds*. Boulder, Colo.: Westview.

Vigil, James Diego. 1988. *Barrio gangs: Street life and identity in Southern California*. Austin: University of Texas Press.

Volpp, Leti. 2002. The citizen and the terrorist. *UCLA Law Review* 49:1575–1600.

Von Drehle, David. 1999. To killers, model school was cruel. *Washington Post*, April 25, A01+.

Walcott, Rinaldo. 1997. *Black like who?: Writing black Canada*. Toronto: Insomniac Press.

Wallace, Michele. 1992. *Boyz N the hood* and *Jungle fever*. In *Black popular culture*, edited by Gina Dent, 123–31. Seattle: Bay.

————. 1995. Masculinity in black popular culture: Could it be that political correctness is the problem? In *Constructing masculinity*, edited by Maurice Berger, Brian Wallis, and Simon Watson. New York: Routledge.

Warner, Michael. 2000. *The trouble with normal: Sex, politics, and the ethics of queer life*. Cambridge, Mass.: Harvard University Press.

Watanabe, Satoko. 1998. From Thailand to Japan: Migrant sex workers as autonomous subjects. In *Global sex workers: Rights, resistance, and redefinition*, edited by Kamala Kempadoo and Jo Doezema, 114–23. New York: Routledge.

Waters, Tony. 1999. *Crime and immigrant youth*. Thousand Oaks, Calif.: Sage.

Watkins, S. Craig. 1998. *Representing: Hip hop culture and the production of black cinema*. Chicago: University of Chicago Press.

Werner, Emmy. 1998. *Reluctant witnesses: Children's voices from the Civil War*. Boulder, Colo.: Westview.

Wenz, Peter S. 1996. Just garbage. In *Faces of environmental racism*, edited by Laura Westra and Peter S. Wenz, 66. Lanham, Md.: Rowman and Littlefield.

Wijeyewardene, Gehan. 1981. Scrubbing scurf: Medium and deity in Chiang Mai. In *Mankind* 13(1):1–14.

Williams, Patricia J. 1995. Meditations on masculinity. In *Constructing Masculinity*, edited by Maurice Berger, Brian Wallis, and Simon Watson. New York: Routledge.

Willis, Paul. 1977. *Learning to labor: How working-class kids get working-class jobs*. New Columbia University Press.

————. 1990a. *Common culture: Symbolic work at play in the everyday cultures of the young*. Boulder, Colo.: Westview.

————. 1990b. *Common culture: Symbolic work at play in the everyday cultures of the young*. Buckingham: Open University Press.

Winant, Howard. 1998. Racial dualism at century's end. In *The house that race built*, edited by W. Lubiano, 87–115. New York: Vintage Books.

Wiretap Magazine. 2002. Generation incarceration: Juvenile justice and the war on youth. In *Wiretap Magazine*, http://www.alternet.org/wiretapmag/Rights/juvenile.html (cited October 26, 2002).

Wojnarowicz, David. 1991. *Close to the knives: A memoir of disintegration*. New York: Vintage.

Wolf, Diane Lauren. 1992. *Factory daughters: Gender, household dynamics, and rural industrialization in Java*. Berkeley: University of California Press.

Wolf, Susan. 1994. *Multiculturalism*, edited by Amy Gutmann. Princeton, N.J.: Princeton University Press.

Wulff, Helena. 1995a. Inter-racial friendship: Consuming youth styles, ethnicity, and teenage femininity in South London. In *Youth cultures: A cross-cultural perspective*, edited by Vered Amit-Talai and Helena Wulff. New York: Routledge.

————. 1995b. Introduction: Introducing youth culture in its own right: The state of the art and new possibilities. In *Youth cultures: A cross-cultural perspective,* edited by Helena Wulff and Vered Amit-Talai, 1–18. London: Routledge.

Wylie, K. C. 1977. *The political kingdoms of the Temne: Temne government in Sierra Leone 1825–1910.* New York and London: Africana Publishing Company.

Wyn, Johanna, and Rob White. 1997. *Rethinking youth.* London: Sage.

Yang, Mayfair Mei-Hui. 1997. Mass media and traditional subjectivity in Shanghai: notes on (re)cosmopolitanism in a Chinese metropolis. In Aihwa Ong and Donald Nonini, eds., *Underground Empires: The Cultural Politics of Modern Chinese Transnationalism,* 287–319. New York: Routledge.

Zingler, Peter. 1989. *Die Seuche (The plague).* Frankfurt am Main: Eichborn.

Index

Acknowledgments

The initial idea for this book was born of a long-standing friendship and intellectual collaboration between the two editors, and the process of making the anthology has felt considerably more collaborative than either of us had expected. In fact, we gained a clearer understanding of the meaning of youthscapes only from our ongoing conversations with many of the contributors and our engagement with their work and ideas. Our participation in *Youthscapes* showed us that the co-production of a multiple-author text can be a vehicle for individuals to connect with others—scholars, educators, and artists—who see the value of undertaking collaborative projects within an academic context that tends not to reward such endeavors fully. So first and foremost, we want to thank the contributors to this volume, for their innovative research and also for their patience and graciousness throughout this process.

Our editor, Peter Agree, showed early enthusiasm and faith in the project when it was still just an idea. We are grateful for his unfailing good humor and sage advice at every stage in the development of this work. Thanks also go to Erica Ginsburg and Ellie Goldberg, both at the University of Pennsylvania Press, and to Winnie Tam for preparing the index. Sunaina is indebted, for powerful inspiration and support, to her comrades in the South Asian Committee on Human Rights and the New England Committee to Defend Palestine. Lissa would like to thank the storytellers at Youth Radio and Youth Speaks.